THINKING THROUGH THEORY

John Levi Martin

W. W. NORTON & COMPANY, INC.
New York · London

W. W. NORTON & COMPANY has been independent since its founding in 1923, when William Warder Norton and Mary D. Herter Norton first published lectures delivered at the People's Institute, the adult education division of New York City's Cooper Union. The firm soon expanded its program beyond the Institute, publishing books by celebrated academics from America and abroad. By midcentury, the two major pillars of Norton's publishing program—trade books and college texts—were firmly established. In the 1950s, the Norton family transferred control of the company to its employees, and today—with a staff of four hundred and a comparable number of trade, college, and professional titles published each year—W. W. Norton & Company stands as the largest and oldest publishing house owned wholly by its employees.

Printed in the United States of America.

Editor: Karl Bakeman
Associate Editor: Nicole Sawa
Editorial Assistant: Lindsey Thomas
Manuscript Editors: Patterson Lamb
Project Editor: Sujin Hong
Marketing Manager, Sociology: Julia Hall
Production Manager: Vanessa Nuttry
Permissions Manager: Megan Jackson
Text Design: Megan Jones
Composition: Westchester Book
Manufacturing: Quad/Graphics Fairfield

Library of Congress Cataloging-in-Publication Data.

Martin, John Levi, 1964–
Thinking through theory / John Levi Martin. — First edition.
pages cm
Includes bibliographical references and index.
ISBN 978-0-393-93768-8 (pbk.)
1. Sociology. I. Title.
HM585.M34583 2015
301—dc23

2014030828

W. W. Norton & Company, Inc., 500 Fifth Avenue, New York, NY 10110-0017

wwnorton.com

W. W. Norton & Company Ltd., Castle House, 75/76 Wells Street, London W1T 3QT

1 2 3 4 5 6 7 8 9 0

If I am in error, it is without loving error . . .

— ROUSSEAU, *JULIE*

CONTENTS

PREFACE · vii

CHAPTER 1 ON THEORY IN SOCIOLOGY · 1

What Is Theory in Sociology? · 1
Looking Outward · 15
Problems and Solutions · 20
Awkward Joins · 31
Beyond Straightening · 40

CHAPTER 2 THINGS AND FACTS: WHO CAUSES WHAT CONSTRAINTS? · 45

Culture as Constraint · 45
Defining Constraint · 52
Defining Causation · 56
Causation and Comparison · 62
Comparison, Processes, and Causes · 65

CHAPTER 3 THE RETURN OF REALISM · 77

A Basket of Isms · 77
Realism versus Social Construction · 86
Getting Real in Sociology · 94
Concepts and Reality · 98
Supporting Claims · 105
*Talk and Scientific Inquiry** · 110
*Talking about Truth** · 116
Conclusion · 128

CHAPTER 4 RATIONALITY AND OTHER LUNACIES · 131

The Debate over Rational Choice Theory · 131
What Is Rationality? · 136
Producing Paradox · 138
From Irrational to Rational Uses of Rational Choice Theory · 149
From Rational Actors to Rational Genes · 158
Conclusion · 172

CHAPTER 5 WHAT DOES THE SOCIOLOGY OF ANIMALS TEACH US? · 175

Fear of Animals · 175
Where Is Complexity and Intelligence? · 182
Roles · 191
Morality (Rules) · 199
Having a World · 206
Conclusion · 215

CHAPTER 6 "THE GENTLEMAN IS TO LET THE LADY ENTER THE DOOR FIRST": OR HOW THE ENVIRONMENT TELLS US WHAT TO DO · 217

Motives and Tendencies · 217
Who Follows Rules and When? · 225
I Can Only Open the Door · 231
Conclusion · 243

CONCLUSION · 245

On Luck · 245
Bonus: The Newest Rules of Sociology · 247
From Here On · 254

REFERENCES · 255

INDEX · 271

PREFACE

WHAT THIS BOOK IS ABOUT

This book is about the improvement of sociological theory. The focus here is on good thinking. I'm not saying that no one thinks well in our discipline, but we often can do better. Unfortunately, few theorists are explicitly concerned with the issues of how to avoid thinking in circles, how to know when we are contradicting ourselves, how to avoid thinking tautologies are meaningful.

I have four main points to make about what theory is in sociology, and what it can—and cannot—do for us. First, we often have relatively good knowledge about the social world, but not very good knowledge about knowledge. Instead of learning more and more about the concrete world we mean to study, the minute we have a finding that seems robust, we run off and arrange it somewhere in the heavens of a world of imaginary entities. And this is because (second) we allow ourselves to take aspects of the way we think about things and to inject them into the world. While we might need to do this *somewhat*, we do it *a lot*, and without apology or hesitation. We are like kids who think they are doing real archaeology by digging up fossils that grown-ups have placed in a sandbox. Third, it doesn't have to be this way. We can become much more rigorous in making our thoughts. It isn't that hard to do, but you do have to *want* to do it.

And so the implication is the following: we've often assumed that the kinds of people who think that sociology can be or should be something like a "science" are temperamentally the opposite of those who want to read works of "theory" closely and argue about the minutiae of this or that claim. I think it would be great if that were true. But right now, we're in a place in which we've got a lot of engine, and no steering. In that case, there is a kind of theoretical work that we need to do if we are to really be scientific.

And this leads to the fourth point: the sort of theoretical work I'm talking about is a formal examination of the architecture of theoretical structures; this turns out to be surprisingly easy for a trained mind, and the training is a lot less painful than mastering arcane vocabulary. It's something that we can, and should, all learn to do.

WHO THIS BOOK IS FOR

This book is written for students, first and foremost. They are the ones who are most likely to suffer from the problems that we have in thinking, and they are the most likely to be interested in changing how they think. They have much to gain, and nothing to lose. Because of this, I write clearly and bluntly, without a lot of defensive qualifications. Further, I don't provide examples of every sort of problem that I am talking about.[1] This bothers older (read: employed) sociologists on a number of fronts. First, it is a violation of the implicit citation-cartel agreement (you cite me, and I'll cite you), and understandably, no one (and this includes me) likes to see a book or article on something we have worked on for a decade that doesn't even notice our contributions.[2]

Second, an absence of citation can be interpreted as an absence of evidence. I think we do this even when we know very well that there is plenty of evidence around. In any case, my argument is not that these problems exist, but about how to solve them. If you *really* don't think there are problems, then by all means, read something else. If you actually know there are, let's not have to drag out a sacrificial victim for each one, okay? If you're new to sociology and aren't sure how common these problems are, start reading around; it shouldn't take long before you learn just what I am talking about.

Of course, we *should* be wary of people who argue against one sort of claim by finding a "straw man." At least, that makes sense if we are talking about taking one *side* in a debate. But if we are talking about clarifying problems, we *do* want to focus on the clearest forms of those problems. Although our examples shouldn't necessarily be those with the *worst* problems (they need, for one, to possess admirable clarity), they aren't always the strongest contributions.[3] So here, when I do use negative examples, they are in no way intended to be representative, nor are they engaging with my opponents on their strongest terms. Rather, I choose the works that magnify the fundamental problems so that they can be

---

[1] I also don't shovel in citations. Chances are, if I am saying something about thinking straight, I'm not quoting either the first or the last person who said this before (and chances are, there are plenty of philosophers or logicians who have), and chances are, if I'm saying something substantive, I'm not listing everything I ever read on the topic, just what happens to be a nice example at hand. Finally, there *are* in many cases more complex treatments and counters to some of the arguments that I make here more simply, but they just aren't helpful for what we need to get done at this time (many involve changing the meanings of our terms in ways that won't work for sociology).

[2] At the same time, since my focus is on *bad* thinking, no one should really be sorry to find his work not referred to herein. Indeed, you should thank your God that I *don't* cite you.

[3] The fact that *your* work doesn't have this problem, oh published author (though this book will be read by students, it will be reviewed by professors, and that's whom I'm addressing here), and that the last few published things you read don't have these problems, at least not in this stark a form, doesn't mean that there *are* no problems. Look at your students' papers and you will realize that just because not all published work suffers from these doesn't mean that there aren't serious problems in our discipline. It's just that they are so serious, they often produce intellectual stillbirths.

seen easily by others. Think of this as an operating theater, with specimens chosen for what they can teach us, not because they are average.[4]

WHAT I HOPE CAN BE ACCOMPLISHED

My last book seems to have led a number of my (remaining) friends to tell me that I write as if I think that everyone else is stupid. I don't understand this, but for the record, I certainly don't think that everyone else is stupid.[5] But (as they say in Chelm) sometimes stupid things happen to smart people, and I think they do, a lot of the time. In those cases, the only thing that being smart gets folks is delaying the inevitable moment when they realize that everything they have been thinking about and saying makes no sense.

But it doesn't need to be this way. We can recognize the five or six most problematic cul-de-sacs where our thinking gets stuck, and use our thinking where it is most likely to do something good for us.

HOW THIS BOOK IS ORGANIZED

The plan of this work is as follows: in the first chapter, I will discuss some of the most common ways that professional sociologists have understood the role of "theory" in their discipline. I then present an argument for one kind of theory-work that is, I believe, underappreciated in sociology, if it is not dismissed as ludicrous altogether. I give a few simple examples of this theory-work in action. The next chapters deal with a set of problems — causality, reality, rationality — that can easily gobble up a few years of a student's brain-life without much to show for it.

To be more specific, the second chapter then begins with what has become a mantra in the sociology of culture, the idea that culture "constrains and enables" action, and uses this to unpack the differences between things and facts about things. With this, we can then begin to investigate what it means for one thing to "cause" an action. We end up being able to avoid imputing aspects of how *we* want to think about things to the things themselves.

[4] For example, I happen to have an extremely well-defined and large optic nerve. I know this because at Berkeley when I would go for my free eye exam, all the students would troop in while my pupil was dilated because I was such a great example of what an optic nerve looks like. Students who learned on me could then learn to identify the same structure in other people. I am not making this up.

[5] I do think that most of them are *wrong*, but in fact, it's because they are probably much smarter than I that they've managed to do so well despite holding incorrect ideas. I, on the other hand, have only managed to stay in the game, given my limited intellectual powers, by seizing upon true ideas, because this makes everything a lot easier on you.

In the third chapter, we build on this newly gained facility to investigate increasingly prevalent arguments for what is claimed to be realism. We find that rather than rescuing the objective world, this legitimizes tendencies for us to conveniently put our own ideas into the world and "discover" them there ("Yay! We were right!" we think). Taking these problems seriously allows us to consider the classic pragmatist solution with perhaps more sympathy.

In the fourth chapter, I examine the problems associated with totalistic rational choice theorizing, which tend to have a particular form of indeterminacy at its heart. We find these same formal pathologies characterizing what is called "evolutionary psychology," which is (I know this sounds mean) basically the biological equivalent of fantasy football. In the fifth chapter, we take a different approach; rather than invent biological-sounding scenarios for long-ago humans, we take a look at what has been learned about animal behavior as a way of developing theoretical tools that might be less prone to import our own convenient ways of thinking into our subjects. The sixth chapter builds on these conceptions to flesh out one particular approach to human action that I think has been underappreciated. The conclusion gives a few additional useful "rules of sociology."

HOW THIS BOOK WAS WRITTEN

Large portions of this book originated in dialogue and debate with others, including Jan Fuhse, Maggie Frye, Matt George, Philip Gorski, Barry Lawson, Dan Little, Doug Porpora, Allison Pugh, and Christian Smith. I was encouraged not to drop portions by Omar Lizardo (who read an earlier version of Chapter 6) and by Jacob Foster (regarding the animals chapter: I've also learned from students in a class I taught on nonhuman animals).

WHO SHOULD BE ACKNOWLEDGED

Of course I thank those who actually read this work. First is Robert Owens, whose rigorous critique pointed to a number of problems, and in many cases I have followed his suggested solutions.[6] Second is Omar Lizardo; were I to indicate every place in which I draw on an idea or respond to a critique made by him it would be unreadable, so I simply indicate here how fortunate I have been to

[6] I offered to pay Robert for each logical contradiction, tautology, or vacuous statement he uncovered. Despite the critique of rational choice theorizing I will make in Chapter 4, I do believe that this, at any rate, is a remarkably effective place for rational choice to enter the realm of theory construction, if we actually want to make our claims better (as opposed to merely fancier).

have such an astounding interlocutor. Third, I was privileged to have extensive comments on certain chapters by Steve Vaisey (1 and 2), Jan Fushe (2 and 3), Graham Peterson (1 and 4), and Jeff Guhin (3); I am grateful for readers whose critiques are as deep as their friendship. Fourth, Will Lewis Sims and Nicole Sawa both read the penultimate manuscript and indicated where things had to be clarified and turned problems into solutions; I am grateful for their careful work, as well as to Lindsey Thomas and Patterson Lamb at Norton for theirs. And most pivotal was Karl Bakeman. He has convinced me, as he has convinced a few other sociologists, that we can have books that are clear and accessible but argue a strong point; that we can talk to students with precision and from a particular position. It is hard to overstate the importance that following through on such convictions can have on our discipline as a whole.

I want to conclude with an unusual set of acknowledgments. Should sociologists remember their mothers and fathers? Arthur Stinchcombe (1982) asked this question in a piece a long time ago regarding the reasons to read classical theory. It's a fine question in its own way, but our mothers and fathers aren't Weber and Durkheim; they are the sociologists a generation above *us*. And so for special acknowledgment and dedication, I want to thank not my own mentors (whom I can never thank enough), but members of a generation of great scholars who at different points were willing to support me, talk to me, and encourage me even though I wasn't their student and whatever ideas I had weren't theirs. I am thinking of Herb Gans, Charles Lemert, Stanley Lieberson, Steven Lukes, Harrison White, and Arthur Stinchcombe himself. But above all, I dedicate this book to the memory of Jerry Marwell, who did so much for all of us and who continues to do more. Pass it on.

CHAPTER 1

On Theory in Sociology

In this chapter, I'm going to introduce a formal problem-solving approach to theory construction, and then illustrate it—and draw out particular lessons—using the examination of one particular theoretical argument. But first, I'm going to handle the question of what theory is by considering what it might mean to do theory-work.

WHAT IS THEORY IN SOCIOLOGY?

To know if something is good or bad, we generally think we need to know what sort of a thing it is. Is this a too-salty cookie or a too-sweet cracker? And so sooner or later, we'll need to know something about what we mean by theory. Usually, the way one approaches this question is to put together a meta-theory of what sciences are, what role theory has in these (or which role it *should* have), and so on. The problem is that few of these theories of science seem to fit what we actually do in sociology, so there's no reason to think that the related conceptions of "theory" are accurate for us.

Instead of starting by trying to determine what the role of theory in sociology should be, let's see if we can figure out what the activity of theory-work (in the sense discussed by Levine, forthcoming) might be. If you were learning how to do theory, what would you learn? What would you *do* when you were done learning it? There isn't much agreement on this, and I think to the extent that there is agreement, it has fixed on a poor use of the term *theory.* So in this first section, I want to consider the different ways theory has been understood in sociology, and to suggest the utility of a somewhat different understanding, that which guides the current work.

Let me begin, then, with a few ideal typical uses or understandings of what we mean by "theory" in sociology. Some have strong elective affinities, such that those who adopt one also tend to adopt another, and others can certainly be held jointly if one wishes. But the differences are no less the real for that.

Theory-Ology

We can begin with the one theory of theory that we all hate, I will call it theory-ology: the study of the work of theorists. The origin myth (perhaps it is true) of this type of theory is that it was created, coterminous with the birth of a new form of sociology and of theory, by Talcott Parsons, who often serves (and probably deserves to serve) as the Snowball for our little Animal Farm. Talcott Parsons became the most important sociological theorist for a few decades, producing a great heap of writings, a long list of definitions, and broad, sweeping claims about humanity, society, evolution, what have you—and he did this with remarkably little empirical study. (It is not at all true that he carried out *no* empirical studies, but almost all his empirical studies came *after* he had developed his theory.)

How did he accomplish this remarkable feat? By studying *other* theorists, most importantly, Max Weber. He began with textual exegesis, which gave him a "place to stand" from which he could move the world. This then (or so we are told) set the stage for other theorists—they would begin as exegetical students of another theorist, first imputing their own ideas to the theorist until they were sufficiently safe to emerge from beneath their aegis. At this point, our budding theorists could boldly proclaim their own ideas. Eventually, if all went well, they could supplant their one-time protectors and in fact claim as their own the ideas of their predecessors. This was the recipe that tells us how one becomes a famous sociological theorist.

When I was in graduate school in the late 1980s to late 1990s, this "theory-ological" understanding of theory was definitely out. There was, we were told, nothing intellectually defensible or personally admirable in being the satrap of one of the theory kings, learning "what he ate for breakfast on Mondays," and so on. Parsons may have achieved his position by climbing all over Weber, our teachers said, but Weber did not become a great theorist by simply analyzing others' texts. Rather, he became great by studying great things.

There was soon to be an institutional implementation of this backlash against theory-ology. At the time, it was common for every graduate department to have "a" theorist (someone whose main works were *about* other theorists), just like everyone had "a" methodologist (usually meaning a very good and creative social statistician). But by the time I left school, there had been a clear shift in hiring procedures in graduate departments, which stopped thinking that they needed "a" theorist, and started thinking that someone who was smart and well educated in theory, even if she was more closely associated with an empirical research project, would be preferred.

Without denying the incredibly painful nature of many theory-ology contributions (especially the dreaded synthesis of the vocabularies of two "theorists"), the turn against theory-ology actually was a setback for the discipline because, as

I shall go on to argue, theory-ologists were often those who were best able to carry out theory-work as critique. With the rejection of theory-ology, theory increasingly meant "empirical generalizations," and so interest shifted to those who made wild overgeneralizations, sometimes peppered with poorly developed neologisms and references to well-known vocabularies in which these neologisms could not possibly survive. The incoherence of the resulting claims might have been avoided if there had been theory-work as critique.

But I anticipate. Let's pursue the shift in conceptions of theory and introduce other conceptions of theory-work that seem to have arisen to replace that of theory-ology.

Theory as Canonical and as Important Propositions

As one conception of theory went into decline, another would have to be raised up. But what would theory be? Descriptively, perhaps the simplest way to explain what one means by "theory" is to point to *theorists*—that is, whoever is consensually called one—and to see theory as whatever they have done. Theory-work then isn't writing *about* theorists; it is doing whatever it is they did. But if theorists do not do anything theory-ological, how do we know who they are? One answer seems to have been that they are promoted to such a position as a result of their importance for the discipline—a circular definition, to be sure, but descriptively, circularity is often the sign of accuracy. "Theory" is then a side effect of canonization. Durkheim has a "theory" because Durkheim was a theorist, and Durkheim was a theorist because we make everyone read Durkheim. Whether this is a result of his institutional machinations and the creation of a school, the result of his intrinsic excellence, or simply a historical accident, is a secondary matter.

A special case of this circular approach arises when we add that we can identify as a necessary if not sufficient criterion for the canonization process that the claims made by the scholar-promoted-to-theorist are big and/or important. This understanding implies that there is no fundamental formal or epistemic difference between what a theorist does and what everyone else does. The only difference is, perhaps, scale.

This was the version of theory explicitly taught to me when I was in graduate school. Theory is too important to be left to the so-called theorists, we were told, along with "we are all theorists."[1] This was said, it seems to me, for a number of

[1] Indeed, as I was leaving graduate school and being interviewed for a job that was pegged as a "theory" job, one tenured professor, who would probably not generally be thought of as a theorist in any of the senses I will discuss, told me that really, *anyone* on a sociology faculty could teach theory, and I think she meant by this that anyone could teach it reasonably well. (I think she meant by *that* that they shouldn't be hiring someone like me in the first place, but we can leave that part alone for now.)

reasons: two local and professional and one intellectual. Most obviously, the idea was to put a stop to theory-ology, which at that time seemed logically to promise an unending series of fractal works like X's comments on Y's reading of Z's discussion of . . . , ad infinitum and ad nauseam. But it was also, I believe, intended to lessen the social distance between theorists and others (where self-professed "theory" types often labored under the illusion that they were of some sort of higher substance than the common sociologist). But a third reason was to express the prevailing epistemic understanding of the production of true statements that was common to mainstream sociology in the 1980s.

A theory, in this understanding, is a proposition: nothing more, nothing less. Well, maybe something a bit more—a series of propositions, a tangle of claims, and definitions—but we are most comfortable when we can grasp the theory as a proposition, because then we know what to do: we attempt to support or test it. When there is support for our proposition, this is good—but it does not thereby become "true," and a contrary proposition does not become false. Falsificationism à la Karl Popper was widely treated as repellent not because a credible alternative had been found, but because of its rigidity; in accepting the law of the excluded middle (things either are or aren't true), it proved itself intolerant, and intolerance was *très gauche*.

This understanding is a stable one—it is simple and definitional; and, by accepting the importance of potentially indefensible social processes of canonization as an explanation of why some are theorists and others not, it dispenses with the need to justify invidious distinctions. So it's not a bad definition. And note that it implies that there is no place for "theory-work" as such; after a short spell of coming up with ideas, one should begin investigating them.

There turns out, however, to be a grave practical problem with this common idea of theory: it seems to accept the idea that a theory is something we make *before* we begin our investigations. (I would think that we already have a fine word for that, which is prejudice.) As a result, students often spend a great deal of time formulating their theory *before* they know very much about the subject. This means that they personally invest themselves in coming up with a particular conclusion at the time when they should be learning how to winnow out error from truth.[2]

Would that producing scientific error would be enough to lead us to question our definitions! In actuality, there wasn't any push-back to this conception on

[2] It isn't necessarily the case that we *should* think of theory as the "before" research; this seems to have come from an idea of "testing" theory that most sociologists recycle but don't really believe in. Before this, as in many other sciences, we had the idea that what you were working *toward* was a theory; it was something that came *after*. And funnily enough, in those days, you'd feel that you had to justify your *research* by claiming that it would (someday) lead to a theory, while now, we feel that we have to justify our *theory* by claiming that it will (very soon) lead to research.

the grounds that it tended to the enthronement of prejudice. In fact, this seemed to be its biggest draw. The more common modification seemed to come as a response to its most admirable feature: its flatness, its refusal to consider any statement more theoretical than another. This might be intellectually defensible, perhaps even unimpeachable. The implications, however, were anarchic. We started from the idea of theory as canonical—basically accepting the fact that, for whatever reason, some were theorists and that was that. But far from being able to justify this canonization, our thinking suggested that we were all theorists, and that all our efforts would be, at least in some phase of their formulation, equally theoretical. "Theory" becomes coterminous with sociology.

Theory as Generalization

And I think it was this puzzling implication that has pushed many sociologists to the position that theory is not just *any* proposition, but is a *general* proposition (or series of propositions). How do we distinguish the particular from the general? A few people still attempt to defend a rigorous two-class model, in which we have statements of particularities that are pure data on the one hand, and general theory on the other. This works well enough as a theory of science, especially experimental science, but it doesn't fit much of sociology very well, and so more common is a gradation of propositions from the less to more general. To the extent that it can be pulled off, a more general argument has a better claim to theory.[3]

I admit that the more general claims seem to be more theoretical, and that they certainly seem more important. Thus if we start with the "canonization" idea of theory—namely, that theory is what is done by theorists, and a theorist is someone who does something that we believe important—then generalization provides a way of getting a little bit outside the circle whereby anything canonical is, by its canonical status, important, and its canonical status is confirmed by its importance. Thus it has some practical advantages. Further, I think we would be mad to deny that the project of reaching toward generalization is key to any science, if only because what we mean by "science" usually turns on generalization (and thus, by this usage, excludes a rigorous history that shies away from generalization). However, there are two problems with the way we use the idea of generalization in sociology.

---

[3] Thus if you were to argue that capitalist activity in Antwerp in the sixteenth century was only slowed by the Protestant Reformation, that would be an interesting historical argument, but if you were to argue that this was *more generally true* you would have an important theory. Of course, since it would be sheer madness to argue that capitalist activity *at every place and at every time* was slowed by increased Protestant fervor, the generalization would also increase fuzziness, taking a form more like "Protestantism actually slowed capitalism."

First, the very important types of productive generalization that take place are hard to distinguish via definition from those that are wholly useless. A classic example of a good generalization is the law of force $F=ma$, which can encompass the case of a simple spring (where $a=-kd/m$) and that of objects in free-fall ($a=g$) and so on. And so we can equate the two types of force ($-kd/m=g$) and predict how much an object in free fall will compress a spring (that's how an old-fashioned bathroom scale works). Now consider the theoretical claim "people always act in their interests" which can encompass the case "people don't give their money away to strangers" when we note that in this case "their interests" are "don't give money away to strangers" but also can encompass the case "people *do* give their money away to strangers" when we note that now "their interests" are "give money away to strangers" and so on. (We'll return to this example with more precision in Chapter 4.) The question is whether this is more like the physics case, or something like the general argument that "all animals have a single physical oomper that is used to achieve their greatest purpose" (where for robins, the oomper is their legs and their greatest purpose is to hop, while for turtles, their oomper is their shell, and their greatest purpose is to hide, and so on). We can't deny that generalization can be stupid as well as smart, and the further one gets from mathematically formalized empirical observations and inference, the harder it is to tell stupid from smart.

Second, we tend to have a hard time understanding the relation between the particular studies we do and the general propositions we are supposedly counting as theory. No one wants to do what Lieberson and Horwich (2008) have called "worker bee studies" and just come up with findings that could be used, eventually, to produce generalizations, and if they did, no one would publish the results. Thus we have a recurrent temptation for each particular study to attempt to develop a generalization. That this is so obviously pernicious has in no way dissuaded us from doing it.

Having done some work of generalization, after writing my dissertation on a particular set of data, I found that generalization was an activity very different from what I had done before. ("I specialize in generalizations," Daniel Bell used to say, and he was right—it's a specialty like others.) One has to determine the range of cases one is interested in, find a common way of examining them, survey examples from across the range, reject language that is too closely tied to one portion of this range, and so on.

But our idea that theory is general, coupled with the idea that everyone is a theorist, leads people to attempt to link their work to general claims—while they throw out the one straightforward way of making such a linkage, which is classic falsification. If there's a general claim that says that something should be observed and you find the opposite, that claim *should* be in trouble. Instead, everyone wants to make his or her own theories, which means that each overgeneralizes from his or her own case. Over time, some contradictions do appear, and one might imagine that this would be the place where we would root out false generalizations.

Unfortunately, we also seem to have developed a disciplinary conviction that one can't analyze anyone else's theory but have to take it on its own terms. This naturally encourages the devolution of sociology into a game in which, by definition, everyone wins. It's like a version of that patronizing mealy-mouthed multiculturalism that passes for social justice on high school campuses ("I totally understand. In *your* culture, that's considered art."). So, too, we say, "In *your* theory, that's true." Indeed, I was explicitly taught in graduate school that since we tested theories, and enough asterisks meant we had at least made it to the next round,[4] there was no reason that different theories couldn't *all* be true. And that is correct — if theory is simply a proposition that something, sometimes, some places, occurs.

Now it is possible that we could retain our genial tolerance for contradictory generalizations by looking for the scope conditions that lead (to use the above example) one's interest to be "don't give money away to strangers" and those that lead that interest to be "do give money away to strangers." There are a few cases in which subfields had debates that *did* lead to such greater clarity. Yet many sociologists seem to have an innate fear of being dragged away from abstract generality and toward the concrete — thus there was, in all seriousness, a debate in sociological social psychology as to whether power *was* (in *general*) about legitimate authority or *was* about domination — as if "power" was something like the Loch Ness monster that, once clearly found and photographed, would give up its secrets, as opposed to a word used loosely by many different people in constantly changing ways. All the participants involved had brains. Yet the argument is fundamentally brainless (and was easily solved to the satisfaction of each by setting up precisely that sort of experimental situation that corroborates her or his prejudices — that is, confirms her or his theory).

This comes, I think, from the deep-seated conviction that theory should be as general as possible, and this vision increasingly threatens the intelligence of our work. If you have ever been traveling and stopped off with friends in a bar, you might encounter a large fellow, a regular, who has had quite a good deal to drink. He is not necessarily unfriendly or mean, and certainly wants to talk, but — buoyed with the alcohol and sense of being in his home range — he does not particularly want to listen. Many of his statements begin with "I'll tell you what!" and sometimes he gets so carried away that he pokes his finger into your chest.

---

[4] Asterisks are used in tables of coefficient to indicate that one is "statistically significant," which basically means we're allowed to talk about it. Many of our theoretical propositions turned out to be tested just by whether a coefficient could be distinguished from 0.

This, unfortunately, is what often passes for theory these days: someone who for whatever reason has a sufficient sense of entitlement that he or she will simply "tell us what." One almost pines for the days in which theory was a complex vocabulary that could be slapped on any observation, to make the mundane seem scientific. Indeed, there may be more in this conception of theory than we have assumed.

Theory as Vocabulary

Making substantively significant general statements from a single case is asking too much, but one can still aspire to generality without needing to develop broad general knowledge if one provides a vocabulary that can be used to describe a wide variety of situations, and we often seem to believe that the essence of a theory is just this vocabulary. Indeed, some students often believe that it is a theoretical advance simply to re-tell a story in the vocabulary that they like.

We always use a vocabulary, so there clearly can't be anything wrong with making one. Further, one vocabulary can have advantages that another does not; in fact, I see no reason to think that one vocabulary can't be better than another—that simple. (It does, however, seem reasonable that there isn't a single best one, though this hasn't been proven.) But we have been burned too many times by word-hawkers whose proffered vocabularies are like the cut-price knock-offs one can buy on the street, seemingly a wonderful bargain but falling apart under serious use (which is usually why our neighboring disciplines were so eager to unload them on us in the first place). Further, we are all driven to distraction with work that seems to substitute the chanting of terms for serious thought (or, at least we have this reaction to *others'* terms).

Yet, the idea of theory as a general vocabulary is, I believe, currently somewhat underappreciated. Just as classical physics was hampered as long as there was no verbal distinction between what we now call *force* (which we associate with acceleration) and *momentum* (which we do not), we too may have problematic vocabularies. Let me give an example: as we'll see in Chapter 4, the idea of "interests" as we use it now in sociology first arose when it was assumed that everyone knew what people valued—money and stuff. But as this concept became generalized, it covered other things that people seemed to value. Now there were and still are many heated arguments about whether regular people "really know what is in their own interest." For example, let's say workers oppose closed shop legislation, and others say that they are failing to understand that this is in their interest and are being distracted by ideological talk of "freedom."

Do they misrecognize their own interests? When you think about it, *of course* people don't always know what's in their best interests. The future is uncertain, and the best-laid plans come to nothing, or worse. Yet critics correctly felt that something smarmy and patronizing lay behind this claim that others don't know their interests. How can that be? It's because "interests" often combine two things: first, a valued state that one hopes to achieve (e.g., higher wages), and second, a belief in the *means* best to achieve that state (e.g., a stronger union movement). It's the second that we must acknowledge to be fallible in all persons, yet the *fusion* of the two in the notion of "interest" was used to suggest that people couldn't even be trusted to know what they *valued*. That's a pretty demeaning way to think about others, and so the critics were right—but the problem could have been clarified, and perhaps dispelled, by a better vocabulary.

So sometimes vocabularies make it hard to ask the right questions. Further, many vocabularies assume too much of what is in question; an innovation in vocabulary can inspire us to ask questions that we did not know to ask before. Finally, even where a new vocabulary does not have such obvious analytic improvements, it can, just as its adherents will aver, awaken a capacity to think somewhat differently. Of course, the same can be said of a stiff swig of absinthe—different is not always smarter. Further, with the repetition of our new terms, we find the advantages that come with them dissipating, for when we fall in love with words and use them over and over again, they lose their meaning (say "smock" to yourself a hundred times. Did that word *ever* have a referent?). Indeed, I will argue below that it is important that we change our vocabulary regularly if we are to get anywhere.

Critics of theory-as-vocabulary will note that the creation of an exhaustive and exclusive partition of all possible observations into a set of terms always has an irresistible appeal over weak minds, who appreciate the false certainty of having a phrase for everything. As this leads to fragmented schools of convicted zealots, no one now thinks there is an advantage in such complete theoretical recastings of the obvious into the high-falutin'. Yet there might be something to taking vocabularies seriously—not to propose complete idiolects, but rather, to work on them, gradually pushing them to greater coherence. Thus, this recasting of theory-work as vocabulary-correction may be related to that of theory as critique.

Theory as Critique

By "critique" here I do not mean an empirical or evaluative critique—you are wrong or bad—but rather a consideration of the internal consistency and possible scope of the use of terms, ideas, arguments, and so on. In sociology, our penchant for such critique has been weakened on all sides. On one side, since no theory could ever be "wrong," just more or less "useful," there was no point in criticizing anyone else's theory. She would respond that she still considered the theory "useful" (meaning it aided her in thinking what she wanted to think anyway). On the other side, the social overlap of sociological theory types with social theory types meant that theories were vulnerable for criticism in terms of their political implications — so why bother looking closely and carefully to determine if a theory's terms were mutually compatible if it could simply be dismissed as reactionary?

But critique is an important part of any attempt to develop ideational structures. Rather than be understood as akin to "attack," it should be seen more like "repair." For example, when Andrew Wiles proposed a proof of Fermat's last theorem, it turned out that he had made an error; this was caught by his colleague Nick Katz among others. After many months, and consultation with others, Wiles was able to repair the problem. Katz didn't break it — it was already broken — he just let Wiles see the break so that it could be fixed.

Of course, no one likes to be *told* that he is talking nonsense. It is reasonable that we react angrily to those who dare suggest it. Yet few of us really want to be talking nonsense, either. And most of us *are*, at least some of the time. It seems to me that this is where theory as a specialized endeavor can come in handy. Just as statisticians can tell you (and they will, trust me) when you cannot conclude what you want to conclude from your data, so theorists can tell you when you cannot say what you want to say. And they can tell you when you know something that you do not know that you know. It is hard to do this without what we call "critique." Yet it may be that there is room for a certain kind of theory-work that can identify problems *before* they bring down an entire system. And this brings us to the conception of theory-work that guides the chapters in this book.

Theory-Work as Orthologics

If we attempt to think consistently for very long, it almost always turns into what would be called philosophy or math, and I am not saying that theory in sociology should be the importation of either of these. Still, there is room for us to learn how to improve the precision, clarity, and coherence of our ideas. Theory-work, then, is the application of mental habits that would be familiar to a philosopher or mathematician to the cases that are important for us.

For lack of a better word, we can call this sort of work orthological, as it involves the application of "right reason" to our formulation of ideas and statements. This is, I now believe, a skill like any others, and it can be taught.[5] Some of the issues are those of style, some of logic, and some more particular to social thought. At the simplest level, that of style, we are perhaps merely speaking of habits of rigor and honesty. One important habit for theorizing is just the following: as one

[5] Although the word *orthological* now generally refers to using the right *word*, there was a time when *logos* was understood as having a wider connotation.

writes a period at the end of the sentence, to stop and ask oneself "am I sure this is true? Let me entertain the opposite. Do I have any reason to reject it other than my desire to go forward with my own argument?"

But many of the problems that we run into in creating theories do not yield to the mere application of elbow grease. Some pertain to the logical relations of our terms (as they are used in sociology). In a few cases, we can identify certain problems without a full analysis. Often we profit from a rule-of-thumb check: we take an argument we make and see whether it holds when we radically substitute other terms in. If so, perhaps the reason it is persuasive is that it is a tautology, and hence not as important as it seemed. Further, we learn to distinguish between good contradictions and bad ones, between those sorts of circles that we shouldn't be able to rule out, and those that undermine our whole approach.

In other cases, however, we face logical problems that have to do with specific combinations of thoughts, each of which is seemingly fine in its own right. Yet together, they produce paradox. Pursuing any such problem might seem pointless for any general treatment, were it not for the fact that there are sets of thought-chunks in sociological theory that turn out to be formally similar. An example that became clear in theology had to do with the puzzle of whether God could make a second God, whether He could make a rock so heavy that He couldn't lift it—all of which turned out to be formally equivalent to the puzzle of what happens when an irresistible force meets an unmovable object. The answer, it turns out, is that we have produced a contradiction if we attempt to produce a world, even a purely mental one, in which there is both an "irresistible force" and an "immovable object," or two Gods each of whom is supreme. That just can't be. Once this is understood, similar puzzles are resolvable.

So, too, in sociology, we often have certain types of chunks, some of which have close formal parallels. Not all of these chunks can go together without contradiction. When these are put together, we can expect certain formal difficulties, though these may be fixable with careful attention. Any existing theory will involve many such chunks, and they may be more or less central. But if we find an inherent problem in *one* such theoretical chunk, we know that we will find it in formally similar chunks. That does not mean that any theory that includes such a chunk is invalid, but it does suggest that a valid theory will deal with the problem—to modify the architecture as a whole in some way. We'll be exploring some of those ways below.

Similar things have been investigated in mathematics; for example, a wide set of combinatoric problems (those considered nondeterministic polynomial time [NP]-hard) have a formal similarity, such that if you can solve one, you can solve them all. It can be hard to understand afterward, but such formal similarities can be overlooked for many years. Bertrand Russell's paradox, pertaining to the set of improper sets, undermined Frege's life's work. Russell eventually realized that it was formally related to the "Cretan's paradox" (the self-referential statement that "I am lying"). That had been known for millennia, but not understood was what it meant when transferred to the realm of infinite recursive sets.

Let me give one example of a family of potentially formally fallacious arguments—one that I found myself struggling with—that may in some instances be true, but is equally plausible where it is not true. It's actually related to Russell's paradox, though here applied to finite sets. There turn out to be a fair number of claims that take the form "When we don't know what it is, we know what it is." This is clearly a worrisome type of argument, and it seems attractive to us when it allows us to say something like "even the things that are [in between / not / opposing] members of class T are also of class T!" I think the (fallacious) logic is

Some of S are T; the rest call ~T.
All T, by virtue of being T, have property B, and this is the
most important T property of interest to us.
All ~T also have B.
Hence ~T are T.

A charming example comes from an interaction I had quite some time ago at an organization where I was somewhat unknown. Strongly supporting a policy that I believed correct, but that brought me no personal advantage and indeed incurred the grouchy hostility of almost all others, I found at least one colleague disturbed and puzzled by my behavior. "I just don't understand what game you're playing," she or he said. I explained that I didn't play games, I just thought that this was the right thing to do. "Ah ha!" exclaimed my co-worker, both triumphant and relieved. "So *that's* your game!"

Perhaps a more pertinent example, one from the world of theory, is from Dewey, who argued that we always see things in our visual field as things-in-particular. He admitted that we don't always know what things are, but in these cases, we see the thing *as an ambiguity.*[6] Perhaps we do, but an "ambiguity" probably doesn't fall under what we previously thought we meant by "things-in-particular."

It is not that this is a simple fallacy—and hence we should never think this way, just as we should never divide by zero. Often we learn something from the exercise of concluding that ~T is T. For example, Niklas Luhmann, in his book with Habermas (Habermas and Luhmann 1971: 32), writes: "All meaninglessness . . . has meaning again through its strangeness."[7] This is true in a way, but

[6] I obediently recycled this idea (Martin 2011), though I now blush to think of it. I still think that the claim is empirically correct (in that ambiguous things are seen as thing-like as they are chunked and assigned an object index in the mind), but I would now suggest a very different formulation, one that does not attempt to erase the difference between things that are recognized and things that aren't.

[7] I adopt the translation of John Bednarz, who brought this example to my attention.

what way? Although linguistic theorists may be exasperated, let us return to an outdated theory of linguistic meaning for a moment, and imagine that you are seated at an old-fashioned teletype machine, communicating with someone far away. You type "ANY NEWS?" and soon, clackety-clackety comes the response: "THE FORTY-NINERS WON THE SUPER-BOWL." The statement THE FORTY-NINERS WON THE SUPER-BOWL means that the Forty-Niners won the Super Bowl. This is a simple sort of semantic meaning that only grazes the surface of normal linguistic communication, but works for some purposes. Now imagine that you type "WHAT WAS THE POINT SPREAD?" and clackety-clack appears on your paper "EWK* @NG+KF!0 *JKFK$$ PKLO." This has a meaning in a sense: it means that somewhere, something is wrong. Something may be wrong with your friend, with his teletype, with yours, perhaps with your glasses, or perhaps with the interaction. But this is a different kind of meaning, a meta-meaning.

Most generally, whenever we find ourselves rushing to claim that "things outside of any set are *themselves* in the set" we may be changing our terminology in ways we do not understand. And if we make a habit of it, we'll end up using meaningless statements. That is, imagine a Venn diagram of two intersecting ovals, marked *X* and *Y*. Our theory is that all $y \in Y$ are *X*. But every time someone tries to disprove our contention by finding a *y* that *isn't* *X*, we redefine *X*—that is, we say, it's not that *y* is *outside* *X*, it's that *X* is *even bigger* than you thought!—eventually *X* will be meaningless. (Let's call this the bigger-not-outside problem.) As I will remark in another place in this chapter, similar extensions have introduced instabilities into certain reasoning processes that took a long time to untangle.

Tautologies and Instability

We've just seen an example of a logically problematic usage (bigger-not-outside) that often sounds, at first encounter, extremely smart. But really, it generally enters theorizing as a *fudge*, that is, as something that makes it harder for others to tell that we are wrong or that something isn't working out in our ideas. (Somewhat different is a *cheat*, which is when we can always prove that we're right.) The bigger-not-outside problem isn't itself a tautology, but it has a relation to tautological statements. In sociology, we do understand that there is a problem with tautologies posing as substantive claims, but we might need to be clearer about good and bad tautologies, good and bad logical circles, and so on.

Good circles are empirical ones. Sometimes we say things like "people try to be good, and good is whatever people say is good." That's circular, but that's the way it is. Tough luck if you don't like it. Bad circles are when we are assuming at one place what we are claiming to prove at another. For an example we'll return to in Chapter 4, let's imagine that someone says that the Bible is inerrant, and we demand proof. Our interlocutor points out that it is written in the Bible that it is true, and we must accept the Bible as inerrant. This sort of circle — one that requires the hearer to accept the authority of another — is unfortunately present in sociology, especially when it comes to destructive critique. ("Don't listen to what these people say about themselves, because they're crazy. I know. They say *I'm* crazy, but that's just the sort of thing you expect crazy people to say.") We can call this the "evil twin" paradox — we have twins, each of whom declares that the other is the evil one, or two people, each of whom claims that the *other* is the lying Cretan. If it works, it's only a *cheat.*

This sort of circle leads to what we'll call *instability. Instability* arises when we can derive contradicting claims from the same premises (in logic, this might be called "inconsistency," but here I'm emphasizing the activity of making theory, not the finished product). This is the sort of formal problem that is most worrisome to sociology (and will be of special interest in Chapter 4) because this means that the only way we pick who is right is to use something *outside* of our logical and empirical coherence: perhaps whoever seemed most confident, whoever used the fanciest words, perhaps the tallest person in the room, or the one with the most Y chromosomes. I think we can fairly call any theoretical structure that not only includes such instability, but can't do without it, and defends it, *pathological.* In a real way, it has cast its lot *against* science — against the possible adjudication of claims using logic and evidence, and *for* personal authority and suppression, and say what you will about how no science lives up to a perfect model, that still can't be good. Thus our goal is not to be pedantic for its own sake, but to clarify logical issues that have allowed us to move away from rigor and systematicity in our work.

There are also good and bad tautologies. If by a tautology we mean something that is necessarily true, there's nothing wrong with that. We often need to use tautologies to manipulate our ideas. The form of the syllogism itself is considered a tautology in logic, though that doesn't mean that saying it is wrong or stupid. Further, there are some sentences that are performatively tautological, but still have a particular content. Thus the statement (which we'll return to in Chapter 6) "you cannot fail to think of an elephant" is true by virtue of saying it, but it's still true and has a real content. What is important for us is not the presence of tautology itself, but rather confusion or instability. Tautologies in a strict form don't *create* either, but they can mask them. And we often have things that *aspire* to tautology, namely, circular logics. So *confusion* arises when we do not understand that we have said a tautology as opposed to a sentence that adds new information (by restricting the set of possible referents of a predicate, for example, as when we say "the rose is white").

When it comes to addressing such logical issues, one could try using a cookbook-type approach — compiling a list of frequent errors that we make associated with certain ways of thinking. The ancient rhetoricians did something very much like this, both in Greco-Roman and Indian civilizations. In fact, you will find the error of "even ~T are T" referred to as a classic error in Aristotle's *Art of Rhetoric* (II.xxiv.13–15). This easily led to a highly scripted way of thinking, equivalent to B-movie kung fu ("Ah, you try your angry crane on me? I respond with the elusive monkey technique!"). But in still other cases, the problematic chunks are not general issues of logic but pertain to ways of thinking that may be specific to the study of social life. These require more protracted treatment and hence form some of the chapters to follow.

It is my contention that this sort of theory-work is important and very rare in sociology, in part because of the decline of theory-ology. There are few ways to learn and implement these skills other than the close analysis of the arguments of others. Consider Stephen Turner, whom I certainly consider to be one of the great American sociological theorists. I am a devotee of his work not because he helps me say things I would like to say. In fact, it is the opposite: he has thrown up spikes that threaten severe tire damage if I were to take the route I'd like to. But he has done this by being right — by being clear about errors that others were making (Colin Campbell has done this as well in places), and I think that this capacity largely came because he had spent serious time going over the implications of others' theories, treating them as worthy of sustained attention. Although most of our ideas aren't worthy of this attention, the mind honed on Weber can then be used to great effect on lesser mortals.

This is what theory-work should be; I go on to say what it can do for us. I first discuss the relatively easy matter of how we should be critically evaluating the theories of others. I then turn to some more general issues that we can internalize to improve our own thinking. I deal with one of the most common formal difficulties for us (one that reappears in various guises across this book), and then issues of how we produce our concepts. I close with a discussion of "unthinking"— how learning about our thoughtways can be used to get a bit closer to what we're trying to study.

LOOKING OUTWARD

Crushing versus Dissecting

As we often do in life, here we will begin by considering how to critique others, and only after this is mastered, learn how we can critique ourselves. When we are unable to see the beam in our own eye, we are fortunate to see the mote in someone else's. And for such researches, it has turned out that the much maligned "theory-ology" has proved quite useful. The close attention to the ideas of others can lead one to recognize certain problematic patterns of thought — at least in others.

That is, most of what passes for critique in sociology is not particularly compelling. Such would-be critiques can involve dismissing something we do not particularly *like*, or saying that we ourselves find something else more interesting (often this is couched as the author "missing the *real* point"). Dismissing others for not being ourselves hardly counts as critique, but it not for that a true critique can only evaluate a theoretical contribution "on its own terms" ("By the standards of contemporary paranoid neo-Nazi thought, this book was quite compelling . . ."). For better or worse, the project of critique implies certain commonalities and shared evaluative standards that different works can be held to.

But how do we hold them to such standards? We must analyze, and to do this we must focus, which means that one has no choice but to simplify arguments. This does not mean to *label* (as in calling others' ideas "-isms"), which doesn't add much, and certainly not to *dismiss* on the basis of naming, which is morally bankrupt, the hate speech of the intellectual world.[8] But we may need to see a particular argument as having chunks that are of a certain class, and we will almost certainly need to determine the core structures of an argument.

Such simplification is easily contested in sociology—though that is not to say that it is not done all the time. There are, however, two different ways of simplifying. One we can call reduction, but crushing would be better. Here we take an argument and turn it into something very simple, but only for the purpose of dismissing. If you want to throw a piece of paper in the wastebasket, you need to crush it to a little ball first. So if you want to throw Marx's work in the garbage can, you need to reduce it to something obviously stupid (such as "all humans only act on the basis of non-idealistic motivations"). This is simplification with violence.[9] Watch for people giving a quick summary of someone else's argument and then dismissing it as "simplistic."

Although not all theories can be turned into directed graphs, let us for a moment imagine that this is the case. One theory might begin with premises p and q, then say that $p+q \rightarrow a, b$ (that is, p and q together imply a and b); $b \rightarrow d$, $d+p \rightarrow e$; $e \rightarrow f$. One form of crushing is to say that the theory claims that $p+q \rightarrow f$, which is false, and therefore reject the theory. Another is to focus on p (which we

[8] Beware of people who "defend" their own theory wholly on the negative grounds that unlike other vaguely defined theoretical currents (say, X-ism and Y-ism), it is, by definition, free of various "errors" or "fallacies" that are given equally opportunistic labeling (say, the fallacy of B-ism)—with no close attention to details. Usually, all they mean is that the *packaging* of their theory contains a misleading and possibly meaningless claim, such as "all the explanation of X-ism with none of the B-ism!"

[9] I have noticed that many current graduate students at least initially believe such crushing to be a form of intellectual *assistance* to their perhaps doddering forebears. "I think I know what he is trying to say," they helpfully say of a serious thinker, as if our theorist's verbal complexity was a simple result of fatigue and mental strain, like that of a stoned valley girl attempting to explain to a police officer why her Mazda is in the middle of a football field, and that a friendly emendation would reduce, say, Marx's theory to something that he could have tweeted to his followers ("Karl: Yo ho mateys, capitalism be double-plus-ungood ☹. @IWA"), confusing clarity with newspeak.

personally reject) and not *q* (which we can't deny), and so claim that this theorist *really* is saying that $p \rightarrow f$ which is wrong and this shows the stupidity of the whole *p*-ist theory. This sort of crushing is neither helpful nor necessary for critique.

But it is also possible to simplify without violence; here we attempt to find the intellectual skeleton of an argument. Rather than crush, we open up. We do indeed trim away, or at least ignore, much of the fat, but we do not do violence to the core of the argument.

Although I used the metaphor of dissecting, the best one is to compare the theorist to a structural engineer.[10] The idea is to find out where the real support is. In many buildings, especially newer ones, walls that you might think are structurally important are actually hanging on the frame. A structural engineer wouldn't confuse hanging walls with supporting walls and therefore think that a building was stronger than it really was.

This sort of activity is usually *not* welcomed by theorists, who tend to be the shady developers of the intellectual world, looking to unload their timeshares before they blow town. Further, this sort of structural approach is considered nearly dirty pool, as if it were off limits to X-ray behind hanging walls to find rotten timber. "But we spackled *over* that!" our theoretical entrepreneur wails in rage and despair—although in sociological theory what we say is that we have added "nuances," which are generally some sort of ornamental plasterwork concealing the actual supports. Looking behind the ornamentation is often dismissed as 'reductionist.'" But finding the core principles of such a theory is not the same thing as *reducing* the theory to these principles alone.[11]

For example, consider Pierre Bourdieu's theory of practice. At the core of this is a version of a habit theory, and it shares a great deal with other habit theories (such as that of John Dewey). Being clear on this is vital for understanding and for appreciating Bourdieu's work: there is nothing demeaning in pointing to similarities. And this does not mean that it is *only* a habit theory, that habitus is *nothing other* than habit, or that his theory can only deal with habit.

Critics of Bourdieu, in repeating the common argument that he has no "room for change," are usually being silly, because they are deducing this from the mere

---

[10] Here I know whereof I speak. Recruited by the University of Chicago I was given a generous housing allowance that would help me to purchase any house in the area, so long as it looked like it was falling over. I have had a number of interesting conversations with structural engineers about what actually holds up a house, and what you do when some of it has been stolen by previous residents.

[11] The analogy to ornamentation is also worth taking seriously. Sometimes the surrounding theoretical claims are not quite fat, nor merely spackle, but are more akin to ornamentation, as it was used in, say, baroque keyboard music. A performer would add certain types of runs and trills where they might add to, and hopefully not subtract from, the written piece. They would indeed be part of the performed piece, but might be done differently at the next performance. So, too, much of the ornamentation of theory is ingeniously tied to the core structural principles, but we don't doubt that had the same basic book been written at a slightly different time, much of this would be different—although the theorist would presumably tend to believe that all such claims were rigorously derivable from the core principles.

fact that Bourdieu's theory *is* largely a habit theory. But just having a habit theory does not mean that one says that habits *always* work, or that *everything* is habit, or anything obviously stupid like that. Sometimes the critiques of Bourdieu that simply start from the habit theoretic nature imply that merely acknowledging the *existence* of habit would be theoretically fatal!

But one can acknowledge the existence of habit, its importance, even its centrality, and put forward a habit theory without this meaning that one cannot grasp things that *aren't* habits. It *does* mean that habit theories, like other good theories, face a decision when they come up against the bounds of their applicability. Either they need to do hard work when it comes to the places where habits don't work, or they need to stay out. The work needed is hard because it involves more than just denying the implications of one's ideas and turning the theory into mush, nor can one just glue on a *second* theory. So the second option, staying out, makes a lot of sense, and there's no shame in it. We aren't going to have very good theories if we reject all that are about something in specific (see the legislative analogy below). It would be like rejecting a theory of magnetism because it doesn't explain gravity, unlike the wonderful all-purpose demon theory—that is, for any physical phenomenon one wants to explain, one posits invisible demons responsible for its occurrence.

Hiding Premises

Thus, identifying core premises alerts us to where certain types of work will need to be done. We become more attentive at these places, attempting to see whether this work is being done well or poorly. Unfortunately, theorists may, more or less deliberately, attempt to confuse us here. Indeed, while adherents tend to respond to critical dissections with claims that this does violence to the integrity of the theory, such violence is quite often done by the theorists themselves.

Why? First, we must recognize that aficionados of a theory tend to elevate the theorist to such a position of cognitive authority that he is allowed to pass judgment on his own theory. Thus if a theorist had a theory with a set of wholly materialist and egotistic premises, if she closes her book by saying "my theory is *not* materialist-egoism," then any investigation of the theory that emphasizes its wholly materialist and egotistic premises will be countered by those who cite the one unimpeachable authority we have, the theorist herself, to the extent that the theory is *not* as it was made out to be by the ignorant critic. So when a theorist hits problems, it is tempting to blatantly just deny them.[12]

[12] Windelband ([1882] 1915: 52) noted that the theorist may be completely unaware that these ideas cannot go together in a system—in fact, since they've "gone together" so nicely for so long in *his head*, he is convinced otherwise!

As Marx would say, we do not ask people their opinions of themselves, and we should not allow theorists to tell us what their theories are all about. Very often, most of the work that constitutes a theory is an attempt to deal with the key problems that come with the theoretical approach. In some cases, these attempts are important and theoretical work is done when they are valid. But in some cases, this theoretical work is basically a heap of inconsistent or meaningless claims that serve to distract us from the core issues. Like the couple in the story of Baba Yar, throwing behind them the magic comb that springs into a dense woods to slow down the pursuing witch, theorists often throw complexifications around the core of their theory (pretending these are protecting belts, although they are more like blubber) largely to bog down the critic. It isn't uncommon for a sociological theory to start with a core premise that leads to two conclusions, one of which is desired (it solves a theoretical problem) but the other of which is considered by the author and likely readers obviously problematic. And as we'll see, theorists can use different means to grapple with this, but sometimes they prefer to simply distract us.

Finally, there are times when it is not one or two implications that are disliked, but practically all of them. Almost all of the theoretical work involved here requires backtracking, ripping up, or stopping the most obvious conclusions from entering the readers' heads. I am going to call this the Lagadosian tactic. Jonathan Swift (1960 [1726]: 146) spoke of the wise men of the Grand Academy of Lagado. One of these was hard at work on "an operation to reduce human excrement to its original food, by separating the several parts, removing the tincture which it receives from the gall, making the odour exhale, and scumming off the saliva."

In the same way, one might, say, take the model of rational choice, and "scum" off the various postulates until one had re-created everyday action. The only question is, why on earth would one want to? Sometimes it seems that people just like a certain *name*; you can call yourself a Marxist (but renounce dialectical materialism), or a pragmatist (while embracing conventional epistemology), or even call yourself a Red Sox fan and root for the Yankees. It's rarely a promising way to start—the chances of being able to start from a set of premises and successfully derive not just one or two but a complex of fundamentally antithetical doctrines aren't great, and so, unless one has good reason to think that you'll be able to "get there from here," one may have to face facts and renounce one's supposed axioms.

Talcott Parsons—our running example for this chapter—wasn't in that situation. He wanted *most* of the implications of his axioms. Just not one in particular—the one that would lead his readers to walk away in disgust, namely, a strong prediction of the necessity and preferability of stasis.

PROBLEMS AND SOLUTIONS

Was Parsons and/or His Theory Conservative?

To aid in our explication of how to analyze the role of premises in theoretical architectures, I introduce what will be the running example for this chapter, namely Talcott Parsons's systems theory. I use this because no one really minds if we show that Parsons's thought was problematic, and so I don't get angry emails. Parsons attempted to construct a systems theory of society and to tie this to individual action in a potentially bottom-up way. He was, as a result, accused of being conservative, often with a "crushing" argument that did violence to his system—some of which was interesting and important (although not the work we will be examining here, his mind-numbingly dreadful *The Social System*).[13]

And perhaps we can start with the question of whether Talcott Parsons was a conservative, what this might mean, and whether it matters. If you are thinking that this is a stupid question, I agree, but it was a commonly discussed one, and addressing it will allow us to approach an orthological consideration of Parsons's approach, conservative or not. So . . . was he?

First, in many cases, our critiques—even those made by and of sophisticated thinkers—boil down to being based on another's general mien, and not that person's specific claims. We don't find fault with his writing—we hate his guts.[14] Often, at base, these "discussions" might go, "A conservative is someone you long to sock in the nose, while a liberal is someone you want to slap silly. I want to punch Parsons in the nose, ergo, he must be a conservative."[15]

Surely we can do better than that. So let's understand that by this question of Parsons's conservatism, we don't mean in his personal character, or even in his own political convictions (he was a progressive), but whether his theory has conservative implications. (In the wonderful words of Alvin Gouldner [1970: 332]: "Functionalists, then, constitute the sociological conservation corps of industrial society.")

Talcott Parsons's functionalism, like many (not all) functionalisms, assumed that certain social institutions had to be understood in terms of their contribution to the overall functioning of society and its capacity to successfully meet the challenges posed by its environment. Now, not all that Parsons did was this func-

---

[13] We should note that one bad book does not make one a bad theorist. One of the many things I love about Parsons is that he was always moving in his thought, always changing, and hence writing "this week's" version of the theory. Perhaps as a result, there wasn't much orthodoxy he could enforce on his students and so he was much more tolerant than many other big ticket theorists of his students thinking on their own.

[14] The importance of this distinction was made to me in conversation by Richard Avrut.

[15] Owens (2010) helps explain *why* so many sociologists after 1951 wanted to sock Parsons in the nose.

tionalism, even during the years that he was a functionalist, but that isn't relevant. In the turbulent 1960s and 1970s, this view was widely dismissed for being conservative because it was taken to imply that society was okay the way it was, since things were functioning, and that the conflict the radicals hoped to introduce would be bad (akin to a fever in a body).[16]

Defenders of Parsons argued that those who believed that Parsons's theory was conservative were wrong. They pointed out, for one, that he acknowledged that there were always some sorts of conflict, that he saw society as a moving equilibrium, and so on. Further, they would point out that Parsons *himself* denied that his theory was conservative!

Of course, it is true that certain types of functionalist argument that make reference to a whole will indeed always be a fertile ground for thoughts that will strike many as conservative, for such thoughts necessarily imply a reference frame other than that of the arbitrary voluntaristic imposition of absolute standards of justice to which many radicals may appeal. Parsons's theory is not that simple, but this issue is. He was no fool, but we are if we think that emphasizing the "changing" or "unsettled" nature of the equilibrium in an equilibrium theory changes the key issues here.

But this isn't really the point. First, there's nothing wrong with this sort of conservatism: most theories that have strong predictions that tomorrow will be a lot like today have a "conservative" element, and may we ever be preserved from living in a world in which that alone is grounds for criticism. Of course, some criticisms of a theory like this will not (explicitly) be rooted in political side-taking — rather, the theory will be rejected because it isn't "true to life." It seems too "one-sided." That is, it doesn't fit our prejudices.

Theory and Prejudice

The greatest impediment to any theory in sociology has been the drive to make its results immediately approximate our prejudices about how the world works. Rather than develop clear thinking, which might be useful in certain circumstances, we expect any theory — at least, any general one — to produce a world that looks like ours: a critique of any biology that doesn't immediately lead to dioramas we find enjoyable.

This is problematic for two reasons. The first is that this is just a terrible way to make theories — to insist that they jump to the end point of investigation and account for everything. To use the common physics analogy (cf. Lieberson 1985),

[16] Funnily enough, the same theoretical structure can appear very anti-conservative . . . so long as one *grouches* about the fact that everything seems to serve a function for the "system." DiTomaso (1982) wonderfully shows the structural parallels between Parsons's theory and that of Althusser.

we would never have a theory of gravitation if it were expected to immediately account for magnetism, the fact that not everything falls at the same rate, and so on. The way to sink a bill in Congress, experienced politicos know, is to attach so many riders and additional parts that it can't possibly be passed without bankrupting the treasury. So, too, the way to sink a promising theory is to try to make it account for everything.

The second thing is that many of our prejudices about how the world is and, hence, how our theories should look, are totally indefensible. But we distort our theories by making sure that they look familiar, constantly fudging and smudging so that our theories have no strong implications (akin to altering the theory of universal gravitation so that as objects got *really* light, they'd actually accelerate more slowly, since that's what we all know is true from experience).

And this gets to why I think that what in other circumstances might be pure pedantry—asking ourselves, at each step, "but am I sure?"—is often the basis of profound insight in sociology. Then theory-work can open up new directions of progress, as opposed to merely coming up with fancy language to disguise the fact that we are regurgitating prejudices. And some seemingly wacky statements, like the pedantic ones, are to be preferred to the seemingly reasonable (that is, comfortingly familiar) ones, if they come from plausible premises. Thomas Metzinger's (2003) careful work that leads to the argument "There are no such things as selves" is important and rigorous, not *because* it challenges our prejudices, which most theories attempt to treat as valid and explain, but because it challenges our prejudices because it is gutsy and rigorous.

For this reason, some of the intellectual traditions that are often dismissed by those with a passion for true science are actually the more scientifically rigorous ones (a point to which I return in Chapter 3). The fact that they don't immediately confirm our everyday lived reality *within which* we do our scientific researches does not justify our dismissing them. Analogously, it is obvious to most of us that only a single line can pass through a point and be parallel to a different line. But once someone asks, "Am I *sure* that this is necessarily true?" and spends the time generalizing to other cases, as did Bernhard Riemann, only the ignorant would try to drum him out of science; and in this case, the resulting geometries turned out to be both radical and necessary for physicists' models of the universe.

So, too, those who emphasized that the "motivations" for actions were things that empirically, observably, came *after* the actions as social explanations, and those who noted that scientific truth was the *product* of social action and not its cause, have been, and continue to be, dismissed as if they were willfully making things harder or sillier for the rest of us. Now in a few cases, truth be told, some *were* clearly enjoying making things harder for the rest of us, and sometimes they wrote in a silly way. But they were good scientists, better than the rest of us. They were largely ignored by our discipline not because they were stupid or hairsplitting, but because if we accepted what they have said we would have needed to throw out half of our work and start from scratch, laboring much harder for every article published than we do now. (We'll return to this in the last chapter, so if it doesn't make sense yet, maybe it will then.)

In sum, we need to put on hold our judgment that a theory gives "too much" weight to one or another "side" of some issue. The first issue for a critic is whether the theory works as advertised; whether it makes sense, whether it is internally consistent, whether its premises imply what the theorist says they imply, or whether they imply something different. And so here, we attempt to start with core premises.

Parsons's Premises

It isn't always easy to tell what the premises of a theoretical work are, for not all works start with them. But this seems like a promising candidate for a fundamental premise: Parsons (1951: 205) gives as the "first law of social process" that "complementarity of role expectations"—that is, that the interactants' ideas of what is going to happen mesh with one another—"once established, is *not problematical.*" Clearly Parsons does not deny that this is a crucial axiom for his theory. He develops it as follows: "An established state of a social system is a process of complementary interaction of two or more individual actors in which each conforms with the expectation of the other(s) in such a way that the alter's reactions to ego's actions are positive sanctions which serve to reinforce his given need-dispositions and thus to fulfill his given expectations."

Now the first thing that we cannot help noticing is that there is indeed a very conservative feel to this set of assumptions—that the core of a social world is people being pleased that everything stays the same. We can understand why Parsons's theory reeked of conservatism, and why those for whom this was a dirty word immediately began looking for weak spots to tear it down. However, there is no intellectual sin in having a conservative temperament, nor from starting from conservative premises. Indeed, conservatives may be constitutionally favored when it comes to dealing with all sorts of theoretical and empirical puzzles. Further, it isn't even obviously empirically unacceptable to suggest that people—*all* people, at least for the purposes of creating a theory—prefer to preserve the status quo. (Subordinate people, contrary to what rabble-rousing intellectuals assume, might be extremely worried about any breakdown in a plausible order because they have a hard time protecting themselves.)

However, Parsons's theoretical argument here goes beyond this, and directly implies that all people have a need-disposition to have others confirm their expectations—that every time someone violates our expectations, it pains us, at least compared to the gratification we would experience if she conformed. Parsons here (and elsewhere, as I [Martin 2001a] and previously Dennis Wrong [1994: 68] have noted) rules out the possibility of a "pleasant surprise." We may expect the bully to hit us as we walk by, but (as Parsons would have no trouble acknowledging) be pleasantly surprised that he does not hit us. (Although participants may be disconcerted when everyday social order is brought to a crashing halt by seemingly *meaningless* refusals to meet expectations [as in the breaching experiments of Garfinkel], this in no way implies that all have an interest in expectations being met, and usually a relatively short bout of introspection is sufficient to demonstrate this. When I walk down the street in Hyde Park, I fully *expect* people to pass by me with rigid fixed unhappy stares, or to glance at me as if I had just informed them that I was a representative of the IRS here to collect their gonads in lieu of a fine. I certainly would be upset and frightened if instead they were to flap their arms and crawl around me on their knees. But I'd actually prefer an [unexpected] "howdy" to either of these.)

The premise, then, is factually false. And a demonstrably false premise isn't good (and having a false premise isn't the same thing as a general feeling that the theory as a whole isn't "true to life"). But still, false premises sometimes turn out to be a reasonable place to start. (It also should be noted that not all starting places are axioms: sometimes a theorist starts with a simplified version of the axioms that illustrate key aspects of the theory, but then replaces these axioms with more accurate ones.) Unfortunately, Parsons's premise also tends to imply that the role system that produces society can never have such pleasant surprises. We all must want things to be just as they are. This is obviously silly, and I think Parsons knew it—he did not want to draw the conclusion that all people, all the time, want things to stay as they are. So what did he do? Here it helps to stop and consider this problem in more general and formal terms.

Handling Problems

We left Parsons in the position common to many theorists. They begin with a set of propositions S that jointly imply a, b, c, and d, while they would like to conclude a, b, and c, but not d. What to do? Let's assume that the issue of S implying d is well recognized and so the theorist cannot just ignore it and hope no one discovers that her axioms imply it. What are possible responses?

A. *Disprove the entailment.* In some cases, it is widely believed that $S \rightarrow d$, but the theorist attempts to demonstrate that this does not follow. If that effort is successful, this is an impressive solution. In fact, it's really the only decisive one.
B. *Use an ex cathedra denial.* A surprisingly common attempt is to take advantage of the fact that the author is alone in a room at the time of

writing, and is likely to be read only by those who are sympathetic to the endeavor, and thus unpoliced; hence, she simply denies that $S \rightarrow d$, perhaps saying that only a fool would believe this in the first place.

C. *Introduce new axioms.* Sometimes a theorist introduces a new axiom, T, such that $S + T \rightarrow a$, b, and c but not d. When this axiom T is simply "*S* does not lead to *d*," we call this ad hoc (there are other forms of ad hocery, but this is the most blatant form).

D. *Recast S.* In some cases, a theorist attempts to open up *S*, recast and rearrange it into $S*$ so that it no longer implies *d*. This is very difficult, and even when it succeeds technically, it often fails rhetorically, because readers lapse into old habits and read $S*$ as *S*. On the other hand, theorists sometimes *claim* to have done such recasting, when in fact, they are really doing a form of (B) here. (Watch for claims that they have a "nuanced," "critical," or "sophisticated" version of the old axioms; chances are all they'll say about their new secret formula is that new-and-improved *S* doesn't imply *d*.)

E. *Introduce (intuitively plausible) substantive claims.* But in other cases, it is not a new axiom that is introduced (as in [C]), but a *substantive claim*. It might seem hard to distinguish a substantive claim from an axiom, and we can acknowledge that the difference is relative to context, and yet it is palpable. When a theorist introduces an axiom, he labels it as such, and in a sense "loses" something, for axioms are costly. The more that are made, the weaker is the internal structure of the theory. Instead of being connected to *one another*, portions of the theory are now connected to the (putative) nature of the world. Further, the reader understands that while she has granted the axiom provisionally, to see what can be made of things, she mentally retains the right to withdraw assent to the axiom at any time. It is different when a substantive claim is used to neutralize *d*. Then the reader's *own* empirical knowledge is drawn to support the claim, and it is "free" to the theorist. Thus these days, to us, "all people maximize their well-being" is an axiom; "we really love our kids" is a substantive claim that is costless.

F. There is one last solution, related to (E), which is to *construct an open-ended substantive claim*. This is a trump card that can be played at any time, because it has the form of a substantive claim and yet can encompass any particularities. I'm going to call this the Tigger principle. When Winnie the Pooh and Piglet meet Tigger, he assures them that he eats *everything*, but whatever he is given, he tastes and decides that this doesn't quite qualify as part of his everything. By "I eat everything" he meant "I eat everything *but* honey, and thistles, and . . ." A common version, well beloved by Durkheim, is to implicitly exclude "pathological" cases from the scope of the theory. (If you think that pathological cases are those that the theory doesn't cover, good guess.)

Paying attention to when solutions of form (E) and especially (F) enter a theory turns out to be extremely useful in figuring out where a theory is going wrong. I expand upon this, and then return to our example.

Formal and Substantive Statements

The reason we need to pay special attention to responses (E) and (F) is that while they are formally very bad news for a theory, they often seem to readers to be very good indeed. We will have occasion a number of times in this book to draw on the distinction between substantive and formal rationality—a distinction (used frequently by Weber) that can be applied to actions. For example, a welfare bureaucrat who applies a poorly framed rule that ends up denying a deserving citizen benefits may be said to be acting in a formally rational manner, because the form of the action (deduction from rules) is rational—even though the action does not reach the intended goal (providing assistance to the deserving). This bureaucrat would be substantively rational, even though formally irrational, were she to throw the rulebook out the window and make an exception, because then the *substance* of her mission—helping the deserving—guides her actions.

I think a similar distinction can be made regarding theoretical statements. A statement *a* in a set of other statements *S* is formally rational if it is consistent with the implications of the other statements (*S*). For example, if we assume that people are economically rational and seek to maximize their expectations of hedonic enjoyment, that they use laws of probability to do so, and that they estimate the likely hedonic enjoyment of the next year, the next ten years, and so on, we can conclude that there must be *some* odds at which they would be willing to bet their lives for a dollar.

Yet most of us would not wager our lives for a dollar, no matter what the odds ("I'll give you seventy quillion-quadjillion to one!"). Here we seem to be acting in a substantively reasonable manner, because we don't think someone is irrational for turning down this bet. We may not be able to explain precisely *why* this is rational, but that doesn't mean that it isn't. I'm going to propose that we consider a substantively rational statement to be one that has a "reasonable feel" to "reasonable people," given what they know about the world.[17]

---

[17] This sort of social basis to the definition is necessary, for in contrast to Weber's examples, we don't have a clearly identified goal state that analyst and actor agree upon.

Theorists often don't like producing statements that seem substantively irrational, even if such statements are formally rational, and they often come up with different ways to qualify the implications of their arguments. And one way is to include substantively reasonable assertions that possess congenial implications for the theoretical conclusions. In other words, even those who resist making their theory immediately look familiar and satisfy our prejudices may balk at including something that seems really weird, and if they have to, they'll insert a reasonable claim to keep weirdness at bay. Yet this, I will argue, completely undermines the value of their theory.

It is not that substantive rationality has no place in sociological theory. Indeed, one of the more compelling branches of social thought, often associated with British empiricism in its "sentimentalist" mode, bases its understanding on the assumption that human beings are substantively reasonable creatures and that we need to understand their capacity for ethical and harmonious action on the basis of this substantive orientation to what is reasonable. Similar ideas are often now developed from a neo-Catholic tradition, and sometimes considered Aristotelian. This is because Aristotle may have been the first recorded to grapple with the fact that human beings must be able to make judgments that they cannot defend through deduction.[18] Somehow, the anchor of such judgments is not found in an *axiom* but in the constitution of the person. This resolves some problems but raises others, leading to theoretical investigations that are certainly worthy of serious consideration. But it is one thing to develop a theory *of* how people are substantively reasonable, and quite another to insert substantively reasonable statements *in* a theory.

A theory is in some ways a recipe for making statements; if it is anything other than a collection of "my favorite words," it offers promise for others to make substantive statements that the theorist herself may not yet have made. My great-great-aunt Sadie was an excellent cook of traditional Jewish dishes. My mother often would ask her for a recipe so that Sadie's techniques could be passed down. (This is all true, by the way.) Aunt Sadie would describe the steps: next you add in the potato starch. "How much?" my mother would ask, pencil at the ready. "Oh you know, not too much, not too little."

The problem here was that the embodied knowledge couldn't be passed on: as long as Aunt Sadie was there, things were fine, but without her, there was no recipe at all. Similarly, when a theorist injects such substantive statements, often to the effect that "you don't want too much change, or too little," we don't really have a theory at all. The seemingly close fit with the reader's expectation is deceptive.

---

[18] Previously, skeptical thinkers surely pointed to the *difficulty* of such judgments (later known in philosophy as the problem of how many grains make a heap—if you start with one grain, it isn't a heap, but as you successively add one, then another, at what point does it become a heap?), but they may not have attempted to *solve* the problem.

The theory is not doing *well* because it seems "accurate"; it is doing horribly because it has built in wiggle room in which anything can happen. People are selfish, except when they're not; all history is moved by class struggle, except for a few people; and so on. All such claims sound reasonable, but none should be allowed to be granted the title of theory.

Pathologizing and Other Forms of Subjective Judgment

So we left off with Parsons starting from the false premise that we all get gratification when others fulfill our expectations. Sometimes we start with false premises because they are good enough, or because even though they aren't *always* true, there is a class of situations in which they might hold, and that's what our theory will explain. Other times we start with false premises but revise them later, usually by making them less restrictive. This is not inherently invalid, but it is tricky because we need to make sure that we are not using a set of premises S to derive one set of conclusions C, and then changing our premises to S' which imply D, and claiming that our theory explains C and D—when $S' \rightarrow \sim C$. For an example of a successful change of premises, one can first define a simple equilibrium and then generalize one's presuppositions to a case of a moving equilibrium without pulling out one's own supports. And that's what Parsons was doing. But *how* did he do this? And *how* did he deal with the problem of seeming to rely on a personality structure that approved of all stasis, which seemed implausible and objectionable?

He did two things. First, he constructed a theory of the personality that explained that this "complementarity" was true for properly functioning personalities, but there were some defectives out there who just came out wrong and had a perverse need-disposition to *violate* expectations. Such an answer would make anti-conservatives absolutely howl with rage—that any apparent dissatisfaction to a regime of conformity to inequality came from the absence of a quality control mechanism to weed out the unfit—but it is a conventional type of fudge.

Unfortunately, it is one of the more troublesome aspects of theorizing. On the one hand, it *isn't* reasonable to reject every theory because of a few exceptions, if those exceptions are what really should be rejected. We don't forbid ourselves from calling horses, quadrupeds, or saying that they nurse their young, just because one in a million is a mutant. So, too, in sociology, there's nothing in principle unacceptable about wanting to be able to rule out muties. On the other hand, practically every incorrect statement can be defended if we are allowed to cherry pick our examples and discard as "pathological" whatever doesn't fit our preconceptions. Durkheim (e.g., 1933 [1893]) was famous for this—developing a theory of society that he himself claimed did not fit his society, or any others. His conclusion was that this spoke poorly of society, not of his theory. Most of us have not been moved by this logic.

Usually there is no formal way that we can decide how many "exception" cards a theorist is allowed to play in advance. If the theorist can describe the origin and etiology of the exception-ness independently of the theory, we tend to cut her a bit more slack, but usually we have a sense of unease that is roughly proportional to the number of exceptions but inversely proportional to the explanatory power of the theory.

But to return to Parsons, he did not simply rest with this answer for the same reason that Durkheim did not rest with it. Both were indeed conservatives in a way, but in a more important way, they were not conservatives, but progressives. That is, both saw progress and development as normal states of society. Parsons understood this in terms of a moving equilibrium, which is an extremely sensible and powerful way to think, and (as Parsons's defenders correctly argued) undercut the dismissals of Parsons as a reactionary. Thus Parsons would not say that failure to enjoy stasis comes *only* from pathology, because there must be some sort of way in which some actually existing people reject old ways in favor of those that are more appropriate for the near future. (And this is his second response to the problem of stasis.)

This is something that Durkheim himself expressly put forward, but he had the intellectual honesty to admit that he wasn't able to completely figure out how to incorporate it in his theorizing (see Durkheim 1979 [1908]: 57). Parsons, characteristically, made it seem as if he had solved this problem by restating the folk theory of his sympathetic readers in excruciating double-talk; predicting the existent and chalking it up to the scientific stature of his theory, when (as in the vast majority of *The Social System*) his statements are simply ad hoc claims. It is true that in one way, he did successfully change and expand upon his core premise without violating the implications that he had drawn from it. That is, although he first derived the expectations from the existent (more obviously in Parsons and Shils 1954 [1951]), thereby implying that ego's expectations for alter's behavior at time t come from ego's memory of alter's actions at times 1 through $t-1$, by expanding the role of the shared social values, he replaced these empirically generated local expectations with transcendent shared ones derived from overarching value commitments. I believe that this is in many ways a successful technique: although he had replaced the ground under which he began building his structure, none of the conclusions he drew from the earlier derivation of expectations are upset by this new form of expectations.

Yet something more was needed. If there are valid expectations that do not correspond to the actual state of things, how do we tell the valid from the invalid?

That is, which ones are fundamentally compatible with the healthy development of the social whole and its core principles? *You* may expect that I treat my neighbors fairly (even though I do not), and *I* may expect that you shall shovel my walk for me every day (even though you do not). How are we to determine whose expectations are valid and whose not? It wouldn't work to stress "shared" values because we already must have noticed that there is some sort of *lack* of sharing here. We can't root things in the majority, say, because that is again to define the *ought* by the *is*. If that worked, we wouldn't be in this fix in the first place.

And indeed, Parsons did believe that sometimes an *ought* that doesn't correspond to the *is* is a *good ought*, and sometimes it is bad. His explanation goes as follows: there are "vested interests" coming from the nature of equilibrium maintenance (1951: 491f), and any change means overcoming resistance of such vested interests; for example, slavery may be incompatible with democracy, but slave owners don't want hear that. But not all changes are compatible with the survival of the system; that is, sometimes change doesn't destroy the system (e.g., plants and animals can *grow*), while other changes imply destruction of the system (e.g., being cooked). With a moving equilibrium, then, there are two main ways things can go wrong: either the system *doesn't* move where it should because of "vested interests" and the resistance that arises, or the progressive sectors experience too much strain so that they end up as an "alienated revolutionary movement" (520).

This may be called the Goldilocks theory of change. Like Goldilocks, Parsons can tell whether what people want is too hot or too cold. In other words, when confronted with whining hippies like Meathead in *All in the Family*, who want to have their cake of capitalist prosperity and eat it too, Parsons smartly sends them packing, but if he then turns and faces stupid reactionaries like Archie Bunker, who's been cheering and repeating "incompatible with functional needs! That's just it!" Parsons has an answer that would do Meathead proud.

We see, then, that he is relying on the interjection of a personally arbitrary substantive judgment (how much change is just right) at a vital place. If so, it is hard to see why we should consider it a theory at all. If the system as a whole has a regress to a personalistic judgment that Parsons has to make, why not cut to the chase? We have a case of social conflict: well, is this a case of the implementation of true societal values against the resistance of "vested interests," or only "alienative motivational elements" in the population as a result of strain (521) who, holding out for some sort of unrealistic utopia, get their hands on a "latent reservoir of legitimation possibilities" and effectively (if irresponsibly) link it to demands "incompatible with the functional needs of the institutionalized order" (296)? When push comes to shove, you have to run off and find Talcott to see if this is too much, too little, or just the right amount of change.

AWKWARD JOINS

Turbulence

We've seen in Parsons's work a potential problem in a core axiom; by tracing the adjustments made to the theory in an attempt to deal with the problem, we find the areas that need to be scrutinized for weakness. And in fact, we find a key weak spot in the theory. The problem is delayed, but not fixed: it requires an arbitrary Goldilocks judgment, undermining the seeming clarity of the initial structure. This is a fine example of how an architectonic approach to criticizing theories of others helps us understand what they do and do not mean.

Further, we've found that in this case our problems ripple outward from a typical point of structural weakness in theories, one pertaining to fusing the "is" to the "ought." It seems that in one sense, Parsons hoped to get the "is" from the "ought," by positing that people produce and reproduce patterns of action because they think that others *should* observe these patterns; hence, ego sanctions alter for deviance, reproducing the pattern. To aid this derivation, he first proposed that the "ought" came from the "is" (as we form expectations based on what happened in the past, and consider those legitimate expectations). This sort of fusion is stable, but it has three disadvantages. One, on which I focused, is that we know it isn't true. A second is that it makes all change exogenous. This is sometimes misstated as the theory being "unable to account for change," which is incorrect; we could feed changes in the external environment into such a circular theory and account for change very well, although our predictions could be extremely sensitive to the proper specification of what we feed in (often known as the initial conditions). And this would in no way be a stupid theory: many students of social revolutions have in fact hit upon such a model, as they realize that what seems to motivate most of the rank and file of transformational movements is a desire to keep things *the same* in a changing world.[19]

The third reason, and what I think is most empirically important, is that nowadays we think that people are creeps for saying things like this (whatever is, is good), and so no one wants to start with a premise that affirms this, even if it works in architectonic terms.

Hence, most of us look for other ways of dealing with the problem of the *is* and the *ought*. One stable solution is to jettison one of the two completely, and it is always the *ought* that gets tossed. This can be done either by treating morality

[19] And it isn't really true that habit or reproduction theories make all change exogenous. The American composer La Monte Young had an influential piece, "Arabic Numeral (Any Integer) to H.F." in which the score is merely for the performer to make a sound, repeat it, and then repeat the sound previously made, as exactly as possible, *ad astra*. Rather than being a recipe for stasis, the result (if performed with a proper instrument) is continuous and marvelous change.

as an uninteresting social illusion or by ignoring the oughtness of motivating communications. But this tends to leave many of us unsatisfied, and so we get many other attempts. I won't here argue that most of them are likely to fail (although I will explain why this is so for a large family of them in a forthcoming book). But just as a good architect or plumber knows that if you try to join steel pipes with zinc plating to copper pipes, you can expect corrosion to begin, so a good orthologician will expect trouble to begin where theorists attempt to fuse the is and ought.[20]

Inside Out

We can return to the running example of Parsons's (or almost anyone's) functionalism to help clarify another common sort of problem that arises due to a joining (though in this case, one that is often unrecognized as such). The issue at hand is how we theorize "roles"—facts such as that some people bake bread and others grow wheat. In Chapter 5 we will find that examination of animal social behavior casts considerable light on this issue, but we can make some headway simply through orthologics.

The first thing we can do is bear in mind that as we (possibly all humans, certainly contemporary Westerners) have a strong tendency to interpret action in terms of intention and purpose (I will return to this below). We also should understand that the way we ask questions tends to orient us to certain forms of answer. Thus if we ask someone, "Why do you think this person goes to work every day?" the answer will likely be "to make money"; if we ask, "Why does the baker bake bread?" our answerer will probably focus on the fact that the bread is going to other people who will eat it (even though the two questions might be the same in denotation, if our first person was a baker). Thus we need to watch ourselves carefully to make sure we are not assuming that our answer will turn on the social purpose accomplished by the person inhabiting a role. There's nothing wrong with this being an answer, so long as we're sure that there *is* a social purpose. In that case, we can go on to see whether the fact of the purpose could be

---

[20] It is extremely common, especially these days, to hear that the divide between the "is" and the "ought" has been overcome, and that only an old-fashioned stodger would willfully refuse to acknowledge that this is no longer recognized as a problem. But one will note that the justifications for this are always things like "in practice, no one can separate values from factual statements." That is, they pertain to the "is"-ness of the is / ought distinction, while the stodgers who maintain their belief that this is a fundamental distinction usually are insisting that they *ought* not to so be intermixed. The fact that it *is* the case that the is and ought cannot be separated does not compel these thinkers to believe that it *ought* to be the case; this fact itself seems to me to support the stodgers and not the fusers. I'll return to this in Chapter 3, but I think this is a very serious point: not only does it not *logically* follow that one *should not* pursue a goal simply because one *cannot* reach it, but I suspect the opposite is true; our reach *must* exceed our grasp, or what's a science for? Although I do think that there may be places in which *is* and *ought* are necessarily and justifiably fused, pursuing this requires careful attention to the possible objectivity of requiredness, as given by Köhler (1938).

responsible for the action, but even if the purpose exists, we might find it doesn't explain the action. We must avoid a hasty acceptance of a claim simply because it feels good.

Bakers do bake bread, and others eat it, and it might seem like one was being purposefully difficult were one not to accept "baking of the bread" as the answer for the question "why is there a baker?" But (in a simplified feudal order) knights protect peasants, which seems very good. But it doesn't explain why there is a knightly order, since no one but knights particularly wants things this way (especially the protected peasants, because this order is one that forbids peasants to have arms and involves knights attacking peasants). The knightly order was—and most political societies are—for better or worse, an elaborated, modified, mitigated protection racket. To give an analogy: my dog is honestly convinced that she performs a vital function for the house. This is to instantly alert us if any *other* dog comes within 500 yards of our front door, at any time of the day or night. I am sure that all the dogs wonder together about how people ever got by without them.

Now the issue is not that we need to separate "good" jobs from "bad" jobs. There is a formal problem here that has perhaps not yet come clearly to the surface. Here is a different example (Lieberson, 1985, works this through quite nicely): a regression equation tells us that high school dropouts are far more likely to be poor than high school graduates. Concerned with the problem of poverty, we embark on a dedicated campaign to end dropping out. It succeeds perfectly, and yet we find that poverty has not been reduced at all.

What all these examples have in common is a confusion of action within some order and the creation of the order itself. (It is often assimilated to the issue of cross-level inference, but I think that this is formally quite secondary to the issue of inside-outside.) This problem has been repeatedly clarified, and repeatedly remuddled. Rational choice and / or analytical political theorists such as Jon Elster, Adam Przeworski, and Erik Olin Wright gave us some tools here; Karl Mannheim formulated a version for thinking about what it meant to say that something was "utopian," and statisticians struggle with this now under the name of the stable unit treatment value assumption, but the common issue has to do with the collapsing of an "outside" question with an "inside" one. An "outside" question might be something like, "Given all the different occupational distributions that there might be, why does this society here have the sort of occupational distribution it does?" An "inside" question might be, "*Conditional on the fact that* (in other words, *assuming that*) this society here has the sort of occupational distribution it does, why do *these people inside* this society have this occupation and not that?" Answering the second doesn't answer the first. This does not mean that the "inside statement" is irrelevant, but it often turns out to be something different from what we originally asked.

For example, let's say that there is a new religious group, call them the Church of Smok, who smack themselves on the head every morning when they rise. We wonder why this is. We study a set of different individual Smokkers, understanding what this action means to them and to others and so on, and we then explain that they do this action because it is deeply intertwined with all the rest of their lives. We can perhaps communicate this to the reader with dense and well-written prose. However beautiful this description may be—and it may indeed have serious scientific value—we need to understand that formally, it is reproducing a simpler argument that we reject when our children make it (though most of us basically accept its validity in our own lives): we did it because everybody else was doing it.

We could reach this understanding of the formal characteristics of our explanation if we were to substitute "kiss a chipmunk" for "smack self on head" and find that the explanation was pretty much the same. By dropping to the "inside," we answered a somewhat different question from "Why do Smokkers smack themselves on the head?" which is what we started with, for we turned it into "Why, *conditional on the fact* that Smokkers are known to smack themselves on the head, does any *individual* member smack herself or himself on the head?" Or confusing "Why are there knights and peasants?" with "Why *conditional* on the knightly system, does any peasant accept a knight's protection?" Or confusing "Why are dropouts poor?" with "Why *conditional* on the economic and occupational organization of a nation, are the dropouts the poor ones?"

This elision has been responsible for the remarkable profusion of work pointing to the importance of institutional logics in the explanation of action. Those who have put forward theories turning on such institutional logics will have different and in many cases deep thoughts along these lines, but the heart of all still seems to me that an institutional logic is a "way things are done" in such-and-such a place, or in such-and-such circumstances. (Often the deep theorizing here has to do with the connection between this practice and subjectivity, though this isn't crucial for the point I am going to make.) A focus on institutional logics has become increasingly interesting to students attempting to explain why people do the things they do. Indeed, this is often held up as an alternative type of explanation to individual-based accounts, or as an alternative level of analysis, showing that there is a need for a vocabulary of social explanation not reducing to individual actions. It seems associated with the introduction of more and more "culture" into organizational studies, in part because it turns out that explaining why middle-level managers at Bear Stearns do what they do is a lot like explaining why Melanesian fishermen do what *they* do—if they're not to be dismissed as simply insane, we need to be sensitive to their cultural understandings. As you might guess, however, we start to run into Smokker-type problems.

Consider Vaughan's (1996) justly famous *The Challenger Launch Decision.* This is a wonderful piece of research that uncovered not only important information about this particular case but about organizational decision making in general. Yet it was seized upon by others (and to some extent used by Vaughan herself) as supporting the idea of an institutional cultural explanation. Indeed, when Vaughan boils things down to a (general) sociological conclusion, it seems of the form "institutional culture caused this decision to be of this sort." As I am sure a number of people have pointed out, as institutional culture is itself nothing other than the pattern of social action that takes place in the institutional setting, this is to take the pattern of action, pull out one part, put it by itself, draw a line from the rest of the pattern to this one part, and write "causes" on the line. Such answers are quite valid if we mean that *my* action was conditioned on everyone else's. But it pushes off the bigger question, in the same way that we push off the question when we explain authoritarian actions by pointing out that they tend to be carried out by authoritarian people.

Although this book is about theories, not methods, a related confusion is actually seen in the widespread use of change score models, and perhaps working through this will clarify things for some readers (for those for whom it doesn't, my apologies, and let's meet at the beginning of the next section). This is when instead of doing a conventional statistical analysis in which we compare the value of some dependent variable (e.g., income) to another (e.g., education), we compare the *change* in each person's income to his *change* in education (although we realize that there are all sorts of reasons why this particular example isn't a good candidate for a change score model, itself an important lesson). The statistical logic underlying the technique is fine[21]—if indeed one variable is a linear function of another, and we have observations over successive times, we should be able to subtract the equation for one time from that for another and produce a model for the changes that will retrieve the correct original coefficients without having to worry about any unmeasured

[21] If the income of person *i* at any time *t* (denoted $Y_{i,t}$) is a linear function of a set of other time invariant variables *Z* and time variant variables *X*,

$$Y_{i,t} = \beta_0 + \sum_j \beta_j^A Z_{j,i} + \sum_k \beta_k^B X_{k,i,t} + \varepsilon_{i,t}$$

then we can subtract this from the same equation for the next time (*t*+1) and get

$$\begin{aligned} Y_{i,t+1} - Y_{i,t} &= \beta_0 + \sum_j \beta_j^A Z_{j,i} + \sum_k \beta_k^B X_{k,i,t+1} + \varepsilon_{i,t+1} - \beta_0 - \sum_j \beta_j^A Z_{j,i} - \sum_k \beta_k^B X_{k,i,t} - \varepsilon_{i,t} \\ &= \sum_k \beta_k^B (X_{k,i,t+1} - X_{k,i,t}) + (\varepsilon *_{i,t+1}) \end{aligned}$$

That is, all the time invariant disturbances cancel out—whether or not they are measured and included in the model, and the new errors can be assumed to behave nicely, leading us to get the original parameters from a change score model.

confounders that don't change over time (since these will drop out, being the same in both equations).

The problem is that it is extremely unlikely that the linear function, should there be one, between two variables is really anything other than an outcome of a set of processes that we should be investigating, and there is no reason to think that these processes are expressible in such a linear law. What we end up doing, then, is not explaining the relationship in which we are interested (call it the "pattern"), but instead, we examine the deviations *from* the pattern. The pattern and the deviation *from* the pattern are not necessarily related in a simple and obvious way (although not all organizations of deviations are compatible with preservation of the pattern). For example, in his wonderful study of the relation between bowling scores and status, William Whyte (1981 [1943]) found, overall, a positive correlation among the "corner boys" he studied. And it might well be that if someone's status increased, his bowling score might increase. But if someone of low status increased his bowling score, it wouldn't lead to an increase in his status. Rather, the pattern would be preserved by the others "razzing" him and *lowering* his bowling score (and perhaps his status as well).

The difference between the overall patterns and deviations *from* the pattern is most wonderfully seen in the common practice of including a lagged dependent variable back in the change score model.[22] We almost always find this coefficient to be negative, implying that to him who hath, something shall be taken away, and from him who hath not, something shall be given. If this sounds funny to you, that's because in the real world things tend to go the other way—the phrase Merton (1968) stole from the Gospel of Matthew: to them that have, more shall be given (or in my dad's more folksy language, "them as has, gits"). But in statistics, this is a common phenomenon entitled "regression to the mean" (hence the name of the statistical method being used).

This isn't because all phenomena are attempting to commit suicide—that money gets rid of itself (although actually that would explain a lot about my finances), and so on. Rather, it is that if you get lucky one year, chances are you won't the next year (otherwise, it's not luck—it's something about you, which has been taken out of the change equation). Even if you don't do *worse* than usual the next year, if you do *usual*, still, your *growth* will be less than it usually is (given you were lucky last year), and so the term is negative. Even though those with money tend to get more money (and more and more and more), we can get a misleading view from the change model.

[22] That is, we fit

$$Y_{i,t+1} - Y_{i,t} = \beta_Y(Y_{i,t}) + \sum_k \beta_k^B (X_{k,i,t+1} - X_{k,i,t}) + \varepsilon*_{i,t+1}.$$

Now the same general problem haunts the more prosaic terms on the right side of the equation. The things that help explain *deviations* from a pattern aren't always the same as those that explain the pattern. In many cases, we're looking at short-term errors, luck, mistakes, and other things that reverse themselves shortly. But we can think we're understanding the main pattern itself.

In sum, there are times when we begin with a question that is *not* conditioned on certain facts, but find that it seems easier to answer it when we *have* conditioned on these facts—yet this turns out to be an answer to a wholly different question. This problem of conditionality, as we shall see, recurs in a number of guises.

Outside In

We can make the reverse error, assuming that our answer to a question about action given certain conditions can be explained by the examination of those conditions themselves, but this is rarer and rarer given our increasingly fine data sources. Instead, the "outside in" error that we tend to make is somewhat different; it is thinking that the gross outside pattern (the marginals, if one is thinking statistically), itself constrains the inner (the cell frequencies) so that they produce the aggregate pattern. This is often extremely tempting because we have good reason to think that *something* should be leading the aggregate pattern to be stable. This is especially true when the pattern we're thinking about is something *good*.

It does seem reasonable that *something* should make sure that there are always farmers, because if there aren't, bad things will happen—like, we run out of food—yet the importance of farmers doesn't itself lead people to become farmers. More generally, this error involves taking an *outcome* of a set of actions and making it *itself* the cause of the actions. If you have what seems to be a good explanation for why we see something that *does* exist, see if it changes when you substitute something that *doesn't* exist (though it would be good if it did). If our explanation for the existent thing is just as strong a "predictor" of the nonexistent, we've got a problem. It's a well-known error in philosophy (at least, to nondeterminists), to assume that just because something exists, that proves it *had* to exist.

Sometimes, though, we are hesitant to propose so simple a solution and just declare the effect the cause—and so we worry about what bridges the two laws, as if the outcome were itself something other than an outcome. But this is still putting a force where it shouldn't be—akin to wondering what bridges the law that water runs downhill with the law that lakes are formed where they are (the good places where they need to be for us to fish in them). But lakes don't *pull* the water down from the mountains and hence cause streams. Lakes are lakes because that's where the water ends up. Sometimes people do things to make sure lakes stay lakes; so, too, there can be all sorts of social factors that try to keep outcomes the way they are (and if the lakes don't dry up, we know something about the water cycle, and so on). Just as there can be cases in which the individual conditional action can be used to explain the aggregate, so, too, there can be cases in which the aggregate pattern *is* imposed on the internal workings (action conditional on the pattern). Sometimes the marginals *are* fixed (e.g., there are only so many seats in Congress), other times, there are processes that tend to restore an aggregate (well-functioning markets do this in all sorts of happy ways). But we need to have good reasons to expect that this is the case, not simply assume it because, were it true, it would justify our thinking in more "sociological" terms.[23]

Levels of Analysis

This brings us to a recurrent confusion in sociology, namely, that of how to understand the relation between different "levels of analysis." The "level of analysis" chosen for the purposes of theorizing (though not of data analysis) is often treated as if it were a matter of personal predilection, somewhat akin to the way drivers in New Jersey seem to feel about traffic lanes (the passing lane has a nice view of the park, good for a leisurely trip . . .). Do we want, for example, to start with individual-level actors or collective-level actors?

That, at any rate, should be an easy question, because there are no collective-level actors. Action is something that is done by individuals, and only them. Of course, one may respond that I am here defining "action" in the way I want, and then making it seem as if everyone must agree with the definition, and this is true. However, think about the word "contraction." Suppose the muscles in your body were having a debate about how to understand living movement. One said that it wasn't simply muscles that could contract, but living bodies as a whole could contract, since they clearly were responsible for initiating their own spatial displacement. Another argued that although bodies certainly did *something*, what they did shouldn't be called "contraction" because it had nothing to do with contraction as all muscles until then had understood it, and broadening the usage was simply losing a term, not making an intellectual advance. I'd side with the second.

I'm not sure I know the best way to define action, but I know that we won't make headway on this if we include every change that we can think of as a case of action. It is no more plausible to say that an *organization* "acts" when a CEO signs a directive to cooperate with a federal investigation than it is to say that his

[23] Similarly, in models for occupational mobility, we make a mistake if we don't fix the marginals of the destination classes at *all* (implying that a certain associational pattern within cells *could* make the next generation all lawyers—scared you!), but also if we fix them *exactly*. Perhaps best would be some sort of penalty for going more than a standard deviation outside of predicted trends. Again, this isn't a work on methodology, but I have always believed that, like the knowledge one is soon to be hanged, numbers have a remarkable concentrating effect on the mind.

arm "acts." This is not to say that there are not times when we want to treat collectivities as units of analysis, and even attribute directive force to them; for example, we might want to allow them to "move" around in an organizational ecology. But we lose the possibility of understanding what *action* is if we think that it is any change attached to a unit that provokes other changes.

Eating is also something done only by individuals. Ecologists often model relations between species in collective terms: sheep in a certain area will consume so much grain and grass; wolves will consume so many sheep. There is nothing wrong with this. But they don't go from this to the idea that the same principles of food consumption that we see in the individual hold in the aggregate. It is not that the sheep, collectivity, "eat" in a way somewhat different from, but fundamentally the same as, the way that an individual sheep does; it is only the individual eatings seen in aggregate.

Of course, not all collectivities are such simple aggregates; many have internal organization. Our CEO who has, as an individual, signed a directive, may have just been consulting with lawyers inside his organization; they may have talked to other lawyers outside the organization, and done so *as* representatives of the organization. If we are interested in organizations, we may find that they can be studied to great success as organizations — that is, as units. We can loosely and analogically speak of the "interaction" of organizations and their "action." But when we treat collectivities as "actors," we obscure, reify, and fetishize — and we introduce strong tendencies toward bias.

For example, many analyses of the relation between the state and challengers (such as social movements, or other states) assumed that states were actors. They therefore imagined that the state, as state, confronted an opponent, and, mindful of its own interests and resources, took actions that were most likely to allow the state, as state, to realize its goals.

This is untrue, and so leads to error. Specific individuals do the acting. Sometimes they valiantly attempt to be mere agents of something else, but even then, it is quite rare that it is clear to impartial analysts, or even to the actors themselves, whom they represent (the state? the government? the nation? their party? the voters? those who voted for them? their protectors? their immediate supervisors? and so on). More generally, states are assemblages of actors pursuing their own goals at the same time as they are responsible to other claimants. Generals do not just fight the enemy; they fight other generals, or at least compete with them. They urge battle plans that are good for their careers. The same is true for all other aggregates, even the friendlier ones.[24]

[24] The chances are unfortunately not zero that the people in control of the organization *your* livelihood depends on are basically ransacking it for their own purposes, even if they're continually working on their "mission statement." Are you working on a theory that legitimates their piracy by hypostatizing a collective entity?

This is not usually the case for individuals: although we aren't quite as whole-and-entire as we like to think, it is rare that one encounters someone whose actions are due to delimitable subselves with coherent, abiding, and competing visions. When you do get a sense that there's a whole bunch of little people inside that thing, taking turns peeping out of the eyeballs, it's downright scary.

We've seen, then, a few repeated formal problems that tend to come with thinking about action. There are other problems that come with thinking about action that are, I think, outside of orthologics proper; they pertain to the relation between action and will, and raise philosophical issues on which we are unlikely to agree. In such cases, we cannot banish those who disagree for simply not "thinking straight." But in other cases — for example, the problem of understanding when we are "conditioning" on things we shouldn't be — we are able to fix some errors by being attentive to the places in which intellectual turbulence is generated by improper joins. I close this chapter with what I find the most promising implication of an orthological approach, although the most fraught with difficulties.

BEYOND STRAIGHTENING

Thinking and Unthinking

This conception of theory-work as orthological may seem antithetical to that of theory as wild, sweeping, and inspiring claims. We might imagine the pedantry of orthologics in the form of the aged scribe gleefully restraining bold genius with a pointless scholasticism born of resentment.

And yet I think that it is far more likely that punctilious attachment to exactitude breeds bold arguments. Because when it comes to social life, an area about which we all know so much, in ways that are usually sloppy even if profound, rigor can lead to novelty. And this is related to a second issue, one that may seem quaint to raise. Here I am forced to the uncomfortable position of putting forward a key conception that is impossible to defend, and indeed is easy to attack. It is this: before we have a scientific knowledge of the social world, one that builds on but goes beyond our everyday knowledge, we need to know about knowing, about how people, or at least people like us, think. Only after we have mastered this can we begin to account for the most obvious distortions and packagings that come with the thought process.

This might seem to imply some sort of perfect knowing without human knowing, which would be silly, and not what I mean. And at the same time, I cannot say exactly what I mean, because I am putting forward a sense of "better" that is not defined by *best,* but rather by *worst.* (Thomas Kuhn [1962] did something similar regarding our understanding of scientific progress, which he believed in but argued must be understood as a movement *away from* and not a movement *toward.* I find that his ideas here are quite reasonable.)

Thus I believe that in social science, some sorts of knowings are worse than others; further, we can learn to recognize some of the characteristics of bad ones by looking at how we think. Awareness of our tendencies can lead us to correct initial ideas. For example, many of us have no trouble with awareness of, and correction for, social bias associated with our having friends and enemies. We can think about this using the language of what is called balance theory, which formalized our tendency to approve of (believe, accept) propositions and claims made by those whom we like, and to disapprove of (disbelieve, reject) those made by those whom we *dislike.* Knowing about this tendency, and that it might influence our own thinking, we may force ourselves to give extra consideration to claims made by our enemies that might be true, and so on. The inability to define a perfect knowledge does not prevent us from correcting such a tendency.

But things get harder when the biases are not *overlaid* on our normal intellectual tools, but are part and parcel of them. And sometimes our biases are interwoven with our theoretical assumptions and approach, and require painstaking analysis to uncover. Just as when we approach matters on the subatomic level, we may need to let go of our ideas of what "space" and "position" are; so, too, when we approach action, we may need to get rid of some of our ideas. Much of what passes for theory in sociology consists of people attempting to shore up our normal (pretheoretical) ideas at all costs, and missing the wonderful opportunity to think something new, and perhaps, to a wee extent, see something we have not seen before.

Many of us accept that our intellectual production involves a "working-up" of the world (or at least, of our sensations of the world). Although I do not exactly agree,[25] this is a good enough way to begin. Imagine we say that our ideas are indeed such a function of the world: $I = f(W)$. Of course, we don't know the world directly (following this way of thinking about things). Yet can we know something about the function $f()$? Why not? If so, it doesn't seem impossible that we could describe an approximation to the inverse of f, call it f^{-1}. We then are free to construct $W' = f^{-1}(I)$, with the assumption that $|W' - W| < |I - W|$; that is, our new estimate is closer to the way things are than was our first understanding.

If you think this is necessarily impossible, imagine having a car that pulls to the right when the steering wheel is in the neutral position. (Again, I know whereof I speak.) If you were driving at night at the great Salt Flats, you might have no

---

[25] Like the Gestalt phenomenologists, I would reserve "world" for a compiled, organized, and integrated set of places that forms a ground not so much *for* but *of* possible experiences; we'll return to this in Chapter 5.

idea—everything would be relative. But if you are driving on Route 90, you will notice the guardrail coming frighteningly closer (again . . .). So you can take this into account. Similarly, if we did nothing but ponder, our conceptual distortions would be impossible to uncover, and this is why, as Harriet Whitehead (1987) has argued, in regression-type settings our cognitive propensities assume dramatically simple and strange shapes. But if we have to act, to try things out, to fiddle with the world, we can find our failures all lining up. Practice is the guardrail of the highway of theory.

The "inversion" of our own ideas is nearly impossible when it comes to the more concrete engagements with the world, paradigmatically seeing itself. Things look a certain way to us, and when we try to get around this, we end up inventing an equally human world (the Hobbesian world of gray silent objects, a sort of Tim Burton movie version of social life). But when it comes to more abstract concepts, such an inversion turns out to be far from impossible. In the easiest exercise, all we need to do is think about what we'd *like* to be the case—some sort of "assimilation" of the world to our schema—and then back up a bit. We force ourselves to entertain the possibility that what we'd like to be the case just *isn't* the case. More difficult instances require us to focus on what is most "good to think"—that is, what sorts of thought come easiest to us and seem most obviously to be true—and see if we can invert that.

Often going further in this sort of inversion requires rejecting our vocabulary. As I've said above, there's nothing wrong with using a particular theoretical vocabulary; in fact, new words often give us a head start on new insights. But if we use the terms for too long, we stop seeing *through* them and only see the words themselves. We get so used to our terms that we often see them as if *they* were the real. And worst of all, sometimes we convince ourselves that there is no other option. Then our focal point zooms in to the tip our noses, and we live wholly within the constructs of our mind. When we do this, we tend to become more sure of ourselves and of our knowledge, because everything "is" as it "looks"—even though we are knowing less and less.[26]

And of course, we seem to have iron-clad arguments as to why things *must* be so—why we can never peek around our schema for sorting and presenting the world to ourselves. Yet those who make these strong arguments always convince me of the opposite—though their logic sounds reasonable, I cannot but help notice that those most insistent on these points are the least curious, least interested, and least likely to *learn* of anyone that I know. They live in a prison of their

[26] It was for this reason that Fichte never used the same terminology for his central ideas, but instead restated his fundamental insights differently over and over again. He believed that his listeners had to follow him and simultaneously undergo the same enlightening thoughts he was reexperiencing, as opposed to using the dead system that, like a shell, survives the living animal that produced it. I believe there was much wisdom here, even though I never understood what the hell Fichte was talking about.

own making—shackling themselves to the wall of the cave, secure in their knowledge that no one else is even able to crane his head to peek outside. In contrast, those who look for more may never find what they seek, but they seem to often find *something*.[27]

Animals and Unthinking

It is for this reason that Chapter 5 uses the study of (nonhuman) animals to generate insights that might be used to see around our normal preconceptions about human behavior. But even without using animals as a ground for thinking, we've learned a few things about some of our own biases in thinking about human action. Attribution theory in particular has given sustained attention to how we tend to ascribe the action of *others* to their internal state and motivation; we are more sensitive to the importance of the external situation when it comes to our own action, but we often interpret this in terms of *restraints* to our exercise of morally approvable action.[28]

That is, we tend to see things in terms of *intention*, although not always—there are times when we emphasize chance, usually when we're trying to wriggle out of something we did wrong by pointing to the factors around us. But we are big believers in intentionality, our own, too (see Wegner 2002). We also think that things are meaningful. Gary Alan Fine (2002) found that "gamers" who play fantasy role-playing games that turn on a roll of the dice—often people with a fine understanding of modern science—cannot help but reject the idea that the roll is actually random. Because so much rides on the outcome in the game, and it is the one physical thing that they *do*, they are forced to conclude that one can be more or less skillful in throwing the dice.[29]

Knowing this, we can check ourselves when we assume that every event linked with a human body can be mapped to a corresponding intention. That doesn't mean that we have some principle that requires that we always *deny* intention. But we hold back a bit before making an overly convenient assumption. In contrast, poor theorizing assumes that we should not only give into our prejudices, but formalizes this as dogma (e.g., even when there is no empirical evidence of an intention for a body to give rise to a phenomenon, that indicates at least *two* intentions, first an intention to do the act, and second, an intention to cover it up . . .). And

[27] Pippi Longstocking pointed out that being a successful thing-finder often turns on being open to appreciating the things you *do* find, instead of implausibly holding out for just what you happen to want (let alone sulking when, as might have been predicted, it does not fall into your lap).

[28] This is what Goffman (1974) referred to as our "primary framework," the division of happenings into those that are guided by will and those that are natural.

[29] Thus although the gamers may come together to *pretend* magic, the *real* magical thinking enters in their interpretations of their real-world actions, the dice-throws.

more generally, we can look for when we are trying to make our theoretical structure *define* us to be right, before we even start looking around.

Onward

This, in outline, is what I think theory-work can be for sociology, and why I think we need it. The next chapters apply this in more detail to issues that have led to recurrent problems in thinking straight. We start with some puzzles about what can constrain action.

CHAPTER 2

Things and Facts

Who Causes What Constraints?

We begin our orthological investigations by attempting to clarify some of the most problematic usages that bedevil sociology. And when I say bedevil, although I do not mean it literally, it will not hurt if the reader visualizes imaginary demons springing to life and then tormenting humans, because that is more or less what our incoherent arguments do; they people the social world with imaginary actors reminiscent of the "demon theory" used as the humorous alternative hypothesis in scientific epistemological puzzles. Somehow, there are things that compass us about — they "constrain us" and "cause our actions"— although we cannot see our invisible tormentors. The reason, I believe we will see, is because they are imaginary. This then has serious implications for how we understand possible explanations of action.

I begin with one particular (but particularly bothersome) instance of confusion regarding our understanding of causality, namely, our arguments about the effects of culture. I then go on to consider how we should (or can) think and talk about causation more generally.

CULTURE AS CONSTRAINT

Finitude and Being Something

It increasingly seems as if the one thing we are sure of in sociological theory is that culture "constrains and enables" action. One might object that such a statement is vague or tautological, or that to make culture a subject that acts upon persons is problematic. I think that the second of these is closer to the mark, but the problem with this idea is more fundamental. I believe that there is no way of parsing such a claim so that the words "culture" and "constrain" have anything approaching their conventional meanings. While it might be well and good as an informal saying — akin to "I love chili, but it don't love me!"— actually incorporating it into our theories would put us on a very shaky foundation indeed.

Here, I want us to see what happens when we take this formulation seriously—that culture constrains and enables (we'll call it the CCAE thesis). Now although, as DiMaggio (1997: 268) says, "this position has become virtually catechismic among sociologists of culture," it's hard to find concrete examples that illustrate the core idea with much clarity. Sometimes (e.g., Turco 2010) culture seems to *enable* some people's actions and *constrain* others, but this seems equivalent to saying that "guns both help and hurt," as it depends which side of the barrel one is looking down. In other cases (Messner 2000), it seems that every last bit of culturally defined action (e.g., a soccer team of four- to five-year-old girls chooses "Barbie Girls" as their name) is by definition both constrained and enabled by culture. So to figure out what CCAE means, we may need to start from scratch and move slowly.

The goal is not to banish from our theoretical lexicon what I think will turn out to be a meaningless phrase—given that it is at worst a conceptual tinnitus, it doesn't do much harm. Because it lacks architectonic implications, it leaves most theoretical structures as they were. But attention to this case can bring to the fore certain more general issues and difficulties. So what does it mean to say that culture constrains us?

First, it is important that if such a statement is worth making, it must use the words "constraint" and "constrain" such that their meanings are similar to their meanings in other usages. It wouldn't make sense to say that "culture constrains," but then to have to, like Humpty-Dumpty, add that *here* where we use the word "constrain," it actually means "suggests" or "inflates." Most important, we need to make sure that here *constrain* does not mean *cause*. In other realms, we are able to use the two terms distinguishably (a match causes but does not constrain a fire; a fence constrains but does not cause a lion). If we cannot keep these distinct in our realm, that suggests a misuse of terminology.

To constrain means to limit, to hold back, or to check in some way. Have we ever identified a definition of culture that could do this to a person? Here the quest is not for the highest degree of precision. As I argue below, we can reach for too much precision in the social sciences; still, our words do and must mean things, and when we use them against their meanings, we think we have said things we have not said, learned things we have not learned, and ruled out things we have not ruled out.

I will go through three somewhat different, though all overlapping, ways that people have used this idea of culture constraining. I won't pick on anyone in particular, as they are my friends or my friends' friends. Of course, there are plenty of ways in which each of us, as an individual, is constrained by our culture—if we treat others as loyal agents of the culture. One way to transform the CCAE thesis would be to break it up into "me and everybody else." If we think about the example of the Church of Smok from the previous chapter, we could say that the

Smokkers' culture constrains them to slap themselves on the head, if we mean that any focal individual might be forced to smack himself on the head, because of all the *other* Smokkers, who believe the church doctrines (or Smoktrines, we'll call them). The true believers aren't constrained, because they *want* to slap themselves on the head, but the heretic *is* constrained. We can even imagine a case of pluralistic ignorance in which no one actually believes the Smoktrines, but everyone enforces them, and thus everyone is constrained, by everybody else.

Now it doesn't have to be that the constraint comes from a fear of punishment. The thing about semiotic codes, as Ann Swidler (2001) has said, is that the "meaning" isn't about what *you* are trying to get across, but how your actions (or "gestures" in Mead's [1934] terms) are interpreted by others. Swidler gives the example of the institution of "secretary's day," an artificial holiday that is acutely embarrassing to many administrative assistants (secretaries) and their immediate supervisors (bosses). Everyone might prefer that there never was such a thing. Conditional on there *being* a secretary's day, however, if a boss *doesn't* give a gift to her or his secretary, it *could* well be because the boss assumes the secretary agrees that the whole thing is ridiculous. But . . . it *could* be that the boss doesn't appreciate him or her. Better be safe and give a gift; so, too, on the secretary's side, better respond with shows of appreciation. Thus there can be an institution that everyone participates in—and everyone has "in his or her head" in a way—yet the constraint comes not from the inside, but the outside. In that way, it isn't crazy to say that we are constrained by culture.[1]

CCAE 1: MCMU

But the way in which people propose CCAE is not that it motivates *others* to constrain us, but that our *own* culture constrains each of us. One version of this, which was extremely influential among graduate students in sociology in my day, assumes that the reason culture constrains us is that it so totally defines our universe and experience and so on, that some things are impossible to think, or to appreciate, or something like that. (I will call this the "my culture, my universe" or MCMU, view.) For example, as a twentieth-century American, I cannot see human sacrifice as a beautiful and moving religious experience, I do not like fertilized duck eggs, and there are parts of Amazonian myths that have never made any sense to me. The reason this is, argue MCMU-ers, is that my culture has prevented me from having the subjectivity according with these understandings or appreciations.

---

[1] Formulaically, if each person's subjectivity is denoted x_i, and the set of all subjectivities is X, and we denote $X \setminus x_i$ as X^i, that is, all minds *except* our focal person, we can say that any person (i) might be constrained by X^i, but not by x_i.

But who is this "me" who has been held back by his culture? It must be some precultural me, an abstract individual who, but for the stamping of culture, would exist as some sort of *Homo genericus*. Of course, one thing sociologists will unite on is the impossibility of such a being. Everyone is a some-sort-of-person, and all some-sorts-of-persons are, to the MCMU-ers (and I think correctly so), cultural persons.[2]

What we have stumbled upon here is a basic philosophical idea that to determine is to renounce possibilities—in Spinoza's formula, *omnis determinatio est negatio* (all determination is negation). A baby has if not infinite, still amazing, potential. For one, she can make many different sounds with her mouth and recognize many as well. But as she learns *one* language, she loses the ability to learn to make other sounds (English speakers not quite getting the difference between X and Sh in Mandarin; Mandarin speakers not quite getting the difference between L and R in English). But the baby isn't an "individual" in the way most of us understand. Babies are potential individuals, but anything that we would recognize as an individual is already something, and hence has limits—is finite. But the precultural me, the abstract individual being posited by CCAE, is, to use the language of Schelling and other idealist philosophers, an *infinite* subject.[3] That is, there is a way in which this me is unbounded precisely because it is not (yet) determined. There are coherent ways of starting with the idea of an infinite subject and following the sequence of determinations that lead to the concrete and to finitude. This was the dialectical approach of Hegel.[4] Then each stage in which a

---

[2] One of the theorists to take the idea of cultural constraint seriously is Alexander, who therefore must split the self into two parts, one of which is compelled by the other, and thus (2003: 4) quite logically proposes that his theory must be "a kind of social psychoanalysis." The problem with this solution is that psychoanalysis is well known as an approach that has the sort of instability pointed to in Chapter 1. If you need proof, this was authoritatively demonstrated by Martin (2011). If after reading that, you *still* don't believe me, then you must be crazy.

[3] It is somewhat funny that this historical tradition started with the assumption that it is not our *culture* that constrains us, but our *desires*, for to the extent that we act on the basis of immediate desires, we are as robotic as animals. (Here it was understood that the "true us" was what could be thusly constrained by our animalistic side—it was the God-given reason in each of us.) The German solution to this problem (centrally raised by Rousseau) was increasingly to make *culture* that which allowed us *not* to be determined by our desires, but to still be something in particular.

[4] Indeed, I do not know the origin of the mantra that "culture constrains and enables" but I suspect that it can be traced back to Kant's (1950 [1787]: 187; B187) argument in his section on the schematism of the understanding, that the sensible aspect of the schemata "realizes the Understanding in the very process of restricting it." But it probably was the Birmingham School of Cultural Studies who developed the idea in a sociological direction in the early 1970s (see, especially, the essays in Hall and Jefferson 1993 [1976]). This then became widely influential because of the work of Anthony Giddens, who first worked out the manta of constraining and enabling. For Giddens, it was "*structures*" that both constrain and enable (Giddens 1976: 161), and we might indeed expect a structure to have more constraining capacity than other things. Unfortunately, for Giddens, structure *was* culture, as it is "rules and resources," things that exist only as memory traces (1984: 377). Giddens thereby took something ("structure") that had previously been understood as *outside* of the actor—and which could indeed be easily understood to constrain and enable—and put it *inside*, without rethinking this notion of constraint. Thus although Giddens (esp. 1979) used his admirable intellect to resolve a number of formal problems, in this case, he made quite a few for others.

predicate is attached to a subject is indeed a constraint, and a constraint that must be overcome in order for dialectical progress to be made. But it does not make sense where all subjects are considered inherently finite.

In other words, that we are some things and not other things is indeed an important part of the human condition, and it may, in some circumstances, even make sense to use the lack-of-some things as explanatory factors in arguments based on counterfactual dependence (e.g., "were I only five inches taller, I would have been able to serve as a pilot"). But it does not make sense to go from this to the claim that what I *do* possess constrains me, simply because it is not something *else*. Thus if my height is 5′2″, it would indeed be reasonable to say "if my height were 5′7″, I could reach the cookie jar," but not that "my height constrains me from reaching the cookie jar," for had I no height at all, I also would have no cookies.

We must accept that there are things that we may reasonably say, and expect others to understand, that do not rise to the standard of exactitude required for something to be graced with the name "theory." Consider a closer parallel to many ideas of CCAE. We are at home in a room with a window. A friend calls and tells us that he is parked outside and that we should look at what he has tied to the roof of his car. We run to the window, but no matter how we position ourselves, we cannot see him. "I'm sorry," we say, "but this window was placed in a stupid position. I cannot see you. The window constrains me from seeing you, though it enables me to see a stupid tree."

The chances are good that our friend will understand us, but if he were to take our words in a more precise manner than intended (perhaps he is a theorist), he might be surprised, and say, "The window is preventing you from seeing? Would you be better off without one?" We would need to explain that actually, the window really does not constrain us at all; it is actually the wall that is the constraint. The window is the relaxing of a constraint. Unfortunately, it is just not the relaxation that we happen to want right now. "I see," our friend might reply. "It is not that the *window* constrains you, it is *the fact* that the window is where it is, and is not somewhere else, that is the problem."

There is a great deal of difference between saying "culture constrains us" and "the *fact that* we are of *this* culture and not *that* one constrains us." What we have found (and to which we will return below) is confusion between a *thing* and a *fact about* the thing.

CCAE 2: Culture as Language

Let's consider two other specific versions of the CCAE thesis (other than the MCMU variety), which might be seen as being immune to this critique. The first is the culture-as-language version. The argument goes like this: there are some things that my language makes easy to say, but other things that my language makes hard to say; so, too, with culture, it makes some things easy to do and some hard.

Now I must confess the idea that our language makes things hard to say or hard to think is an eminently reasonable idea. In fact, the alert reader will notice that I claimed exactly this in the first chapter, when I said a poor vocabulary could make it difficult to ask the right questions. The question will be, however, just what this means, and what the implications are. We'll find that it needs to be unpacked before it can be defended. So let's first think about how language might constrain, and then see what the implications are for culture. We will have to imagine that the language does not prevent us from *thinking* this or that; otherwise we return to the first (MCMU) case.

In language examples, we often seize upon cases in which there is a term in one language that is difficult to translate into another, often a subtle idea that requires a long string of words to communicate, if it can be done at all. Perhaps an even clearer example would be color terms. Languages differ in the number of basic color terms that are used—some have no word for "green."[5] Yet I will provisionally accept that we cannot claim that speakers lack the visual ability to distinguish between what we call green and what we call blue (e.g., Bornstein 1987; though see the work of John Lucy [1997] for the other side). Are they, therefore, constrained not to be able to comment on the beautiful greenery?

It does seem that in many cases, they can do a reasonable job with wordier circumlocutions. Our person lacking the term "green" might say "the kind of blue that is almost yellow." In other cases, a new word can do the trick: although my son's lexicon lacked a term for a particular genre of movie that he found abhorrent, when explaining why he refused to join others to see the Disney movie Wall-E, he was able to explain that it was a "robomance." But we do not need to deny that it can *ever* be the case that the lack of a word means that a potential speaker does not even reach for the circumlocutionary technique, because she seizes upon a near equivalent. An emotional state a Korean might identify as *Han* might be described by an American as "I'm depressed," as opposed to "I feel the subdued rancor and grief of resentment at lifelong oppression for which I take full responsibility, even though this bitter pill was forced on me by others."[6] Yet even here, it seems hard to argue that it is the *possession of English*, and not the *ignorance of Korean*, that is relevant, as someone who had both might not only have no trouble speaking of *Han* in Korean but even be able to explain the feeling in English to non-Korean speakers.

---

[5] For consistency with most work on this issue, we'll ignore the important fact that languages aren't restricted to their basic color terms: but look at all the names in your 64-piece Crayola set!

[6] Here I draw on Schwartz and Kim (2002).

Thus in almost all of these cases, it seems to be not that people are constrained by their language, but rather by "the fact that" they do not have a different one. Although I can think of a few cases in which one might think the actual possession constrains, these wouldn't be used to explain the CCAE thesis.[7] Once again, we seem to have confused things and facts about things as we try to determine what cultural constraint might mean.

CCAE 3: Culture as Tool Kit

We found that the MCMU understanding of CCAE seemed to require that there be a "precultural" person to be constrained *by* her or his own culture. But (as I noted), one might get around this by saying that it is not one's culture *tout court* but one separable aspect of it that produced the constraint. Thus, although it might not make sense to propose a John Levi Martin who has no culture, and then propose that his American culture constrains him, we might imagine a counterpart very like him but lacking one particular cultural element (e.g., his revulsion at the thought of eating living creatures). Thus, if we were to reject the idea that culture is such a seamless web that no element can be removed without it being spontaneously regenerated (and most sociologists *do* reject this idea), we might be able to propose that particular elements constrain, even if we can't say that culture as a whole does.[8]

And this revised version seems to be compatible with what I think is now the most popular version of the CCAE thesis. Here we argue that, contrary to the MCMU, culture is not an all-embracing way of being and seeing, but a tool kit. As different tools are good for doing different things, some tool kits allow for some things, but not others, and we pick them up and put them down depending on what we are trying to do. Thus having a hammer does not prevent us from loosening a screw, but having a tool kit without a screwdriver constrains the approach that we will take to loosening the screw: we will either give up the job, use something else to loosen the screw (e.g., a vice-grip), or drill out the screw completely.[9]

---

[7] For example, a German speaker might be confused by the Yiddish use of the word *verschimmelt*, which means *rattled, confused, not all together*, while in German, it means *moldy*. We might be able to imagine a world in which persons know more than one language but cannot keep their understanding of one word from bleeding over into their understanding of a close homonym. Thus a German speaker who understood in some sense that Yiddish speakers used the word differently might never shake the German meaning. But we all probably have somewhat different senses of the connotations of different words, so this doesn't seem to be a very significant wrinkle.

[8] To use the notation of note 1, if each person's subjectivity (x_i) is composed of K cultural elements c_{ik}, and we denote $x_i \setminus c_{ik}$ as x_i^k, that is, all of our cultural mind *except* for this one element, we might now say that any person (i) might be constrained by x_i^k, but not by x_i.

[9] Although the "tool kit" view is commonly associated with my advisor, Ann Swidler, I don't think she ever said anything remotely like this tool kit version of CCAE.

One might argue that the constraint comes in the missingness of the screwdriver that is associated with possessing this tool set. But then once again, it turns out that we are making an *absence* the root of constraint. This has worrisome implications. Our tool set may have seventy tools but it lacks an infinite number of things—not only this screwdriver, but a posthole digger, a computer-assisted die cutter, a liquid oxygen engine, and a George Foreman grill. If we were to similarly maintain that our tool set constrained us from making a fence, producing fasteners, reaching the moon, and having lunch, we would throw the accursed thing away, since it seems to prevent us from doing oh so many different things.

It appears that if a tool kit is a set of tools, and the hammer does not constrain us not to take out a screw, nor does a wrench, nor a tape measure, then the set itself cannot constrain us. Again, it turns out that if we are to speak of constraint, it lies not in the tool kit, but "in the fact that" we have the tool kit we do, and not a different one.

The last recasting of this objection argues that what the cultural tool kit constrains is not so much our actions, but our subjectivity, by making things hard to think. But since culture itself is just this subjectivity, this is a strange sort of constraint, in which the same thing enters twice in our statement, once taken to be a constraint, and another time as the constrained. The only way anyone can make sense of this is to recognize it as a very simple logical fallacy, namely, claiming that whatever is, had to be.

But if we stick with the more common formulation, whereby our actions are constrained by our own culture, we have found two serious problems. The first is the flagrant equation of determination and negation, with its implicit contrast to indeterminate infinity. It may be true that if I have $1,000 in the bank I am enabled to buy a used motorcycle and constrained from buying a new one, but it doesn't seem at all right to say that "money constrains and enables." There are times when we might well want to argue that there is something constraining in a lack, but we have seen that in the undisciplined form in which this was introduced for culture, we said all sorts of silly things.

The second confusion was between *things* and *facts that.* As we pursue this issue, we will, I think, understand the relation between the two confusions, for they have a formal relation to one another, and to other puzzles we will explore.

DEFINING CONSTRAINT

What Does It Mean to Constrain

I hope that the reader has been convinced that we are wrong to think that culture constrains, and that this comes from our confusion of *things* on the one hand, with *facts about* things on the other. The reason being, if the reader *is* so convinced, she or he won't have wasted money on this book, because I want to go on to show what is wrong—or at least incomplete—with this way of thinking I've put forward. We are making progress, but not there yet.

One of the difficulties in orthological work is often that if we attempt to increase the precision of our terms indefinitely, we end up not being able to say *anything* at all. Like the "New Academy" of the Roman world, we will chalk up as theoretical excellence our refusal to assent to *any* statement. Or somehow, we will try to zoom in closer and closer, leaving human beings behind and end up in a world of just stuff or just idea-vibrations or something that isn't very useful. We need to find the level of precision that allows us to marshal our thoughts with greatest clarity and to be able to say things, but not just any old thing that happens to sound cool.

A reader who accepted the arguments above might go on to reason as follows: I accept that culture does not constrain actions; rather, it is the fact that I am of such and such a culture that is constraining. But what can it mean for a "fact" to constrain?

Come to think of it, what does it mean for *anything* to constrain human action? There is one way (indeed, a way which I think is correct) in which *nothing* can constrain an action, but this involves equating constraint with causality (for I will accept that it makes sense to say that nothing can "cause" an action, but this awaits exposition). But there is another way to speak of constraints on action, one that I think is clear and plausible, which we owe to Thomas Hobbes.

Hobbes (1909 [1651]: 161, also 99) defined freedom as a merely *physical* quality of bodies, "the absence of Opposition; (by Opposition, I mean externall Impediments of motion;) and may be applied no lesse to Irrational, and Inanimate creatures, than to Rationall." Thus, thought Hobbes, it is silly for people to march around demanding freedom, because if they are moving about, they certainly have freedom (as opposed to being in chains). However, he recognized that to approach issues of political and social importance, he would need to make an analogical step and treat certain social institutions *as if* they were constraining, even though they did not *physically* constrain us. Thus he termed the law "Artificiall Chains" (62; *sic*), because if we let the law guide our actions it is *as though* we were physically constrained.

Following Hobbes (and Locke, who accepted this), we can consider constraint something that prevents us from doing what we want, and we recognize that this term best applies to physical constraint, but perhaps next best to threats of physical constraint or retribution, and then perhaps next best to laws, and so on . . . At some point, we will need to stop using the term "constraint," but we may not be able to define it in advance.

Certainly, however, the Hobbesian version is very clear that nothing *inside* the actor can constrain the actor (any deficit here Hobbes calls "want of power"). I also think that this is extremely reasonable; as we have seen, it becomes very paradoxical to say that I am constrained by things inside me, or by me myself,[10] for if we allow this usage, the word *constraint* rapidly loses any meaning at all, and in fact becomes the exact same thing as *enables*. That would explain why we think culture constrains and enables—it has nothing to do with culture, but only with a warped understanding of *constraint*.

How Do Facts Constrain?

In any case, what could it mean to say that a "fact" constrains things? We may need to determine what we mean by a fact. There are many circularities in our definitions of facts, and I think this is one of the cases where this circularity is not a problem to be solved but something to be accepted: there isn't any way to get out of these circles because they only become stabilized via social agreement. For this reason, I will give that sort of definition that is sometimes called "constructivist" but might better be called "cop out." That is, if we really need to talk about, say, "the beautiful," but find that no matter how hard we try, our definitions have problems, we may fall back on "by the beautiful, I mean what is commonly taken to be beautiful in such and such a time and place." This usually works because the reason we're talking about our central term (here, the beautiful) in the first place is that it has some sort of role in lived experience and thought. Yes, it can be a cop-out, but as I think we'll see in the next chapter, sometimes it turns out to be a strong finding: that some concepts (and beauty is often seen to be one) can be anchored *only* in the jointly created experience of a community.

So I'll unashamedly be copping out here with my definition; I have no objection if the reader wants to replace this with anything she or he thinks will work as well or better, but I suspect that's impossible. In any case, a fact is the sort of thing that, for a human community of interlocutors, makes a proposition that is potentially true, actually true. In turn (and circularly), a proposition is potentially true if there is agreement among said human community that it can be (or could be) true, in the sense that there is nothing in the nature of the terms to

[10] Certainly one might point to certain physical characteristics of oneself—especially ones that are temporary, new, or pathological—as constraining one (e.g., "I can't keep up with you because of my sprained ankle"). In such cases, however, we seem to treat our body as outside "us" as actors; when our body smoothly accomplishes our will as opposed to frustrating it, we tend to feel that our body *is* us. As Alexander's approach (see note 2) indicates, *when* (and if) we identify something in our *own* subjectivity as undesirable and pathological, we can also identify it as constraining us (e.g., "my religious upbringing still makes it hard to relax at the be-in!"). Identifying things in *others'* subjectivity as undesirable and pathological is very rude, and it turns out to also make for bad science.

make such truth inherently impossible.[11] The fact, then, is that which casts the shadow of a true proposition when exposed to the light of inquiry.

The conceptualization here means that there may be some communities, say, *A*, *B*, and *C*, in which the proposition "Motörhead kicks Beethoven's ass" is potentially true (even though in *A* and *B*, this is considered true, and in *C*, false), while in other social communities, say, *D* and *E*, this is considered a proposition that could never be true or not true. The *fact* (for communities *A*, *B*, and *C*) is what makes Motörhead kick, or fail to kick, Beethoven's ass.

Further, one key attribute of a fact is that, as Ludwik Fleck (1979 [1935]) emphasized, it serves as a *constraint* against arbitrary thinking. It's something you can't make go away. We might think that a "theory" is true, but later rip it down entirely without feeling like we were total idiots for accepting it. But with a fact, we can sometimes rotate it, see it from a different angle, describe it differently, but we can't accept with equanimity that something we thought was a fact "wasn't." And finally, it does indeed seem to me that for most sciences, especially simple ones, things work best when facts are anchored in the here and now (and I'll make a few suggestions as to how we can do this). But that doesn't mean that we can simply declare that all facts *are* thus anchored, and indeed it isn't at all clear to me that it could *ever* be possible to have all facts thus anchored.

Now what does it mean to say that facts, as opposed to things, constrain? We can return to our example of the window. If our friend says, "Put your head against the wall on the right side of the window, and I bet you can see me" and we say "I can't; there is a shelf there" it might seem quite reasonable to locate some form of constraint in the shelf itself. Of course, we *can* locate the constraint in "the fact that" the shelf is there, but it isn't clear that we *need to*. We can *feel* the constraint of the shelf as we jam our head against it and push. But when it comes to locating constraint in the window, we *can't* locate it in the window itself. Nothing about the window as window blocks our view the way the shelf interferes with putting our head somewhere.

So then to return, how does the *fact that* the window is here constrain us? The language examples above make clear our answer—it is not actually the *fact that* the window is here that is constraining; it is the fact that it is here *and not elsewhere*. And this seems to be generally true of the facts that constrain—it is not

[11] I understand that this implies that in some cases, an authoritative pronouncement is as factual as anything else. Thus the thing that makes it true that the substance of the wafer changes is that the church says it does. If you find this, or other implications of my definition, unsatisfactory, I don't blame you; I've never found a better definition. Other attempts at definition make a fact into a proposition or a thought, which doesn't seem right to me; or they make it something about the "real" world, but the "real" world itself then becomes warped beyond recognition as it expands to include all the sorts of things that we would want to make our potential facts true. (This doesn't help us with *true*, but we can push that off for now.) In the next chapter, I'll be forced to side with those who see the real as something that emerges from facts, and not vice versa. I don't like it any better than you, but there it is.

so much the facts themselves, for we use them as shorthands for a more complete expression "the fact that it is this way and not that way." It is for this reason that the collapsing of things and facts turned out to be the same as assuming that all determination was negation. Both have, at base, a confusion of negativity and nonexistence with positivity, what we have at hand. Indeed, were a *second* window added in the right place, "the fact that" the first window is where it is would have no constraining power, would it? For by "the fact" we almost always mean not "the fact that it is *this*" but "the fact that it is not *that*."[12]

We have, then, not completely come to an adequate understanding, for we seem again to be relying on the idea of something that *isn't* as a constraint, which we have already seen to be somewhat problematic. On the other hand, we might be encouraged, because the formulation of "this but not that" is related to how we often pose our theoretical questions more generally. Even more, it is related to how many of us formulate causality. Hence we may do best by turning to these more general issues of how we think about causality in sociological theory.

However, things will become a bit more difficult as we turn from constraint to causality because we have a clearer understanding of what we mean by "constrain" than we do by "cause." So we will need to understand not only what we mean by causality, or how we might define it, but also, what we mean by definition.

DEFINING CAUSATION

Definition, Typification, and Delineation

When we strive for exactitude in our thoughts in sociology, we generally begin by attempting to be clear and explicit about our *definitions*. What could be wrong with this? More than we are generally told.

As I briefly discussed in *The Explanation of Social Action*, and return to in more historical detail in a forthcoming work, sociologists are, to use a crude version of a well-known distinction, strong nominalists. To anticipate the next chapter, in contrast to realists, who think that generalities are "out there" in themselves, nominalists think that only particularities are real, and any conceptual collection of them arises through the mental act of determining the boundaries of collections through definitions. It is *we* who create the whole by attaching a name to the collection (hence "nominalism"). Because of our nominalism, when we are confused, we usually believe that we can get analytic clarity by demanding

[12] And it is for this reason that the above definition of fact, which might have seemed like hairsplitting, may be important. If a fact is what makes a proposition true, but is not itself the proposition, then we see that there is something problematic when we take the tight relationship of the fact to its shadow-proposition to import into our thoughts about the fact something that comes more from the nature of the proposition, which is a connection to *other* propositions. We'll look more carefully at this soon.

or offering definitions. But it turns out that this is not always so, and one such case may be at hand.[13]

I can still remember being dumbfounded when reading the reviews accompanying the rejection of one of my first article submissions (never published). The reviews pointed to something taken by the editors as a fatal theoretical mistake, namely, that in an article about power, *I had never defined power*! But this was an examination of data produced in response to questions asked of respondents regarding their power relations with one another. If anyone was defining power, it was they, not me. Were I to impose my own definition of power, I could only be confusing things. Yet this critique seemed, to the editors, right on.

This is because power is a confusing topic; it doesn't always appear clearly labeled, like a zoo animal ("The common coyote [*Famishius vulgaris ingeniusi*], native to the American Southwest, now endangered due to the human encroachments and improper disposal of anvils . . ."). It *is* hard to know what we're talking about (and my paper *did* stink). It seems as though starting out with a definition might help; a nominalist believes that there's no other way to start.

Now whatever anyone's personal predilection here, one has to recognize that there may be times in which our instinctual nominalism may not work. That doesn't mean we have any *better* alternative, but before starting off down a road, it's nice to know if it really goes where you think it does. Our first impulse is invariably to define our abstractions as conjunctive, subsumptive concepts: we give a list of criteria that a particularity must satisfy to be included in the concept. (Henceforward, I will use the term "concept" only in this restricted, technical sense.) So we consider a particularity. If it fails any one of the criteria of our definition, it is not included as an instance of the general concept. Thus the concept is equivalent to a set, say X, to which particularities can belong, say, $x \in X$. Occasionally, we are forced away from this form of definition to allow for disjunctive concepts (something that satisfies one criterion *or* the other) or in other ways, but these take considerable mental effort.

A classic, still (worthily) used today, is Weber's (1946 [1918]) definition of the state: it is a "human community" that "(successfully) claims the monopoly of the legitimate use of physical force within a given territory." If we are wondering if a particular human community is a state, we need to ask ourselves if it satisfies the definition. If it claims the monopoly, and so on, but *unsuccessfully*—not a state. If it claims the monopoly of the legitimate use of *spiritual* force within a given

[13] I believe we should prize analytic clarity, although it is our beginning, and not our ending point, as thinkers and researchers. When, in our training, we pass beyond this beginning, we find that in our works, clarity is always our ending and not our beginning. In this work, I will not go into the mysteries of the dialectic, which is indeed necessary for social thought, but one thing that we have learned from the hash that was called "logic" in Stalinist Russia is that dialectics cannot be approached without a strong grounding in analytics.

territory—not a state. If it claims the monopoly of the legitimate use of physical force over only *selected* persons, say, all those whose names begin with a "J"—not a state. This one works well (which is why Weber lifted the definition from Ihering [1913 / 1877: 238]!), in part because particularities that don't completely satisfy the definition are often on their way to being gone. So there doesn't seem to be too many ambiguous cases.

But other times—when particularities are more "spread out" than "clumped" in a space of possibilities—definition doesn't always work the way we want. Someone studying "domestic violence" among young couples will need to make decisions, somewhat arbitrary, as to which couples to consider "domestic" and what acts to consider "violence." Is domestic violence every time a person strikes his romantic partner in anger (as opposed to in fun)? If so, one might find that more females are domestic abusers than males—they may be more likely to hit, but less likely to hurt (see, e.g,. Whitaker, Haileyesus, Swahn, and Saltzman 2007).

There are, however, two other possible approaches to creating our ideas that have been proposed for thinking clearly in the social sciences.[14] One is ideal typification. Although ideal types, as defined by Weber, are *related* to concepts and the process of concept formation, ideal types are not "concepts" in this technical sense. That is because rather than being *sets* into which we place our objects, they are single constructs that we use to *shed light* on the members of sets—of which they may or may not be members.[15] That is, we may construct an ideal type of economically rational action (x^*) to shed light on the set of empirical actions (X), yet not a single one of these is ideal typical. In many cases, we end up saying something vaguely like $y_i - y^* = f(|x_i - x^*|), x_i \in X$—the degree to which a certain outcome (y) for a case (case i) deviates from our theoretically claimed expectation (y^*) is a function of how much this case (x_i) deviates from the ideal type.

There are no good justifications for using ideal types in the social sciences, except for the fact that we are going to do it anyway. Call it "stereotype" and you start to see the problems: it allows the analysts to simplify reality in the sort of way that is conducive to their clinging to their preconceptions. Science, when it works, throws up resistance to arbitrary thinking. Ideal typical thinking doesn't.

However, it seems that it is a close approximation to how we generally think. We all—at least sometimes—think in stereotypes, although we can follow Rosch

[14] There is also exemplification, when we attempt to drag other people around and point them to examples of what we're talking about. I'm not sure if this really qualifies for "thinking clearly," but it often works pretty well.

[15] In a few cases, this set may have a single member, but this turns out not to radically change the nature of ideal-typification and so I don't emphasize this distinction. It is, historically, associated with the question of how one grasps an "individual," for in many cases, we need an ideal type to understand even a single case.

(1978) and others and call these prototypes.[16] If we did a Venn diagram of *prototype* and *ideal type*, we'd see an intersection between the two, but there are prototypes that are not ideal types and ideal types that are not prototypes. For one, a prototype may arise through inductive experience and it may not accentuate any particular ideas we have. We may not even be able to explain why a daisy is more prototypical a flower than a rose. And an ideal type may not be a prototype because a prototype is generally assumed to actually be an existent member of a set.

And this seems to be a common way of grasping a set. That is, instead of defining our generalities through definitions that set up the borders and boundaries, we focus on the *central* case and assimilate others to it more or less. Thus a sparrow is a very birdy bird, an eagle somewhat less, a penguin less, and a cassowary (flightless and furry) even less. So, too, when we try to think about things like the relation between dropping out of high school and delinquency (if we think at all, as opposed to simply throwing variables in and out of equations), we're likely to be trying to imagine the relation between our prototypical dropout and our prototypical delinquent in our minds. At least that would be the case if our imaginary case actually existed; if not, we're not even using a prototype, just an ideal type. I am going to argue that although there are cases in which (just as Weber said) an ideal type that isn't a prototype is defensible, most of the time, this should be a cause for worry. Our real problem, then, is twofold. First, we often use ideal types to define sets and imagine that they are not simply prototypes, but modal (that is, most common). Second, although we *think* in ideal types, we *work* using nominalist procedures, and so we catch a lot of fish in our nets that are very different from our prototypes. (I have discussed this in the piece on *The Authoritarian Personality* [Martin 2001b].)

Now I want to discuss a third way of approaching generalities, which we can call delineation. Delineation is what a realist is likely to do if she wants to be analytical. Here, rather than establish boundaries and declare that all within them is homogeneously subsumed in a generality, one attempts to establish a perimeter around the range of phenomena one thinks should be seen as part of the generality. In contrast to the conceptual cleansing that must accompany the erection of borders through definition, delineation allows minorities to remain on the wrong side without threat. One may be imperfect here without the attempt being worthless, and it is easily recognized that some particulars that may satisfy the delineation are not instances of the generality.[17] Thus we might use the same words to delineate that we do to define; the difference turns on how we under-

[16] Or one could go back to Plato and call these "forms" or "ideas," and then avoid the question of whether prototypes, unlike ideal-types, need to exist as examples.

[17] One optimistic explanation for the increased interest in fuzzy set approaches in sociology is that they allow for such ways of understanding our relation to generality that do not have the problems of strong nominalism. But a contending explanation would be that existing fuzzy set methods are good for turning minor numerical differences into very large ones, which seems to me a very wicked thing indeed.

stand when words and cases don't match. Using a definition, when we find a case that doesn't fit the definition, we throw out the case. Thus we might say that since the United States government actually doesn't claim a monopoly on the physical use of force, since it recognizes the right of state and local authorities to use physical force, it isn't a proper state. If we were only trying to delineate the phenomenon, we'd shrug our shoulders and say, well, then again, some federal states are different.

Defining Causation

Now let us turn to the matter at hand: how we approach the issue of causality. "Causing" is clearly a very general idea, which seems to encompass many processes, such as "burning," "creating," "killing," and so on. Is it really obvious that there must be a single definition that can unite what we think is essential in all of these (a point made by Cartwright 2004)? It is, of course, possible that we hold a nominalist position here, and think that there really isn't any "causality" in the world, but that it is a convenient way of organizing our experiences for purposes of action (often called a "Humean" perspective). If that is true, however, we will have a great deal of work to do if we are to claim that all true scientific explanation *must* be causal. At best, it seems that we could try to claim that we are burdened with a need to see things in causal terms, not that this promises our salvation.

But if we hold a fundamentally realist position on causality, it is not at all clear why we are attempting to define it, as opposed to trying to delimit it, or to use a prototypical approach. Let's consider both of these possibilities, starting with the first. How could we delimit what we mean by causality? Here we could come up with a few cases we think of as being Ur-causal—as causal as causal can be—and see if we can find some things that all of the cases shared. We could then use these features to construct our lines, saying that pretty much everything we want to call causation should lie on one side of the lines established by some of these shared properties.

We may disagree here, but I think that we find very, very little that we can say. Causes can be either necessary, or sufficient, or neither; they may come before their effects, or they may be simultaneous (especially in the relativistic sense in which events within light-speed distance apart are simultaneous, as one can find a reference frame in which one precedes the other, and a second in which the reverse is true). They may be reversible, or they may not; they may be compatible with willfulness, or they may not. The exercise is profitable insofar as it leads to the equivalent of a negative ontology: we know what *not* to put in a definition of causality.

The other possible way to proceed is prototypical. I've suggested that this is always a worrisome choice for us; it is a concession to prejudice. But given that it is the way we normally think, it sometimes turns out to be helpful to at least understand *how* we are thinking. There have been two prototypes that have been used to anchor understandings of causality. One is mechanical collision. A second possible prototype is human willfulness. These are very different, and our sense of causality is likely to be very different depending on which we choose. In Chapter 1, I suggested that one of our problems is the way we see everything through our human lenses, which lead to particular distortions. Yet I also think that in this case, we are better taking the latter (willfulness) as our prototype, and not the former (collision).

And this is because I believe that what really lies at the heart of our intuitions about what makes a relation "causal" or not is one which comes from our interpretation of willfulness, and it has been *already* projected into mechanical relations; we then use this to reinterpret our idea of "will" in a distorted form. That is, our idea of mechanical collision is itself so overladen with our interpretive glosses that it is not an acceptable prototype. The relation between one ball bouncing off another is not quite the same as how we understand it, because we are up against the limits of our understanding.[18] We also may come up against our limits when it comes to understanding the willfulness of our action[19]; however, we may begin with the phenomenological experience of the world's *resistance* to our willfulness.

Or at least, that is what seems to me the most encouraging way of proceeding if we wish to clarify the nature of our ideas. Certainly, we would need to do this if we were going to use the presence or absence of causality as a criterion for determining what was or was not a good explanation. (Did we not know what we meant by causality, we would have a problem using causality as a criterion.) The other way—which we seem to do in practice, though we don't understand it as such, is to use our feeling of a good explanation to define "cause" in any particular case. Although this solves many problems (or would solve, were it recognized that this is what we do), it brings a few of its own.

[18] Philosophers of science are used to the puzzle of whether "forces" are real or simply letters that are used in equations with no existential analogues. But Wolfgang Köhler (1938) had a different question—are billiard balls or magnetic filings ever "forced" in the first place? I am forced to wait at red lights, show up for work fully dressed, and pay income taxes, none of which I would do if I weren't forced, and I don't like it one bit. I'm not sure I would be forced if one couldn't properly append "and I don't like it one bit."

[19] Indeed, I think this is why Schopenhauer considered as noumena not only the human will but gravity and all natural forces—if we realize we can't grasp the causality of the natural world, nor the freedom of the will, why not just bundle them all together? It's not a bad idea.

CAUSATION AND COMPARISON

Smart Questions and Stupid Answers

In both sociology and everyday life, we wonder "why did this one thing happen, and not another?" This is an extremely reasonable thing to do, and there is hope that sociology can help us answer such questions. Further, no one would deny that if we ask questions of the form "why this but not that?"—as the "that" can be different—we may expect different answers, all equally valid, for why "this" happened. I have never denied this.[20] In fact, we'll see that we often don't want to drop the "but not that" part. However, there seems to be a very deeply held conviction in sociology these days that, by definition, the answer to any such question is a "causal" one. That is, if we like the answer, we *call* it a causal one. This is then used (with glorious circularity) to argue that our science of explanation must be based on such causality, because there is no explanation without causality. I am going to call this the "casual causal" view (because of this easy generosity with which any answer is considered a cause). Unfortunately, we don't have an equally generous vision when it comes to our *definition* of causality, but we'll get to that below.

Now, given that we aren't all clear and agreed on what we mean by "cause," I can't simply say that this casual causal definition is wrong. Yet it does seem to me problematic to have a sense of causality that throws together higgledy-piggledy things that are generally seen as antitheses (most important, internal human motivation and external mechanical causality).[21] And as said above, I see some advantages in retaining the word "cause" for a narrow class of events turning on the prototype of effectual human motivation. But this is in some ways a matter of preference. I will go on not to continue arguing *against* the casual causal view, but examining what happens when we try to define it clearly, and apply it to the case of human action.[22] Thus I completely acknowledge that we (at least, Westerners) often do use the casual causal terminology in everyday life—but that doesn't mean that it can attain the degree of precision that might be required if we were to claim that we could use this conception to push our thoughts further toward something that would deserve the name of a social science.

We find ourselves, we recall, asking questions about why this and not that, and in the conventional understanding of causality, our answers are of a parallel

[20] I have found that *The Explanation of Social Action* was read (when it was read at all) as arguing against posing *these* sorts of questions, which was certainly not intended.

[21] If these *can* be brought together, then there's no problem, but put your "sciencie" feelings to the side for a moment and don't assume that it's been done yet in a way that would survive serious critique.

[22] Thus from here on, we are only considering the role of causality in explanations of human action as carried out in sociology. Things that don't work for us might work for a very different field.

form: because of the fact that this and not that was the case. There are thus two different comparisons being made, one of the cause (call it x) and one of the effect (call it y). In some cases, one of these is of a very restricted kind, namely, this (x) and the absence of this ($\sim x$). Often, however, we find arbitrariness for both, in that we may be comparing this (x) to that (x'), where there are many, perhaps an infinite, number of x's that could enter our comparison.

There is nothing wrong with asking questions like "why this and not that?", and it isn't the worst thing to treat any answer to this question as a cause. But this open-mindedness doesn't necessarily sit well with a narrow definition of *cause*. This has proven to be the case with the most popular current definition in the social sciences, which is to argue that the cause of things being this way and not another is identical to the issue of the presence-as-opposed-to-absence of a putative cause. (This is known as the *counterfactualist* approach to causality which we'll get to soon — the counterfactual has to do with the putative cause first and foremost.) There are, then, two different comparisons being made. Neither by itself is problematic, but tying the two together and calling it cause has defeated many of the best minds.[23]

Here is an example I have used before: the question is, "Why did you not come to work yesterday, as opposed to coming?" The current understanding of the nature of this question is that *any valid answer* is a cause. Thus my projectile vomiting, which I might raise as explanation, was indeed a cause, but so are all the infinite factors that led to this and not that. For example, had bandits arrived at my door, kidnapped me, and taken me to work, I would have been there, so logically, the absence of the bandits kidnapping me was also a cause. Perhaps they seem a little stupid, but at least they are true.

Consider the same tolerance for stupid answers in the context of a different science. We ask, "Why does a projectile make a parabolic arc?" and we accept the answer, "Because it did not hit a bird." We ask, "Why does a wolf mother moving her cubs one by one return one last time even after all the cubs are gone" and we accept, "Because she was not kidnapped by aliens." Not a promising beginning. I am not saying that researchers in other fields have a better definition of cause than we do; I'm saying that they don't seem to need to start with it as a central concept at all. The key is that sciences work well when they pursue the specific sorts of things that they are all about. Although sociology isn't *only* about action, still, action — especially social action — has to be at our discipline's core (or so I believe). And when our investigations have to do with human action, our methods should take us *into* that. Comparison is a means to an end, but never an end in itself.

[23] One reason for the difficulty, not explored here, is that is it not so much the absence of the cause ($\sim x$) that we are interested in, but the *world* without the cause ($W \setminus x$). But it turns out that this can't always be neatly constructed, because eliminating x from the world requires eliminating *other* things, too.

We have, to an extent that seems difficult to account for, accepted an understanding of causality that is not wrong, but is neither obviously true nor carries with it any explanatory advantages. It *is* related to an important advance in thinking through the notation that should be used to describe statistical and quasi-experimental results, but as a theory of causality, it is at best trivial, and at worst, deeply stupid.

Events and Propositions about Events

How do we get into this puzzle? Our previous investigations regarding the supposedly constraining effects of culture point us in the right direction. To a considerable degree, we have confused explanations of something with explanations of *the fact that* this thing exists or has occurred. Indeed, most of us will not initially be able to accept that these are different. What is the difference between "the French Revolution" and "the fact that the French Revolution occurred?" Return to the example of the question, "Why does a wolf mother moving her cubs one by one return one last time even after all the cubs are gone?" What is the difference between explaining "the fact that she returned a last time" and explaining "her returning the last time"? The answer must be that we can explain the first successfully without having learned anything about the second. That is, the true statement "the wolf mother returned to the den because she was not captured by aliens" has not moved our science of animal behavior one step closer, and a theory of explanation that denied this would be a travesty. We might not be able to make any theory at all of what we mean by cause, but whether we do or not, we need to be focusing on the second type of explanation, not explaining "the fact that she returned a last time," but explaining "her returning the last time." What could this latter mean?

It must mean that we know something about her returning. It is not that knowledge about the fact is knowledge of a single event as opposed to a more general set (for aliens-not-kidnapping is a general cause of all such returnings). It is that the lack of aliens coming does not tell us anything about the returning itself. Can we formalize this principle? Probably not. Or at least, not unless we accept that there are returnings, and that they share an essence. That is, we might say that the fact of the return was *contingent*, accidental, largely happenstance. Something irrelevant to our concern could prevent her from returning, and we should not be distracted by this. What we are interested in is the *process*, not the outcome. We joke about doctors who say "the operation was a success, but the patient died," but sillier things have been said. Where actors have incomplete control, we have to expect a potential divorce of process from outcome.

Yet making this distinction is unlikely to do much for us. We really don't want to try to defend our focus on the returning by arguing that it has an essence.

Essentialism is a dirty word, basically because we know that when we are talking about groups of people, essentialism has in the past been associated with things like genocide. Of course, that doesn't mean we should refuse to be essentialists about *anything.* Still, there is a problem with a theory of knowledge that incorporates essentialisms — it's the nuclear option of epistemology. It flattens anything and gets out of hand very quickly. But the fact that we can't define what it means to pursue the core phenomenon and not the contingent things around it doesn't mean that this principle is wrong. So I see much virtue in the general idea of focusing on "causal powers," but I haven't seen any way of defining it analytically that is stable.

We know* that in some cases, our explanations of the fact take us away from the explanandum (that which is to be explained)— such as with the kidnappings that did not occur. We know* that in other cases, our explanations of the phenomenon take us *into* it — such as when we conduct tests to see if wolves can keep track of numbers. In some cases, we are not sure, and of course, sometimes what we "know" is wrong (hence the asterisk by *know,* to indicate that this is "that-which-counts-as-knowing," the sort of cute textual effect Garfinkel would use). But science does not work by being foolproof, *ab initio,* by definition. It works by picking itself up, dusting itself off, and resuming the trail when it has been thrown or gotten lost. Even so, it often ends up lost. Nothing better is promised mortals.

This distinction allows us now to approach the issue of comparison and causality. In a word, while comparison is enough to settle many explanations of "the fact that," it is only a first step when it comes to our quest for knowledge.

COMPARISON, PROCESSES, AND CAUSES

Comparison and Etiology

Consider what it meant for Robert Koch to decide that the cause of anthrax was the bacterium *Bacillus anthracis.* It clearly did not mean the same thing as "the reason these guinea pigs have anthrax (as opposed to not having anthrax)," for there are infinite reasons that could be invoked (e.g., that a toss of a coin led them to be assigned to treatment as opposed to control groups, that they had the misfortune to be sold to his laboratory, and so on, all as necessary for the *fact that* they had anthrax as the presence of the bacillus). One thing that we clearly mean is that if we are to look at the events that we call anthrax — especially the respiratory collapse — we find those little buggers plugging away. Although we can try (as did David Lewis) to interpret each link in the chain that leads us from symptoms back to the causal agent as a counterfactual one, we can also imagine it as the opposite, one of sufficiency, for example, via mechanical interactions according to mechanical and chemical laws — if we want to, that is. Fine with me if you don't.

Now consider what it means to say that a gunshot wound was the cause of a man's death on a certain day. If we interpret this as "what are the reasons for *the fact that* he died today," we cannot exclude the fact that he did not die the day before. Yet we would be very silly to imagine that this was the cause of the *death*.

It may help to make what first might seem a strange distinction (though in Western metaphysics it has been well understood since Aristotle [*Posterior Analytics* II.7] and emphasized again by Avicenna). This is to distinguish between a thing and that thing's existence. The first we can denote x and the second $\exists x$. We also may need to distinguish between $\sim(\exists x)$ and $(\sim\exists)x$. The first denotes that x does not exist. The second is a nonexistent x. There is a difference between saying "we have no bananas today" and "a magic dragon," even though both "bananas here today" and "magic dragon" are not existing. Both involve mental manipulations involving some sort of transcendence of the sensible and empirical; but in the first case, we manipulate our idea of an absence, and in the second, we manipulate something in the imagination. This difference comes in handy later.

We'll also notate certain facts using an ad hoc notation $x \lozenge p$ to mean x is p; in traditional logic this might be denoted $p(x)$, but in our case we want to leave open whether it makes sense to consider p a set, an attribute that cannot be understood in set-theoretic terms, or what. We will use $\rightarrow$ to mean causation, either definite (referring to a single instance or a delimited set of instances) or indefinite (referring to any instance); thus $x \rightarrow y$ means that x causes or caused y. We will use " " to denote a proposition, and we will assume that every proposition needs a copula of some form, whether *is* ($\lozenge$) or *causes* ($\rightarrow$) or something else. Thus "x" is not a valid proposition while "$x \rightarrow y$" is one. We allow as a special case existence propositions; that is, "$\exists x$."

Finally, for ease of exposition, I'm going to constrain us to a timeless world (though I'll only do that temporarily . . . that's a joke, son). That is, we're only considering the present, and so we'll bracket the puzzle of existences that once existed, but do so no longer, and so on. We can then call "the real" that place where our facts seem to live — as we'll see in the next chapter, I think this is a correct description of where "real" comes from, but let's just use this as a convenience for now.[24]

[24] Now it isn't necessary, given the way I have defined facts, but if one wants to try to ground all facts in something other than belief, I'd suggest that we declare that a statement that "it *is* a fact that Napoleon *was* the loser at Waterloo" or, similarly, "it *is* true that the train *will* come at noon" must be interpreted as "it *was* a fact that 'Napoleon *is* the loser at Waterloo'" and "at noon it *will be* true that 'the train *comes*.'" This doesn't get rid of time, but it takes it out of factuality and truth and allows it to find its way to where I think it behaves a little better, namely, in terms of our collective inner experience, whatever that might be. If you don't accept this, you're on your own.

The puzzle that we are facing now has to do with the relation between different types of causal statements. One kind is "$x \rightarrow y$," a statement that would be true if, in the real, $x \rightarrow y$ is factual. A second is "$\exists x \rightarrow \exists y$" which, if interpreted definitely, is true if, in the real, $\exists x \rightarrow \exists y$ is factual. If either of our causal statements is indefinite, it is difficult to evaluate (the Humean problem), and we push these to the side for now, and consider only definite statements. We can see that the first and second are not necessarily the same. A match can cause a fire without the existence of the match causing the existence of the fire. This is going to prove very important, because the most influential understanding of causality in the social sciences right now, simple counterfactualism, deals not with relations between things, but relations between existences, sometimes merely the existences of attributes.

Now of course, it is reasonable to object that the mere existence of something is never a cause. The existing thing has to be implicated in some sort of process somehow. That's perhaps all very well, but that doesn't change the issue for the logical status of the terms in our theory. For example, let's say little Billy foolishly picked up a popsickle on the floor and licked it, thereby allowing little *varicella zoster* virus bodies to stream into his body and cause him to display the symptoms of the chickenpox. Because of this, the school authorities would not allow him to return to kindergarten for a week. We might well say "the cause of Billy's quarantine was the existence of his chickenpox symptoms," but we mean this in a different way from "the cause of Billy's chickenpox symptoms was the *varicella zoster* virus." In the second case, we can say that the virus itself ran around doing all the bad things that led to Billy's unhappy state. In the former, however, the symptoms did nothing. The activity was due to the principal of the school, who reacted to *the existence* of Billy's symptoms.[25]

The two potential causes enter our arguments differently, and we should recognize this difference. For when we investigate the *thing* as cause, we are led *into* the phenomenon in question, in the same way that we wanted to explain the returning of the mother wolf. But when we investigate the *existence* of the thing as cause, we may or may not be led toward the thing (the chickenpox). In the case of Billy's quarantine, we are led away from it. Put another way, in a world without

[25] You might say that Billy's immune system, just like the principal, reacted to the existence of the virus. I admit the force of this argument, and even would confess that I am stumped. However, I know that if we go down this road, we end up joining most simple counterfactualists in declaring, for example, that anti-black racism is caused by the presence of blacks, and such not. All I can say is that this is one of those (not infrequent) cases in which we must tune the precision of our logic to the point where it allows our thinking to work best for us, and in this case, the degree of precision we need is a bit higher than it currently is. (I would note that counterfactualists also conclude something very similar—we need to tune the parameter of the "fragility" of the world in order to make useful statements [Lewis 1986: 197–199; 2004: 85ff].) But here is where the delineative approach comes into its own. I might indeed not be able to catch all the causality on the correct side of my thoughts. But I can still go to press, confident that these thoughts are going to help us pursue the phenomena, even if they're not wholly adequate to the world's organization.

observers, indeed, without any mind at all, we might have $x \rightarrow y$ (the virus producing the chickenpox). We also might, somewhere else, have $\sim(x \rightarrow y)$—that is, there is an organism that lacks the virus and the symptoms.[26] But it is only mind that takes these two cases and puts them together to make a statement of the form $\exists x \rightarrow \exists y$.

It would be a lot easier on us if we could deny or negate the difference between things and their existences. It is, I believe, partly because of this problem that a number of theorists of causation wish to restrict causation to something that pertains to relations between *events*. Of course, there is an immediately attractive aspect to the focus on events, for causation seems a very *active* sort of relation, and with events, it seems that something is happening. That is, since causation is active, it is indeed reasonable to want our cause to be more on the verb side of things, and less on the noun side. But there is a more formal reason, one that, when not brought to surface, can introduce all sorts of confusions. For events are a curious class of entities whereby $x = \exists x$. In fact, I think that this identity could be used to *define* what we mean by an event, and indeed, some theorists of causality have basically done this (e.g., Humphreys [1989: 24f] who defines an event as any property of a system in a trial).

And it turns out that it is this property of events—that they are the same as their existences—that is key for counterfactual explanations. Their seeming "activity" is less important, and indeed, turns out to be counterproductive. For example, imagine we ask someone why the eight ball went into the corner pocket, and she were to reply that the cause was the cue ball. This doesn't seem right; perhaps she has spoken too loosely, because she has ignored the active nature of the process. It is not the cue ball itself that is our cause, it is the *striking* of the cue ball against the eight ball. Bam! Action! Causation!

Unfortunately, we have started down a road that leads to a very bad place. What do we mean by the *striking*? Presumably we do not mean the touching, for a cue ball can rub up against an eight ball without sending the eight ball flying. We really mean the (nearly) elastic collision of the two, which is to say, that sort of touching in which momentum and kinetic energy are conserved.[27] But this is to say that the *effect* is part of the definition of the *cause*—a common problem if we try to define causality as a process. (Precisely because we use the process to link one thing to another, it's usually got a bit of that second thing in it. If it didn't, the link wouldn't be there. And so processes don't lump off into nice separable units.) Of course, we can revise by saying not that the collision was the

[26] We might say, $\sim x$, $\sim y$, but this is inexact; more properly, in the world without mind, $\sim x$ must not be interpreted as the absence of x, which is something only mind produces. We can say that a dog is not a cat, but not that a not-cat is here.

[27] That is, $m_1v_1 + m_2v_2 = m_1v_1' + m_2v_2'$; $\frac{1}{2}m_1v_1^2 + \frac{1}{2}m_1v_2^2 = \frac{1}{2}m_1v_1'^2 + \frac{1}{2}m_1v_2'^2$.

cause, but "the fact that" the cue ball hit the eight ball is the cause. But that's what we've been trying to get *away* from.

The second problem with this restriction to events is that (unless we follow Humphreys and propose a degenerate definition of events, which has its own problems),[28] every theorist with an intuitive sense of causality finds that this rules out *something* that she or he would like to include. For some, it is that "gravity" can no longer be a cause; for others, it is that an inquest that finds an anomalous situation cannot call this the "cause" of the effect, since it was not an "event" (e.g., the cause of a building collapse being that the ground underneath turned out to be very sandy). It seems there is almost nothing we can say about what sorts of existing things can be causes.

The third problem is that we find, perhaps most strangely, that existence and nonexistence turn out to be very hard to tell apart! You might think, well at least we know that a nonexistent match cannot cause a fire. But many disagree. For another way of making a causal statement is "$\sim\exists x \rightarrow \sim\exists y$"—had x not existed, y would not have existed. This relation, plus the fact $\exists y$, identifies x as the cause of y. This is known as a counterfactual definition of causality. It is often believed to be the same as "$x \rightarrow y$," but philosophers understand that this is not invariably true. Still, "$\sim\exists x \rightarrow \sim\exists y$" is often a reasonable way of terminating an inquest and so often does seem like what we mean by a cause. So, for example, imagine that we are trying to figure out why there was a huge fire in the Berkeley hills in California. The best minds are put on the question, and they blame me. Why? Because when reports of a brush fire in Orinda were received, I had the job of lighting a counter-fire—to make a small, controlled fire that would eliminate the flammable material in the fire's path. If the fire came this way, it would reach an area with no fuel, and it would be unable to cross it.

Unfortunately, I forgot to bring a match with me. Unable to light the counter-fire, I ran away, and the fire spread across Wildcat Canyon and into the Berkeley hills. Thus the absence of a match caused the fire ["$\sim(\exists x) \rightarrow \exists y$"], though it wasn't that a nonexistent match caused the fire ["$(\sim\exists x) \rightarrow \exists y$"].

Let's pause for a moment and consider what might seem to be a very silly question. If the nonexistence of things [that is, a $\sim(\exists x)$] can be a cause in our world, why can't a nonexistent thing [a $(\sim\exists)x$] be a cause? If my absence-of-a-match can cause a fire, why can't a fire-breathing dragon? What is the difference between an existing absence and an absent existence? We might be tempted to say that it's because the dragon doesn't exist, but that the absence-of-a-match *does* exist. I

[28] For the record, the biggest problem with this is that it simply doesn't make sense. To say that an event is the property of a system under a trial (e.g., we measure the ground and find that it is sandy) is to make the *attributes* of things the causal agents, and not the things themselves. Were this true, we'd have no trouble, because all our existing techniques would make perfect sense. But we attempt to understand causality because we know that attributes themselves *don't* have causal power.

think that's pretty silly, or at least, an abuse of the word "exist." More important, this leads us to realize that it doesn't matter whether we're talking about a match or a dragon, so long as it *isn't* existing! Because, according to counterfactualist logic, the *nonexistence* of the nonexisting thing *can* be a cause, though the nonexisting thing itself can't! Even though we can't say "the fire-breathing dragons were the cause of the fire," we *can* say "*were there* fire-breathing dragons, fighting fires in these hills would be a lot tougher." That isn't a foolish or wrong statement, although it does sound sort of strange. Whether it properly is a *causal* one, however, is a different matter.

Thus looking for relations of counterfactual dependence — what we observe wouldn't have been observed were it not for something else — makes a great deal of sense in many cases. In those cases, we often are fine with the idea of focusing on things that *didn't* happen. But a causal interpretation struggles with the fact that our proposition refers to a nonexistence; we can attribute causal power not only to the absence of things that are absent, but even to the absence of things that don't exist and in fact could *never* exist![29] We might want to know why we have a science in which so much causal power is attached to what *isn't* here, and so little to what *is*. And the answer is, as we shall see, that what we mean by causality is no more or less than a form of our imagination, and so it works best the more imaginary things it has to manipulate. A single billiard ball on a table can't do much; at best it might be able, if properly directed, to knock another ball in the pocket. It can't, by itself, say, *make* a billiard table. Just looking at the balls on the table, there aren't a lot of causal relations going on. But shift to the realm of imagination, bring in the jet fighters that didn't crash into the table (and hence are claimed to be a valid causal answer to the question of why there is a billiard table), the dinosaurs that didn't eat it up, well, *now* we're talking! Now *there's* some real (that is, imaginary) casual power for you!

Further, the assumption is generally that when we say "$\sim\exists x \rightarrow \sim\exists y$," we are talking about a counterfactual nonexistence, because we use it when in the world we *have* seen x and y. For example, a man has died ($\exists y$), and he has been shot ($\exists x$); a counterfactualist says that the shot caused the death because had there been no shot, there would have been no death ("$\sim\exists x \rightarrow \sim\exists y$"), meaning that the nonexistence has not been observed. Clearly, if a "fact" is that which makes a proposition true, in this case, the fact can't be defined as "the way things are in the real world," since this absence-of-being-shot was *not* in the real world.[30]

---

[29] It gets worse, because according to the logic that treats the existence of things as if it were itself a thing, the nonexistence of things exists just as much as existence, which means that an existence is itself the nonexistence of a nonexistence, and so on, and pretty soon, you're staring at the back of your head, only it's upside down . . .

[30] Now you see why I couldn't define a fact as being based "in the real" (or, technically, "in the actual"), though just like you, I'd prefer it if we could.

For this reason, sociologists tend to use comparisons to things that *are* in the real world. Let us find non-shot people and see if they are non-dead. But this raises new puzzles as opposed to solving old ones. It would be extremely foolish, would it not, were we to deny that the gunshot wound was the cause of death, merely because we, standing in the city hospital, find one person over here who has died and was *not* shot, and another who actually *was* shot but has not died? Despite the retreat from the strongest forms of such claims made by Skocpol, there are few sociologists who recognize that our approach to explaining events such as revolutions using comparisons is just as implausible.

Does that mean comparison can never work? Of course not. Indeed, epidemiologists often use comparisons for precisely this endeavor of determining the cause of a death or a disease. What might all the victims have in common? Were they in the same place? Did they interact? Have they engaged in similar behaviors? The usefulness of such comparative procedures, however, is (in principle) restricted to a preliminary stage of focusing the attention on possible explanations. The fact that many men who came down with AIDS had done poppers (alkyl nitrites) was not, in the long run, considered sufficiently strong evidence of Peter Duesberg's theory of the causes of AIDS to lead people to reject the alternative theory, the theory that AIDS symptoms are caused by the HIV retrovirus. Although comparative evidence has been an important reason for this decision (that is, there are populations with none of the risk factors that Duesberg focused on that do develop what seems to be the same syndrome called AIDS in others, and they are HIV positive), another important reason for the consensus is that more researchers believed that they understood the processes linking the retrovirus to the symptoms.[31]

Mechanical Men

Processes like those that link a virus to a symptom — chains of cause-and-effect relations — are now often called "mechanisms," and there is nothing wrong with insisting that such processes be part of a complete understanding. Terminology aside, we might simply say that any scientific pursuit that does not involve a love of analysis — of breaking apart, looking more closely, and so on — is doomed to irrelevance; of course, fanatical attachment to analysis is no guarantee of success. Attempting to understand the optic system, say, of an animal is going to lead us to

---

[31] Of course, there are cases in which this evidence is lacking; Koch himself was frustrated in his inability to repeat his success with tuberculosis when it came to cholera, because he could not successfully transmit the disease via the pathogen to animals, as he had decisively done with tuberculosis (Brock 1988: 162). For this reason, he had to fall back on epidemiological studies — comparisons of where cases occurred — which led him, like John Snow (well loved by statistician David Freeman), to propose contaminated water wells as crucial for the spread of the agent.

want to look a bit more closely, and this will involve, sooner or later, cutting into one. But there have been plenty of researchers who confused chopping with studying, and whose spectacles were so covered with blood that they were unable to see very much.

In any case, there is nothing wrong or petty with wanting to look closely, and to the extent that this is what is involved in the call for the examination of mechanisms, all is well and good. Yet in American sociology, there has recently grown up a wholly indefensible conviction that mechanisms are *causes* that explain individual action, where "mechanism" does not mean the thing you get when you cut into, but rather, an explanatory regularity. Further, it is argued that this supports a kind of causal analysis that does not resolve itself into the causality of human actors choosing to do things and getting them done.

This latter type of causality (where the causation comes from people acting), or "first person causality," seems to make a great deal of sense, but often strikes the sociological imagination as disappointingly trivial and nonscientific. Here causality must refer to the prototype of willful human action. But such human will seems to confound our understanding that what opens the door to true science is the presence of the *opposite* of such willfulness. Hence, the quest for a different vocabulary of causation, a "third person" one, in which the causes aren't just people doing things; rather, the prototype of causation is one billiard ball smacking into another. Put a chain of billiard ball interactions together ("cue ball's going to hit the seven into the nine, nine off the side into the corner pocket") and you have a mechanism, at least if it happens over and over the same way. Here I want to use as an example my favorite writer on these issues, who also probably put forward the most influential version of this argument, namely, Charles Tilly; as a historical sociologist, he presumably got it from Norbert Elias, though there are plenty of other possible sources.

Tilly identifies recurring patterns of social action and calls these "mechanisms" because they can be envisaged as discrete parts of a clockwork that, assembled in a certain way, will produce a certain result. In itself, this is a laudable endeavor; the word "mechanism" to describe the pattern nicely highlights the modular nature of these explanatory nuggets, at the cost of some misleading imagery. I'm not arguing against most of Tilly's approach here, I just want to consider whether it makes sense to call these mechanisms "causes" of action.

Some may argue that the mechanisms aren't causes of *actions* (like Lenin getting on a train), but of *outcomes* (such as the Bolshevik seizure of power). I think this is a plausible argument, but given that these outcomes are nothing other than lots and lots of human actions, this sort of response raises a second problem that we'll have to put off until the next chapter, namely, how we think about aggregates. In a nutshell, if one has a causal argument, one usually wants to be able to identify some *X* that can do something to something else. It is harder than it looks in sociology to get something other than a person or group of persons to be that *X*. We can still make arguments of the form "the reason that the Bolshevik revolution succeeded as opposed to failed" was due to "the pattern of coalitions," but that doesn't mean that we want to say that we have a scientifically defensible understanding of "causality" that should hang not on persons but on things like "the pattern of coalitions."

So the problem, then, isn't that people have identified mechanisms, but that some sociologists seem to think that these mechanisms can be a causal force that allows us to dispense with the causal powers of persons. That idea seems very puzzling to me, for the mechanisms themselves are nothing other than patterns of action. They do not *explain* the action; they *are* the action.

For example, Tilly (2004: 20) lists "coalition formation between segments of ruling classes and constituted political actors that are currently excluded from power" (henceforward, CFBSORCACPTACEFP) as a "mechanism" tending to "cause" democratization. Speaking loosely, this is all well and good, but it cannot be seen as a successful form of third-person causality. That would require us to imagine some form of CFBSORCACPTACEFP that is forced upon persons as opposed to arising from their own actions. Why? Because a relation between CFBSORCACPTACEFP and democracy that we interpret in *motivational* terms doesn't support the doctrine of the existence of third-person causality. Now not all cases of mechanism are so obviously tied to motivated action, but no case can perfectly satisfy this vision of human action being caused by such mechanisms, because it requires action without action.[32] The more seriously we take the causal language, the sillier or crazier our thoughts become.

An analogy might be to think about a wave in water.[33] If we were to think impressionistically about why some molecule of water first moves up and then down, we might well say that this was "caused" by the wave. This might then be our evidence for a theory of fluid dynamics that says that the cause of fluid motions was the wave. It would seem right to us, and we might abuse any colleague so simple-minded and stubborn as to deny that waves deserved to be considered real and possessive of causal power ("vulgar reductionism," we would smirk—if we did not consider him a traitor to fluid dynamics entirely). But the wave doesn't cause the motion of the molecules—it *is* the pattern of their motion, each causing the other.

At the same time, I emphasize, it is fine to say that the "mechanism" is the "casual cause" of many *outcomes*—that is, that this happened as opposed to

[32] Indeed, Daniel Little (1991: 14–19) emphasizes that such causal mechanisms "are typically grounded in the meaningful, intentional behavior of individuals" because the regularities we see "reflect facts about *individual* agency." This seems to make a great deal of sense to me and suggests that accepting the importance of causal mechanisms requires a robust restriction of our understanding of causality to first-person causality.

[33] This was proposed by a commenter on a blog discussing my book; thank you Peter T., whoever you are.

something else—in the same way that we may loosely say that the wave caused the wave. And of course, there's nothing wrong with talking about the effects of "the wave" on something *else* (the cause of the wall being knocked over was the strength of the wave). But that's not about explaining the motion of the *water*, which is our analogue to human action.

Processes and Comparison

We began with problems of constraint and culture, and found something paradoxical stemming from the attempt thinkers made to have one part of us (our culture) constrain another part of us. We pulled apart a number of the confusions inherent in this way of thinking about things, and then moved on to apply some of our lessons to the issue of causality. We found that in sociology, we tend to do two things. First, we think that *any* good answer to a question of the form "why this and not that" is, necessarily, causal, and yet we also think that there is a single definition of causality (the counterfactual) that applies to all the things we think of as causes. This justifies us using comparisons to get at causality.

Just as it is reasonable to wonder "Why this and not that?"; so, too, it is reasonable to compare different cases. But there are no guarantees that comparison will lead us to an answer—it can be a fall-back until we understand processes, and it can help orient us to the right processes. But we lose as much ground as we gain if we assume that the processes *themselves* are the causes, simply because we *call* them mechanisms. Thinking analytically, even mechanistically, is all well and good, but we easily confuse ourselves and make action itself seem as if it were an actor.

Finally, we saw two differences that are often confused: the first is that there can be a difference between things and their existences, and we need to keep these distinct when thinking about causation. A way of highlighting this is to remind ourselves that the world as such is a "base one" counting system. The way that the world has six sheep, say, is to have six sheep like this: sheep, sheep, sheep, sheep, sheep, sheep. Things are either there ". . . or they're not," we add. For it is only we who add the possibility of their not being there. Even though existing things exist in the world, and I'm fine to say exist in the world whether or not there are any people, their *existence* isn't in the world—it is in the heads of the sorts of beings that can comprehend the nonexistence of things, as well as the existence of non-things (abstractions, imaginary animals, and so on). $\exists x$ is a proposition—the sort of thing that is only in some sort of mind, and hence is manipulated by mind. (In contrast, things themselves are manipulated by our hands, among other things.) Indeed, it is well recognized that statements like "$\exists x$" presuppose the *idea* of x (*that* we can treat as established; the question now pertains to the existence of the idea).[34] When we forget this, we allow ourselves to attribute to the world characteristics of our own thinking.

The second confusion comes when we ignore the difference between things and facts about things. We have seen a relation between the two confusions because in almost all cases, when we are saying that the existence of things, or the fact of things, does something, we are smuggling in an inherent comparison. It is no wonder that we find that these transformed versions of things (their existence, the facts about them) do much better for us in completing the sorts of mental constructs that we want to develop—because they are themselves prefabricated to have these constructs inside them. They are not things, but comparisons. We define cause as "that which would answer a question I have about a comparison," and so we deploy as our causes not things in the real world, but a new compound unit of comparison-containing-units-easily-confused-with-things. That makes our job a lot easier.

Because the things we group together as causal are too disparate to have much in common. Asking "what is the commonality between the relation of lighting a match to an explosion, the relation of gravity to the moon's orbit, and the relation of my thoughts to my actions?" is like asking "Now what is it that has four pair of pants, lives in Philadelphia, and it never rains but it pours?" The only answer is to make one up. That is, I'm saying that our idea of "cause" is anthropocentric. That's not a problem if we acknowledge it; indeed, I think it's the way things should be.[35] But if we don't acknowledge it, we confuse our minds and the world.

It may indeed be that such confusions are, to some extent, unavoidable here (a theme we return to in the next chapter). However, we see that the extent is not necessarily total; we are able to do a partial inversion of our tendencies and make certain corrections.

But to do this, we will need to be vigilant in looking for our tendency to confuse things and propositions about things. For we have a tendency to make overly convenient worlds that have the characteristics our mind would need them to have were it to be able to assemble them in the way that feels most comfortable to us. But we often allow ourselves such importation of mind while we also claim that we are making knowledge about mind-independent things and processes. You have to love how IKEA made it so easy to get a shelf to attach to a side with just that little wrench, but you'd be a fool to claim that this was inherent in the nature of wood, and in fact, explained how trees held together. Yet that's what we do.

---

[34] It is for this reason that many medieval proofs of God's existence were successful; by starting from the idea of God, which included perfection, it would be contradictory were a perfect thing not to also have existence, QED.

[35] In fact, one of the good things about our anthropocentric idea of causality is that by asking "why did *A* do (or become) *X* as opposed to *Y*," instead of simply "why did *A* do (or become) *X*," we in effect make our question conditional on the existence of *A*, and therefore eliminate the infinite number of counterfactual answers that merely point to the things that made *A* be there in the first place. Sure, we still have an infinite number of potential causes left, but we're moving in the right direction.

CHAPTER 3

The Return of Realism

A BASKET OF ISMS

Guide for the Perplexed

In this chapter we explore a tangle of problems revolving around the issue of what is called realism in sociology. I'm going to begin by laying out, in simplest schematic form, the bare bones of the issues that people are using the word realism to denote. This isn't to reduce all realists or their opponents to these positions, but to show their starting points. And so adherents of the most important contemporary approach to realism, called critical realism, will be disappointed that I don't deal much with the body of any of their arguments. But most of these arguments are separable from the "realism" part, and it's there — in the first paragraph, as it were — that I think the problems lie for us. So I'm going to start by focusing on the issue of realism at its most basic level.

In Chapter 2, I brought up the fundamental distinction between *nominalism* (the philosophical position that the general concepts or "species" we use to grasp particularities come from our mental definitions) and *realism* (the position that the generality is in the world, and only for that reason, in our minds). Confusingly, we often use realism in a different way — to mean the philosophical position that the knowledge we have is knowledge of the real world, as opposed to knowledge of some fundamentally mediated construction that our minds toss over the real world. The confusion comes because the two kinds don't always go together: there are people who are anti-nominalist realists but not realists in the second sense. It's the second sense we're going to be focusing on now, and I'll use "realism*" to indicate realism-in-opposition-to-nominalism.

So we all have experiences, phenomena, measures, or what have you, that we can denote with E, our experience. Most of us think that these experiences are related in a nonrandom way to the real world, which we'll call R. I'll say "the real world" over and over, as opposed to simply saying "the world," and this is because in Chapter 5 we'll start using the idea of "world" in a different way, one compatible not with realism and idealism but with phenomenology. In a few places, I'll use a different distinction, but it means the same basic thing (though I think with a bit more precision); instead of talking about experience and the real world,

I'll talk about the phenomenal realm and the trans-phenomenal realm. The former is the world of experience—a rose before me looks red and smells fragrant. The trans-phenomenal world is what realists call the "real" world—it is something outside of, beyond, or behind my experience. It is about the cellular structure of the proteins that make up the flower surface, and about the molecules that drift off the surface of the petal, diffuse in the atmosphere, and bind to receptors in my olfactory epithelium. Most anti-realists (such as the subjective idealists we'll turn to shortly) don't deny that there is a trans-phenomenal world, they simply insist that our knowledge is knowledge of the phenomenal world. And they don't pick and choose (as did the earlier critical realists, who largely followed Galileo and Locke here) and say that some phenomenal properties (e.g., scent) *don't*, while others (e.g., extension) *do* exist in the trans-phenomenal realm. Anyone who has seen the movie *The Matrix* has a fine understanding of the difference between the two realms. The question then is: What is the nature of this relation, that between our experience and the "real world"?

One simple way is to propose an identity: E = R. However, there are two ways of making this argument. One (often called naïve realism) may be denoted (E) = R. The world is the primary thing, and our experiences are nonproblematic reflections of this. This doesn't really stand up to much philosophic scrutiny, and so no philosophers of import were ever really naïve realists. However, some—most important, the Scottish common-sense realist school, associated especially with Thomas Reid—did argue that we can establish this "=" because the shape of our knowledge is a necessary joint function of the world and our sensory system, and we can trust the latter, because God wasn't a sadistic jerk playing a joke at our expense by giving us an unreliable set of senses.

The other way to propose an identity (generally called idealism, sometimes objective idealism) may be denoted (R) = E. Our mental experiences are actually the real thing; the world is secondary. To the extent that the world exists, it does so *as* mind (if not ours, *someone's*). This argument is associated with Bishop Berkeley. Finally, there is consistent phenomenology, which argues that the whole idea of a world beyond experience (a trans-phenomenal world) doesn't make any sense, and so there isn't anything to equate. We start with experience and find that the world is just a kind of experience. To some, this is seen as a version of idealism, but to its proponents, it is a rejection of the ideas of E and R altogether.[1]

[1] There are two other approaches of historical interest, though not currently influential in the social sciences: monism (also known as duality—or it should be), most famously associated with Spinoza, in which the same thing looks E-like when viewed from one side, and R-like viewed from the other (call it ER); and preestablished harmony, associated with Leibniz, in which the E and R realms proceed in parallel tracks but do not influence one another (E||R).

The above approaches solve our problem by fusion. If we aren't going to fuse, we still need to link. The hypothetico-deductive approach says that we begin by posing something about a world (R′) and then make conditional deductions as to what would be experienced (E′) were this world the real one. If E′ = E (that is, it's what we *do* experience), we tend toward believing R′. This is a delightfully consistent approach in the abstract and has been used as our basic model for theoretical—and statistical—logic in sociology. The problem is that it is underdetermined, in that there is usually a class of potential real worlds (call it $R = \{R\}$) that imply our E′. Choosing between them becomes the difficulty.

Let's introduce a little bit of notation. "$\Rightarrow$" means "goes from / to," and so in hypoethetico-deductivism, $R \Rightarrow E$. "$\supset$" means "implies," and "*a*." means *a* is true. We'll also define $\subseteq$ as "is a subset of," though we won't need that for a while. So if (1) $a \supset b$, and (2) *a*., then (3) *b*. "~" means "not," or the negation of something (this will turn out to be more complex than it looks at first). Note that according to logic, if (1) $a \supset b$ and (2) ~*b*., then (3) ~*a* (this is the same as the logic of counterfactualism we explored in the last chapter). We'll use capital R (and E) to represent the real world (and experience) in general, and lower cases to mean particular things about the real world (or experience). Hypothetico-deductivism logically "works " (that is, leads to ironclad arguments in the abstract) only for falsification (disproving things); a systematic defense of this approach is most closely associated with Karl Popper, who argued that this is how science could / should / did progress. That is, the logic is

1. $r' \supset e'$
2. e'

but from this we can't conclude

3. r'

However, were we to have

2′. $\sim e'$

we could conclude

3′. $\sim r'$.

With this under our belts, let's progress to what is sometimes called transcendental idealism, and associated most famously with Immanuel Kant. This approach actually takes a form similar to that of hypothetico-deductivism. It states that if our knowledge is to be what we mean by true knowledge, then a set of conditions C about the joint constitution of world and mind must be true. That is

$$\sim C \supset \sim K.$$

This turns out to be logically a very strong theory, but also sociologically, it is one we often fall back on (although we may still deny that we do). For example, at the end of the last chapter, I argued that our idea of causation, one that relied on relations between *existences* as opposed to relations between *things*, imported into the world ideas of comparison that were properly only aspects of *mind*. If you found yourself irritatedly thinking, "Well, of *course* we do this to some extent; that's not news, it's *obvious*," you were thinking according to the general planks of transcendental idealism. The thing is that we want these necessary things we do when we think to be *absolutely true*. The doctrine that this is so is what was called transcendental realism, which became important for critical realism in sociology. It goes as follows (Bhaskar 1975: 29):

1. $\sim C \supset \sim K$.
2. Science exists (S.).
3. Science is just that sort of knowledge that we are talking about ($S \subseteq K$).
4. Hence C.

This logic is just fine, though of course it begs the question. That is, we understand that airplanes fly pretty much as they would if we knew what we are talking about, bridges also stay up, mostly, and so many of us are willing to grant (3). It doesn't, however, rigorously follow (and I'll make this point briefly below for those who are interested). But usually the people who accept (3) aren't in the market for an epistemology anyway. Further, although this particular plank was reasonably treated as obvious in works that focus on the physical sciences, it seems to become more and more problematic the closer we get to something like sociology. I don't know of anyone who has explained that we *do* have "science" in sociology, just a promise that if we *were* to do what people tell us, we *would*, which undermines the transcendental realist logic.

In any case, those who follow this approach do share with naïve realists the two basic planks of realism. The first of these is that the things we know about are things with properties, and these exist (and their properties exist) independent of mind. The second is that when we know these things, what we know are the mind-independent things, even though we know them with our mind. Naïve realists say this holds for all of what a sane person counts as knowledge; critical realists claim that it holds only for a subset of things produced by good science.

The last approach would be notated $E \Rightarrow R$. We go from experience to the world. This (what in statistics was known as the problem of "inverse probabilities") might seem obviously the best way to go forward; the problem is that it turns out to be a lot harder to justify logically than hypothetico-deduction. I'll be arguing that pragmatism is the most consistent version of such an approach, though I'll consider it $E \Rightarrow W$, as the world W is a world but not necessarily the one (R) that realists are looking for. Still, getting to *any* world is pretty good, and I'll argue that the pragmatist approach works for us, basically because if you are trying to run a cable from one place to another, and aren't really very sure about the location of the second, you're better off tying the cable firmly to where you are at the first location and then setting out, being willing to retrace your steps a lot, than you would be if you untied your end, and threw the whole reel off into the distance, hoping that you were hitting the right place and could get it back. The big difference between the pragmatists (and phenomenologists here) and the realists is that the former are satisfied with W and think that it gives you pretty much everything you could reasonably want from a world. Realists think this doesn't live up to the real world they've constructed (in their imaginations, it should be noted), and so they keep on throwing their reel out into the bushes (and yelling, "Hey, please throw one end back!").[2]

Making this argument will actually take a bit of time, even at the simple level that I'll be staying on. Before starting, we need to deal with the other way that realism is often used, namely, as an alternative to nominalism. But before *that*, I return to the point about the nondemonstrated nature of the pivotal assumption (3) in the transcendental realist argument; those who are not interested can skip to the next section without loss.

Mapping Phenomenal to Trans-Phenomenal Lawfulnesses

I have argued that there is something unsatisfying about assuming what is generally at issue, namely, what the epistemic status of our scientific productions actually is. Simply declaring that science is what we think it is seems to make a bit of a mockery of the whole idea of a realist "philosophy." But this assumption could be defensible on empirical grounds—even if it can't be proven, we have good enough reason to treat it as such, and I think this was the way the logic worked. The assumption seems to be that because we can successfully and cumulatively intervene in the world, our science is not only all-that-we-would-want-of-a-cognitive-relation-with-the-world (which subjective idealists, objective idealists,

---

[2] This is what critical realists call "retroduction"—making a statement about the real that would explain what we actually experience. It seems all very well and good, but I think we'll find that there turns out to be a problem in treating the real as if it were sitting out there, patiently waiting for us to derive things from it.

and pragmatists would generally acknowledge), but "knowledge," in the sense of propositions about attribute-bearing things that are true because the attributes to which the propositions refer exist in the real world and have the purported relation. (Bhaskar himself steered clear of this sort of idea of truth, but not all his social scientist followers have.) That is, it isn't that you can successfully drive a car down the road without hitting things—you could do that by "feel" without really needing scientific knowledge. But if you could write a program to successfully drive the car, you'd need to employ various ideas such as that velocity is distance / time, that on a straight flat plane the size of objects to you differs by the inverse of their distance, and, I suppose, all the basic principles of the laws of gravity and momentum; and it would work. This implies that our laws aren't simply things that work "for us," but the laws of the world itself.[3]

Except that you might be driving in a simulator. The lawfulness exists—not only in the phenomenal world that you experience, but even in the trans-phenomenal world—but that does not mean that the entities that you experience have corresponding entities with all the same properties in the trans-phenomenal world. The lawfulness of the real world does not imply the reality of *any* properties of the phenomenal world (for the lawfulness is about relations *between* properties). The realist equation is not one that can be supported by evidence or logic.[4] One is free to say that it doesn't matter—that all trans-phenomenal worlds that have the same lawfulness that we experience are what-we-shall-call-real worlds—but that isn't the realist position (it's a lot closer to the pragmatist).

In this case of the driving simulator, we might have what we should call a "one to one" or a direct mapping of the two lawfulnesses. A one-to-one mapping is where, given two sets of elements, the mapping links every element of the first to one and only one element of the second, and vice versa. In this case, we might say that although the elements are different, the relations between the elements are the same, and thus there is a way in which the proportionality of "distance traveled" to time is the same in both realms, although certainly "distance traveled," and perhaps time as well, are not the same thing across realms. The "distance traveled" in the first realm, which comes from the fact that going sixty

---

[3] Now most realists will point out that they deemphasize the importance of "laws" (which are themselves ideational constructs of scientists) and instead focus on things in the real world, and their causal powers. That's quite true and may well have significant implications. However, the way we learn about the causal powers of the world is generally to make use of the regularities we find in the world. But I'll go on to speak of "lawfulness"—that there is enough regularity in the world for us to exploit in our investigations—and not require that we come up with irresistible laws.

[4] You might say, but then we'd *know* that we were in a simulator. But as Morpheus would say, not if you were born there. Then you might say, what is it a simulator *of*? The pragmatists I'll draw on would agree with the implicit thrust of your question.

miles per hour for thirty seconds means going half a mile, has a corresponding operation in the second realm that we can call "multiplication" (even though this might be shifting a sequence of bits left or right in a computer register).

Now we might think that the existence of such a one-to-one mapping implies some sort of fundamental relation between the properties of the phenomenal and the trans-phenomenal world. But this isn't necessarily the case. Herbert Simon (1996) gives the example of two games, each involving two players taking turns: the first in which the numbers 1 to 9 are laid out on separate cards, and one successively chooses cards so as to be able to take a set of three cards and make a sum of 15 (the cards, once taken, become the property of the chooser). Although each can see which numbers the opponent has chosen, most of us find this a surprisingly difficult strategic game.

The second game is tic-tac-toe. Most of us find this an extremely *easy* game, so easy that we know that it is always possible to draw. But Simon shows that there is a one-to-one mapping between these lawfulnesses, in that there is an arrangement of numbers into a magic square such that the two are equivalent. That is, if you wrote down the laws of the number game, someone else could replace each *element* in your description with an element from tic-tac-toe, but the structure of relations would remain. Someone could "be" choosing the numbers but "think" she was only playing tic-tac-toe. Thus a one-to-one mapping doesn't imply much about the "reality" of the properties that are united in the lawfulness.

But are we so sure that we can count on such a one-to-one mapping between the phenomenal and trans-phenomenal lawfulnesses anyway? Certainly, the success of science in intervening in the world suggests that there should be *some* sort of mapping, but there are other possibilities. Consider a many-to-one mapping between lawfulnesses in the phenomenal world and that of the real world. That means that many different phenomenal lawfulness are really linked to the same underlying trans-phenomenal lawfulness. In fact, we generally believe that this has, historically, been a pretty common state of affairs. We believe that we make fundamental scientific progress when we realize that two or more lawfulnesses, previously established and used to success in our interventions in the world, are really the same lawfulness. The greatest example of this is Newton unifying the two chief successes of early modern physics, the Keplerian laws of planetary motion and the Galilean laws of the motion of bodies on earth; ever since, as it is in heaven, so shall it be on earth, but this was not the case previously. Before that, we had found different lawfulness that mapped on to the same lawfulness of the world, but we weren't wrong for all that.

Now consider a one-to-many mapping—this means that something that we understand as a lawfulness in the phenomenal world is collapsing and making indistinguishable lawfulnesses that are not identical in the trans-phenomenal world. It is clear what this implies—probability—and indeed, this was close to the Einsteinian critique of quantum mechanics as an "incomplete" system: by lacking a place for every real property, so Einstein argued, quantum mechanics was treating as the same case cases that were not the same.[5]

Finally, it isn't even true that there can't be laws to the *phenomenal* realm that have no simple counterpart in the trans-phenomenal world, and yet allow us to make important, sustained, and cumulative interventions in the world. I don't know how the newest television screens work, but I did understand how the older, cathode ray tubes worked. If I remember it all correctly, electrons respond to an electro-magnetic field, which means that if you can figure out how to get a stream of them shooting out of something, by altering an electric field you can direct where they're heading. You can make a planar shape out of a florescent material, which means that if an electron hits it, an atom's electron will go into a higher energy state and then will release a photon. So imagine you have an electron beam going across the screen just like the type on this page—horizontally until it gets to the end of a line, and then down one space to the next line, and so on—and for each place you traverse, you turn the beam *on* where you want light and *off* where you don't want light. You create a fine pixilation that will look to us like a black and white and maybe gray picture.

How do we do color? Well, as we all know, the three primary colors (red, green and blue) can be added in different combinations to make all the other colors (or at least a big range of them at a given brightness). Further, some florescent materials emit red light, some green, and some blue. So if we could lay thin strips of the three successively, then we could excite some combination of the three at nearly any point. To our eyes, it would look like the three sets of photons are coming from the same point, and so we see a single color there.

Now here's the thing, most physicists will say that *some*, but not *all*, of the lawfulness involved herein is present in the trans-phenomenal world. Most physicists (even if not all philosophers!) believe not only that the electrons are real, and the laws relating the motion of the electrons to the strength of the electric field are there, in the world, but that these laws are the laws that would govern these sorts of things even in the absence of human beings altogether. But the laws that mean that red and green together make yellow do not exist as such in the trans-phenomenal world. Most physicists would say that this comes from the three-color receptor nature of our own optic system and is in some ways almost

[5] I recognize that the usage of the idea of a "complete" system had a technical meaning that not all accept, and indeed, if I remember correctly, this holds for Einstein himself, who rued using the terminology in his classic paper with Rosen and Podolsky. Or at least, this is what Karl Popper told me that Einstein told *him*, when, as a young student, I had the opportunity to ask Popper a question. I hope I am remembering this correctly.

a trick played on the brain. Indeed, Goethe's (1970 [1810]) approach to the theory of colors — which opposed Newton's attempt to replace phenomenal coloration with trans-phenomenal frequencies — was largely dismissed because it was believed to be pointless to further explore the lawfulness in the phenomenal world once its trans-phenomenal substrate had been identified. But they wouldn't deny that it was possible for cumulative expertise and control to develop (not only in art, but most noticeably there) given a lawfulness that was wholly in the phenomenal world. True, it isn't the kind that means airplanes stay up, but it is the kind that means you could make a picture or a photograph so realistic that a person would swear he was looking out a window, and hence shapes the behavior of people.[6]

In sum, we can't go from the fact of our increasing mastery of the world around us to the idea that science constitutes the sort of knowledge that the philosophers went out hunting for. Now I understand that it is possible that some adherents of transcendental realism would object, first, that they do not actually claim that the issue of laws is at all relevant to their claims, which pertain to *mechanisms* that operate in the world; their argument, it will be said, is that these mechanisms are (1) the sorts of things that will produce certain lawful statements in laboratories; (2) real; and (3) that (1) is not the key issue, while (2) is. But this is one of those objections that transcendental realists make that involves them embracing precisely the arguments that they are supposedly rejecting. The issue was, we recall, not simply that *something* happened, but that this something could be known in the sort of way that anyone would want to call knowledge-of-reality, and this way is (they do not object to this) a way turning on the idea of lawfulnesses, even though not necessarily the explication of laws.

Thus it seems to me that the undoubted success of modern science — which is not simply that planes stay up and all that, but that we have a sense of *getting somewhere* with our science[7] — is compatible with a wide variety of mappings between the lawfulnesses of the phenomenal and trans-phenomenal realms, wider than is compatible with any but the most vacuous sense of realism. It therefore follows that the key assumption, used to transmute transcendental idealism into transcendental realism, is an extremely weak one.

Well, whether you accept that or not is perhaps a personal matter. Let's rejoin the main thread of the exposition and see how realism has been opposed to nominalism, particularly in sociology.

---

[6] If you reply that "and hence [it] shapes the behavior of people" isn't a strong enough criterion to use this case as an example of phenomenal-but-no-trans-phenomenal lawfulness, then you're saying that realism isn't applicable to sociology, and so I guess I agree.

[7] This sense of getting somewhere isn't the same thing as believing that "we now know the truth," which many nonscientific fields have instilled in some practitioners, often to their detriment. I'll get back to this at the end of the chapter. See, we're getting somewhere!

REALISM VERSUS SOCIAL CONSTRUCTION

The Reality of Species

Nominalism means that the generalities we treat with our minds are constructs of the mind and lack any fundamental trans-phenomenal justification. The species "badgers," the idea of "liberty," the class "weekopreebie" consisting of all red objects that are made of plastic and have never been in a barber shop are all assemblages that are held together by our *names* for them. Hence "nominalism" is the hallowed philosophical term, but in sociology, we generally think of this in terms of "social constructionism."

One of the things that is most difficult about dealing with social constructionism is that it is a widespread set of ideas that (it seems) no one has ever put forward . . . at least in print. That is, those of us who oppose this social constructionism have a hard time citing any cases of the sort of thinking that we would hold up as a strong example. Yet I don't think people are wrong to think it exists. I know that it *does* make an appearance, time and time again, in the medium of graduate student papers (and in discussion). The fact that these papers tend not to be published is not a reason we should *not* deal with the ideas. On the contrary, it's why we need to clarify things, so that students can put their effort into things deserving of publication.

Further, it has to be recognized that radical social constructionism isn't radical at all; it is a logical extrapolation of some of our most fundamental beliefs about the unordered nature of the world, and the heuristic nature of our mental tools. That's because mainstream social science tends to assume nominalism. *We* group things together and call them something —we, and not nature. Our knowledge is knowledge that is *for* us, but that doesn't mean (or so we think) that it is *of* the real world. In sociology, this is what often troubles us, as it often logically seems that we can't really know all that much about what we think we know.[8]

To some degree, the debate between social constructionism and realism has been one of complete nonengagement, in part because the two talk at cross purposes. (Indeed, just as we saw regarding the issue of Parsons's conservatism in Chapter 1, in many cases, it seems that people understand the debate more in terms of *habitus* or style than epistemological planks—the uptight and complacent on the one side, the fuzzy-minded and directionless on the other.) Fortunately,

---

[8] Our ideas here are inchoate and with his wonderful simplicity Bruno Latour (2004) has recently highlighted the inconsistent logic that lies behind what is called social constructionism in practice; here we will not be worried about the second moment of the two-stroke engine of social constructionism, that in which the constructs are *explained*, and only focus on the epistemology.

some of the results of the previous chapter will allow us to make some clarifications. One error that has prevented the two sides from engaging is related to that whereby we confuse things and propositions *about* things.

We will denote particularities that are perceived by a human with lower-case letters like x, and the species to which they (may) belong with upper-case letters such as X. Thus Fido here is a dog, Mr. McFeely is a postman, and this is a lump of coal I have in my hand. You will note that the species enters as a predicate of the particularity: we say x is X ($x \Diamond X$ here meaning $x \subseteq X$). This issue of species does not have to do with "levels of analysis"—this would be the case were we deciding, say, how close to zoom in or out on Fido, such as to look at him as a set of organs or as part of a household. But to say that Fido *is* a dog is to say that the particularity here is united with things that are not-here as being equally members of the species.

Now it turns out that in general, we don't have terms for particularities, only for species. When we do have labels for particular things, these things are "individuals," which, as Rickert said (1902: 504; also 1986 [1929]: 100), means that they have a certain form of *value* for us (Fido isn't just any dog, the way that squirrel over there is pretty much interchangeable with any other squirrel, at least for *us*). We also don't have *terms* for them, we have *names.* Without accepting all of Rickert's thoughts here, we can follow him in imagining that sociology is basically a generalizing science, and so our terms are X's. (We'll for the moment push all individualizing concept formation into the discipline of history, though we won't pull tenure from all historical sociologists just yet.)

Now, social constructionism usually has to do with the species. One is saying that it is not this particular x (Fido) that is a social construct, but the species (X). There are two ways of interpreting this. One is a bit sophistical, and true by definition, and this is to say it is not the species as *content* that is socially constructed, but the idea of species itself. That is, if our species X is the set of all dogs $\{x_1, x_2, x_3, x_4, \ldots\}$, what is socially constructed here is not the choice of members x_1, x_2, x_3, and so on; rather, it is the *form*, the brackets "{}" *around* the set members, which we can call the "species form." (This is basically the argument made by Locke 1924 [1700] and again by Durkheim [1995/1912] in *The Elementary Forms.*) It seems hard to argue against this sort of claim—if we point to something that looks like categorical thinking among animals (and there is indeed such evidence), one can counter that monkey-species-form is not human-species-form (which only those who have had the experience of living as both human and monkey can judge; I haven't but perhaps some other sociologists have). Or one could claim that therefore social construction extends to monkeys and pigeons and so on.

But the more common interpretation of the statement that X is a social construct is that it is the *content* of X that is socially constructed—that the members of the set have been arranged by human cognition in a way that could be otherwise. This is basically an empirical question. It seems that it is extremely difficult to deny that certain categories are social constructs, when these social categories are actually produced by groups of people. For example, the category "criminal" is a social construct because it is defined by laws that are written by some people and enforced by other people. Hard to deny that crime is a social construct. That doesn't mean, of course, that that fellow who knocked you down and is running away laughing with your wallet is imaginary. On the other hand, it seems very very difficult to claim that, say, all animal species are such constructs, since probably without human beings around, animals do a reasonable job of finding others in their species and mating and rearing their young (though actually many animals are a bit more interested in cross-species dalliances than we might at first expect, and in some cases, the boundary between species *does* seem to turn on how *we* define it). And in between there are cases in which humans may organize things in a certain way, but we don't think that, given the circumstances, there really is any other way they *could* be arranged.

This suggests a simple resolution—all particularities are simply real, and in many cases, the species into which they are sorted are constructs, but not all.[9] However, there are two wrinkles: first, how we assign particularities to species can change how we think of them. Because we accentuate some attributes for the purpose of assignation and downplay others, these are likely to be more salient in our own minds. That means that if we think about the particularities, we might be guided by our placement, even if these placements are somewhat arbitrary. If smoking cigarettes were made illegal, then all smokers would become deviants and criminals, and we might understand their actions in a very different way from how we understand them now. Our explanations of their actions might have a lot to do with general explanations of deviance (they come from disadvantaged backgrounds, they have cognitive shortcomings, they are poorly adjusted, they are signaling rebellion) and not the explanations we might use were they not seen as deviants (e.g., we might point to the pleasing qualities of a good smoke). And of course, we can imagine that the ideas we have about some *X* can be arbitrary even if the *membership* of the set is nonarbitrary. Thus, even if there just were males and females at birth, we could consistently claim that "gender" is a social construct if by this we mean that our ideas of boys and girls (blue / pink, fireman / ballerina, and so on) don't come from the nature of the collections themselves.

---

[9] This is basically the approach taken by Bhaksar (1975: 210) who argues that some things are natural kinds if they have a real essence in common, whether or not we know it. So "all dogs" and "all carbon compounds" have such an essence, but "tables" and "chairs" do not. Whether or not one wants to try to defend something like this for dogs and tables, I think it would be pretty hard to take into the realm of sociology (unless you don't mind having your a** kicked).

Second, and more complex, it might be that there are cases in which precisely *what* species some particularity is placed in changes not only how we think about it but also its own nature. One of the things social constructionists and realists like to argue about is the social construction of mental illness. We might think again that the two sides are talking past each other, since to say that "schizophrenia" is a social construct in the sense of gathering together a disparate set of particularities that could be organized differently (some but not all considered "possession" in one social formation, or "dissociation" in another, and so on) doesn't mean that the particularities aren't real (that this or that person has something seriously wrong). Yet some social constructionists might argue that calling one person schizophrenic does not simply collapse this person with others and accentuate certain particularities, but changes the nature of the phenomenon itself. After all, the thing about studying social life is that our conceptual work can escape from our offices and infect the minds of citizens. In contrast to possession, schizophrenia cannot be cured with a single violent struggle of expulsion, and if schizophrenics know this, exorcism stops working (perhaps). Thus when it comes to constructs that are of humans and their actions and attributes, it is possible that things are more difficult to untangle. For this reason, many debates shy away from these hard cases.

In any case, the talking-past often happens in the following way. Realists scornfully ask if the social constructionists do not believe that x is real, while social constructionists think the realists are completely unimaginative (or ignorant) to think there could not be (or has never been) an X^* very different from our current X that could also encompass x. But both sides accept that we basically *sense* particularities first and foremost; social constructionists are perhaps more ready than their opponents to accept a form of scholasticism that assumes that we can only *know* species, but many of their opponents seem to accept this as well.[10]

Here we need to pause and make a distinction that accords with general understandings, although it isn't always borne in mind. (As we'll see toward the end of this chapter, I personally don't think it gets to everything we need to know about these matters, but that's for later.) This is between *real* and *true*. We're going to want to use the word *real* to refer to things-in-the-world.[11] We'll use the

---

[10] This doesn't mean that there aren't traditions of thought in which it *isn't* accepted that we necessarily begin by perceiving particularities. In fact, various forms of stable neo-Platonism exist in political theory and in cognitive science. But that doesn't seem relevant for untangling our ideas here. Thus although in philosophy there is a use of realism to designate those who believe that species are, *qua* species, real in the world, no sociologist I know of has had both the desire and the wherewithal to defend such a statement in close epistemological terms.

[11] Technically, I'd prefer to call this "actual," but though Bhaskar does, most sociologists don't make a distinction between real and actual and so here we won't either. I think a clear pursuit of the definition would only strengthen my argument, as "real" would turn itself into something very different from what realists imagine it is. Here I would follow Pepper (1961), who argues that we have to understand the "real" mental extrapolations from the actual, though that doesn't mean that they aren't defensible, perhaps even necessary extrapolations. Thus "time" is something we draw out from the actuality of the present, because we need to, and we consider it "real" even though the past and future aren't actually anywhere.

word *true* to refer to propositions *about* the world. That is, some x may be real, while "$x \Diamond P$" could be true. But x itself can't be "true," and although there may be a fact "in the real" that makes "$x \Diamond P$" true, the proposition "$x \Diamond P$" itself isn't real. We often get confused by saying things like "x is *really* P" which blends aspects of the two. This is, as you will see, related to the confusion between a thing and its existence; the latter, which *seemed* to be something in the "real" world, turned out to be a disguised form of a *proposition*—something that could be true or not true.

Now, given our disciplinary ways of thinking, sociological realists are in some ways confusing things when they say that this or that *species* is real. That is, if you dip your toe in the Atlantic Ocean, you are touching something real. However, the idea that these waters are part of "the Atlantic Ocean" is well considered a "social construct." In our current understanding, it would be clearer to say that the proposition "x is X" is *true*—yet this does not itself mean that X is not a social construct. Indeed, it isn't even the case that saying "there is a matter of fact in the real that makes '$x \subseteq X$' true" is incompatible with social constructionism, at least of the Weberian (voluntarist neo-Kantian) stripe. In this view, we *do* construct our species on the basis of some sort of intellectual interest, make different statements about them, and let the world tell us if these statements are true or not. Thus we might make a species "pra" composed of all things that are red and smaller than a breadbox, and another "pri" composed of all things that are made of wood and spherical. We could wonder whether most pra weigh more than the average pri, and if we find that they do, this is a true statement grounded in a matter of fact, even though pri and pra are human constructs, and stupid ones at that.

In sociology, the opposition to social constructionism rarely turns on the argument that we can directly perceive species *qua* species. Instead, the issue is that of the basis of the species that we do assemble. We can call whatever makes a species a species completely "arbitrary" if it has no necessary relation to the nonhuman world. Although it's hard to specify what arbitrary and necessity mean here, a way to think of it is the following: imagine we were to restart the earth's history, and maybe this time it was from the cat family that intelligent life developed. Do *they* divide things up differently? Do Martians studying earth use different divisions? If so, these divisions must have something arbitrary about them. The other pole would be that this basis to speciation is solely found in the organization of the world itself. And we can probably imagine things in between (even though we may have a hard time figuring out how we'd *know* where any particular case sat). We can probably find a lot of good examples of things toward or at the second pole (the nonarbitrary), but these tend to be things far from sociology (things like animals and minerals and vegetables). The ones we care about as sociologists (things like morality, domination, and so on) are harder to peg as totally nonarbitrary. And so critical realists, who claim that science must attach casual powers to entities (Elder-Vass 2010: 65), need to have a coherent answer to these questions, because they are generally attaching their causal powers not to particularities but to *species*. If the species are arbitrary, there's a real problem.[12]

Reality of Attributions

We've so far examined the question of attributions of reality for cases of the form $x \subseteq X$, which, as I've noted, is a central one for issues of realism as opposed to constructionism. Still, this kind of predication (x is a subset of X) has certain particularities that might mislead us in forming our general ideas about realism. So let's take another example of $x \Diamond P$ that has a different functional form; further, it is one that has been the subject of great interest for quite some time. This is the example from psychometrics: we give, say, 1,500 persons a pen and paper test. We add up the number of right answers, perhaps doing additional statistical manipulations, and assign persons a score. The question is how we evaluate statements such as "your IQ is 105."

The social constructionist view obviously has a head start in this race. First, the scale itself is exactly a social construct (a set of people made it, after all). Second, we can compose sets of questions that produce similar numbers (even with similar scaling properties) that no one would defend as tapping real traits (thereby spreading guilt to the measurement of other traits by association).

What is the realist position here? Well, it turns out that the most straightforward one doesn't actually oppose the social constructionist one. This would be to claim that (1) the persons studied are real; (2) real properties in the real persons are responsible for the statement "your IQ is 105"; and thus (3) "your IQ is 105" is factual. But we could say the same for any mishmash scale we were to fabricate: if I multiply your age by the number of Captain Beefheart records you have, take this to the power of 1 + the number of Caroliner Rainbow records you have, and then divide by 1+ number of Elton John records you have, subtracting 10 if you have a moustache, I get a number that is grounded (or so I believe) in factuality, and yet my "cool quotient" isn't thereby demonstrated to *really* measure coolness at all.

---

[12] Sayer (2010: 88) recognizes that we need to abstract from the concrete (and thus produce concepts), but he doesn't seem to worry about the specter of nominalism at all—he merely advises us that "abstractions should distinguish incidental from essential characteristics." This seems to assume what needs to be demonstrated as possible.

One coherent response to this has been to renounce any attempt to attach *meaning* to these constructs. Instead, we simply let the concept in question *be* the extent of the operations used to measure it. It doesn't matter what we *call* it; all is denotation, not connotation. This is most associated with positivism, and critical realists reject this—treating it as if it were antithetical to social constructionism, although as we have seen, the two agree as to the fundamental problem of the underdetermined nature of our underlying measurable traits.

A realism, noticeably different from constructionism for the IQ case (which I'll call realism*), then, says not merely that our measurement owes itself to real properties but that it successfully measures that which it believes it measures. A single number corresponds to a single trait, and our label of this trait is damn close to the nature of the trait itself. The key to such realism* is that things are the same whether or not there is an observer mind. Even though it would be silly to insist that the numbers themselves would exist without us thinking about it, or that the trait would be called "Intelligence Quotient" in English, we do need to think that the trait would exist as such, as opposed to being called into being by our measurement (as is my coolness score).[13] Anything short of this is compatible with social constructionism. That is, you may think there are indeed really stupid people and smart people; but if you do not believe that IQ measures a single trait (even if with noise) the way a bathroom scale measures mass, then you are not adopting a realist* account of IQ, which means that you do not have a realist* account of any analyses that involve IQ, and this is not changed by stomping around swearing that you believe in the real world, not even if you would risk your life on the bet that "mental tests measure *something*" (see, e.g., the wonderful work of Michell 2012 and elsewhere).

Of course, a realist may respond that it isn't that realism says that anything in particular *is* real, just that we should study the things that *are* real. Toward the end, we'll return to this statement—though it may seem totally empty and unsatisfying, I'll suggest that there is wisdom here (even though it doesn't fit with the way most realists talk now). But we still have a problem in knowing how to talk about the reality of attributes more generally.

Substance and Accident

Historically, there have been two families of approaches to some of these problems. Here we'll switch from examples that are familiar for thinking in terms of social constructionism to those that are more familiar to philosophers: I see an angry fireman (after, say, someone has pulled a false alarm). I say "the angry fire-

---

[13] I personally can't make sense of this approach for *any* cases, but a realist* needs to be able to make it work for *some*.

man is real." Most will accept that the *fireman* is real, but there will be disagreements as to whether we consider his *anger* real. One way to approach this, initially extremely satisfactory, is to make a distinction between the object (which can be real) and the attribute (which is not, in itself, real, though it is predicable of a real object). Thus the *fireman* is real, and it is *true* that the fireman is angry. Hence, given any $P(x)$, we turn it into x and "$x \Diamond P$", one real, the other true.

The problem with this is that it isn't always clear what is the object and what is the attribute. What if instead I were to say "the angry man who works in the fire department is real," and therefore say that while the *man* is real, the firemanishness, like the anger, is merely a predicate that can be said to be true. We can keep going (from the angry *man* to the angry, human *animal*, to the angry, human, living *carbon assemblage*, . . .) and eventually we end up with the idea of "substance." The *only* real thing *anywhere* is substance—everything else is a predicate. But once philosophers had followed this chain, they realized the substance was logically something with no properties—the only thing that was real was nothing.

One possible response to this is to make a distinction between two sorts of predicates, essential ones and accidental ones. Just like it doesn't make sense to call a person "John Levi Martin, who just happens to be human," though we can say "John Levi Martin, who just happens to be nearsighted," so we can divide the predicates of anything into those that our object could not lack without ceasing to be itself, and those that we can imagine varying without it being such a big deal. The first, *essential*, predicates, are part of the object. The second, *accidental*, predicates, aren't quite part of it in the same way; hence, the common opposition of "substance" and "accidents."

This works okay as long as we all agree as to what is essential. But the minute disagreement surfaces, all hell breaks loose. It's because of this that "essentialism" is such a dirty word in sociology. No one really thinks that *nothing* has *anything* essential about it, but no one wants to say it, because even if we don't turn out to be wrong (and we usually do), someone's going to hate us for it.

So what do we do? The other response involves saying that the anger is real. Not "the man is *really* angry," nor even "the man *really* is angry," but "the man's anger is real." For this case, we can imagine two different ways of supporting this. The first way is that we make the anger an empirical phenomenon susceptible of measurement. Anger is a measurable state, like momentum, and so just as we might decide to say not only that "the billiard ball is real" but "the momentum of the billiard ball is real," so we say the anger is real. The problem with this, we recall, is that not everything we can measure is what we'd want to define as real—because even if it's *something*, it might not be what we think it is. (Thus, when the early IQ tests involved items such as whether the subject knew that a tennis court was supposed to have a low net, one could say "intelligence" was "measured" and therefore was "real" but none of us now would defend this claim.) So this isn't really doing much for us.

The second way of supporting this is to focus on a thing's capacity to provoke responses *in us*. That is, we accept that our understanding of the object is a relation, not a simple attribute that can be attributed to the real. The "trait" is understood as a quality, something that is defined by its *potential* to do something else, most notably, to evoke a certain sort of experience. This solves a lot of our difficulties, though in Chapter 6 I'll propose that we need to be cautious here—the idea of "quality" turns out to have a number of potential problems for explanation. Still, overall, this seems a defensible way of proceeding. However, it really is that associated with subjective idealism, and not the approach of realism. It doesn't allow us to get *ourselves* out of the statement. It drives realists crazy, because they want us to be able to say things like "even if there were no humans ever alive, this rock would weigh 7.4 pounds." Unfortunately, they don't want to be able to say, "even if there were no human beings ever alive, Elton John's records would be totally lame," and it turns out that there isn't any way one can support the thesis of an intrinsic difference between the two sorts of claims other than by yelling at people, blaming them for delivering this piece of bad news, insulting them, or kicking them.[14]

GETTING REAL IN SOCIOLOGY

The Resurgence of Realism

And here we turn not just to realism in general but to the widespread enthusiasm for what people are calling critical realism. As said above, I'll be ignoring most of the work that goes by this name, and not merely because I haven't actually read that much of it (a good discussion by one who apparently has is Reed 2011). (I have indeed picked up the central work here by Roy Bhaskar and begun a number of times, but when I awake, I always wonder whether I really need to devote any more

[14] You might say that the assessment of Elton John's records as "totally lame" includes a valuation while the mass of the rock doesn't. The problem is that this distinction works okay for some polar cases, but poorly for many others, a fair number of which are important for sociology, which must deal with the experience of human beings and often has to blend the two (what are called "thick" descriptors). One early response (e.g., Tetens 1777: 556) was to attempt to say, for example, that all those with sound taste will *sense* sweetness in, say, a dessert wine, but not all will find it *agreeable*. However, it isn't really obvious that we do all have the same sensations. For one example, it seems that popular wisdom is correct and that some people are far more likely than others to sense cilantro as having a "soapy" taste (in part for genetic reasons: see Eriksson et al. 2012). Thus all we can say about the sweetness of sugar or the soapiness of cilantro is that sugar (or cilantro) is that-sort-of-thing that has the potential to induce an experience of sweetness (soapiness) when brought into contact with a being-of-that-sort. This also holds for the lameness of Elton John's records. I've suggested, and indeed believe, that we should try to minimize the valuation in our terms, but that doesn't mean that we can *define* the problem away by positing that our claims can be *value*-independent because they are *mind*-independent.

time to a tortured formulation of my own prejudices.[15]) But that won't be a problem, because we'll see that the problems come from what is at the core of realism, and about what critical realists *haven't* done.

Now critical realists don't agree on much, and indeed, the variation is, in a way, part of the commonality. For I've observed that the degree of enthusiasm that converts have for critical realism doesn't seem to correlate with the degree of actual reorientation of their practice. Conversion to critical realism appears to be a rather quiet and dignified affair. A man may leave the office in the evening an unrepentant epistemological sinner and return the next morning a critical realist, and even his closest friends may remain none the wiser. What he does at work, and how he interprets what he does, seems precisely the same (we may see why below). Perhaps there is a little more spring in his step.

And this is because what people take away from critical realism is pretty much what one already thinks as a practicing sociologist. We have knowledge, incomplete knowledge, which is knowledge of real things. These real things have their own mechanisms, and these are what we're trying to learn about, though since the mechanisms aren't necessarily always on, there's no guarantee that we'll see them in operation, though perhaps with experimentation, we can turn them on, and so on. All of this is close to what most of us believe—the problem is that epistemologies aren't about what we believe, but about what and how we know, and that ontology, a set of statements about what the real world is like, is never a good substitute for epistemology. That is, you may not need an epistemology, but if you do, don't let someone peddle you an ontology.

It's a reasonable question whether one *ever* needs an epistemology. Many of us dismiss all these issues as nonissues, and there is a very good reason for this. When a science is going well, usually none of this matters at all. You can think there is a single real world, or you can think you're a brain in a vat and I'm just part of a program, and it may not matter at all for whether we decide that a particular claim has been proven or rejected. This is especially so in the many sciences that turn on production of phenomena. If you can make the cold fusion happen, you are right. You might need money, assistants, all sorts of allies to do it, but maybe even with them, nothing will happen. That means that there is a refreshing freedom from epistemology in many (though not all) cases. The naïve realist and

[15] I haven't read that much of the works of the central figures here, for the same reason that I have never eaten chalk. Although I am aware that some children do eat it without obvious bad effect, doing so has never seemed to me either appealing or useful. Indeed, I find critical realism distinguished from all other philosophical approaches by its complete inability to arouse my interest. I never think, "that's an interesting idea" or "that's strange!" or "I never thought of that!" And as we shall see, I suspect that this is precisely why it has become so beloved. Regarding whether my not reading all of the key works means I am unfit to judge, I must appeal to Oscar Wilde's point that a critic doesn't always need to finish a book to know that it isn't worth reading—let alone a restaurant reviewer eat *all* of the food on his plate to pronounce a dish unpalatable.

the person who believes he is in the Matrix simultaneously mail their papers to *Nature* and the reviewers don't need to know about anyone's epistemology.

In sociology, people can't win by making a phenomenon happen (Stalin didn't become right that the next phase of agriculture was a collective one by forcing people into collective farms). People disagree, and unless we define their disagreement as insanity—a strategy so very enjoyable that it fueled continuous enthusiasm for psychoanalysis despite the research tradition's notable lack of success—we find that sane people disagree about what is real, and hence their explanations for things are at odds. Sometimes we find empirical ways of deciding who wins, but there are times when this breaks down, because each side thinks that they have something really strong, but the other doesn't recognize this strength at all.

Now we can all come up with attributes of a better explanation, but most of these just rephrase the problem. We can say the better explanation should be insightful, but whose is insightful? (Hint: Which is yours?) We say that they should be reflexive, but whose is more reflexive? If that guy's theory was truly reflexive, wouldn't it reflexively include that it was stupid and wrong?

Epistemology is for times like this, when things look like they may be going badly, when we're suddenly not sure if something *could* be true, no matter how hard we tried to do things right. It's a court of last appeal, to see whether or not we're standing on what we think we are. Sociology can't always be talking about these issues, but there are going to be times in which *not* talking about it is worse than talking about it. But worst of all is *seeming* as though you're talking about them, when you're not.

And that's what I think is generally happening when we bring up realism in sociology. Critical realists may (reasonably) respond that they aren't giving an epistemology but changing the issue to one of ontology (what is the world like), but this does not seem binding to most adherents of critical realism who seem to think that these claims are relevant to issues of epistemology. But bringing "realism" here is akin to turning a serious philosophical discussion into an awards ceremony. It pretends to address problems but simply declares that no one should recognize the problems.

For critical realists argue that *in principle,* one shouldn't respond to their arguments with epistemic questions, and that these have already been handled. I recognize that the critical realists seem to know a great deal more than I do about all sorts of complex and subtle aspects of social reality. It's just that I can't tell *how* they know this, and when one asks, one is somewhat haughtily informed that one is committing a social blunder, the "epistemic fallacy."[16] Now when I

---

[16] As an aside, there is something very puzzling about Critical Realists' mantra that their opponents make the mistake of focusing on epistemology as opposed to ontology (which, as I have noted, is akin to criticizing parents for making the mistake of teaching their children to walk instead of run). Presumably "realism" is an epistemology—the term doesn't make much sense as an ontology. My guess is that the Critical Realists have a strong dislike of anyone reconsidering something they believe they've settled—which is fair, I suppose, but hardly makes for interesting reading.

was a lad, my pappy told me, "Son, one day a man's going to come up to you—he may be one of your friends—and he's going to promise that if you invest with him, he'll double your money in six months. He'll show you all sorts of official looking documents and contracts and securities. He may even introduce you to people he's made rich. But if you ask him precisely what he's going to do, he's going to dismiss your question and try to make you feel foolish or ungrateful for asking. Don't you give him a nickel. All you'll have at the end is worthless paper."

Although I am completely trusting of their good intentions, I would hope that the recent adherents of critical realism are not getting in at the bottom floor of what is basically an epistemic Ponzi scheme, in which the apparent success of declaring some things real is used to encourage even more wild speculative claims. For, somewhat surprisingly, realism here doesn't seem to tether anyone to the sorts of things that most of us would understand as real—quite the opposite. And so it seems that realism isn't the cure for the problems of idealism; it's just a problematic idea.

Form and Content

Let me start with where I think critical realism might have a head start over the rest of us in terms of formulating key questions, and then show the problem with its general answer. The problem, one well pointed to by Porpora (in preparation), is this. Many of us in sociology can't understand how to say something like "social structure is real," because social structure seems to be a set of relations, and relations aren't existing stuff. But to deny social structure seems very silly—sociology is all about social relations, and to say these don't exist is pretty much to write yourself out of a job. More generally, we might say that our way of understanding existence privileges *content* over *form*, although things in the real world have both. They all do, necessarily. We will need a way to acknowledge the reality of form.

The problem is that we can *see* form in all sorts of things. The stars are in the sky, and they actually *do* have certain reciprocal relations to one another (gravitational attraction, however negligible, for one). Does that mean that the Great Bear is *real*? In a way yes, but not in a way that would rehabilitate astrology as astronomy (or so one would hope). It's only *we* who see it as a bear.[17] Where we and the Romans saw a Great Bear in the sky, the Maya saw Seven Macaw and the Egyptians, the thigh of a bull. The stars are real, really there, and you get to connect the dots any way you want.

But imagine what would happen were we to simply declare that all relations are in the eyes of the beholder, which is the classic nominalist response that

[17] As an aside, I want to indicate that I actually am impressed with the cogency of arguments by the Gestalt school that *some* configurations are nonarbitrary in that any being with a visual system like ours would "see them as constellations." But since most sociologists don't accept this, I won't rely on these ideas here.

many sociologists have been taught. We basically say that there is no "right" way to see society—if you want to think that it is connected by relations of organismic cooperation, that's just great; if you want to see these relations as oppression and exploitation, why that's peachy keen, too. If we really move all relations to the realm of "nonreal heuristics" that we use to study reality (whatever "works for you"), not much of what we're interested in is left in the reality side to study!

There are indeed problems with the conventional approaches here. And that might be why critical realists tend to spend the body of their discussions of these issues doing what Kurzman (1988) calls "alternative-knocking"—a logically useless but rhetorically powerful way of "establishing" one's own point. Because, as we'll see, the critical realists have nothing to say on this issue.

CONCEPTS AND REALITY

Working Up and Messing Up

The key problem is that our debates here don't have to do with ultimate reality. I can't help being struck by how often critical realists want to shift the conversation to the debate over whether *anything* is real, and oppose an imaginary interlocutor, perhaps John Lennon, who claims that nothing is real ("and nothing to get hung about").[18] But in sociology, the problem has to do with the status of our key *concepts.*

To simplify this discussion, I'm going to use the case of general concept formation, as it nicely parallels the realist-nominalist and realist-social-constructionist puzzles, though our example of "IQ" is also an example of a concept. Most conventional philosophies of social science don't worry about whether, say, people, or hats, or even possibly languages are real. They worry about when we "work up" reality into concepts and talk about, say, "whites" or "catholics" or "the Romany people," whether these concepts should be treated as real or not.

Thus I think Porpora's point—that if we don't think social structure is real (or at least, *real enough*), we should pack up and go home—is a good one. But if I am claiming that the most important characteristic of contemporary US society is the division between the bourgeoisie and the proletariat, whether or not we agree that "social structure is real" won't matter. We can be pretty sure that "the bourgeoisie" isn't "real" in *that* sense—it's some kind of general or abstract term created by our intellect, for better or worse.

---

[18] To the extent that they choose to reject this null hypothesis, they are going to be able to hold themselves to remarkably lower standards than other philosophical schools over the past four hundred years that have uniformly taken this for granted (including idealists like Berkeley). I recognize that they believe that their generous *diagnoses* of why others have made the various "errors" that they have should be accepted as in-kind compensation for the weakness of their own positive program, but most of us don't agree.

This is where the rubber of the mind hits the road of the real; what is the critical realist position here? Somewhat astoundingly, there doesn't seem to be one. Different people have written different things, but if there is consensus on a position that connects these ideas to core principles of realism, it has certainly escaped me and other critics. Indeed, treatments of concept formation in critical realism tend to be extremely perfunctory and simplistic, along the lines of "do a good job." Bhaskar (1979: 63) himself says that fortunately, "most" of our concepts will come from actors, since they need concepts to orient their own activity. Beyond this, he suggests that good concepts of social structure might be identified by "their effects," and then lets it rest at that.[19]

So how do we decide what it is that is producing the effects we see? Elder-Vass (2010: 74) claims that a social structure is real and bears the causal power for actions seemingly carried out *by* the individuals if the said individuals would be unable to carry out the same actions *outside* the structure. But if you take this logic seriously, it implies that the only causal powers individuals possess are those that they would have naked, alone, in a vacuum. That can't work. Sayer (2010: 89; emphasis added) argues that we can identify social structures as composed of what Bhaskar called internal or necessary relations—those "in that *what* the object is is dependent on its relation to the other."

Bhaskar (1979: 54) claims that this holds for the relation between the bourgeoisie and the proletariat. If this essentiality doesn't seem obvious to you, it does to Bhaskar, as he claims that such results are established "a posteriori, in the irreducible empirical process of science." But as a general criterion, this is obviously assuming what we were wondering about (were the concepts that we used good ones in the first place). Sayer attempts to give a more abstract specification: a capitalist is no capitalist without an employee (even though he doesn't disappear as a human). But this holds for totally arbitrary relations that we can compose, such as zookoe partners (the person whose left eyeball size is closest to yours). A zookoe partner without a zookoe partner is no zookoe partner.

So how can we evaluate the reality status of different concepts of social structure? Porpora (in preparation) tries to erase the distinction between form and content—to make the relations "material" because they exist. But even were that true, what sets of relations, say, classes, are real? Elder-Vass (2010: 17; 2012: 22) suggests that we can say that certain groupings of individuals are real entities because the members are connected by social relations. The problem with this answer is that if you were to actually trace these relations out, you would find that people

---

[19] Well, to be fair, he does launch into a few pages of gobbledy-gook designed to cow the general reader (another of the strategies identified by Kurzman 1988), and eventually reaches the sage conclusion: "If one denotes some social phenomenon in S_1 [our subject matter at hand] as 'P_1', then the most adequate description of P_1 in L_2 [never defined] will be that description—let us call it $D*_2$— . . . entailed by that theory $T*$ (formulated in L_2) with the *maximum explanatory power*" (76). Quite.

don't sort themselves into groupings — things like social organs. As even Spencer knew, we (unlike the "contiguous" cells that form an organ) aren't clumped. Manual workers have relations with foremen, with clerical workers, with their children, their neighbors and so on. And so we don't find that in social life these relations lead to neatly bounded entities — we get one big mass of humanity, or perhaps all life, or, if Latour is right, almost everything in our world, as our real entity.

Emergence and Realism

We are finding, I think, a surprisingly casual treatment of a key part in what adherents find so promising about critical realism — namely, that it gives us a firmer grasp on the reality of the higher-level concepts that we use to study social life. Indeed, this gets to what is often seen by critical realists to be their most important plank: there are multiple levels of reality, and the higher ones that emerge from the lower are no less real than the lower. That is, reality conveniently shears itself into the same layers that we do in our sciences — thus there is no fear of, say, a reduction to bitty-witties (what used to be called "ultimate" elements).

The problem that we've seen regarding form and content reappears here. Certainly, it does seem pretty dumb to say that a hedgehog is less real than its organs; its organs, less real than its cells; the cells, less real than the molecules; and so on. But that doesn't make it smart to say ". . . and therefore, the bourgeoisie is just as real as Andrew Carnegie." No one in sociology thinks that we are a branch of applied particle physics. Further, almost everyone accepts *some* form of the idea of emergence (though some may still hold that this is only an *epistemic* and not an *ontological* emergence). So why all the fuss about emergence in critical realism?

For one thing, it is believed that this would ensure the autonomy of sociology and explain why it can produce robust knowledge. Indeed, critical realists often make the (logical) error of thinking not only that their idea of emergence would imply that sociology, say, could develop its knowledge without reduction to bitty-witties, but that the reverse is also true—that the appearance of robust social regularities explained on the social level could only occur given strong emergence.[20] But the role of emergence is even more fundamental.

[20] Unfortunately, even if the rest of critical realism turns out to be correct, this is not implied. It is quite possible for orderliness and lawfulness at one level of analysis to be a product of a mechanism operating wholly and solely at a different level (though we would believe our wrong-level theoretic mechanism to be the "real" one). For example, certain patterns produced by cellular automata (e.g., rules 73 and 90 in Wolfram 2002: 26, 59) can give rise to orderlinesses of different scales. If we lived in this world, we'd come up with different levels of analysis. But everything is generated by processes at the same level. It isn't obviously true, but it isn't obviously untrue, that this might be the case for our universe. In that case, while there is nothing wrong with saying that it's a good idea for us to make those concepts that are most useful for us, we're wrong if we conclude that the mechanisms these invoke are necessarily "real."

Reality talk is about establishing an anchor or foundation. Most of the problems we have in sociology come not from the nature of the anchor but from everything after that. Those who have struggled with the nature of concept formation generally walk away worried about the long chain that connects our claims to this anchor. "Emergence" as a doctrine is used by critical realism to "restart" reality again and again—to declare that the fourth floor is *also* a foundation . . . and therefore we can make a wood frame building higher than current building codes allow. I'd say . . . get out!

You don't have to accept any particular theory of concept formation. Indeed, you can hold to a philosophy of social science that doesn't involve concepts at all, or at least, doesn't require that we "make" them (restricting itself to the ready-made), or one that posits that we must "get past them." Most sociologists aren't enthusiastic about these alternatives (though I am!) and critical realists don't buy any of these. They're still using concepts like the rest of us, which means that somehow, we need to know what to put in the box and what not, where to trim and snip away connections. But as a general philosophy, critical realism doesn't offer us anything helpful, and at its worst, it gives us something positively hurtful, namely, a temptation to play the epistemic trump card of declaring what *we* believe in to be real. Some critical realists play this card more than others, but they all have it, which is worrisome. Because when we go from fun to serious, a trump card becomes an H-bomb, and we need a nonproliferation treaty.

One last metaphor: you can have a stamp that says "PAID" on it, and rush around stamping all your bills "PAID," but this doesn't change the minds of any bill collectors (trust me, I've tried it). Same with stamping "REAL." I'm going to tell a story that will probably not make any converts out of aficionados, but I think will explain things rather well to the beginner. It's an allegory that attempts to communicate how Bhaskar's work has become influential in sociology.

The Fable of the Fish

A while ago, in a place not too far from here, professional fishermen got together to see if they could figure out a more satisfactory method for ocean fishing. The problem that they had was that for some sorts of fish, they had to use hook-and-line methods, and the hooks had to go very far down and come back up very slowly. Sometimes on the end would be a big fish, but sometimes it was just an old tire, or a rotten dead carcass, or a mass of seaweed. Further, because the fish were coming from great depths, they often exploded as they were brought to the surface due to the pressure change. It wasn't always easy to tell a fish that had been caught live, but had then exploded, from one that had been caught dead—and wasn't to be eaten.

Of course, once they got it on deck, they knew if they had a fish or not, even if they weren't always sure if it was good to eat, but they wanted to know *before* that, so that they could fish in the right places, and get rid of nonfish they had caught without bringing them all the way up to the deck. Some people suggested using past results of where fish were likely to be. Others tried to attach the lines to various sensors to see if the weight and resistance of the hooked object was like a fish. Some argued that all things on the end of the line should be referred to in the same terms, others that different terms should be applied depending on what the sensors said, and some people were working on trying to build more sophisticated sensors. No one could guarantee, however, that what you pulled on deck was a fish. And the biggest problem of all was that even when you were out all day, you might not get a single bite.

Then one day, a man came around announcing that he had solved all these problems, and would give a talk about this to interested fishermen. Everyone came that evening and crowded into the hall. This is (in essence) what he told them (his version was somewhat lengthier): his theory combined the *reality* of the stuff in the ocean (he called it the intransitive) with the *active nature* of human work. Previous people had made all sorts of mistakes, and did not understand that the reason fishing worked as well as it did was that there *really were* fish in the ocean, although *not all things* in the ocean were fish! To fish correctly, what one needed to do was to have one's hook go into a *real fish*, and then *pull* the fish out—and thus without their *agentic deployment of effort*, no fish would be caught, but this in no way meant that the fish were not *real* fish.

He stopped and looked around triumphantly, expecting plaudits from the fishermen. But they had all sneaked out. Fortunately, many of their seats had been taken by social scientists, who promptly gave the speaker tenure.

Thus it seems to me that critical realism offers a fine vision of what science should be: there are goings-on out there, and we are trying to understand these goings-on. Further, critical realism says not simply that this is what science *should* be, but that it *can* be. It seems that few would spend their time doing science seriously if they did not agree. But we turn to epistemology when we want to know *how* this can be, or to determine when it *is* this, and when it is *not*. And here I find that in practice, critical realists substitute professions of faith for serious analysis. That is, the problem isn't that critical realism has the wrong epistemology, it is that it doesn't have one at all, but gives its adherents the *feeling* that they have one.

Stop Stopping

As any schoolchild knows, one way that LSD seems to induce hallucinations is by binding to and activating serotonin (5-HT) receptors 5–hydroxytryptamine subtype 2 ($5\text{-}HT_2$), as well as $5\text{-}HT_5$ and $5\text{-}HT_6$, thus inhibiting serotonergic cell firing "while sparing postsynaptic serotonergic receptors from upregulation / downregulation" (Passie et al. 2008: 305). The activation of these receptors probably in turn leads to an increase in phosphorylation of Ser^{130}-DARPP-32 (DARPP-32, or Mr 32 kDa, being a Dopamine regulated phosphoprotein), which in turn inhibits the multifunctional serine / threonine protein phosphatase, PP-1 (Svenningsson et al. 2005), which in turn disturbs the extracellular regulated kinase cascade. Since 5-HT inhibits other neurons from firing, decreasing its activity allows other neurons to become more active, and LSD inhibits certain cells from releasing serotonin. In other words (ones that I have a chance of understanding myself), imagine a traffic policeman being relieved by someone dressed as a policeman for the next shift, but with no intention of asking *anyone* to stop. All the lights are green, our grinning lunatic beckons everyone forward, and a hallucinatory mess results.

Similarly, to think straight, some inhibition is necessary, and a serious epistemology is such an inhibitor. (Theodor Adorno [1973 / 1966: 388]: "The Kantian system is a system of stop signals.") Critical realism steps in to where an inhibitor should be, and says "go on! Go on!" Thus critical realism becomes a sort of hall pass that will allow its adherents to do whatever it is they want to do anyway. (This is nicely given as a point in its favor by Steinmetz [1998: 174].) And thus it isn't at all strange that some critical realists (e.g., Smith 2011: 491) see much of American sociology as critical realist without knowing it.[21] This is not a problem in most cases, since what we do is okay, mostly, but it is a problem to have an epistemology that fails when we need it.

It is worth emphasizing that the logical problem here is that in practice, critical realists are fusing transcendental realism and hypotethico-deductiveness, and proceeding with illogical confidence. That is, let's accept both sets of planks:

1. $\sim C \supset \sim K$.
2. Science exists (S).
3. Science is just that sort of knowledge that we are talking about ($S = K$).
4. $r' \supset e'$

[21] As Lizardo (2012: 8) has pointed out, the same is held by "analytical sociologists," that it is a movement that considers itself a radical alternative while admitting that many others do it without knowing that they do.

Now it seems to me that critical realists are proposing that we can boil this down to

5. $(S \wedge e') \supset r'$

(read $\wedge$ as "and"), which is not a valid conclusion. That is, even if you accept that the real world is the sort of world that allows us to have valid knowledge, that does not mean that the things we could validly say about the real world that are consistent with our experience are correct. In fact, this doesn't solve the indeterminacy issue of hypothetico-deductiveness at all. As we saw above with the case of social structure, it almost seems like the insistence on the reality of *something* is believed to support the more difficult issue of the status of this or that mental construct. Critical realists recognize that we necessarily use concepts to grasp the real, and that the concepts themselves aren't real, but don't seem to be interested in paying close attention to the relation between the concept and the reality. Instead, they emphasize the fallibility of all knowledge, which might be relevant to explaining why scientists might once have believed in phlogiston and now believe in oxygen; but it doesn't shed much light on our everyday problems in sociology, which have to do with the nature of general terms that we make to manipulate reality.

Or perhaps we might say that it works until it doesn't. Insisting that there *are* natural kinds, that copper really is copper and iron really is iron, might pass muster if you're attempting to explain why chemical science works (as it does). Because you're not going to be arguing with someone who thinks that copper *isn't* really copper. But when it comes to sociology, be prepared to insist that, say, Western culture really *is* Western culture; that exploitation really *is* exploitation; that girls really *are* girls, and to have your interlocutor respond, "Nuh-uh." The question is, who is the better scientist—the one who is so attached to an imagined reality that she is frustrated with the critic who doesn't accept that kinship isn't a social construct but a natural kind, or the critic?

Form and Substance in Scientific Orientation

It may clarify matters to begin with a familiar story from the 1980s, a heated dispute about the nature of science. Scientists often angrily reject work by sociologists of science who claim to explain how some scientific truth gets accepted as a "social product." The scientists dismiss this obviously cockamamie idea by emphasizing that the reason scientists believe, say, that the attraction between nonmagnetic macroscopic objects in a vacuum is proportional to the product of their masses is that it *is* actually such. End of story. Science is right, scientists are right, and no one needs stupid sociologists, who can't even understand the basic math involved, saying otherwise, and trying to pick apart the findings that scientists now feel confident in treating as solid, as "black boxed." That which scientists have joined, let no sociologist set apart.

Now in a way, such statements are supportive of science as an institution, and we can call them *substantively* scientific, for they aim to shore up what is commonly understood as science. But as arguments, they are little more than a profession of faith, often with an additional support of authority. This is of course the kind of thing that modern science grew up in opposition to. *Formally*, then, these arguments are very unscientific, and the social constructionists were actually the scientific ones, putting their personal faith in the belief that the attraction between nonmagnetic macroscopic objects in a vacuum is proportional to the product of their masses on hold, and empirically observing the actual processes that led to the acceptance of this belief.

Sometimes being a good scientist requires following where science leads you, even if it seems unfamiliar and not what we thought science would look like. By temperament, I'm the sort of fellow who would like to take a strong commonsensical realist position. In fact, I started brushing up on what was known about the visual system and the neurology of vision to combat the stupidities of the sorts of voluntarist social constructionism that drives the realists crazy. Sure, lots of that "it's all in your mind" stuff didn't jibe with what we've known about vision, but neither did my own prejudices. If you want to believe that, say, seeing is a simple, passive internalization of the real things in our real world, I'd advise you not to crack open any books about it.

To the extent that realism (as it is currently claimed by sociologists) as an epistemology is such a profession of faith, it can have that strange characteristic of feeling, and seeming to some to be, substantively scientific, while in fact being formally unscientific. Without doubting the patriotism of our fellows, we shouldn't allow shouts of "science, love it or leave it!" to prevent us from carefully checking the papers of those who want to enter our camp. Some of the nicest, freckled, lemonade-selling kids turn out to be spies.

SUPPORTING CLAIMS

Needing the Real

We've seen that in many technical ways, there isn't that much separating critical realism from the subjective idealism it claims to oppose. Yet people insist that adherence to realism is of vital importance for their sociological work. What, then, do realists get out of being realists?

There is a way in which we are all realists, for anyone who isn't is a madman or is lying or is being purposively silly, for we believe that the world we are in is real. And no one claims that because we live in a real world, we all are right in our ideas about the world. Whatever realism means, it can't be about either of these. I think that here, as wherever things get hard, it's nice to look at *when and where* people fall back on the realism. The microsociologist David Gibson once commented to me that in reading over his own rough drafts, he realized that whenever he began a sentence, "in fact," he was about to introduce a claim for which he had no evidence. These were the places to which he needed to direct more attention.[22] So, too, I have noticed that people in sociology turn to realism when they want to justify seeing things their way, even though they suspect that what they are saying is not obviously a universal truth that all will recognize. In other words, realism is a bit like the coating that allows us to swallow a pill—in this case, a substantive assertion that one would like to make but that can't be proven.

A common justification for making such substantive pronouncements is to declare that "the proof is in the pudding," and such statements are accepted because they lead to satisfactory results. Unfortunately, given that we don't do the equivalent of put airplanes in the air with our knowledge, our criteria for "goodness" in theory are so subjective and malleable (e.g., "it gives me insight") that by themselves they are worthless. Hence the justifiable suspicion that we have (as I said in the first chapter) of such substantive statements being introduced in sociological theory.

Now *no* serious theoretical contribution in sociology of which I am aware is completely free of substantive statements about the way the world is. That is, any statement made can be (1) established as a deduction from ideas we already accept, (2) a hypothetical (if we believe *X*, we must also believe *Y*, often used to introduce axioms), or (3) a substantive claim. These latter may involve appeals to research (psychologists have found *X*), to widely held understandings (parents usually feel love for their children), or in some cases are merely examples that may not need to be accurate for the theory to be valid. But in other cases, the theory involves substantive claims that are particular (not universally held) and not easily supported with an appeal to research.

In Chapter 1, I said that such claims are costly, in a way. Like "buying a vowel" on *Wheel of Fortune*, you need to buy them with your explanatory winnings. Some substantive statements, however, are very inexpensive. The cheapest are those that only a maniac would deny—for example, that people are conscious[23]—

[22] This is a great example of the sort of critical self-examination that *is* possible (and don't let any facile arguments suggest otherwise), and why Gibson's work is so much more rigorous than that of someone who would only blush with pride when reading his rough draft, and at every "in fact" think, "Go get 'em, tiger!"

[23] I use this example because I suspect we're actually *not* conscious in the way we think we are, but I'll be damned if I'd try to buy *that* vowel!

and the next cheapest are those that are common, and known to be such to all members of a certain school. If a rational choice theorist were to claim that people make trade-offs between different possible good things proportional to utility that each thing would bring them and to its likelihood of realization, we'd think,"Well, if I didn't want to hear that, I shouldn't have picked up this book," and so we don't count it as heavily as we would if this same theorist proposed that the value of a commodity ultimately came from its socially necessary labor time of production. Finally, we seem to have an intuitive sense that tightly related or integrated substantive claims aren't as costly as less integrated ones. That is, even if the first claim doesn't logically imply the second, if the two flesh out the same sort of substantive understanding of the world, two claims aren't twice as costly as one.

But what can we do when our theoretical vision requires the introduction of a large number of substantive statements that are loosely integrated and not invariably accepted by the target audience? It seems that in such cases there is something appealing about a claim of realism. It promises to convert a very costly theoretical strategy, a liability, into a credit, by claiming the epistemic high ground. It is, then, a stabilization strategy.

Stabilization

We saw some of the problems that Parsons had when it turned out that his theory was only "finished" when he himself had passed judgment on whether some sort of change was a good change or a bad change (or whether the absence of change was good or bad). We can refer to this sort of thing as the "stabilization" of a theory — a theory is "unstable" when the same structure can produce wildly different predictions given the same inputs.[24] Realism can become attractive to sociologists as a stabilization strategy — we have too many moving parts, so we need to nail some of them down by professing our faith in their reality.

Just as a theory can be unstable, so an epistemology for social explanation is inherently "unstable" if, given two different explanations, there is no way to adjudicate between them to anyone's satisfaction without an appeal to an exogenous status of those offering the explanation — exogenous meaning that the different statuses aren't generated by the research itself. There must be an authority that is treated as fixed and stable if the knowledge creation is to be stable. The degree of exogeneity required may actually vary from none to total; but as we approach total, we necessarily will produce what Lakatos (1970) called degenerative research programs — or no research programs at all. (It is possible for research programs

[24] I'm not talking about when a theoretical structure is open to producing different claims given different empirical findings. There the stabilization is where it should be — in the measurable world.

to degenerate even when the status that orders them is endogenously generated, but that seems to be unimportant for sociology.[25])

Now in sociology, we're used to studying all the human, the imperfect, the dirty aspects that go into making scientific truth, and we may not understand the differences in the role that authority plays across the several sciences. It is indeed true that in most physical sciences, authority helps, as does money and everything else. But it is rarely sufficient. When, in May of 1989, Linus Pauling used his personal authority to get a letter published in *Nature* explaining how cold fusion could take place, he did indeed get a publication. But he didn't get a truth because cold fusion couldn't be made to happen enough times in enough ways. Having a Nobel Prize winner as an ally to your claim is great, but as Latour has said, sometimes microbes are your best allies. And it doesn't necessarily matter whether you think that microbes are real, or even if electrons are real. What matters is if they'll do what you want them to do (cf. Hacking 1983).

In sum, there's a way in which what makes a science a *science* (and not just any old field of intellectual production) is that authority *can't* be relied on as a permanent stabilization strategy (nor can popularity). It can be used for a long time, but if it becomes totally invulnerable, you no longer have a science. We therefore need to look very carefully at different stabilization strategies; it might not be that there is any *one* that is the best for us all, but some could kill us.

Peephole Epistemologies

Realism works just fine when we all agree about what is real. But that's basically saying, it works just when you'd never be looking around for an epistemology in the first place. In such cases, realism doesn't seem to do much for us that we don't already have going. In fact, varieties of realism that are not simply naïve realism share something with most Kantian epistemologies, which they normally see themselves as opposing, and this is that they start with the (hypothesized) reality and use this to explain the (derived) experience (e.g., perception). As a result, they demote the experience to the status of a suspect. Some suspects are innocent until proven guilty and others guilty until proven innocent, but all can be remanded by the judge to the prison of illusion for contempt of reality.

Thus critical realists may shore up our conviction that our sensation of the *texture* of an object is real and that we don't have to second guess ourselves here, but when we say that the object is red, the classic critical realist (the version from the early twentieth century, that is) says that in the real trans-phenomenal world

[25] For the record, an example is when people are accorded status by their capacity to see patterns in environments with very low signal-to-noise ratios. You might be king of a subdiscipline by virtue of your sensitivity to the presence of, say, N-rays, and one could only prove you wrong if she were *more* sensitive. This could lead to a sustained investigation of something that isn't there.

there is, say, a solid mass composed of intertwined molecules arranged in a set of layers in turn coiled that disproportionately reflects light with a wavelength of approximately, say, 690 nanometers. This can then be used to make other statements about the trans-phenomenal world, such as "this material is oxidized iron" or "this star is receding 10,000 kilometers per second from us," because everything needs to be linked to those processes or mechanism that the realist thinks are in the real.

As a result, such realism turns out to have a great deal in common with what Theodor Adorno (1973 [1966]) called "peephole epistemologies"— those that posit that we get a wee peek at the trans-phenomenal reality, and see something real if we angle our head the right way. But what about when others swear that *they* are seeing the real through *their* peephole, and it doesn't look like what we are claiming that we are seeing through ours? We are likely to conclude that the problem is that they are looking through (or perhaps have their heads up) the wrong hole altogether. Without any recognized procedures for determining which linkages are real (and this doesn't mean vague criteria of "giving insight"), we basically depend on each one's authority to declare that what each sees through his or her peephole is the real.

Further, unlike the first generation of early twentieth-century American critical realists who were providing epistemologies for the physical sciences, there's no agreement on what one *can't* claim to see in the real. Some can see emotions, others oppression, a third faith, and a fourth, perhaps, ancestral spirits. Formulaically, we all accept that the statement "$x \Diamond P$" is true if there is some matter of fact in the world that makes this true. But the emphasis on realism seems to tempt sociologists to go from "$x \Diamond P$" to "x is *really* P" to "$x \Diamond P$ is real." But this is to collapse truth and reality, and to imagine that the forms we use to grasp reality are those that structure reality; in other words, we make ourselves the measure of all things.

The reader may think that I am here *assuming* the Kantian (subjective idealist) position, and so someone who rejects this does not need to accept the arguments here. But that is not quite so, for this position itself is in many ways a zetetic one — which means not saying that x is the case, but pointing out that $\sim x$ has not been proven. Thus although I do assume that certain aspects of human thought are *not* likely to be identical to the fundamental nature of the world, I'd be happy to learn that the opposite was the case. But I'd want to have a good reason for believing this, as opposed to its simply being stamped REAL.

This plank — that we cannot assume that the trans-phenomenal world has the same properties that our projections of it as reality have — is often considered by practicing scientists to be ignorable even if undeniable because, to the extent that we understand it (and much about it may be incomprehensible to us), we think there is no other possibility. If the world had some sort of arrangement that wasn't consonant to our minds, we'd never know about it; hence, there is no reason not to assume that it *is* consonant with our minds. That's all well and good, but it isn't a *response* to the subjective idealist position — it *is* the subjective idealist position.[26]

Although that position is a relatively robust one, it isn't the only alternative to a claim of realism, and it actually isn't mine. I want to close by saying that the most important alternative to realism isn't idealism (a negation), but pragmatism, a reversal.

TALK AND SCIENTIFIC INQUIRY*

Truth and the Pragmatists

There's a different way of starting, one that was developed by Peirce, James, and Dewey.[27] In this light, we start not with a hypothesized trans-phenomenal world in which we honestly believe, in other words, with our *faith*. Instead, we begin with our *experience*. We have experience, certainly singly, and it seems often jointly. We are not prey to it, buffeted about without any capacity to master it, because we have some sort of cognitive system that allows us to do many smart things with experience. Knowledge, in this understanding, is not about a set of abstracted propositions but a function of a living organism dealing with its environment; rather than human knowledge being a "fallible" version of a more perfect knowledge that doesn't exist, knowledge is an intrinsically human way of dealing with our world. If knowledge helps us in our world, then it is meaningful; if not, it isn't much of anything in particular.

This is often where pragmatists lose people. The idea of a truth that just "works" seems like a pretty sorry second-best compared to a *true* truth. But let's look at this more closely, focusing on what are known as "correspondence" theories of truth. Here the idea is that our statement is true if it corresponds to the world. (I'm going to focus on the simplest form of such theories; we can then see whether any particular emendation solves these problems. You might believe one does, but we learn what the problems are by focusing on the simpler version.)

---

[26] Technically, such defenses are an appeal to a regulative principle of reason — that we must treat the world as if it fits our minds; otherwise we won't get anything done. This is antithetical to the principles of realism but may be claimed by some who think of themselves as realists nonetheless.

[27] Yes, I am aware of their differences here. I tend to rely on Dewey for most things about the relation of knowledge to the world, on James for the nature of experience, and on Peirce for logical considerations. And yes, I'm aware of how difficult it can be to sort out Peirce's changing use of reality-talk, and to sort out his protestations of faith from his epistemology. We'll take what we need, and leave the rest.

First, we need to recall that we found that merely having our proposition be grounded in matters of fact wasn't enough to make things "true" by commonly understood standards. (For example, think of my empirically grounded 'coolness' scale—It isn't true that you really *are* uncool if your number is above average, is it?) Our correspondence has to be tighter than that. Thus we say things like the statement, "the ball is red," is "true" if the ball is *really* red—that is, in the real world, it *is* red.

You might be wondering whether the problems that we saw in the last chapter, turning on the differences between things and facts about things, might arise here. Good guess. Let's look more closely at what we have on each side of this successful correspondence. On the one side, in the realm of our ideas, we have "the ball is red." On the other hand, in the real world, we have: the ball *is* red. But take away the italics on the word "is," put there to give us a feeling of finality. What we have on our first side is a proposition; what we have on the second side is . . . hold on! It's the same proposition! No wonder they correspond: we're not establishing a relation between a proposition and the world, we're establishing a relation between a proposition and itself! So no wonder it all seems so airtight. We haven't been comparing our knowledge to the world—we've been comparing our real, empirical knowledge to another form of knowledge, a God-knowledge, that we invented and didn't realize we were thinking of. We got this confused with the real world.

You might object that of course there's a proposition on the other side. We're talking (or writing) here, after all. Unless I get out a hot glue gun, and glue a red ball to the page, there's not much *else* that can be done. One can't demand a definition of truth that, by definition of its being a definition, can't be expressed on paper. But the pragmatist takes away a very different lesson from this objection. If the logic up until this point has been valid, there is no reason to run away now. The implication is that the definition of truth *can't* be a paper definition, but *has* to be a real world, an in-practice, definition. Truth then is no longer about the correspondence between two things, one of which is empirically existent though second-rate (fallible and all that) and the other is hypothesized to be realer than this, but never actually seen.

In the previous chapter, we saw that, although it was hard to explain, we wanted to focus our science on things and not facts about things, so that our inquiry took us "into" the things themselves (the mother wolf's returning, and not "the fact that" she returned). It turns out to be hard to specify in the abstract how to do this—and sometimes we all acknowledge that we can't get "into" the things. (Think of magnetism: one can go into the magnet and learn a great deal, but it wasn't possible in classical electromagnetism to really get into the phenomenon of magnetic attraction and repulsion. Still, it was studied nonetheless.) But one nice thing about the emphasis on taking practice as our criterion is that it tends to take us into where the action is.[28]

Now I am not claiming that all realists adopt the correspondence idea of truth; indeed, Bhaskar (1975: 249f) himself ends with a very clear and powerful statement of just the points made here regarding the difference between propositions about things and the things themselves. Yet I don't see many sociologists following him and concluding that "truth" is a matter for each science to define internally, probably because this is something that assumes consensus and doesn't help one side gain the moral high ground. Instead, sociological realists seem to easily be truthists (for an important example, Smith 2011).

In any case, what is truth to the pragmatists? Knowledge is something produced by the human community, and truth is what they arrive at. This isn't because whatever a million idiots agree on will be treated as true, although this does seem to be empirically correct. We may not *like* the way in which Latour (1987), say, has talked about truth as an outcome of scientific success and not an explanation of it, but it's empirically rigorous and defensibly circular; further, it is a stable way of talking about truth. Truth is what we do all agree on, and it is what we *should* agree on, because we're constitutionally fit for an engagement with the world. We have critical faculties, we can intervene, we can reason, we can connect, and we have insight—insight that, as Peirce emphasized, has a head start because our minds developed in the sort of world with the sort of lawfulness that surrounds us.

This is a radically democratic way of thinking and we need to adopt it not because it's good to be fair and equal, but because it's stable. As far as I can see, in the social realm, there are only two stable ways of grounding sociology: one is a mechanical-objectivist version in which formal procedures are decided in advance (e.g., whoever has the biggest R^2 wins). This isn't as crazy as we often make it sound, but I don't know anyone who thinks that such a mindless criterion is all that we need. The other stable grounding is a democratic intersubjectivist one that is unsatisfied with any honest disagreement. When two people disagree, if they are realists, each believes that his or her ideas are the real ones and the other person is the idiot. But if they are pragmatists, they realize there *is no truth yet*. False things aren't those that we *should* discard, they are those we *have* discarded; the things we can treat on faith aren't those that we *shouldn't* doubt, they are those that empirically *are* never doubted. Don't tell me, said Peirce, that

[28] And this also shows what is incomplete about attempts such as Groff's (forthcoming) to specify casual powers as *dispositions* of one thing to affect another. The mother wolf may, among other things, have the disposition to frighten me should I see her, because I am the sort of being who takes fright at wolves of any form, and this may be essential to her (if she lacked this power, she would not be a wolf). However, investigating the *fright* (and not the fact that I was frightened by her) would go into me, and not into her.

we should doubt everything—we only doubt what we *do* doubt, and we doubt the parts that look like they're not working.[29]

This seemingly arcane issue of philosophy thus has, I think, a serious bearing on how we think about sociological research. I am saying that it's time for us to stop each one setting up his own soapbox, and only being able to agree that at most one of us has it right. We have to stop assuming that the reason others disagree with us is that they aren't sufficiently attached to reality, or aren't sufficiently critical. We need to be able to study the social world but also the dispersion of understandings of and attitudes to this world, as opposed to relying on personal faith.

Thought Outside Human Minds

The pragmatist conception of truth is, I suspect, usually dismissed because it is not actually understood. Of course, we all like to imagine that the only reason people disagree with us is that they are too stupid to *really* understand our point (sort of like a person who makes a bad joke grumbling that the hearers didn't really get it). But in this case, we may well need to free ourselves from our initial understanding of terms so that the pragmatist argument becomes correctly understood in its own terms, rather than translated into terms in which it no longer makes sense. In the European rationalist approach, knowledge is fundamentally a set of propositions that can be expressed in linguistic form, and (as we've seen), a piece of knowledge is true if it corresponds to what is going on in the world. So think of two pieces of knowledge:

A1. "The sun goes around the earth," and
A2. "The earth goes around the sun."

We say that the proposition A1, even if it is subjectively held by someone, isn't a good example of knowledge, because it is *false*, while the proposition A2 is *true*, because the earth really does go around the sun. When pragmatists say things like "if an idea successfully guides practice then it is true," they are often interpreted as saying "if believing A1 helps someone get up in time for work, then it is

[29] For example, see his "Lectures on British Logicians" (1869), "Lecture I. Early Nominalism and Realism," p. 313 in *Volume II* of *Writings*. It is here that he notes that "in science a question is not regarded as settled or its solution as certain until all intelligent and informed doubt has ceased and all competent persons have come to a catholic agreement, whereas 50 metaphysicians each holding opinions that no one of the other 49 can admit, will nevertheless severally regard their 50 opposite opinions as more certain than that the sun will rise tomorrow. This is to have what seems an absurd disregard for others' opinions . . . ," which seems to me to well describe the fix the current interpretation of critical realism tends to get us into.

true." This seems silly, and it is basically silly, and so pragmatism is rejected as inadequate.

To approach the pragmatist understanding of truth (and here I mean that held primarily by Peirce and Dewey, who agreed to this extent), it will help first to make some distinctions, and then to make an analogy. The distinction is a simple one. When someone defines truth, she might mean it in one of three senses.

1. *Descriptive.* Our theorist may be describing how in actual social life, things become understood as true.
2. *Prescriptive.* This is when we try to formulate criteria by which we can determine what should "count as true" (e.g., we may say that true statements should be replicable).

But we may also have a somewhat vaguer sense of truth, which I shall call our (3) ontological. This is the belief in truth that keeps us going and means that we can argue about versions of (2), comparing them to an inner sense that we can't necessarily define. This is when we say "truth just is true, dammit!" And we're upset because we *care.*

Somewhat analogously, we might have a descriptive definition of morality, one that holds that it is whatever any society treats as sacred. We might have a prescriptive one we'd want to use in our own society (e.g., focusing on equal rights and the preservation of the autonomy of the individual). But many of us retain a different sense of morality—that certain things simply *are* bad, no matter whether we can quite justify it—even though we might despair of completely justifying or capturing it through prescriptions. This analogy turns out to be useful in clarifying the nature of the pragmatist understanding of truth.

The Young Hegelian Ludwig Feuerbach made a critique of orthodox Christianity (and a formally parallel one of orthodox Hegelianism) that was crucial for the development of dialectical materialism. In essence, his argument was that "Man—this is the mystery of religion—projects his being into objectivity, and then again makes himself an object to this projected image of himself thus converted into a subject" (Feuerbach 1957 [1843]: 29f). That is, human beings have various qualities that vary across time and place. Some people, say, modern Europeans, are very loving. When they think about God—and Feuerbach's assumption was that there is no God as a sentient person other than humans—they naturally imagine that God is better than they in every possible way.

That means that He (and He alone) is *truly* loving, is absolute love. When Europeans look at themselves, rather than recognizing themselves as a rather loving bunch, they see themselves as only deficient, indeed, absolutely deficient, by comparing their finite (but respectable) amount of love to that of God. They therefore see themselves as worthless, hateful sorts of people—unless they can make an alliance with this absolute love in the form of the-God-that-does-not-exist, and then use their alliance with their imaginary friend to hoist themselves above others. Rather than their love being something that *unites* the human community, it becomes something that severs it and sets it off against itself.

You probably get the point. Imagine that instead of God's love, we are talking about knowledge's truth. Just as Feuerbach's Christians' mistake was to think that there was some extra-human love, so in conventional social science we seem to think there is an extra-human truth. We imagine that there is, outside us, some sort of absolute knowledge that would only make sense if we were to posit a superior, indeed infinite, intelligence, a God. And not just any God, but one who shares our basic form of reason. Then we compare *our* pathetic, worldly, knowledge, to his truly true truth, and find that ours is usually flawed . . . unless we somehow make an alliance with reality, and get the priestly power to transubstantiate limited human thought patterns into truly real, really true, truth.[30]

Pragmatists are often believed to be confusing the descriptive and prescriptive definitions of truth (if four billion idiots believe it, it must be true, end of story), and of lacking the human commitment to the ontological kind of truth entirely (supposedly only asking "Where is the 'cash value' in this?"). If anything, pragmatists are collapsing the descriptive and our personal-commitment, our ontological, versions because they are saying that what truth *is* is a human effort to grasp the world; it cannot be compared to an absolute knowledge that is held by our imaginary friends, but to itself. That is, what truth *is*, what we believe in when we believe in truth, is the collective efforts of a human community. That doesn't mean it can't be done better or worse.

Further, we have to understand that there is already a tendency toward distortion and confusion in our focus on propositions (which I have stressed for the purposes of clarification). When we attach truth to propositions (as we should, if we are to think conventionally, though at the end of the chapter I'll suggest something different), we are already squeezing a great deal of the world's mystery into narrow boxes. The conventional approaches (not only the realist, but almost all the nonpragmatist versions except for the objective idealist) believe in their hearts that knowledge is a nonhuman abstract entity—that is, we have to think about knowledge that no person knows—and yet this knowledge is (remarkably) necessarily expressed in *propositions*, which take a linguistic form that, so far as we know, is unique to humans. Yet the emotional commitment that we have to truth suggests—and I think it *should* suggest—something more fundamental.

[30] I mean this very seriously. You will note that in his *Disputed Questions on Truth*, Thomas Aquinas began with the problem that confronts us here, namely, that it seems difficult to separate Truth from Being (Qu. 1, art. 1), and even harder to have Truth be an attribute of the world as opposed to just our minds (art. 2). His solution was, "Even if there were no human intellects, things could be said to be true because of their relation to the divine intellect" (1952: 11).

I'm going to use "truth*" to describe this *non*-propositional truth that pragmatism is often talking about.[31]

When we realize that our conventional ideal of truth is restricted to propositions, we may realize that this truth is, in some ways, truth*—*conditional* on the acceptance of the propositional form. This logically, and I think correctly, implies that there is a great deal of truth* in the propositional form *itself.* Recall from Chapter 1 that "critique" is not about negating ideas but finding their actual limitations; this critique of nonpragmatist conceptions of truth does demonstrate their limitations, but as we recognize limitations, we make our thoughts more concrete, and find we can appreciate our (limited) subject of investigation better than we did when we preserved vague and implausible ideas about it. So, too, as we recognize that our "truth" is conditional on the propositional form, we recognize that the propositional form has been remarkably effective at grappling with the world, which is to say, it has truth*. But truth isn't truth*.

TALKING ABOUT TRUTH*

Truth and Propositions

In other words, we need to do a little of that reverse-engineering, the unthinking, that in the first chapter I suggested was more possible than we might think. Otherwise, in our quest to make a simple, attractive, and reassuring answer to the question, "How can our thoughts be true?" we make the world something that it is not—we import a great deal of the linguistic structure of our knowledge into the world itself, and confuse (nonpropositional) reality and (propositional) truth. When we assume that *any* sufficiently smart mind comprehending the world would *have* to produce our idea of truth, because it would *have to* think propositionally, we take our ignorance and limitations (I can't imagine *X*) and turn it into knowledge (therefore, *X* is impossible), which has got to be one of the worst theoretical methods out there.

We just can't start out by assuming what we need to question, and this is that the implicit world that would justify all our habits of speech is the actual world. Although I'm fine to say that the actual world isn't a human construct, this implicit one, until proven otherwise, should be assumed to be, which means that it may well be tied up with one particular cultural philosophy of thought and knowledge. To unthink this, let's imagine a race of people who for some reason are very intelligent, but lack a language. (Chimpanzees might come close, but let's make our folks even smarter than chimps.) They have thoughts about their environ-

[31] Here the differences between Peirce, James, and Dewey become a bit more noticeable, given that Peirce could tie this truth* to semiotics and hence push it closer to "truth."

ment, but they do not turn them into linguistically structured propositions, even if they are capable of abstract symbolic thought—that is, having a sign stand for something, even though signs aren't arranged in propositions.

I'm here going to follow conventional ideas and imagine that all mind is in the brain. I'm not sure that this is correct — nor even that it's all in the nervous system — but it will simplify our exposition. Let us imagine that someone has developed a brain-scanning technology that is able to represent the pattern of neural activation of their brains in a parsimonious and decomposable way, such that when someone is thinking about the sun and the earth's relation to one another, a particular state of mind can be measured and described to the exclusion of other brain activity that might be going on at the same time.

Let's say that, in fact, the neural pattern of a member of our species, one who is envisioning the sun reaching up over the horizon, ascending to its apogee over the course of the morning, and slowly sinking, can be notated in this parsimonious visual structure as

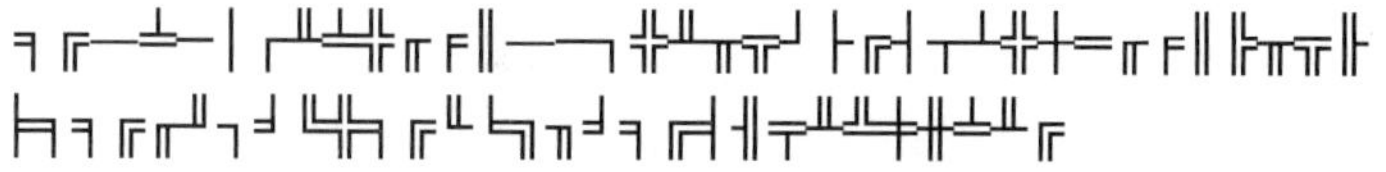

(Recall that there is no linear syntax to this, it is simply something that would allow us to re-create the three-dimensional pattern of neural activation.) There is a way in which, to a consistent pragmatist, this way of thinking about knowledge is *superior* to our propositional form, which, by necessarily using shared symbols that have their own syntactical restrictions, may be distorting the actual cognitive relationship that an actor has to his or her environment. This latter is what knowledge really is — it is an actual, empirical, relation of a sentient and intelligent organism to its environment. It is used by this organism to help coordinate physical responses using the motor system, as well as further cognitive processing using the central nervous system.

Now what does it mean to ask whether

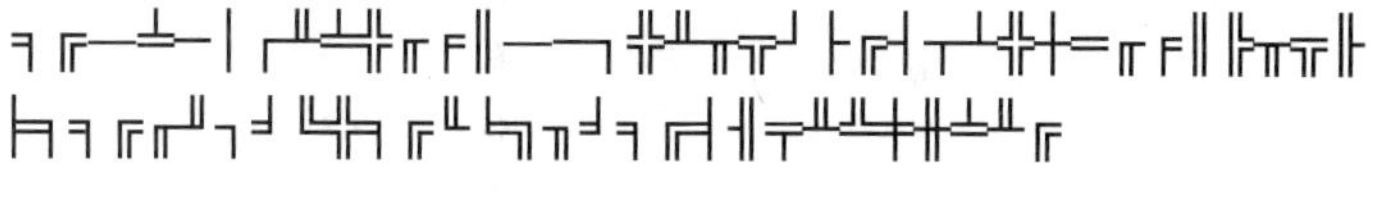

is true?

If this were a linear syntax, we might be able to say that we mean,

Does 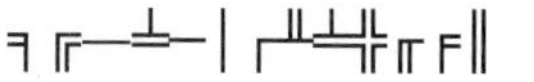 *really*
 in the 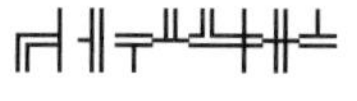 ?

But that is not the case.

Let's ask a different question. Suppose that the neural representation of the identification of a cup at eye level, center, is 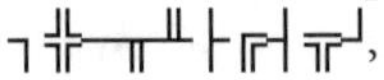, and an actor with this neural pattern, should she also want a drink of water, will reach out her hand to grasp the cup. What does it mean to say 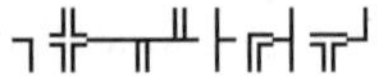 is true? Presumably that the actor will be able to have a cup in her hand at the end of the motor sequence. Abstract beliefs are not the same as this, but they are not different in their substance. They are more general and potentially generative, freed up for manipulation by intelligence—but they are mental activities designed to help us to get by in the world.

Now we may feel sorry for the nonlinguistic beings here, who have all sorts of disadvantages related to their deficit. They believe, say,

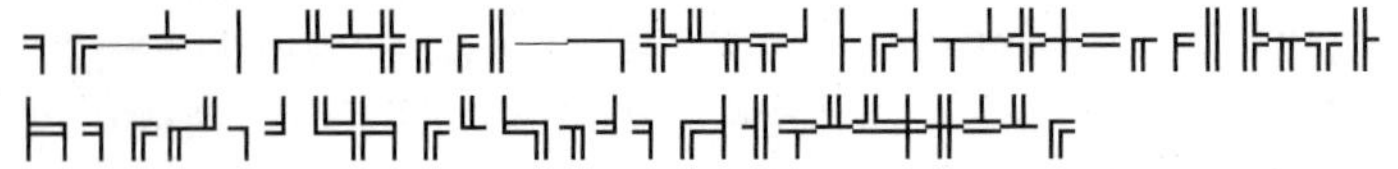

while we believe

The Earth goes around the Sun.

Not only is our version true (because in the world out there, if an omniscient being could know everything, *He'd* say "The Earth goes around the Sun"), it is a shorter and clearer way of expressing our belief than the brain dump.

Or that is what we believe. Unfortunately, this is not empirically correct. We have learned to assent to the verbal formulation "The Earth goes around the Sun," but to call this our *belief* is not much different from insisting that kindergartners in Russia believed that "In the Soviet Union, all property is in the hands of workers and peasants" or that American children believe that when swimming they should watch out for the Undertoad, or that elemeno is the twelfth letter, or other confused verbal formulations that draw assent.

Go out of your house at 8:00 AM and point to the sun coming over the horizon, imagining a line (call it A) passing through your arm to the center of the sun. Do the same thing at 12:00 noon, pointing to the sun up high, imagining a line B. Now point to where the two lines cross. Most of us will point to our own shoulders. That would be true if the sun went around the earth; if the earth were to go around the sun, the two lines would meet in the center of the sun. The fact that we have learned to assent to the verbal formula "the earth goes around the sun" does not seem to have much to do with the neurological organization that we use to coordinate our motor actions.[32] The pragmatist does not need to insist,

[32] I get this example from Hutchins (1995).

as did Sherlock Holmes, that the knowledge that the earth goes around the sun is therefore useless and should be thrown out. But it does mean that the pragmatist theory cannot be rejected in favor of a different one that has folk plausibility to us but is descriptively inadequate. Our beliefs cannot be the sets of verbal formula to which we assent, because many of these (often those that in our theories of knowledge we imagine are the "rock bottom" of our worldview) have no motor correlate beyond the assent, and no representational content. When we do try to fill them in with some sense of what we mean when we say "everything is made of atoms," we tend to get something haphazard and preposterous, hardly a good mark of the "true."[33]

When we *deny* that

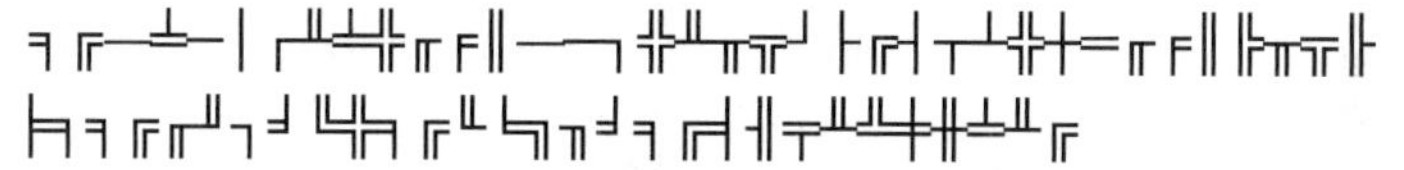

is true, we do this by engaging in a number of flights of fancy, even when it comes to our own knowledge. These flights are so ingrained (habitual, a pragmatist would say) that we forget that they are all indefensible, even if we might want to make them on the basis of faith.

1. The first thing is to equate our own linguistic representation "the sun goes around the earth" with

   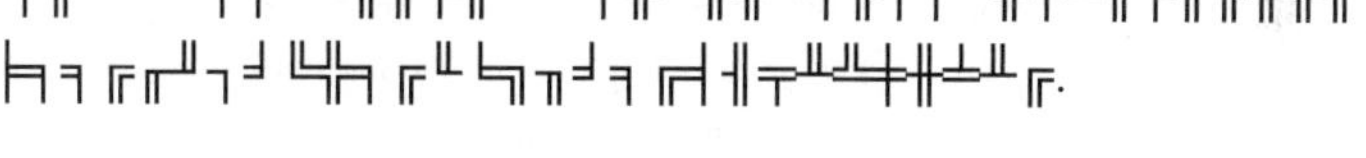

   As we all know from personal experience, it sometimes turns out that when we try to put our beliefs into words, we find that they do not precisely express what we mean. Sometimes this is because we are confused, and it helps to clarify our thoughts, but sometimes it is because our knowledge remains vaguer than words are good for, and perhaps in a few cases, there are no words for what is in our head.
2. The second is to imagine that there is a correspondence between our verbal formulae and the nature of the world, the one thing that we seem to be sure isn't true. With some careful work, one can define "goes around" so that it makes sense given a star in motion around a

[33] Vosniadou and Brewer (1992) show that while almost all young American children (around 6 to 9 years old) will draw a circle to represent the earth, and agree that the earth is "round," they may actually think that the earth is a pancake, that it is a hollow sphere, or that there are two earths. Adults' ideas about "atoms" are probably similar—all may be able to give verbal assent, but the actual mental models diverge from those of scientists (if there are still scientists out there who have mental models of subatomic reality).

galaxy, a galaxy whose center also is in motion, but this isn't true for other very reasonable statements that we want to be true like "Education increases tolerance."

3. The third is to imagine that there is, in principle, a superhuman form of knowledge in which these propositions could be, should be, would be held, so that our knowledge can be true only if it agrees with this divine knowledge. That is, we accept in principle that it could actually turn out that "the sun goes around the earth" is true after all, but that's because we can imagine our godly thinker knowing this, even if all of us think differently.

There's nothing wrong with making a leap of faith—as Peirce argued, some of these seem to be unavoidable, and these things we can treat as necessarily true, because if we can't doubt them, don't pretend we do.

But we haven't gotten much in exchange for the three above leaps of faith; all they do is lock us into a way of thinking that leads us to paradox in those few cases in which we need to be really clear about what it means to know something. And one of those cases in which we need to be clear is social knowledge.

This might have seemed a rather lengthy exposition of a relatively simple idea. But I have found that a number of nonpragmatists seem to understand these arguments in outline and to remain unmoved. When I said that I believed that some didn't "understand" the pragmatist position, I meant that although they had the capacity to repeat the verbal statement ("yes, yes, this is a constructivist argument that truth is just a human product"), they didn't necessarily *feel* what an alternative would be. This is not too different from saying "yes, yes, the earth is a ball" without having any clear internal vision of what this means, nor a way to translate it into particular imperatives for action. Indeed, there is something a bit sad, and something a bit funny, about our human tendency to believe that we understand arguments about the limitation of propositional thought to encompass certain ideas, simply because we can recapitulate the verbal expressions that were used to communicate the ideas.

Our thinking isn't all of the same stripe. We can think more or less propositionally. We think better nonpropositionally when we aren't talking to someone else. Thinking nonpropositionally often takes time and effort. In fact, I think it is comparatively harder, for propositions, even when they are internal, are like a scaffolding that we can rest on as we ascend in thought. There's no reason that just because one instantly understands what is meant by the proposition "truth is a formation of a human community," in the sense of being able to grammatically parse it, that one understands its import. That requires being able to mentally get a wee bit outside that community; often, our rejection of the claims that things can be outside come from our reading those claims wholly inside. We reject the argument that there is more light outside the cave because we all know that caves are dark.

Further Examinations of Nonpropositional Truth

We may have been convinced that there is something inherently propositional about "truth" as it is commonly used, but there is a potential problem here. For saying "our idea of X is bound up with our way-of-talking about X" is one of the forms of argument that turn out to be *too* effective, in that we can substitute *anything* in and the argument seems just as valid. We need to make sure that we have not inadvertently fooled ourselves by, in our very argument against confusing things and propositions *about* things, making just this confusion.

To proceed, we will, rather than assume a completely nonlinguistic intelligence, assume two different partial ones. To get to one, we'll start with Mead's (1934) famous analysis of communication via gestures. And we'll draw a bit on what we've learned from animal studies, unfortunately jumping ahead (since this is the topic of Chapter 5). In any case, the meaning of a gesture made by one animal (*A*) to another (*B*) is, proposes Mead, what *B* is going to do about it. A dog (*A*) baring its teeth to another (*B*) makes a gesture that "means" run away if that's what *B* does.

Now many gestures in animal communication are "ritualized," meaning they are exaggerated and stereotyped, often taking the *beginning* or *preparatory* stages of an act and stretching them out. That's what baring teeth is. It's a getting-ready-to-bite that is slowed down enough to give the other fellow time to run away.

Animal *A* doesn't need to know the effect on *B* for there to be meaning. But *A* might know what the gesture means, and do it for just that reason. For example, you might understand that reaching out a hand, palm upturned, to someone is a gesture that means "help me." Well, there is pretty good evidence that chimpanzees understand the meaning of a set of ritualized gestures (including the "help me" gesture). They can use these to try to arrange their social relations in the way that they want.

Let's call the set of all these gestures a code. And here we can draw loosely on Austin's (1975 [1962]) distinction between three types of speech (or speech act). The first, locutionary, is propositional, such as our famous "$x \Diamond P$." In the second, illocutionary, we actually perform an action in saying words, such as responding "I do" to "Do you take this man to be your lawfully wedded husband?" The third, added later by Austin, is the perlocutionary, in which we hope to bring about an effect on the hearer. The chimpanzee code, in this reconstruction, is one that is restricted to perlocutionary acts.

Let's imagine a wholly *locutionary* or referential language *L*—the sort of pure language that logical positivists had tried to construct and that some computers might be understood to use, devoid of all perlocutionary implications—no enticement, no enlistment. Creatures restricted to *L* could say "it is raining" and presumably even "I don't like that," which means that if you went up to one and smacked him over the head with a fish, he could say "I don't like that" and hit you. Perhaps they even have future conditionals, so that he could say "I don't like being hit with that fish and if you smack me again I will hit you so hard that you'll wish you hadn't." Would they be able to have a sense of good? Would they ever need it?

The answer, "No, they have no sense of good," seems convincing, and there is a sense in which it is technically correct, but I think it is actually a bit less conclusive than it might seem. Why? Because we have, unwittingly, let ourselves be drawn from what we commonly mean by good, which is good-in-itself, to something a bit different, namely, good-in-conversation. As we've seen, it can be hard to separate things from propositions *about* things. My sense is that our people restricted to *L* might well retain a feeling of goodness and badness that is very close to that we have, but one that loses most of its *motivational* aspects—that is, those whereby we attempt to control others' actions by deploying ideas of goodness and badness. But what many of us think of as the core of morality—the goodness or badness of actions—might remain. Indeed, we would probably see that any form of mobilizing-good that did not build on, substantially overlap with, and/or translate a nonlinguistic form of good would actually be a mere form of manipulative hypocrisy.

Now, as we'll see in Chapter 5, there's some reason to think that among some of our nonlinguistic cousins, it is only *badness* that exists, and not goodness.[34] But it isn't at all obvious that our imaginary people couldn't develop goodness as well (and I'll return to this below). Because lacking language does not prevent us from being oriented to the *actions* as such, and if that's what we think morality is all about, it doesn't change things to talk or not talk about them.

Thus we cannot stop with immediately plausible arguments that suggest that the lack of a word for X means the lack of experience of X. Sometimes this is true, but perhaps not as often as we might think. This is good news for our argument, because it means we don't have a tautological conclusion in which anyone without a word for X can't experience X, which would lead to a confusion between "*X*" and X itself.

But now let us return to the issue of "true." Let's now imagine creatures that have only a perlocutionary code *P*. They can make statements like "come over here" or "feed me" or "let's go swimming in the lake" but not "it is raining" or per-

[34] In Christian theology, the notion that badness was only an absence of goodness is known as the "privative" theory of morality. Sociologists and anthropologists—I think correctly—often suggest the reverse, that goodness is the absence of badness, and we may also find that truth is the absence of falsity.

haps not even something like our "I don't want to," though they could of course refuse with their actions. Let's even imagine that they can say things like "shake the tree with me to make rain," and not quibble that it contains an implicit proposition "shaking the tree makes rain."[35] The addressed, let's say, knows full well that shaking the tree will not make rain. Will he think, "It isn't true that shaking trees makes rain"?

Here we are on somewhat stronger grounds. We have not only honest introspection but also some research (discussed in Chapter 5) that suggests that the idea of false belief is hard for all of us, but extremely difficult for nonlinguistic creatures (e.g., apes and human infants)—even though great apes, especially chimpanzees, have some capacity for a perlocutionary code.

It seems to me very implausible that those restricted to a perlocutionary language would have anything like our current understanding of truth. That doesn't mean that, confronted with the scene in which someone they like is obviously about to embark on a wasteful and frustrating course of action based on a false belief about the world, they wouldn't have a sense of opposition, a sort of negation of how things are. For example, watching my dog tensely maintain surveillance over a bush which the weasel she thought she has cornered has quietly abandoned, I am struck with the pathos of my dog's false belief, and I even say aloud, "You idiot! It's not there!" Similarly, our imaginary creatures might understand the *falseness* of the other's beliefs as the problem at hand. Yet if, as I cannot but help think, their attention and efforts were directed at the world itself, and not at a representation of the other's representations, they wouldn't have our idea of truth. The capacity of understanding falseness would lead to an idea of truth only if the mistaken attempted to justify their own beliefs. But these creatures would have something else, and that something else is, at basis, what the pragmatists are proposing as the core, the personal commitment version, of what truth* is all about.

To sum up, our speakers of a purely locutionary language might first focus on *badness*—violation of some code—but there is no reason to think that they couldn't develop an idea of goodness, too. And that's because goodness applies to action or to people, and those sorts of things are observably present, whether or not you're talking about it. But truth and falsity are different. They apply to states of mind, if not to propositions, and these things aren't normally observable. *Others'* certainly aren't, and the truth of our own mental states is transparent to us—we see *through* them, and focus on the *world*. That is, Hume was wrong when he argued that when we think "the apple is red," we also, if only implicitly,

---

[35] We can't, however, indefinitely stretch the limits of our thought experiment—that is, it doesn't make sense to have our people be able to say "come with me and watch the earth make an ellipse around the sun serving as one of two foci." And this suggests the limited utility of this imagination-based approach.

think "it is true that 'the apple is red,'" and hence also "it is true that 'it is true that "the apple is red,"'" and so on and so forth. We "see" mental states—they become opaque—only in failure. Strangely enough, then, our people would have a sense of false, but unless they could talk about it, no sense of true.

*Predicates and Truth**

Chimpanzees don't talk unless we teach them to, yet they can count and add. A chimpanzee knows, in a way, that 1+1=2. But I find it extremely implausible to believe that the way a chimpanzee struggles with this has much in common with our idea of truth. Because there's nothing true in 1+1=2. The "isness" in that expression isn't attached to the predicate "true" but to "2." "True" enters only when we say "the statement '1+1=2' is true." We confuse ourselves because opponents often dismiss the pragmatist conception of truth* with what seems an unbeatable challenge: "but don't you believe that 1+1=2 is true?" The idea is that our speaker must stammer and either say something ridiculous or admit defeat. But I believe that 1+1=2, and I believe that "1+1=2" is true. What we need to understand is that these are different, and in principle separable. Just as we found with the word "cause," that we were unifying many real processes, but not adding anything meaningful by using the same term for all, so with the word "true" we aren't directly grasping all the predicates that can plausibly be attached to real things (the sun *is* gas; the earth *is* round; water *does* conduct electricity)—the only similarity that these things have comes in the statements we make *about* them.

At this point, this may now seem obvious. The reader is likely to believe that she or he always knew this, that this was never an issue. But (from discussions with others) I find that doubtful. Most people I talk to begin by strenuously denying that what we commonly mean by truth has *anything* to do with the linguistic structure of human thought. And I think that is often because it is assumed that accepting this would imply something very unsavory—for example, our language, or even worse, the particularities of any language, so structures our experience that it might as well be writ in the nature of things. That or they've been burned out by Wittgenstein and think this is a dead end. But we've seen that attention to what is "easy to think" can allow us to take a step back, and think a wee bit outside these terms, and perhaps improve our thoughts.

And, most important, this exercise also helps us see the problem with attempting to join a conventional understanding of truth with a commitment to realism. When we say *really*, we usually use it not simply to intensify, in the way we would use the word *very* (which comes from a word originally meaning "truthfully," by the way), but to deny our listener the option of thinking that there is a possible slippage between our propositions and the world. But this is precisely what we should never exclude, if we want to be serious scientists; that is, we don't use the word where there is doubt. Iron is *really* heavy is a colloquial intensifier; iron *really is* heavy is saying that we must not doubt the statement that "iron is heavy." But no one is in fact doubting this. That the atomic weight of iron "really is" 55.8, however, is somewhat different (here see Bhaskar 1975: 211). We are saying that our understanding of the proposition "the atomic weight of iron is 55.8" should *not* be understood in terms of the related propositions that would help unpack it. (For example, that if one were to successively refine iron using a certain set of procedures, and sort it into different isotopes, computing a weighted average among the isotopes that are stable, we will etc., etc, ...) Rather, what we do is attempt to fuse the proposition and the world.

What seems to me a very good retort is that all that I say is correct but completely irrelevant. For science *is* a set of propositions, and so this is exactly the right criterion of truth to hold. But I think that this is incorrect. Attempts to sketch out how science could be understood as a set of propositions (that purely locutionary language I mentioned above) were famously unsuccessful (e.g., that of Otto Neurath [1944]). In *Calvin and Hobbes*, Calvin stares at his math homework in frustration. "What's five plus seven?" he asks Hobbes. "I don't know," answers the tiger. "I don't know either," confesses Calvin. "Then write, 'I don't know,'" advises Hobbes. "Hey! That's a true answer, isn't it! I can write that for *all* of these! We're done!" (Watterson 1990: 242). Calvin shows us that true propositions aren't all we want, though we certainly don't want false ones.[36] We may not be able to completely formalize what we want science to be getting at—how we can know which true propositions are the ones to pursue and which not (something we saw in the last chapter about causality). It is for this reason that we may need to, at times, back up or zoom out or whatever one wants to call our capacity to understand that the truth* we are really pursuing is not simply about propositions but our whole engagement and activity with the world.

Experience and Reality

What, then, is the relation of our experience to our ideas of what is real? Here I want to rely on the approach of John Dewey, most notably in *Experience and Nature* (1929). Imagine we are walking in the woods with a friend. Oh my! We see a snake off to the side! Oh, it turns out, it is just a funny branch. Let me show y—ak! It *is* a snake after all!

Many of us would say that we *thought* we saw a branch, but we *really* saw a snake. That is fine for everyday chitchat, but it if you want to be scientific about it,

---

[36] We can compare this to the tendency of the conventional understanding of causality to accept an infinite number of vacuous statements as true, discussed in Chapter 2. According to such conceptions, Mrs. Wormwood would have to give Calvin an A.

you're in for some real problems. Everything we know about the optic system tells us that the "seeing" of the snake and the "seeing" of the branch were exactly the same sort of seeing. The fact that *it turned out* to be a snake can't be folded into the seeing itself. That is the *outcome* of inquiry, not present in its earliest stages. If we want to deny that we saw a branch (our second take) because it was an incomplete, hasty, imperfect seeing, presumably we also need to deny that we saw the snake at first (when "it turned out," wrongly we later concluded, to be a branch).

What is the relevance? Well, for most of our walk, we also "saw" things that weren't themselves. A pebble that, had we paused to examine it, might have turned out to be a bottle cap. A twig that might have turned out to be an insect. A worm that might have turned out to be a leaf stem. Do you want to insist that everything you saw in your walk through the woods was real? Probably not, because you don't want to commit to them all. Only the ones that matter.

If you came home and said "I happened to see a worm today in the woods," no one would particularly care, and so this might stay real, if you wanted it to be. But if you also calmly added "and I saw a leopard," that might be much more interesting. The reality of the leopard comes into question, even though the way you saw it might be just like the way you saw the worm.

Real, then, *is*, and *should*, be the outcome of debate once agreement is reached, not something used to foreclose debate. We may need to use this to orient and regulate our inquiry—because there *are* things we commit to, dammit, and, by gosh, we *believe* in them. That's as it should be. But follow the logic: reality is about belief, our belief.

*Living Truth**

And so now I think we're in a position to say something a little better, if a little vaguer, about truth* and reality than we could before. This is something that I learned from Peirce, even if it wasn't exactly what he was teaching.[37] Truth*, or at least truth* in science, is not an attribute of propositions, or even of ideas; it is not an attribute attached to nouns, nor a noun—it is a verb. When philosophers of science wrestle with a mass of claims, propositions, definitions, and such not, trying to sort them into true and false piles, they are facing an impossible task, because they are dealing with the discarded casings of truth*, and not the truth* itself. Truth* in science is an endeavor, an effort, and an ethos, and it points to reality; but this is because reality is the virtual projection of the lines of our

[37] It is also similar to the arguments made by Laudan (1977) in equally straightforward prose; my Hegelian language might obscure the similarities, and I'd rather not go into the differences. Finally, I honestly think that this is the sort of thing to which Nietzsche would have assented, on a good day, back when he *had* good days, though it is more commonly associated with Lessing.

effort, the vanishing point, as it were, and not a place that we know about (let alone get to).

We need a belief in truth*, a motivating faith that what we are doing makes sense, whether or not we can say anything particularly intelligent about truth*. As I said in Chapter 1, the fact that we *cannot* reach a truth* free from values and interests in no way implies that we *should not* strive for it. Just like plants might be said to "try" to grow toward the sun, and grow straight and proper as a result, even though they cannot *reach* the sun, so a science, perhaps *especially* a social / behavioral science, will become bent and lowly if it does not strive for the truth*. In Stammler's (1896: 599) poetic words, "Thus the sailor follows the North Star, not to reach it, but in the striving to follow the correct bearing."

And we can strive for truth* without understanding it. Above, we concluded that, outside of dialogue, truth* is transparent, while falsity isn't. Perhaps the lesson here is that the way we pursue truth is to eliminate error—like the (presumably apocryphal) story of the sculptor (I've heard it said of Michelangelo) who explained that the way you carve a statue of a horse from a block of granite is to start with a block, and chip away everything that isn't a horse. Similarly, at any time, truth* is what's left. Of course, we're in a different position from the sculptor because we think we're never done. So truth* isn't the sculpture, it's the sculpting.

Taking this seriously, as I do, implies that the same proposition, the same theory, the same thought, can be true* for one person and false for another—but not because of their general "worldviews." Newton's theory of gravitation was true* when he said it, and it remained true* for someone in 1820 who was willing to discard it if something better came along—who treated it as one rung on a ladder, to be grasped and released. But if this person's neighbor clung to this same rung with fanatical conviction, couldn't be budged, and in fact would kick at the face of anyone trying to climb past him, it was false* for and in him.[38]

Similarly, we each believe in the real, in the sense that the real is what we are consistently and coherently committed to. When that belief becomes widespread, our belief vanishes—that is, it becomes transparent—because it is never questioned, and that is what we usually mean by the real world. In a nutshell, though it might initially seem paradoxical, a commitment to the real is wonderful if it means that we have an impulse *toward* the real, but it becomes pathological when we think we have found it.

Peirce opened a wonderful, subtly and sadly biting review of a textbook with a paean to the habitus of the scientific researcher, whose job is to learn more: it is

[38] Truth in science might well be different from other areas where we might want to use the idea of truth. If so, we will probably have to take seriously Gadamer's (1976 [1965]) conclusion that *anything* said within a tradition, and by implication, within any language community, has *some* sort of truth to it. The puzzle then becomes, as Makkreel (1990: 158) has said, how we appeal *from* tradition. But that's someone else's problem.

always to be dissatisfied with what one knows, to be aware of the infinite ignorance we possess in comparison to the infinite wonders of the world. (He went on at some length here.) Quite different, he then noted, was the habitus of the lecturer, the professor, whose job is to transmit, but whose means are to cow and to impress others. The professor's way is to be extremely complacent and satisfied, continually self-impressed with how much he knows. It is unfortunate, Peirce commented drily, that our philosophy books tend to be written by professors.

Much resentment and rancor lay behind Peirce's words, but I believe they are accurate and profound.[39]

CONCLUSION

We all believe in reality because, by definition, what we believe in is the real. That isn't the issue at hand. The question is whether because of this, we get to stamp our thoughts and ideas with something special, a certificate of authenticity. It might seem crazy if we were to say that we believe in a real world that is the object of our science, but at the same time, to caution that we shouldn't be claiming that the things we are thinking about simply *are* this real world. Or to say that the best scientist is one who keeps in mind the difference between truth and reality, thoughts and the world. But thinking is all about leaving the world — putting it on hold, negating it, resisting it, turning it into a hypothesis—and being able to say "it might rain tomorrow" when it isn't raining now, or even to say, "if you had a brother, would he like fish stew?" If you didn't want your subjectivity to be unmoored from the world, at least somewhat, you shouldn't have started thinking in the first place.

Of course, we do want to have our thoughts be thoughts about the world and to tell us things about this world that make sense and work for us. In fact, when we're done, we want our thoughts to hug the contours of the world as closely as the breading on a schnitzel. But it might take a bit of effort, and you might need to peel up that certificate of authenticity to get at some broken parts. The problem, then, is that realism is a bit less real than it might sound, because realism is about *downgrading* the importance of reality and *upgrading* the importance of human subjectivity and culture. That is, realism is a form of hastiness. We so, so

[39] A good critical reader will notice that while I began by arguing that we must distinguish between "real," which we use to describe the world, and "true", which we use to describe propositions, we have now uncovered a fundamental parallel. This is as it should be: there is all the difference in the world between the confusion of two ideas that are used improperly, and then a discovery, once the ideas are clarified, that they have an inherent connection. In this case, their connection comes from the fact that both are aspects of the endeavor of a human community to make sense of what is going on around and in it.

want to believe that our human constructs are real, that we declare that they are: we make the world in our own image. It's not all that different from what is often called rationalism (as opposed to empiricism), our refusal to encounter anything that is not already us or ours.[40]

Knowledge in its abstracted form (e.g., laws of physics) is not real in the sense of having a direct existent counterpart. Knowledge that is real is the kind of thing that is in the heads of human beings. Of course, we are free to have faith that the knowledge our little human brains produce is in some way mirroring the exact nature of the universe. Indeed, perhaps, we *must*—that is, in Kantian terms, "reality" has a *regulative* function in our inquiry. The problem with "realism" is that it gives reality a *constitutive* role in our epistemology for which it is poorly equipped. Realism thus leads to a confusion between our faith and our findings, and causes us to demand a sort of personal authority that we have no business claiming.

[40] Realism denies that what we bring as human minds is inseparable from the nature of the world, but it seems the only real way to see whether our way of thinking is inherent in the world is to spend some time talking to, say, bees and lizards. We won't be able to do that, but we'll pursue this insight in Chapter 5.

CHAPTER 4

Rationality and Other Lunacies

The man of system . . . is often so enamoured with the supposed beauty of his own ideal plan of government, that he cannot suffer the smallest deviation from any part of it. He goes on to establish it completely and in all its parts, without any regard wither to the great interests, or to the strong prejudices which may oppose it: he seems to imagine that he can arrange the different members of a great society, with as much ease as the hand arranges the different pieces upon a chess board: he does not consider that the pieces upon the chess board have other principle of motion besides that which the hand impresses upon them; but every single piece has a principle of motion of its own, altogether different from that which the legislature might choose to impress upon it.

— ADAM SMITH, *THE THEORY OF MORAL SENTIMENTS*, II–59FF.

The days of heated debates over rational choice theory have, fortunately, vanished; but unfortunately, no lessons have been learned. The participants simply aged out of the juvenile gang warfare that seemed to orient much sociological theory in the 1980s and 1990s—only to repeat some of the errors under different names. Here I want to consider some of the formal errors that those pursuing rational choice theories in sociology often fell into, and to suggest that there are general lessons.

THE DEBATE OVER RATIONAL CHOICE THEORY

The Fizzle

In graduate school in Berkeley in the 1980s–1990s, there was no doubt as to who was the enemy: it was rational choice theory in all its insidious guises. The most humorous thing is that the advocates of rational choice, rather than sidestepping the sometimes pointless dismissals with a few careful distinctions, seemed enthusiastic to enter the lists on the same ludicrous grounds as their adversaries. As this bizarre fight tumbled about, rigorous individual-level modeling developed in a number of sciences basically free from the dogmatism that characterized rational choice thinking in much of sociology. And even in sociology, probably the clear majority of thinkers—and the majority of articles and books—didn't have this character.

That is, I'm not talking about individual-level modeling that started with commonsensical principles about what people want, and perhaps even used utility functions. This sort of bottom-up modeling is in no way a silly or ideological idea; in fact, it's a very good one. I'm talking about what happened when people, perhaps most often young scholars, attempted to defend "rational choice" as a *total* theory of society. This generally provoked other people to come up with "hard cases" ("Okay, so what about a fellow who sells all his clothes and gives the money to the Salvation Army?!"), which were then countered ("Dude, he is doing that to get into heaven! It's self-interested!"), and so on ("But say he doesn't even believe in heaven, he just thinks it's the right thing to do."). It is only this total form of rational choice that I want to consider here. For the sake of brevity I won't continue to make this qualification, but bear it in mind. It's this form that clearly displays the formal problems that can trouble us in a number of realms.

Such "total" rational choice theory as it existed then (and perhaps survives in a few lunatic nonagenarians) was an interesting intellectual phenomenon: it is hard to really call it a "theory" since there was little that all practitioners ever agreed on besides the need to use the words "rational" and "choice" near each other, as well as a hierarchy of preferred explanations. One should begin, if possible, by postulating *Homo assholio*, but allow oneself to be dragged wherever necessary, up to and including *Homo durkheimianus*, so long as one claimed that one had actually *predicted* whatever disconfirmations of one's axioms one found.[1] Yet this rational choice was not merely a broad intellectual trend as was "structuralism" in the loose American sense of the 1970s. Some people were, or said they were, rational choicers, and others weren't. The social division increased the severity of vociferous debates regarding the use of rational choice theory in the social sciences, more recently in religion (Iannacone 1995; Spickard 1998) and historical sociology (Kiser and Hechter 1998; Gould 2000), and previously in regard to the family (Becker 1981; Proctor 2000).

Even more interesting, just as one group of sociologists seemed to be boldly marching like Hannibal into distant territories with confidence that their economic elephants would conquer all that lay before them, another group (inspired

[1] This is a tremendous simplification, but still an accurate gloss, on Coleman's wonderful and important (1990) attempt to create such a total theory. First showing that it could make sense for individuals to create and enforce norms, he went on to allow not only that people's "interests" are wholly defined by their beliefs and indeed include their values, that it can be rational to turn into that sort of being who takes the welfare of others into account, but even that their "selves" can include other people. At the end, the only thing he has conclusively demonstrated that *isn't* rational is to continue to propose rational choice theory as the best approach for the world of normatively driven altruists he has derived! As we'll see, I disagree.

by Karl Polanyi) had, like Scipio Africanus, marched the other way into the home territory of their enemy and declared the inapplicability of purely economistic models to economic life itself—sometimes prematurely.

And yet the monumental clash never seems to have taken place. The two armies each got bogged down in their campaigns and lost their troops to desertion and despair. One will note how few of the above references come in the current millennium. If the disagreements were so important then, why no longer?

I will (not surprisingly) argue that most of the disagreement came from poorly phrased thoughts and contradictory theoretical forms. Yet the debate was potentially important, as it had to do with the study of action. If there is anything we should be theorizing in sociology, it is this. And yet we all agreed to abandon it, largely because we found we could do more work if we didn't know exactly what we were studying. Further, the debate could have been used to identify formal problems that recur in the theorization of action, and which returned under another guise.

"Shtick" and Debate

What was the focus of the disagreement? As with the debate between realists and social constructionists, when we attempt to remember what everything was all about, we seem to have an easier time working things through in terms of personality and self-conception as opposed to substantive claims about the world. There may indeed be truth to these stereotypes, although the exceptions are not only many but seem to increase as we move from students and adherents to the actual formulators. In any case, the personality-type opposition is understood to have been akin to a left-right one. Many on the left here will point to the obvious need for rigid closure that may well have characterized certain rational choice types. Of course, those on the right will, with presumably corresponding accuracy, point to the complete fuzziness of many on the other side, who will believe anything that is vague and ludicrous and accept nothing that might actually have a chance of being true. I don't deny that, at least in the classroom, the debate seemed to pit those whose confidence exceeded their smarts against those whose smarts exceeded their production (even if the smarts were relatively equal across the two sides).

This division was perhaps accentuated because the debate often seemed to lead the sides to align in terms of whether they favored or opposed simplification. No, it was even stronger. On the one side were some who believed that coming up with *any* parsimonious model of action, no matter how patently absurd, made one the sociological equivalent of a Kepler. On the other side were those who believed that any reduction in complexity was equivalent to the Goths sacking Rome.

But there are different kinds of simplification, at least here. We will always make simplifications that are necessary given our limited capacities. For example, if, on returning from a museum we are asked to describe Renoir's painting "Two Sisters," most of us will not be able to do better than to say that there are two female figures, one a young adult, seated, and the other a child (standing?), both wearing hats, a bit fuzzy . . . Then there are unconscionable simplifications, which sociologists have at times confused with science, equivalent to saying, "on average, the painting was brown," because were you to randomly sample points and blend them, that's what you would get.

Our objection to the foolish simplification does not, however, mean we should want to restrain a Newton (or even a Goethe!) who is determined to try to understand the bases of color. One may focus on the simple question of how colors mix, how the reflection and transmission of the colors of translucent objects are related, and so on. Many of us believe that this is not possible for human action, and they may be right. But it hasn't been proven, and so we cannot dismiss efforts to make simple models of human action.

Modeling

I've noted that in practice, rational choice theory could be (and was often) used to refer to a limited and nontrivial set of axioms that can then be used for strong deductive theorizing. The virtue of such an approach can be (as I shall demonstrate) the ability to start from a set of actions that are each explicable individually, propose some sort of aggregation function, and then make strong and counterintuitive predictions that can be relatively surprising, and, maybe, even true. I'm not saying that there were no problems with this approach. For one, like any deductive enterprise, there tend to be a *lot* of false positives. Because if you don't actually know something about an area, you can still make a lot of correct predictions, especially if you're allowed a peek at the data beforehand, and so you never know how very wrong your ideas are.

But there was no reason that this approach couldn't start with simple axioms, find empirical challenges, and revise the axioms—for example, work that shows people don't discount future costs and benefits the way economic theory first imagined they should (see Frederick, Loewenstein, and O'Donoghue 2002). Further, there were even theoretical ways of responding to disconfirmation, ways that weren't pathological. For example, we might wonder why a man who very much enjoys drinking beer and shooting pool joins a religious group that forbids these activities, when there is a very similar group next door that doesn't. One possible response is to argue that there might be a *different* good reason for joining a group that seems to take away fun. Many groups provide collective benefits but are vulnerable to free riders (those who don't contribute but take just the same). Strict groups may do better at keeping out free riders and thus be better providers of collective goods. So maybe it's overall a plus for our fellow to join a strict group. Here, using the initial strong axioms of self-interest that we started with, additional reasoning produces a strong (and testable) answer to what might first seem a disproof.

A second possible response is to propose that we have dual preference structures — we can have a desire for something, but also a second-order desire *not* to desire this. We just need a little external constraint to do what we want to *want* to do. This might be puzzling, but many of us immediately recognize this in ourselves, so it too is amenable to empirical exploration.

A third response is to say that in fact this fellow desires not to have his desires met, and leads to what we can call (taking the words but not the ideas from Freud 1961) "the economic problem of masochism." As we'll see, something puzzling, something unstable is going to rise up if we try to go down that road.

But that's where people went when they tried to demonstrate that rationality is a "true" model of the individual actor. Opponents reasonably listed examples of cases that cannot be profitably explained by rational choice theory. Such cases are legion, but since there are plenty of cases of almost anything, such examples were not in themselves conclusive. Proponents, in turn, attempted to answer such claims by watering down the definition of rationality and by positing invisible utilities that explain whatever case is to be explained. In other words, opponents pointed to deviation from the model (and since no model fits perfectly, there is plenty to point to), while proponents over-fit existing data (which leads to a theory that is less likely to be correct though it seems to explain more — not outside, bigger!). In particular, proponents were led to emphasize the weakest aspect of the theory, namely, its ability to explain *why* some apparently irrational action is rational. That is, by assuming what others doubt (rationality of each and every action), the theory predicts the existence of unobservable theoretical factors that justify the assumption. Such circularity is often a part of scientific progress, but usually only when it leads (eventually) to strong independent predictions. But the watered down understanding of rationality that resulted was too weak to allow for any but the vaguest promises to explain anything that comes along. In contrast, it may be that a narrow definition of rationality, precisely *because* it deviates from actual human action, is most theoretically useful.

Useful, true; contrary to bastardizations of pragmatism, we don't need these to be the same. But we do need to keep straight which is which. Let's see how people defined rationality, and how it worked for them.

WHAT IS RATIONALITY?

Is Anything Irrational?

In previous chapters, we have seen a class of problems that turn on the confusion of substantive and formal approaches to the same concept. This lies at the heart of the problem of rationality for sociology, and it is, as we shall see, related to an uncertainty of whether to consider "rationality" an attribution of *actions* or of *actors*. Let's begin with a definition of rationality taken from our all-purpose example, Talcott Parsons (1949: 58): "Action is rational in so far as it pursues ends possible within the conditions of the situation, and by the means which, among those available to the actor, are intrinsically best adapted to the end for reasons understandable and verifiable by positive empirical science." This is really a *substantive* definition (and one of *action*, not *actors*). The problem is, says who? Whose positive empirical science? Certainly, the definition might work for things like whether to make rain by dancing as opposed to seeding clouds—but is it rational to avoid foods with high cholesterol to avoid heart attacks? Who speaks for empirical science? And what if there's something basic we've *all* overlooked that we should be doing? Is *all* our action irrational?

Perhaps we should amend this definition to say that action is rational when a person uses those means that modern empirical science at that time *says* will reach this end. But as we realize that "science" doesn't say anything (only people say things), we would have to amend this in turn to read, action is rational when a person uses those means that *accredited scientists* at that time say will reach this end. But this raises its own problems! Who are scientists? Do doctors count? What about psychologists? What about sociologists? What happens when scientists disagree? How can our actor choose?

Further, we must note that we have been talking about the rationality of *actions* and not the rationality of *persons*. We don't yet have a definition for rationality when it comes to persons, but we do have one for being *ir*rational; presumably, we would not want to call someone a "rational" person whom we also believed to be out-and-out, full-bore, bull-goose loony. That might be a place to start! The issue of the rationality of *actors* should be relevant for our attempt to specify the nature of the rationality of *actions,* since rational choice theorists often explained their adherence by pointing to their belief that we really were rational actors. But Parsons's definition still seems to put rational actions out of reach of many rational actors. If rational action requires using means that science says are correct, an actor exposed only to incorrect knowledge might end up making consistently nonrational choices as to means. Indeed, we can even imagine a rational person who never carried out a rational action in her life. However, it still seems a bit hard to consign all those who lived before the birth of modern science to the hellfire of irrational action (perhaps there is a sort of limbo of the patriarchs for people like Hobbes and Galileo). Further, the personal traits that would seem to be implied by our definition have to do not with cognitive functioning but with obedience (and obedience to people like us). That's worrisome. Is there anything different in doing what a scientist says one should do and doing what a priest says one should do?

We might therefore decide to focus on the cognitive processes involved—deduction from plausible premises—and revise our statement to read thus: action is rational when a person uses those means that the cognitive authorities in his or her social environment claim will reach this end. In this case, the difference between rational actors and rational action shrinks considerably, which might be comforting. But why focus on authorities at all? The authority of scientists must itself be somewhat circular and hence cannot claim rationality (that is, it is formally like the issue of the inerrancy of the Bible, which we know to be true because it says so in the Bible, and the Bible wouldn't lie, because it is inerrant . . .). Thus we are left with a seemingly general and stable definition of rationality: rational action occurs when a person uses those means that he or she believes will reach whatever end he or she is pursuing. We've replaced our substantive definition of rationality with a *formal* definition, one that brackets any particular truth about the way the world works. The problem is, this seems to well encompass almost all of the action that we would want to call *irrational.*

That is, if the word "rational" is to have any meaning in the phrase "rational choice," there must be such a thing as *irrational* choice. Many users of the term, however, explicitly denied that this is the case—and indeed staked their scientific claim to fame on the ability to turn every irrational act into a rational one by fabricating utilities. Thus Posner (1992: 85) argued that "animals are rational as well as people." The lemming hurling itself off a cliff into the water is making a "rational" decision, since "rational" has in effect been redefined to mean "anything you did."[2]

One must of course sympathetically view the plight of theorists facing an insoluble dilemma—if they are to avoid the most outrageous intellectual imperialism, and second-guess the preferences and reasoning of everyone but themselves, they must take into account others' beliefs and values when determining whether action is rational or not. There is, further, something decidedly *right* about such a preference for rationality—we are less likely to dismiss others whom we just don't understand and are more likely to devote time to understanding

[2] Such conditionality also reveals this sort of rational choice theory as fundamentally parasitic on the rest of sociology—it can connect two very close points but leaves it to others to figure what people *do* want, what they *do* believe, and so on (also see Barnes 2000: 76, and 44). And yes, I know the thing about lemmings isn't really true.

how things look to them.[3] But if we reasonably make rationality relative to beliefs and values — one's understanding of the structure of the world and one's goal in this world — then nearly all conscious action is rational, and the word ceases to have any meaning whatsoever. A complete lunatic who believes that tinfoil may block the malicious thought rays beamed by Evil Eternals is thus as rational as the currency trader looking for minor fluctuations in exchange rates. *Given* the belief, it is rational to wear the tinfoil hat. One is forced into the position of saying, "Because he was crazy, he was rational."[4] The one thing we seemed sure of — that a full-out loony isn't rational — seems to be incompatible with our axioms.

In other words, we have stumbled onto another form of the problem of conditionality, when we end up conditioning on some things that we probably shouldn't. In this case, to be able to prove that conduct is (formally) rational, we must accept the condition that the actors are (substantively) irrational; thereby, we are able to come up with only a weak, even degenerate, idea of "rationality." It's like the explanation of our Smokkers — something unconditionally irrational becomes rational once we condition on everything else. The formal definition of rationality necessarily destroys the substantive one. And yet, it is often interpreted as giving a *new* and more accurate substantive understanding of rationality. It's another form of the problem we first identified in Chapter 1: "bigger, not outside."

PRODUCING PARADOX

The Primrose Path

There is an age, it seems, when every American middle-class child, or at least boy, hits upon utilitarianism, specifically, the idea that all action is designed to increase the actor's happiness, and thus, is actually self-interested. If he tells his father, as mine did the other day, his father is likely to burst out laughing, bitterly if he's in a bad mood, appreciatively if he's in a good mood. Because one thing that a parent knows is that the days you do something to increase your happiness are few and far between. The child's first response will be to try to define "feeling good about yourself" or "absence of guilt" as happiness, and later "consonance with self-concept" and eventually even "the reduced cognitive cost of rethinking

[3] Unfortunately, this same impulse — "there must be a reason for what he does" — leads to a form of quietism when we also assume that "there must be a reason for how things are," a pivotal starting point for Montesquieu and Durkheim.

[4] This particular example of irrational action is a real one, and the author of these acts had less confidence in his rationality than would a contemporary rational choice theorist. See Ashwander's (1999) *Am I Insane*.

habits." (Mine did, at any rate.) But this is then to include as happiness things that have no empirical connection to happiness. Here orthological warning lights should start flashing; any system that turns things into their opposites in order to remain "true" is one to walk away from.

Now that I've sympathetically derived a thin, formal understanding of rationality, I want to approach this same puzzle less sympathetically, by considering sociological rational choice theory in its worst guise—not because this necessarily characterizes most adherents, but because it best brings forward a fundamental formal problem in theorizing that reappears in other areas as well. We're going to start with the fundamental idea of "revealed preferences." Economists are often criticized by sociologists for the fact that a key axiom of their theory—that people have stable preferences that go into a calculus to determine choice—is assuming what needs to be proven. But that's the thing about axioms—you assume them . . . or you don't. Usually, you get something from it, though.

Anyway, the economist Paul Samuelson had proposed that consumers' choices between different spending possibilities (well specified and carrying prices) indicated their preferences and that certain mathematical results could be thusly derived. This basic—and reasonable—assumption was then more widely used to mean that even though we can't always peer inside people's heads and see their preferences, we can get *some* information about these by seeing what they do. Now that's well and good so long as we are seeing bundles of goods that carry prices. But when some people brought it into sociology as a justification of their rational choice theory, others cried foul. Because now, the theoretical assumptions seemed to be self-validating, and the system seemed tautological. And indeed, there was often something pathological here, though it wasn't quite about tautology.

Evil Twins

Consider the puzzle of altruism that we raised in the first chapter. It's a "puzzle," of course, only to egoists, and this is how they might handle it. The egoist (aka the rational choice theorist) holds as a theoretical axiom the major premise (A), "All people always act in their interest." How can this be squared with our observation (C), "Some people give money to strangers"? Well, it certainly might be if we were to use as our minor premise, (B), "For some people, giving money to strangers is in their interest" (because they feel good about themselves, look cool to others, or whatever).

Now if we were *sure* about (A), this would be great, because we can produce (B) based on our evidence. And in economics, one might take (A) as a field-defining axiom, but in sociology, it's considered an open question. (A) is something that we need to support. Yet it seems that it is an untestable, indeed, unfalsifiable axiom. And as I've said, when something makes your theory *always* true, it's a big danger sign.

Unfalsifiability itself isn't the worst thing. And lots of axioms are untestable, at least, by themselves. But there is something particular here, and I'm going to call it "unidentifiability." What is curious about this first assumption, our major premise, is that is *always* has to be coupled with a *second* assumption, the minor. Note that this isn't true for the axiom "people always try to pay the least for any good." This is observable, testable, and generates strong predictions.

But in our examples, for every observation (our C), we seem to have *two* unknowns—two things we are trying to nail down [both (A) and (B)]. And this is why I use the term "unidentifiable," for in an analogy to mathematics, we're going to have as much success as someone trying to solve an equation with two unknowns. Do you want to know what x is, if $x+y=10$? You're going to have *too much* success, because you can say it's *anything*.

What we have identified here is a nugget of instability that will make any theory that contains it indeterminate. This isn't actually the case for all sets of theoretical claims, even those with axioms. Many behave a lot more like a proper set of linear equations that we can manipulate and solve.[5] Now in sociology, we've gotten used to dismissing "falsification" as a wrongheaded way to think about scientific theory, and we try to replace "falsifiability" with vague and weak words like "usefulness." It might well be true that falsification isn't a good criterion to impose on research programs or theoretical schools, or that it doesn't tell us much about what is *good*.[6] Still, I have the feeling that we reject falsificationism with such gusto because we want to reject falsification! But if the world has no leverage on our ideas, our ideas have no leverage on the world. Further, we've become oblivious to the real danger posed by unfalsifiable statements. Some are innocuous, but what we have here is a statement, or rather, a pair of statements, that isn't just unfalsifiable—it is self-justifying. In other words, to use the language from Chapter 1, it is a cheat.

Let's look a bit more closely at this cheat, this pair of statements. If either was true, it could make the other true, but if one was false, we'd never know. The two always go together, like Tweedledum and Tweedledee, and in fact, let's call this

---

[5] Of course, I recognize that in many cases, we have "set" the values of some of our unknowns by convention; further, it may also be the case that things we thought were identified correctly later become seen as unidentified. The analogy isn't perfect, but it points to the key issue with the unidentified aspects of theorizing. Further, the issue of identification, often now seen as if it were only relevant to the estimation of causal effects, is a more fundamental theoretical problem (see Manski 1995).

[6] It is indeed logically true that we can't really test any single proposition but a whole set of them (Hesse 1980). In practice, though, we turn some variables into constants ("black-boxing" them). What seems to be key is that we can break apart sets of propositions and put them in *different* clusters that are, at least in principle, testable (even if we don't hold ourselves to respect the tests we conduct!).

kind of pair a "Tweedle." When you ask Tweedledum to prove that he is correct, he points you to Tweedledee, and if you ask Tweedledee to prove *he's* correct, he says, "assuming my brother is true, then . . ." Like the Cretans, the logic is just as compatible with the opposite premises! So consider a different syllogism:

(A′) People always do the *exact opposite* of their interests;
(B′) There are some people whose interests are that they *don't* give money to strangers;

Hence

(C) Some people give money to strangers.

We fit the same observation (C) with just as much success. Why not run ahead with a theory of anti-rational choice? Presumably, the answer will come, because introspection makes us more likely to see (A) as a plausible account of interiority than (A′). But when we do that introspection, we don't *all* pull out the plum of a**holism. Many of us pull out (A″), "only sometimes do people act in their interests." If it's just about whether you pull out (A) and become an economist, or (A″) and become a sociologist, there's not much worth talking about.

And so I think we realize that (A) isn't a proper axiom, as it is vacuous; because it is always paired with a (B) that can neutralize it or reorient it, it says nothing in particular. (Can we call such vacuous axioms "vaxioms"?) We saw this vaxiomatic nature appearing in our first derivation of this degenerate form of rational choice theory; as we put more and more of our understanding into the "conditions" on which we conditioned (we have to say, "rational *given* your knowledge . . ."), we ended up with something seeming pretty vacuous—something that was ripe for indeterminacy. But we might also see that we've rediscovered an instability we first saw in the form of the "open-ended substantive statement" when we were discussing Parsons in Chapter 1. That is, our minor premise (B) enters as a more particular claim for which we have no independent evidence other than *were* it true, our theory (A) would predict what we observed (C). But we really never thought (B) was true until now.

Thus the Tweedle pair nicely encapsulates the formal problem of underidentification, where for every *observed substantive* fact, we are allowed to invent one *unobserved substantive* claim, thus making it impossible to get any traction on our theoretical claim. (A) could be true, but so, as we have seen, could its exact opposite. If you're debating with someone making a Tweedle claim, there isn't much you can say. In fact, the only possible response was wonderfully given by none other than Tweedledee himself (Carroll 1946 [1896]: 52): "If it was so, it might be; and if it were so, it would be; but as it isn't, it ain't."

Alice has a large number of unsatisfactory debates with the denizens of looking-glass land, but this is the most complete dialogic failure; Carroll (quite a good logician) clearly loved the Tweedledee principle, for Tweedledee closes his statement with the definitive conclusion, "That's logic." And so it is, but of a very degenerate kind. When we find someone making an argument where no rebuttal superior to the Tweedledee version can, even in principle, be made, something is wrong. And that is the case for any system that possesses the philosopher's stone that allows one to turn things into their opposites.

Is It Rational to Be Irrational?

This isn't, one would think, news to sociological theorists, and yet it is. Even sophisticated thinkers can incorporate serious formal problems when they try to embrace rational choice principles in totalistic fashion. One of the most important breakthroughs in twentieth-century social thought, or so I earnestly believe, is Herbert Simon's understanding that the right model of individual action is rarely one of rational action, and instead should be seen as simple action ("satisficing") taking place in environments that often hold a great deal of knowledge in them. Here is a way that we approach this problem. I want to buy new razor blades because the kind I am familiar with is off the market. How do I pick them? (It seems that many Americans will go for the next-to-the-cheapest. You might think this is silly but once I bought the cheapest and what a mistake that was!) I could try to find out all the information I can about the different products, how they are manufactured, the satisfactions others have had, or I can just buy the first one I see, and if it isn't any good, throw it away and blindly try another. And repeat if necessary. Will I get the best one? Probably not. But the time expenditure it would take for me to choose the truly best probably isn't worth it. In many cases, the costs of gathering the information that would be necessary to make a strictly rational choice are prohibitive. It is irrational to be rational.

Well if that is the case, as at least one sociologist has triumphantly concluded, "it becomes rational, from the actor's point of view, to 'satisfice' instead" (Goldthorpe 2007: 142). Despite Goldthorpe's generally admirable critical analyses, here I think he makes an error. Just because it is irrational to be rational doesn't mean that it is rational to be irrational. Given the old definition of rationality, this is true only if our actor can compare the costs and benefits of being rational for some choice to those of satisficing, a comparison Goldthorpe knows very well would be even *less* rational than being rational in the first place.[7] To say that it is

[7] That is, we don't know how good the information out there is until we go out and gather it, which means that we've taken on all the costs of the rational choice itself. But we've also got to figure out the expected costs and benefits of *not* using that information. So we're worse off.

rational to be irrational is to do a switcheroo—"rational" no longer means performing a calculus based on information to maximize utility.[8] We've found ourselves in one of those "bigger, not outside" errors we pointed to in the first chapter. To say that even irrationality and nonrationality are rational is clearly to change the nature of what we are talking about in a way we did not bargain for. Very possibly, we're well on the way to a vaxiomatic understanding of rationality.

In sum, it is tempting to solve the problems we uncovered, problems that are inherent to the idea of rationality as an attribute of both actions and actors, by slowly changing the word "rationality" away from the restrictive meaning we started with. Sometimes relaxing constraints to remove paradox works—we get something more rigorous and new. But in this case, we find people claiming to have a theory of rational choice that is equivalent to the crab salad we served at the café where I used to work (there was no actual crab in it, though should you happen to have some crab, it probably would go nicely with the salad). And just as we should have been shut down for false advertising, so, too, should those theorists who claim to be theorists of rational choice, but really are simply talking about any old kind of choice. Or nonchoice. Or whatever.

Exchange Theory

In sum, we've seen a familiar, and simple, problem of taking conditionality of action to turn substantively irrational actions into so-called rational ones. In such cases, we go from a model of rational action to a model rationalizing action; we can come up with a seemingly good excuse for any observation. We just keep accepting conditions until the irrational becomes rational. Recall that in the previous chapter we saw that taking the properties out of any object and making them predicates (the man who is angry, the animal who is a human and is angry) leads to a completely empty idea of "substance" that we suddenly realize we can do without entirely. In the same way, taking more and more out of people and making them the assumed conditions that we treat as nonproblematic eventually leads to a "rationality" that is also nothing at all.

If this is not recognized, and the substantively empty version of rationality is misunderstood as a substantively meaningful statement, we tend to see people confusing "rational choice theory" with a tedious translation project whereby any

---

8 For example, we give someone a choice between two boxes, one of which (as we tell her) has $50 in it and the other empty, and also give the person the "pre-choice" of whether to look into them before choosing. Now someone could "choose" not to peek. It would be pretty stupid if we were to claim that her box-choice was still a "rational" one (just without complete information) because we know that in *this* case, the search costs were comparatively low. We don't want a definition that makes the ignorant choice under high search costs rational but also makes stupid behavior like this "rational."

action can be described as rational, or selfish, or what have you. This generally provokes disbelievers to side with Tweedledee (if it were so, it would be, but as it isn't, it ain't), and nothing much happens. But the problem becomes explosive when taken to the realm of social action and used (quite illogically) to defend the assumption that "exchanges are always equal."

As anyone who studies exchanges, including economists, can tell you, exchanges *aren't* always equal. You can accept the axioms (1) that any action, including the decision to make an exchange with another, chosen by an actor is fully rational, and (2) that the change in this actor's utility due to an exchange is greater than that coming from any other possible action, and even (3) that the benefits of the action outweigh the costs.[9] This just doesn't imply that the exchange is equal. Yet totalistic rational choice theorists often made this illogical deduction (or perhaps it was an assumption) when they treated exchanges in which the equality or inequality of an exchange could not be directly observed.

Why the passionate attachment to this dogma? Two plausible explanations spring to mind, neither of which is particularly compelling to us on a logical or evidentiary level. The first is the sort of thing that we aren't supposed to bring up because it seems to question the integrity of the theorist, accusing him or her of passing off ideology as if it were science. Here I am thinking about what might be understood as the "desire to normalize"—to demonstrate that the capitalist world is more or less as good as it could possibly be. Optimization was taken to justify optimism—the belief that we are in the best of all possible worlds.

Now, I certainly don't believe that theorists were intentionally attempting to support capitalism by making this postulate. Rather, I think that theorists, like other people, can have an abiding background sense that can lead them to make certain logical slips without knowing that they have. Normalization—and its reverse, denormalization—is a powerful form of such a background feeling. Normalization means that things fall into place and make sense. Those of us who feel that things right now are pretty much as good as they can be in many respects—though of course they can get better, but they can't be made way, *way* better via some sort of gut-wrenching change—well, we may grab for thought-ways that make this falling-into-place formally explicable.

The key to this aspect of rational choice theory is a selectionist logic. Things that don't do good for folks get selected out. If something is still here, there must be a reason. This is actually a reasonable conclusion for a special set of circumstances that different cases approximate to a greater or lesser degree. Everyone

[9] It isn't necessarily the case that (2) implies (3). Sometimes you just have to try to minimize your losses.

knows it isn't *always* true, but sometimes we can stretch it to cover the things we want to. No one says that the persistence of the North Korean government shows that it meets an effective demand, while they do say things like that about Wal-Mart or Halliburton. I'm not trying to erase the real differences between these cases, but all exist on a distribution that combines political power and individual buy-in. We need to watch where we glibly push a case all the way over to the "buy-in" pole in order to stop thinking about it.

Certainly, the theorists who were often seen as most central to the rational choice "theory" program seemed completely unfazed when people pointed to the ease with which their planks were used to construct just-so stories that justified any arrangement as the best of all possible worlds. Many scholars *using* rational choice models did not do this, but we are talking about theory here, not science. Such "rational choice" was rightly seen as an attempt to develop what we can call a "Pollyannalytics" of social action, and rightfully dismissed.[10]

Denormalization also takes place — as when those of us who think that things are pretty bad, and that it would take a fundamental reorganization and reorientation to make them better, assume that no one really in her heart of hearts is anything other than an oppressor or a rebel, either potentially or actually. Confronted with evidence that, say, some women like wearing veils, or that some workers don't want any control over production, such folks have an explanatory problem that they may be tempted to solve with an equally fallacious lemma, namely, that there are not only oppressors and rebels, but idiots, which leads us to a new, lower, form of normalization.

So this isn't an ideological critique of ideology so much as a warning to all to beware of logical leaps made when we want to have our gut feeling about the world translate easily (and, as we might say, nondialectically) into theories about it. Empirically, the issue of equal as opposed to unequal exchange appears (in sociology, not in all social sciences) so closely related to the yay / boo divide that it must give us pause.

The second reason that I think explains why the equal exchange postulate was so attractive to rational choice theorists is that *if* exchanges can be assumed to be equal, *and* we have evidence that seems to suggest that they *aren't*, we have a creative line of theorizing that allows us to account for these, a line of theorizing that may lead to the generation of new theoretical ideas. But I want to go on to argue that this turns out to be one of those classes of formal problems that leads to bad thinking.

---

[10] I believe that D. H. Lawrence coined this wonderful word to refer, self-deprecatingly, to his own ideas. Pollyanna was the heroine of a set of sappy books; the original turned on her ability, temporarily disrupted, to always successfully play "The Glad Game" and see a good side to every situation. See Porter (1913).

The Utility of Disutility

Here I'd like to frankly recycle some examples from work that Matt George and I previously did on the use of exchange metaphors to build theories of romantic / sexual pairing (Martin and George 2006). The argument we made was that in attempting to defend the dogma of equal exchange, theorists of the "sexual market" produced not merely tautology, but paradox.

The *basic* idea of equal exchange in sexual markets is very reasonable; since it's a relatively free country, and a fair degree of agreement exists among people as to who is more attractive than whom, people looking for romantic partners will tend to form pairs that are roughly equal in attractiveness. This isn't because people like similarity — everyone would rather be with the most attractive partners, all other things being equal — but only them as has, gits.

As I said, this basic idea is reasonable and even has empirical support. But there were and are plenty of "is she really going out with him" exceptions. The market theorists, rather than seeing this as disproof, made an extension — an extension that was also very reasonable. If the pairing seemed unbalanced, perhaps, rather than reject the theory, one should broaden the search for factors that went into the exchange. Thus, if we see a pair of people (call them i and j) with different attractiveness ($a_i \neq a_j$), it could be that the pairing decision allows people to bring other things into the mix — there can be other resources, say, income, that explain how this match is *still* equal. That is, if we identify this b, we find that $a_i + b_i = a_j + b_j$.

Not only is this reasonable, but if it *weren't* true, people would be not simply falling short of a particular rational model, they'd be remarkably stupid. Even theorists of social action who emphasize the autonomy of different spheres of life — that is, limitations to the ability to "make up for" a lack of one type of resource, say, scientific credibility, with another, say, fancy clothes — recognize that there is *some* degree of convertibility, even if there isn't a simple linear formula (which would imply that a brain-dead rat could still win a Nobel Prize if his clothes were *really* nice). But the thing about formal problems in theorizing is that one reasonable step, plus another, plus another, plus another, leads to madness.

So let's say we find another case, in which $a_i + b_i \neq a_j + b_j$; that is, there's a difference $\varepsilon = a_i + b_i - a_j - b_j$ that seems to give the lie to our principle of equal exchange. So we look until we find some c such that $a_i + b_i + c_i = a_j + b_j + c_j$. Given that there might be an infinite number of possible letters we could add, one might object that this is stacking the deck — the investigator is allowed to look for confirming evidence. But that isn't the problem here. It may indeed be that cherry-picking for confirmatory evidence isn't the most promising way of doing science. Still, it's very hard to rule out such searches for confirmation in sciences, and even though we can't formalize any way of doing it *right* (so that we can be sure we end up with true statements), sometimes it does seem to work out, although lots of times it doesn't, and the only way to see is to let people run off accumulating all the evidence they can.

Our problem is that even given a near-infinite number of possibilities, we might come up with a case in which $a_i + b_i + c_i + \ldots + z_i > a_j + b_j + c_j \ldots + z_j$. Does this mean that the rational choice theorist needs to call off the search for creative attempts to understand the exchange as equal? No, and for an important reason. We've been casual so far in treating these resources (our *a*, *b*, *c* . . .) as if they were objective quantities, like *x* bushels of soybeans or *y* barrels of crude oil. But how could one say something like 24 bushels of soybeans plus 5 barrels of crude is an equal exchange for 7 bushels of soybeans and 8 barrels of crude? That seems like, as we say, adding apples and oranges. Well, how does this happen in economic life?

We know that the answer is that we have a common metric for both, namely, money.[11] But we don't have that for the things that enter into our romantic pairing. Really, we leave it up to each actor to come up with his *own* subjective valuation of how much each contributes to his or her well-being. So when we say "$a_i + b_i + c_i = a_j + b_j + c_j$" we really mean $u_j(a_i + b_i + c_i) = u_i(a_j + b_j + c_j)$; that is, the "utility" of what i's characteristics provide to j is the same as the utility of what j's characteristics provide to i.

So what happens if we have a pairing that appears to be an objective mismatch? The next step—again a very reasonable one, and one made by Collins (1975: 253) in a classic piece on dating logic[12]—is to see that the very disutility of the less attractive partner is *itself* a utility, or indicates a utility. As Collins pointed out, "A highly secure and (erotically or economically) attractive person can profit from a 'mismatch' to a less attractive person, by demanding greater subservience from him or her as the price of staying."

Now this might seem to have reached the point of tautology. But (contrary to the previous implications of Martin and George) it is not. It is an empirical statement (and the subservience is, in principle, measurable). We could indeed, find a

[11] Here one *must* see Marx's (1906 [1867]) wonderful discussion of this convertibility in the beginning of *Capital*, Volume 1.

[12] Although this isn't my favorite piece of Collins's on this issue (he returns to it with more intellectual precision in later work), I should point out that (as George and I said before), what he is saying not only *could* be correct, but we think that indeed it often *is* correct. The issue is whether the postulate of equal exchange that comes with a market metaphor is the best way to think about this; Collins later moved away from this vocabulary. Further, I'd like to point out that I think Collins—perhaps uniquely among theorists discussing these issues—knew what he was talking about. I once did an investigation of the relation between power, status, and attributions of sexiness that began as basically a challenge to theorists to call the coin flip in the air—I laid out the measures I had and asked them to predict what I would see (I had not done the analyses yet). Most I wrote to completely ignored the challenge; some got it completely wrong. Collins correctly predicted some complex patterns in the data that I had not anticipated. It is one thing to predict the dissolution of the Soviet empire, as Collins did in his (1986) book. But to predict affairs of the heart is impressive indeed.

case in which the more attractive partner refuses to exact any surplus subservience from the less attractive. And yet, a theorist who is less empirically tethered than Collins wouldn't be set back in the least, for she or he is sure to go the next step, and posit that ego gains a sort of pleasure by feeling virtuous through refraining from obtaining subservience. Indeed, it is not hard to imagine the most rarified utility of all being the second-order pleasure taken in *not* taking pleasure in refraining from exacting subservience.

The problem isn't that there are so many ways of supporting the "equal exchange" thesis, it's that what seemed to be a strong, substantively relevant assumption turned out to be completely impervious to disproof. That isn't stacking the deck, it's just out and out cheating. But no one meant to cheat. What happened? We started thinking about equalities in terms of a_i and a_j, which seemed external, visible, and potentially comparable. But once we realized we were talking about something different, namely, $u_j(a_i)$ and $u_i(a_j)$, we were talking about something invisible, internal, and *without any common metric.* Our equation is unidentifiable. There is no way to know whether the pleasure you get from eating *your* favorite food, say, chocolate, is the same as I get from eating *my* favorite food, say, arugula. Given that I see a lot of sad sacks out there, I'm pretty sure their average hedonic pleasure from things isn't the same as mine. But I'm not even sure what this means, if it means anything at all. One is free to define these things as equal on average, or whatever—it's totally a meaningless statement. And a meaningless statement never makes for a good theoretical axiom.[13]

Further, this means that the things that are being held to be equal are unmeasurable. And this explains the reason for the unstable nature of rational choice theorizing—that one thing and its opposite can be derived from the same premises. There's nothing wrong with a theoretical system being able to *encompass* opposite statements—as long as the *reason* is that there are different *inputs.* Even if we don't always measure them, knowing that we *can* keeps us from just saying any old thing and rushing to the presses. But when we know that there is something important that can *never* be measured . . . well, we've left the realm of science far behind.

And that's how we can accept as *necessarily* true something that just isn't true—that all exchanges are equal, or at least, they are if everyone is acting freely in his or her best interest. If it *were* true, it would allow identification of our theoretical arguments. But it just doesn't follow: there can be a *good reason* to make an unequal exchange without that making the exchange equal. In fact,

[13] That is, we can have an assumption that we make for convenience's sake (such as a set of parameters summing to zero, which we impose when we *recognize* unidentifiability and know what we need to sacrifice to retrieve *some* information); things like this that are done to set an arbitrary metric are never taken as key axioms. And so, if the theory turns out to explain the data, we never treat this as support for our axiom ("You see, people's parameters *really do* sum to zero!").

theorists of exchanges see this all the time — for example, network exchange theorists put people in various configurations so that some have more opportunities and some fewer. They assume that each person is trying to do the best she can for herself, and they assume that no one will do anything that makes her situation worse, but what people end up doing in such circumstances is to create visibly, measurably, unequal exchanges. That's life — if you're dealt a weak hand, you make unequal exchanges. I'm not saying we should always be crying about it, but we shouldn't be lying about it either.

FROM IRRATIONAL TO RATIONAL USES OF RATIONAL CHOICE THEORY

Baby Talk

We've seen that a certain kind of adherence to totalistic rational choice theory would lead adherents to be rather irrational, completely unable to tell the difference between sane and crazy, smart and stupid — able to explain absolutely everything, as long as everything was defined in optimistic terms as the best of all possible worlds. But it doesn't have to be that way. Of course, we can use individual-level modeling based on realistic models of the actor for all sorts of problems. Beyond this, however, there are eminently rational uses of rational choice theory even where the axioms *cannot* be held to apply. In fact, this might be where rational choice theory is most important.

Let's consider the decision, famously studied by Becker (1981), as to whether to have a child. There are incredibly good reasons for modeling this decision as one of rational choice. The most obvious reason is that for many people, the decision actually *is* a matter of rational choice, or so I am told. Potential parents evaluate their economic security, competing time demands, their faith in their partner, their relation with their own family of origin, the importance to them of other activities that are difficult with children, and so on, and decide whether to have a child.

For other prospective parents, however, this decision is far from rational — indeed, many make the decision without being aware that they *have* in fact made the decision. While some may have made a different decision (e.g., to have sexual intercourse without birth control), others may not even have made this kindred choice (and perhaps have gotten pregnant merely as a result of contraceptive failure, or simply never to have considered contraception). It might then be argued that they make a different choice as to whether to terminate the pregnancy, but this fails to answer the objection on two counts. On the first, this is to acknowledge that the first decision was not a rational choice and to point to a second decision is largely irrelevant. On the second, there will still be some portion who make no choice, because abortion is not entertained as a possible option. To then insist that these people "choose" not to choose may be ideologically satisfying (and don't forget about the choice not to choose not to choose), but it should be clear that we are moving to a world in which we are always right, by definition.

Thus we have some couples for whom having a child is a rational decision, and others for whom it is not. Yet this does not mean that there is no utility to modeling the decision as the result of a rational choice for *all*. Historical demographers have repeatedly found that economic changes that lead to earlier financial independence of young couples lead them to increase the probability at any time of having a child. This can be predicted by treating the decision to have a child as a rational choice—even if it isn't. A whole set of nondecision, nonrational processes can be moved by financial situations and change the likelihood of a conception and a live birth. And in fact, I think that we have uncovered here a general principle for when such theorizing is the right way to go. I want to go on to derive this from another starting-point.

Unintended Consequences and When to Expect Them

I have argued that the use of self-proclaimed rational choice theory led to a common sort of formal error, one that we have seen reappearing in a new guise. The radical conditionality of its central premise made it unfalsifiable, and there was no clear way of preventing a slide to tautology and paradox. But this does not mean that the rational choice perspective has no utilities—it is just that these utilities are not where dogmatic rational choice theory is most likely to be applied, as the scope conditions are rather narrow. (Note that not all models of individual-behavior should be understood as *rational choice* models; my arguments here have only to do with this latter subset.) When these conditions are met, however, the power of rational choice theory to make important and plausible predictions is so strong that it is nothing short of scandalous to refuse to recognize such theorizing as truly sociological. Indeed, I think that we need more, not less, of explicitly rational modeling—under certain conditions. And this is where we do not know enough about things to explain their state, but may be able to predict certainly unintended, but also often largely unanticipated, consequences of certain types of actions.

There is a way in which what we call economics began as the study of the unintended consequences of individual action. One generally starts with Mandeville's (1924 [1732]) *Fable of the Bees*, which argued that individuals pursuing their particular desires could lead to the greater good: "Thus every Part was full of Vice, / Yet the whole Mass a Paradise" (24). This more than any other work introduced the fundamental idea of unintended *aggregate* consequences that later became key for the analysis of markets under people like Adam Smith. Further, Smith himself, in the *Theory of Moral Sentiments* (1997 [1759]), made a similar argument regarding the unintended consequences of the pursuit of selfishness—were it not for the avarice of the rich, money would stockpile and the poor would starve. But the fascination that the rich have for novelties and luxuries leads the produce of the land—the most important thing for human survival, grain—to be rather equally divided, pretty much everyone getting enough to eat.[14]

With Smith's later work, *The Wealth of Nations*, this sort of theory became used more or less as a mechanism to explain the well-known facts of equilibrating markets, as well as the development of the division of labor. Smith did not rely on this understanding to generate counterintuitive explanations, which were, with a few exceptions (e.g., Ricardo), for some time deemphasized and have been all the more noteworthy as a result. In such counterintuitive examples, it is not that the aggregate result is a happy one not intended by the individuals, it is one that goes *against* what the individuals would want. They are free to choose what to do, but the state that would satisfy most of them is one that "you can't get to from here."

One famous example is Akerlof's (1970) notion of the market for lemons. He proposes that nearly all used cars are "lemons" (in worse condition than they appear). The explanation is as follows. First, given the difficulty of assessing the state of its internal parts, most buyers can be hoodwinked into buying a car that is in worse condition than it appears. And they know this. Buyers therefore adjust their prices to take into account this risk, which leads them to refuse to pay a fair price for a car in good condition. Such cars are therefore kept off the market until they are no longer in good condition.

Similar explanations have been proposed by Schelling (1978). One example is the "tipping" phenomenon in which a group of actors, almost none of whom have preferences for strong racial segregation, but have *varying* preferred degrees of similarity in their neighbors, produce a necessarily totally segregated environment. What is powerful in these examples is, first of all, that the model of the individual actor is simple and general—no special utilities or preferences are invented for the explanation in question. Second, the final prediction is derived from an aggregation of individual actions, often involving some simple feedback, so that the result is not one that would be willed by the participants. This means that the invisible hand is not a substitute for some hyper-rational social body, as in some of the explanations of Coleman (1990) (see note 1).

That is, the importance of such worst-of-all-possible-worlds examples is that they more clearly adjudicate between alternate theories than do best-of-all-possible-worlds cases, because we can eliminate the "it's their collective will" and the "it has a social function" explanations. However, even where things aren't quite so neat, we might be able to use straightforward economic-type models of rational

[14] Significantly, it is here, to describe this vice-driven redistribution of wealth, where Smith first uses the phrase "invisible hand" (1997 [1759]: 249); when he later uses the phrase in *The Wealth of Nations* (1976 [1776]: 477) it is, we should remember, only in the context of the allocation of capital.

choice to make nontrivial deductions where we don't actually have all the information to allow us to make a substantively accurate model of the choice process.

How do we do this? We focus only on *costs*, and specifically, *changes* in costs. Pathological explanations, we saw, often had no trouble asserting that costs and benefits were equal, because the benefits (the subjective utilities) were internal to actors' minds and incommensurable. Although one could argue that costs also are forms of psychic pain, and thus we should treat costs and benefits symmetrically, I don't think that's so, at least not in most cases. The benefits of some action usually have to do with its (unmeasured) internal effects, while costs are how difficult the *means* is to the action, and this often involves many observable external factors. We can make a reasonable assumption that increases in such pain are monotonically related to increases in observable, measurable, and manipulable features of the world. Climbing two flights of stairs may not be twice as psychically costly as climbing one, but it is more . . . whatever we want to call it.

I'm not saying that people actually are making decisions in which they take these factors into account as "costs." But people in aggregate may respond to changing conditions in the same direction that they would respond were they rational actors. Thus even those for whom marriage and childbirth are not rational decisions may be less likely to experience these events in an economic downturn. Let's actually start by imagining a world in which our basic hypothesis—that childbirth is rational and those with more money are more likely to have kids—is actually *false*. Our people (like most of us) aren't rationally weighing the costs of having a child (If we did, that would be the last generation of *Homo sapiens*; that's why sex is fun, right?). Specifically, in this world, desire for children is a latent quantity that is randomly distributed across persons with no regard for their material position.[15] We can still use the false hypothesis to make a smart, and in this case true, prediction.

And this prediction is that if the costs to having a child go up, or the resources people have to pay those costs go down, the number of kids goes down. Even though we can't explain any stable outcome, nor can we really do much about most changes in *benefits*, we can be right about changes in *costs*. Why? In the economic downturn, over here, a boy lacks money to go to a dance; over here, a girl scorns a poor suitor; over here, a depressed man has erectile dysfunction; over here, a woman with a poor diet has a miscarriage; and so on and so forth.

As a result, modeling individual actions as if they were rational, while useless in determining the *static* decisions being made by any or all individuals, can be extremely significant in making predictions about when conditions change, so

[15] Of course, a "rational choice" analysis could "explain" this by sagely informing us that children actually "make up" for the disutility of poverty, and hence rational choice theory "predicts" the observations both when people with less money have more children, and when people with more money have more children. Blah blah blah.

long as we have a sense of how change in conditions leads to changes in costs.[16] And such predictions can be important when changes are deliberately introduced by governments. By assuming that people have stable preference structures, and by assuming that they rationally respond to their environment — assumptions that are not in general correct ones — strong predictions can be made that shed considerable light on likely outcomes, even if the processes are unknown. Although *axioms* are made for the purposes of derivations that may involve the attribution of a certain form of calculus to actors' subjectivities, in contrast to the degenerate explanations we explored above, there is no need to compare the apple of one person's subjectivity to the orange of another's. Instead, we are comparing the same aggregate of people under different conditions.

And that was Smith's point in our opening quotation — that the impulse of the planning spirit doesn't always take into account how people react to planners' plans. Social life is, as a number of commentators have presumably said before, like a game: it's hard to predict, because what one person or side does then gets countered by another. Still, sometimes one can predict the next move. Yet we frequently (in sociology, that is) don't, even when we could. The easiest way is to use a rational action model to predict how a change in "costs" will affect outcomes. It may be pretty simplistic, but it's better than our default, which is to assume that people won't change at all, or only will in precisely the way *we* want them to.[17]

Sociological Laws

Here we may learn from our predecessors in the game of enlightened despotism. Examples may be taken from any number of areas, but for consistency, I will examine a set of attempted reforms by Landgrave of Hesse-Cassel Frederick II (Friedrich Wilhelm, 1760–1785), a fine example of an enlightened despot who put into practice many reasonable rationalizations and reforms.[18] (He is best known

---

[16] Goldthorpe (2007: 129) proposed that rather than claiming that people *only* act rationally, rational choice theory can still be used to express at least significant tendencies in large-scale quantitative data analysis. Hence we can argue that "the tendency to act rationally, in the circumstances that prevail, is the common factor at work, while deviations from rationality are brought about in a variety of ways and a variety of consequences." This seems to be quite a bait and switch — to have a theory called "rational choice" even if a rational factor explains 1 percent of the variance and irrational ones, say, 99 percent. (It also simply doesn't follow that the nonrational parts should be treated as if they were "miscellaneous" and not, say, "culture," but let's put that to the side.) We should only propose theories that we think are true, not ones for which we can scrabble up *any* amount of support. For example, you as well as I know that carrots don't cause mice. Still, if we had 100 mice on 75 percent normal diets, and gave 50 of them a carrot a week, we might find that the carrot-eating ones were a bit bigger and healthier. Goldthorpe's logic suggests that this could be used to save the theory "carrots cause mice."

[17] These points were nicely made by Jane Jacobs (1992 [1961]: 271, 441) in a critique of planners who operated in a deductive way and did not take into account how the persons they were planning would follow through on their own interests.

[18] Here I rely on Ingrao (1985); the original source is a German dissertation, Karl Stein, *Das Waisenhaus in Kassel von seiner Enstehung bis zum Ende der kuhessichen Herrschaft*, University of Frankfurt, 1924.

to Americans as the leader of the hated Hessians who aided the British in the War of Independence; we therefore imagine him as some damned reactionary, but he was the sort of fellow who put into place a social welfare system and introduced a bureaucratic civil service, and even kept up a correspondence with Voltaire [Fischer 2004: 52–55].) One of his projects was an attempt to protect farm owners who might not be able to meet their mortgage payments in hard times; he simply made it hard for the creditors to foreclose. The effect was not what he had intended — loans simply dried up as those with capital refused to lend where they could not foreclose. Now that's the sort of thing that supports the quietist version of laissez-faire economics ("If you raise the minimum wage, that will only increase unemployment, so why do anything?"). Those predictions aren't always right, and the point isn't that our assumption should always be "the poor ye shall have always," but we *should* try to predict the countermoves to any move. When there are lots and lots of intertwined players, it can be hard to make a good call, and the prediction that is right once may fail a second time. But where there are few and relatively free classes of players, the quietist prediction may be closer to the mark than many of us would like to acknowledge.

But one of Frederick's programs is of special interest, in part due to the example of childbirth which has been the guiding theme of this section. In 1763 Frederick built a home for foundlings to decrease the rate of the murder of unwanted, illegitimate children. Frederick reasonably expected that some mothers would be too ashamed to come and signal their fornication publicly, so he had built a revolving door into which babies could be deposited on one (windowless) side of the building and picked up inside.

Frederick's innovation succeeded beyond his wildest dreams, or worst nightmares. The emotional cost of depositing a baby was indeed so much lower that it drew in expecting mothers from other areas of Germany, some apparently making repeat trips. Not only that, but parents of *legitimate* children also found it tempting to decrease the number they had to provide for by making a surreptitious trip to the deposit-turnstile. Even though the door was made only for infants, some of the more determined were able to stuff toddlers into the turnstile. Frederick's *Findelhaus* was flooded with babies and infants, some of whom would otherwise have been killed, but others of whom would probably simply have remained with their parents.[19]

[19] Interestingly, this general case of foundling hospitals was an example used by Spencer (1896 [1873]: 20) to describe the problems of social intervention without respect for the lawfulness of social life. But it isn't really *lawfulness* that frustrates the interventions in his examples — it is that actors are free to counter the planner's visions, just as in Frederick's cases. Sometimes the resistance of actors can be countered with *more* power; we just need more than one barrier to channel their action. Spencer (94) also noted that a law requiring each parish to support its poor can lead landlords to remove the housing stock that would allow the poor to live within the parish. It was illogical for him not to recognize that there *were* counters to this move, even if they were oppressive and difficult to implement. Also, I have to say that much as I admire Spencer, he was a lunatic who even opposed legislation that would forbid chimney sweeps from forcing children up into chimneys where they often got stuck and slowly died. Thus speaks the voice of theory.

There was no way to provide for this many infants, and they began to die: those running the facility estimated that they were losing two-thirds of the infants, and they had to start "out-sourcing" (as we might now say) care by allowing untrained housewives to look after for the overflow. This immense tragedy, however, might have been avoided if this unintended consequence had been predicted. It is worth emphasizing that the usefulness of this exercise does not depend on our accepting the substantive claim that the action *is* in fact the result of rational choice: it is sufficient that there are good reasons to *treat* the choice as if it were rational.

To stick with this example, the decision to abandon a child is certainly one that some parents might be able to make rationally, but others not. These latter parents may make the choice to abandon in a moment of exhaustion and depression, and greatly rue the decision the next morning. There is no reason to call this process "rational." Yet for that very reason, the decision is one that will be extremely sensitive to the costs of abandonment—emotional and anti-rational actions are often the ones most susceptible to manipulation via incentives, since a little friction is sufficient to allow one to cool off. We may have no idea why people commit suicide, but we still may correctly predict that suicides will decrease if we make the fences on bridges higher.

Whether or not the choice process is rational, if it in any way involves attentiveness to costs, even irrational attentiveness, then a substantial decrease in costs will probably lead to *some* increase in the number of actions, *all else remaining constant.* Of course, all else does not always remain constant. Yet in the short run, we may be able to treat it as if it remains constant. Hence the equation for the utility of an action, that spirals off into foolishness when used in Tweedle form, becomes extremely powerful when some change is introduced. Without making overly strong claims about a functional form, we can still expect that there will be a change, say, in an equilibrium point, that has to do first and foremost with the change in costs.

The key here is that by focusing on costs, as opposed to utilities, we concentrate on things that are external and observable; by looking at change, we don't have to make any arguments about subjectivity and motivation at all. Now in econometrics these days, there is a lot of enthusiasm for replacing cross-individual comparisons used to support causal claims with intra-individual comparison (often in the forms either of "fixed effects" models or conditional estimation). That is not what I am talking about here. My argument is not that by focusing on change, we get at the right values. That requires many linearity assumptions that economists will in general agree are implausible for the case of unobserved utilities. (Basically, the marginal utility of any resource depends on the quantity of that resource, and of all other resources, that one has, so there is no linear relation between change in quantity on average and change in utility.) Further, I've argued in Chapter 1 that this practice is often flawed, in that we are wrong to think that the things that explain yearly fluctuations in patterns are the same things as those patterns themselves.

All that matters here is that we can assume that there is *some* distribution of preference structures that will not be changed by some proposed institutional change (a similar argument was also made by Satz and Ferejohn 1994: 77). And our best prediction of what will happen after the proposed institutional change is a simple increase or decrease along the distribution, depending on whether costs decrease or increase. Now this isn't always true: there are some worlds in which a jiggle of the state doesn't lead to either a reestablishment of an equilibrium nor to an obvious linear change. Sometimes decreasing costs doesn't lead to increased purchases. How many toothbrushes do you really need? Other times, a small change can lead to what seems like a disproportionately huge change in behavior. And not all changes can be made holding other things constant, as Lieberson (1985) has emphasized.

Yet for those where we can imagine other things remaining relatively constant at least in the short term, it is simply irresponsible *not* to make a prediction derived from the model of rational choice. And where we are ignorant, a reasonable first guess is a simple monotonic change roughly proportional to the change in costs.

For example, the legalization of abortion in all states in 1973 certainly led to an increase in the number of abortions, though the number of illegal abortions can only be approximated. Levine et al. (1999: 201) find that fertility rates decreased around 4 percent in states that had legalized abortion before *Roe v. Wade*, and a similar decline followed in other states after *Roe*. Thus, while we can conceive a demand for abortion that is completely inflexible (such that if a legal option were not available one would find an illegal one, or travel to a state in which it was not illegal), this does not describe actual decision making as well as does a model including partially (but not wholly) flexible demand. Levine et al. (1999) projected that at the time of their analyses, outlawing abortion nationwide would increase fertility around 11 percent, leading to around 440,000 additional births a year. Similarly, restrictions on funding for abortions probably led to an increase in live births (see Korenbrot et al. 1990). There is nothing scandalous about such projections, so long as we know how far we can plausibly project. The answer is usually, "not very far."

If heroin was made totally legal and unrestricted, more heroin would get consumed, at least initially. But that isn't necessarily the end of the story, for consequences do not stop here. It is not at all hard to imagine that the long-term effects of legalization would be quite different; were all recreational drugs legal, perhaps the collapse of the underground drug industry would leave a lot of industrious persons without means of employment. They might find that it made more sense to sell their guns to collectors and work for the advertising agencies promoting various brands of once-controlled substances. Legitimate industries would no longer be chased out of "bad" areas, offering stable employment to residents who would have an attractive alternative to the irregular lifestyle encouraged by heavy drug use. Demand for drugs (pursuing this scenario) might decrease, which would make use more stigmatized or at least awkward, increasing the decline. Who knows? Here we're no longer extrapolating, or forecasting (Bell 1973), based on changing a single parameter, but "predicting"— trying to guess what the world would be like given a lot of changes — and it's unlikely that anyone has a good handle on this. Once we get a few steps out, or a few moves down the line, it's a parlor game, not social science.

In sum, it would be foolish to let our indignation at the irrational employment of rational choice theory prevent us from undertaking such analyses when they are called for. It is worth pointing out that Karl Polanyi, now considered the guardian angel of the new economic sociology (perhaps first emphasized by Granovetter 1985), had no such compunctions. In his classic work on the Great Transformation, Polanyi (1957 [1944]: 79) analyzed the effects of the 1795 Speenhamland Poor Relief law, which basically established a minimum wage for employed and unemployed alike — a most liberal and modern-oriented law if there ever was one.

"In the long run," said Polanyi (1957 [1944]: 80) "the result was ghastly." Employers could offer starvation wages, knowing that the difference between what they paid and what workers needed would be made up for by the poor relief. Workers lacked a material incentive to work hard or well, and, treated as paupers, they got no pride from their work, and so lacked an emotional incentive. Polanyi's analysis is not necessarily the last word on the results of the Speenhamland law, but for our purposes the significance is simply that the single person who more than others emphasized the falsity and human costs of seeing all action — even simply all *economic* action — in terms of abstract bourgeois economics, did not see anything wrong with analyzing the introduction of changed structures by using a model of rational action.

Theory and Action

It's widely repeated that the model of rational action doesn't have to be true for it to be "useful." This is true, but sometimes adherents make it seem like it is "useful" if it comes up with "accurate predictions," and so it doesn't matter if it is at all true. That's not correct. If we can come up with equally decent predictions using *true* postulates, and we often can, there's nothing other than religious revelation that could support a commitment to other postulates. Further, we should have a good reason for *why* the postulates, even if incorrect, lead to correct predictions. The most important class of cases, pointed to by Max Weber (1978), is that substantively irrational actors (which doesn't mean crazy or stupid) are embedded within an institutional framework that has a selective mechanism so powerful it allows us to treat actions as if they were rational (thus we can use market models originally based on rational action to fit the results of zero-intelligence traders, as shown by a now-classic piece by Gode and Sunder 1993).

Weber emphasized that we are often more interested in *deviations* from these predictions than in making the predictions themselves, since in some cases they are not only obvious but unimportant. Thus rational choice theory gives us a pretty good null model, which is what we compare reality to — not to accept the model, but to know what things to focus on. Nowadays, sociology almost always takes randomness as its null, which is basically the thesis that "there is no order in the world, everything is random, chaos reigns supreme." When we reject that, we think we've had a good day at work. The rational model is perhaps one step up from that. It's not the most profound thing ever said about the nature of the actor and / or action, but it doesn't have to be vacant, tautological, or paradoxical. Because when we study change, we no longer need to make theoretical claims about the subjectivities of actors. The problems came not from the idea of rationality but from the use of selectionist models that allowed for the imputation of optimality based on nothing other than the fact that something was observed.

Rational choice theory of this form disappeared. My best guess is that the disappearance is best understood as due to cohort replacement, for it quickly reappeared under another form, claiming now that it took its inspiration not from economics but from biology.

FROM RATIONAL ACTORS TO RATIONAL GENES

> *The ordinary cock-sure evolutionist ought to have no difficulty in explaining these terrors, and the scenery that provokes them, as relapses into the consciousness of the cave-men, a consciousness usually overlaid in us by experiences of a more recent date.*
>
> — WILLIAM JAMES, *PRINCIPLES OF PSYCHOLOGY* (1890): II, 420[20]

Baby Talk Redux

We have seen that one version of rational choice theory was mired in formal paradox, and that the resulting hullaballoo seems to have led to throwing out any

[20] James also wonderfully says "evolutionary psychology demands a mind-dust" (1890 I: 146).

real pursuit of this approach even when it could—and indeed should—throw light on empirical problems. It is fascinating that the same formal problems have newly arisen in the functional substitute for rational choice theory. This is a doctrine that is substantively completely antithetical to rational choice theory and yet is formally very close to it. Further, it may well appeal to the same habitus as did rational choice theory (hence the decline of one and the rise of the other), and we will see theorists actually attempting to skate from one to the other without missing a beat, despite the incongruity.

This doctrine is known as evolutionary psychology. Although there have been calls for an evolutionary psychology in sociology at least since Ellwood (1899), the current version has a particular interpretation of this quest. The key elements are the following: (1) human actions are indeed controlled largely by mental processes; however, many of these key processes are discrete nuggets, called "psychological mechanisms." (2) These nuggets operate without recourse to consciousness; thus, a subjective introspection that does not find the presence of one of these is irrelevant. (3) It is assumed that psychological mechanisms are largely independent of one another—I have never seen any interest in the sociological evolutionary psychologists in considering whether certain nuggets couldn't sit side by side.

As a result, (4) these nuggets can be selected for in evolutionary terms. That is, if a nugget helps you deal with your environment, you're more likely to have grandkids than others who lack the nugget. Further, in sociological versions, it is assumed (for no reason that I can determine) (5) that the environment of evolutionary adaptation (EEA) for these nuggets is invariably the Pleistocene (although researchers acknowledge that the EEA is not any specific time, they tend to imagine that as a species we have a distinct birthdate), and even more strangely (6) that these mechanisms are universal among contemporary human beings. Not only were these things selected for once-upon-a-time, but they haven't really budged since.[21]

[21] This makes evolutionary psychology opposed to what seems the kindred field of what is called behavioral genetics, which examines variation *within* populations. (That is, evolutionary psychology assumes that basically everything of interest is *constant* across people, while behavioral genetics assumes that basically everything of interest *varies* across people.) There was a time when behavioral genetics was the "bad boy" of the biological sciences, not at all accepted by others (see, e.g., the dismissive evaluation of its founder, William D. Hamilton, by the great primatologist Hans Kummer [1995: 185]). I'll actually speak approvingly of "sociobiology," but by this I mean E. O. Wilson's program; further, although behavioral genetics was an inherently compromised field (sharing with evolutionary psychology a suspicious combination of big claims and weak evidence, and refusing to chase poor scientists from its midst [Panofsky 2006]), in other fields—not yet, so far as I know, sociology—there have been some serious attempts to turn this into a productive research direction. Almost all efforts in sociology, unfortunately, combine opportunistic data mining and overfitting with just-so stories, though these involve haphazard references to certain proteins and the serotonin system (usually) that fall quite short of a plausible mechanism. It would both take me away from the arguments here, and depress the hell out of you, to go into how wildly irresponsible the swindling here has been.

In Chapter 5, we'll find that animal sociology forces us to recognize that we can't understand animals as "no-sort-of-beasts" who can be qualityless substrata onto which various independent psychological mechanisms can be tacked, like a Mr. Potato Head, and possessing no other forms of patterned reactions to stimuli. (So it might be evolutionarily a good idea to be a loving animal, or it might not, but the thing about a loving animal is that it may every now and then keep on loving, even when this sort of loving doesn't help anyone in the slightest. That is, if we don't have separate modules for "love your sister's husband," and "love your husband's sister," and so on, we might love our sister's first husband's second wife's kids, evolutionarily stupid as it might be.) The contrary assumption — that every last part of an animal can be independently tweaked by natural selection for optimum performance — is of course the Panglossian approach to evolution that Gould and Lewontin (1979) criticized. They pointed out that the working assumption in evolutionary biology was often the indefensible idea that any feature of an organism had to be successfully adapted to its environment, when in fact, the interdependence of animal morphology suggested that existing structures might be trade-offs in which some aspects were useless or even counterproductive. Although their own approach was not universally accepted, and I am no expert, it seems that advances in the understanding of how DNA is used in embryological development has only strengthened the already cogent logic of their argument.

There's a second problem with these tenets of evolutionary psychology for a general theory of human cognition: there's basically no way that it can be generally true. In fact, the one thing we know about the human brain is that it doesn't come with a great deal hardwired. Even if the entire genome were dedicated to determining the connections between neurons, we just don't have anything like enough base-pairs to do the job (Spitzer 1999: 37). Instead, the brain is a learning machine. Although it's true for many animals to some extent, it's true for us to an extent that really dwarfs anything else we can say about the brain. Still, we're *not* blank slates, not even close, and so this doesn't mean there couldn't be *any* behaviorally oriented cognitive modules that are the subject of selection in humans. But it certainly doesn't sound like a promising way to start for a general theory.

It is not the case that evolutionary psychological approaches have been a failure in all sciences. One of the most unpleasant successes is due primarily to Hrdy's (e.g., 1977) careful work with langurs in India. These monkeys have a system in which a single male tends to take over a troop of females for a relatively short period of time before being deposed. What Hrdy found was that these males tended to attempt, and often succeeded in, killing the nursing infants of females. Her explanation was that given the short amount of time the male had to inseminate females, any behavior pattern that increased his chances would be selected for. By killing nursing infants, he would lead the mothers to resume their reproductive cycles and hence have a chance of bearing his own young.

People did not like hearing this. It contradicted our belief that most animals are good (only nasty humans do sick things like killing babies), and many of us also had an assumption that animal behavior was selected for by being *pro*-social, not *anti*-social. A number of Hrdy's papers were rejected simply for contradicting presuppositions.

There had actually been previous reports of such male infanticide (e.g., Zuckerman 1981 [1932]: 222, 344), but they had been easily dismissed as due to the pathologies of captivity, where most observations had been conducted (for most primates, being locked in a cage isn't great for your mental health). Yet, once her work was finally published, many other monkey scientists (those who study monkeys, that is), reported similar behavior in groups that have similar structures (see, e.g., Cheney and Seyfarth 2007: 40, 57; Perry 2008: 170). The moral is clear: we should not dismiss evolutionary explanations just because they are evolutionary—they may account for things we cannot account for otherwise. And I do not deny that evolutionary psychology can be of use not simply for animals but possibly by other disciplines; I am speaking of it here only insofar as it crawls into my own.

In the case of human action, we have two things: one is the behavior, and the other is the theory of cognition that serves as an *explanation* for the behavior. We might accept that the langurs' behavior increases fitness and hence can be selected for. Yet what does it tell us about the cognitive correlate? Does it mean that there are discrete psychological mechanisms that are being selected for (e.g., a pro-infanticide-when-you-are-alpha-male nugget)? Very possibly. But imagine that through some remarkable feat of engineering (similar to that used in our nonverbal society in the previous chapter), we were actually able to interview the monkeys. Imagine that we ask an alpha monkey, "What's up with all the infanticide?" and he replies, "Oh, I have nothing against the babies, but I really want my *own* babies, and if those kids are still nursing, I can't get their moms pregnant, so there's nothing to do but kill the young 'uns." We'd have a different explanation—a rational choice one—of the same behavior, and it's just as good.

It's just that we don't really believe that langurs are capable of rational action. They're little bitty brain monkeys compared to us. But we do believe that humans are, at least in some conditions, capable of something reasonably close to rational action, even if they rarely make use of this capability. So why the theory of unconscious nuggets for humans?

We might feel a justification for such an explanatory tactic if there are certain behaviors that *would* have been adaptive in the EEA but are *not* adaptive, or smart, or fun, in our current world, but are still done. So if, say, in the Pleistocene, humans tended to be bitten by rabid squirrels but never understood that this was why they got rabies and died, then any persons who, for whatever random reason, developed an instinctive hatred of squirrels and killed any they saw might be more likely to survive and pass down a set of genes coding this instinctive hatred. Now that we have nonrabid squirrels, there is no reason to fall into a murderous squirrelophobic rage, but if we all did, we might need to invoke this explanation.

The problem is that there don't seem to be any good candidates for this sort of holdover of currently irrational universal behavior patterns that would have been selected for in the long ago. Pretty much the same things that were good for Fred Flintstone and Barney Rubble are good for us. Something that scared them is likely to still be scary to us. (And just because most white Americans in the twenty-first century think or do something, or because the author himself does something, doesn't make it a universal feature of the *Homo sapiens* brain.) As a result, in sociology, evolutionary psychologists at best tend to accumulate a great mass of unimpressive findings, which (if they are not totally spurious) are more parsimoniously explained as goal-directed action, yet are held to be in support of the theory of evolutionary psychology, since this also predicts them.[22] Such are the problems with hypothetico-deductionism when it is not paired with some sense of attentiveness to alternative explanations. At worst, there are flagrant fabrications about what "we all" do that are tied to fantasies about the Pleistocene in support of which there is no evidence other than the fictional universals.

Yes, it really is that bad. But because I don't want people in my field crying too much, I'm going to use a widely cited work by a nonsociologist—David Buss's (1994) *Evolution of Desire*—as a key text.[23] Buss is an actual psychologist, though you wouldn't necessarily know it from this work, which doesn't touch on human cognition much. Instead, he focuses on the pure logic of selection. This gives us a chance to see the parallel in the evolutionary psychological arguments to those of the market-based rational choice theory.[24]

---

[22] For example, Horne (2004) attempted to pit what she called rational choice explanations against evolutionary psychological ones, but here she claimed that the former meant that men and women valued resources, while the latter meant that they valued rearing their young to maturity. Given that evolutionary psychologists *also* claim that we value resources (as a means of ensuring the survival of our young), and as an approximately rational type of fellow I can assure you that I consciously strongly value rearing my young to maturity, this seems a very implausible sort of adjudication.

[23] I admit that I can't bear to read much of this stuff, and so I'll just use this one. Feel free to send me efforts that you think are, finally, the good one that will force us skeptics to admit there's value here. And hang on, Texas Rangers fans! This could be your year!

[24] In some ways, Buss (1994: 12, 21, 50, 147) is somewhat less useful in this regard because he has somewhat strangely tried to mush the two theories together, trying to argue that these unconscious psychological mechanisms involve things like surveying our possibilities and calculating costs and benefits, and by postulating various Pleistocene markets.

The Formal Parallel in Selectionist Arguments

The mutual affinity of rational and genetic explanations is one of those lovely occurrences that keeps the classic sociology of knowledge alive and well. Two very different substantive arguments — indeed, we have seen that they are contradictory — are seized upon to make the same sorts of arguments by the same sorts of people using the same sorts of logic, often fallacious. Part of the appeal is the "answer for everything," part the normalization of the existent, but part seems also that common effect of our hall-of-mirrors whereby we have not sufficiently inverted our thought — we read into genes our (not necessarily correct) theory of ourselves, and then justify our theory of ourselves with the genes.

And part of the reason for the parallel may actually be a product of intellectual heritage connecting "Darwinism" and the competition of classical political economy. Darwin (1958: 120) himself contributed to this connection by writing that it was after reading Malthus's *Essay on Population* that he put his ideas together (involving the necessity of competition for survival). (Wallace also reported such an influence [Becker 1981: 136n1].) Darwin's notebooks, however, belie this simple sequence of events; furthermore, as Marx later caustically noted in a letter to Engels, the ideological corruption involved in this irresistible analogy lay in applying Malthus's reasoning to plants and animals, "as if the joke on Herr Malthus did not consist of the fact that he did *not* apply it to plants and animals, but only to human beings."[25]

Marx's comment — technically incorrect as it may be[26] — is helpful because it points out that the relation between Darwinism and classical political economy was a formal one. In this light, it is especially important to recall that Darwin's single contribution was not the importance of evolution per se (a tenet that was in some degree generally accepted during his day), but the claim that species originated via such evolution, and not, as might be thought, that evolution worked within existing species-boundaries; and, more important, the evidence to support his claim that the mechanism producing this evolution was natural selection. It is the centrality of this selective mechanism that leads to the formal correspondence with political economy. In both cases, a competition between structurally equivalent subunits (individuals, varieties, species, firms) leads to an unintended by-product that has certain advantages for *aggregates* of these subunits (species,

---

[25] The letter is quoted in Cohen (1985: 345); also see Marx (1968: 118ff). Note that Marx, like Engels, greatly respected Darwin for his clear thinking, his intellectual honesty, and his empiricism — and abhorred Malthus. Darwin was indeed a good guy, unusually so, but his weakness was to succumb to the temptations of false memory and to understate his debt to others and the degree to which these ideas were in the air, and to overstate his reliance on "Baconian" induction.

[26] Darwin did not claim that plants and animals do increase geometrically, but that *if all their progeny were to survive*, they would so increase. Darwin took for granted that this is unrealistic.

kingdom, nation). Most important, the emergence of the post facto valuable outcomes can then be "explained" by invoking the selective mechanism without actually observing the mechanism in effect.

Thus as selectionist theoretical structures, the two endeavors share certain formal characteristics. The core of both is largely the claim that somehow elements will be more likely to be replicated if they do something good than if not. Let's first imagine that we can rank units in terms of some quality metric, such as an organism's capacity to take advantage of resources and resist threats in its environment (which we'll call "fitness"), or a firm's capacity to meet the greatest effective demand of buyers with the least inputs (which we'll call "efficiency").[27] Second, let's imagine that we can summarize all the different qualities that might lead some unit to survive into the next round into what we'll call a "target variable." Although similar units can all go up or down together—that is, a sector of the economy can boom, a genus can diversify and grow—when the overall population is in numerical stasis, this becomes a positional characteristic: How much more likely is one unit to survive than another? Sometimes we can do a reasonable job at identifying something that correlates very highly with the target variable, such as "profit" in a free-market society; but we don't need to, because the idea of the target variable is tautological: it's *defined* as the probability of survival, so any nonrandom selective mechanism will tend to weed out those low on the target variable. Still, even when there is strong selection for higher values on a target variable, there might be no increase in average values over time, in the same way that you may walk on an escalator and get nowhere though you are constantly stepping up.

What makes these selectionist ideas so exciting is that sometimes we have good reason to think that there is a high correlation between the target variable and the quality metric: unfit varieties of an animal might have fewer grandchildren and become extinct, or less efficient firms might have less profit and get selected out. But this is not always the case. As we'll see, there are good reasons to think that phenotypes of low fitness (as defined here) can increase due to sexual selection, and firms of low efficiency can prosper if they can externalize their costs. In both cases, selection under one environment can lead to a pool of organisms poorly suited to cope in a new environment, and, as Nelson and Winter (1982: 160f) point out, that new environment can arise because of the success of that phenotype.

Given that the relation between selection and change in our quality metric *isn't* tautological (as is the relation between selection and change in the target variable), when do we accept that we can explain change in quality by recourse to a particu-

[27] You'll soon see why I'm using these terms a bit differently from the way evolutionary economists and biologists do.

lar selective mechanism? Usually when the following hold: (1) we are very confident that there is some nonrandom selective process; (2) the suggested mechanism (e.g., market competition, the struggle for existence) proposed for (1) is highly plausible and, to some extent, axiomatic; (3) we think a defensible position is that, at least for some stretches of time, the target variable of (2) is correlated with our quality metric; (4) we have ruled out most other possible mechanisms.

But this doesn't mean that one is on safe ground making a strong inference regarding any particular state or change (e.g., that it is as maximally adapted to its environment as it possibly could be). Not only may the environment change, such that the same structure can have different value in different environments, but these sorts of processes don't necessarily reach global maxima, even if they (theoretically) exist. If you start near the bottom of a mountain and always walk the direction of steepest ascent, you aren't guaranteed to end up on the peak. You can get stuck on a hill off to the side.

So there's no reason to believe that the unfit are *invariably* wiped out with dispatch; indeed, the degree of selectivity seems to vary dramatically across place, time, and unit for biological evolution. The fact that the time scale of change is quite long means that at any time, we may well be seeing a bunch of Keystone Kops who are terribly adapted to their environment, and hardly anything they do makes sense. It's just taking a long time for anything else to push its way into their niche.[28]

You might have noticed that this way of talking about selection is unusual; more commonly, at least in sociology, theorists begin by listing the assumptions that would make selection on the target variable the *same thing* as selection on the quality metric. That's all well and good, at least as a start, but sooner or later, since we know that these assumptions aren't always met, we're going to want to say something a bit smarter than tautology. Spencer might have been a nut, but he wasn't a fool, and when he coined the phrase, "survival of the fittest," he meant to say something beyond "those who have more grandchildren are likely to have more grandchildren." You might think it is presumptuous to declare that we can have independent criteria for fitness *other* than survival: Who are *we* to say whether having an enormous set of spikes on the end of one's tail is a good thing or a bad thing? But it seems implausible to claim that we can't distinguish between the fitness of a loping, flightless bird that lays a single egg every four years in the middle of a football field and that of something like an octopus. (You have a sharp beak? And you spit poison? And you can squeeze through a tiny hole? And you're smart? And blend in with your background? And squirt black ink? You're not an animal, you're a James Bond car!)

---

[28] Only a brilliant close observer like Jane Goodall (1986: 479) could suggest that much of the behavior of chimpanzees seemed to be of dubious survival value, and not merely because of recent changes due to humans. She thought they might have been in the midst of a slow crawl to a different set of behavioral responses when their own evolution was cut short and reoriented by our own growth.

Although one can say that animals in fairly isolated ecosystems are perfectly fit—just conditional on a very particular type of ecosystem—I think it's pretty much the same thing to say they're actually less fit; that is, there's a way that Mother Nature goes easy on such island animals, because there are only a few tough problems they can have (like, finding something on this rock you can live off of). The increased interaction coming from human travel didn't just change the environment (though it did) for the native animals—and turn their being fit-conditional-on-that-environment into being unfit-conditional-on-this-one—it often brought in new animals who were more fit in *target* (island) environment than the natives they were driving to extinction. According to the Invasive Species Specialist Group (ISSG), of the 100 most invasive species, only one animal came *from* Australia (the brushtail possum)—and the place it's invading is New Zealand.

I understand that this seems like Bart Simpson's ideas about Rock-Paper-Scissors: "Good old rock! Nothing beats rock! D'oh!" Sure, no strategy works everywhere. But that doesn't mean we can't separate strength from success. If we were to have species *A* and *B*, occupying a similar niche in environments *X* and *Y*, respectively, and we move half of *A* into *Y* and half of *B* into *X*, then find that *A* replaced *B* in both *X* and *Y*, it seems safe to say that *A* was (always) fitter than *B*. Reasoning the other way, animals that just had bad luck, like getting wiped out by a meteorite, shouldn't be counted as having "low fitness." We can define their environment to include falling meteorites, I suppose, but we need to distinguish between being scientific and being silly.

But even outside of shocking bad luck, we want to make sure we understand the difference between conditional and unconditional statements. "Fitness" is really "fitness-conditional-on-." We're probably best off saying: given reasonable environmental stability, fitness will correlate with the target variable of selective processes; but given rapid changes, with big die-offs, this relation might disappear. Of course, some aspects of the rapid change are interpretable (e.g., when it gets warmer, fur stops being a help and becomes a hindrance). But given that the survival of any species is dependent on the mix of other species, we can see a lot of chaos in the formation of new niches, such that it can be very difficult to assert what would constitute "fitness" a priori. Similarly, we want to make sure that we understand in economic life when fitness-type arguments are conditional on the assumptions of proper markets, so we don't conclude, for example, that Russian gangsters are the most efficient producers (after all, they were selected for, right?).

In sum, if the tautology was all there was to selective models, no one would care about them. Who cares if less profitable firms go under . . . if maximum profit stays the same (which it can in many models)? Who cares if some animals die out . . . if this doesn't help explain speciation and evolution? But where things get interesting, namely, where we switch to quality metrics, we can't fall back on tautology to defend our reasoning.

There is one additional formal problem: the axioms are such that the first extrapolation we make may be contradicted, and indeed, even *inverted*, by further application of the same axioms. This is why economic thought produced game theory — because when antagonists can make moves in response to other moves, as we have seen, our first guess may be wrong. You can surprise by being unsurprising. Further, as we saw in Chapter 1, it isn't always contradictory to begin with a simple set of ideas and use them as a platform to construct new ideas that contradict the initial ones. Thus not every contradiction that selectionist logic produces is a bad contradiction.

For example, market logic generally assumes that an increase in price will lead to a decrease in purchases, because the supply and demand curves intersect in a new place. But as Keynes (1935) argued, truly rational market participants stop caring about the goods themselves and only care about the second-order valuation of the goods. (Even if a tulip bulb is only worth $4.00 to me, if I know it is worth $8.00 to you, I am rational to buy it at $6.00 if I can, so long as no one else has one to sell to you first.) The trick in such a system is to do what everyone else does, just a teeny bit earlier. This means that an increase in price, rather than decreasing volume of purchases, can increase them by increasing demand.

Yes, things are inverted, but we know why and — most important — we have a way of determining whether our model holds. We can *ask* people why they are buying a bulb for $6.00.[29] But even more, we can observe *change*, which as we saw, can allow us, at least at times, to break out of the circle of tautology. Thus we have a possible lever to pry apart two similar cases: one in which our initial extrapolations from our axioms are disproved because there is a second layer of application, and a second in which our initial extrapolations from our axioms are disproved because our theory was wrong. Nothing like that is possible for evolutionary psychology in sociology.[30] And if it were, there's little evidence that anyone in this world is particularly interested in, say, building on the mathematical foundations that have been developed for genetic change (often based on economic models). The creation of the imaginary stories is too satisfying — too gosh darn easy — to give up. "Explanation" becomes reduced to a ritualized telling of a "just-so" story of origins, just like "how the elephant got his trunk," "how GM got its

---

[29] We can also compare decisions of different persons to see whether we are looking at a shift *along* a demand curve or a shift *of* a demand curve.

[30] It is possible with some animals, if experimentation is made by taking them out of their current and assumed to be stable ecological niche and putting them in a new one. I wouldn't be overly optimistic about the results, though. We'd be looking for what are basically failures, and failure is hard to interpret, because one failure can lead to another. With humans, one might think that we can ask, but remember, the whole glory of claiming unconscious psychological mechanisms is that your claims can never be disproved by what actors say.

institutional form,"[31] or, as in the biological examples we shall see, "how the peacock got his tail." If for any particular existent phenomenon, you can come up with one reason it is good and another reason it is bad, and you are willing to swear as the gospel truth whichever helps you make a case, you may have an excellent career ahead of you as an evolutionary psychologist.

Further, evolutionary psychologists have been extremely happy to explain with total confidence anything that seemed to go their way, without first dealing with the reality that their basic ideas were flagrantly contradicted by some of the most robust findings in social science. The fundament of evolutionary psychology is the assumption that long ago, people who lacked certain psychological mechanisms that led them to successfully rear children to the point of reproductive maturity would be weeded out. Those of us alive all have the mechanisms that, at least in Bedrock, were associated with reproductive success. Guess what really wouldn't be expected? Well, exclusive homosexuality for one. A desire not to have children would be another. And the fact that higher "status" people in our world have *fewer* children, not more. If *anything* shouldn't be here, it's these things, which we know there are plenty of. To keep on trying to explain why American women like firefighters ("in the Pleistocene, the risk of cave fires posed a serious threat to . . .") without grappling with the more obvious and important disconfirmations is—or at least should be—well, I suppose the nice way of putting it would be "penny wise and pound foolish." A less nice way would be to call it anti-scientific. And grappling with these disconfirmations doesn't mean telling yarns of vague possibility ("maybe exclusive homosexuals helped raise their sister's children . . .") with the same degree of support as "if we had some ham, we could all have ham sandwiches, that is, assuming we get some bread, too." That's the form of a Tweedle argument, we recall.

Conscious or Unconscious

I noted that there was a strong *formal* identity between evolutionary psychological and rational choice explanations. Yet in *substantive* terms, the two strongly contradict one another. As we've seen, the evolutionary psychological arguments

[31] This is what we see in the "Transaction Cost Economics" of Oliver Williamson. Williamson (1985) built on what is called Coase's theorem, which states that even economic action that leads to unhappy results for others will lead to efficient allocation if there are no transactions costs. Coase's theorem was understood by many to have an unfalsifiable nature; to adapt a quip from James Quirk (attributed by Davis [1986: 149]), Coase's theorem may be said to be simply that "something will always be found to make Coase's theorem true." Williamson went even further toward unfalsifiability, arguing that transaction costs determined when decisions would be placed in a firm as opposed to in a market—in a nutshell, this would happen under the conditions of asset specificity, bounded rationality, and opportunism. But given that there was no metric for any of these, they could be set to explain the outcome in any particular case and could be adjusted if something "turned out" not to be what it initially appeared. It isn't that Williamson was wrong, but that if he were, we might never know.

must have unconscious psychological mechanisms as their crucial explanatory factor. For this reason, evolutionary psychologists like to retell things as if they were vague hints or "cues" to something that the dim organism cannot directly grasp given its impoverished mentality. Thus Buss (1994: 196) speaks of "Men's value in supplying resources, indicated by *cues* such as income and social status." Income is no more a "cue" of resources than a rap on the head is a cue of a forthcoming rap on the head. Often the idea that only unconscious psychological mechanisms can explain behavior is wonderfully hilarious, such as Buss's crucial evidence of the universal preference of women to have mates who are healthy, and that one study found — of all things — that women considered venereal disease an "extremely undesirable characteristic" in a mate (41).[32] Similarly, Kanazawa (2001: 1138) insists that his finding with Still (1999) of an association of polygamy with resource inequality among men requires that women have a psychological mechanism for just this. They couldn't, say, simply prefer wealth *themselves*. Only by assuming what is to be proven — that the actors are actually not rational enough to find their way out of a paper bag and basically need to leave this up to their genes — could this be taken as evidence of Pleistocene mentality as opposed to 1999 mentality.

Strangely, though, despite the contradiction between the psychological mechanisms and the rational choice arguments, the two quickly make an alliance similar to that between Ribbentrop and Molotov in 1939 — when fertile plains are undefended, we've got to grab while the grabbing is good. Thus evolutionary psychologists like Buss (1994: 180) are not only happy to add "costs" to statements to make them seem more scientific, but in fact to propose rational choice *itself* as a psychological mechanism. I am not making this up. "Humans have evolved psychological mechanisms that consider and weight the costs and benefits of these crucial features of context" (Buss 1994: 15, 209). Unless the unconscious mechanism has its own consciousness to do all this, one that we don't know about, that psychological mechanism is us. That is, our consciousness is an unconscious psychological mechanism.[33]

---

[32] Again, "Pimples, ringworm, facial disfigurement, and filthiness are universally repugnant. Cleanliness and freedom from disease are universally attractive" (1994: 53). Unfortunately, Buss forgot that there is actually no reason to think that pimples decrease one's capacity to bear and rear a child to adulthood. Or was it evolution that made this mistake?

[33] Similarly, Kanazawa (2004) says that our general intelligence, which unlike psychological mechanisms is a flexible and open-ended form of cognitive processing, is *itself* a psychological mechanism that arose to deal with situations that we don't have psychological mechanisms for (note the "not outside, but bigger" move). According to him, these days, that's basically all of them. Fortunately for him, Kanazawa doesn't accept his own logic, or he would conclude that everything else he has written is wrong for assuming the opposite (that our action now *is* guided by psychological mechanisms). I imagine evolutionary psychologists with a psychological mechanism for logical consistency were eaten by tigers in the Pleistocene. Perish or publish, we might say.

And thus, in many cases, the "evolutionary psychology" part of the explanation simply turns into a hand waving, announcing that this or that is of evolutionary importance, that we are all evolved, or what have you. To say "In evolutionary terms, fulfilling the preferences held by a mate, or providing that mate with the sorts of resources he or she initially sought, should be a highly effective method of preserving the relationship" (Buss 1994: 131) is formally identical to statements such as "In evolutionary terms, taking a subway clearly labeled with the name of one's destination, should be a highly effective method of getting where you want to go." Yes, it is that bad. The question then must be, "What have we done to deserve this?" And the answer is, I think, that we have made mistakes that let in not only such obviously pathological theorizing, but more subtle difficulties—ones that allow the false and the true to slip by together.

Sexual and Natural Selection

One can't help notice that an inordinate number of the contributions to ecological psychology turn on issues of mate preference. I confess that it is hard to banish the thought that to some extent, in sociology, this is because the sorts of people who are attracted to just-so stories are attempting to maximize the ratio of the attention they get to the work they put in, and so sex (SEX!) is a good choice. But this substantive focus also characterizes much of the serious work in animal behavior, and, most important, some of the less heinous work in anthropology. Why is this?

I think to some extent it is because one of the marks of the ideological or fundamentalist selectionist is that she or he refuses to acknowledge any principles for selection other than fitness, since only this can truly promise to wrap one in a warm and comforting cocoon of tautology. Yet Darwin himself emphasized that in addition to natural selection there could be sexual selection, whereby some animals are disproportionally chosen as mates, regardless of the survival chances of their offspring. He emphasized the *difference* between sexual and natural selection (though recognizing that in many cases they might be impossible to differentiate), arguing that the former could work against the latter, by producing, for example, stags with antlers so cumbersome that they interfered with running.[34] In the terms used above, this leads to a divorce of the target variable from fitness. One reason Darwin felt that sexual selection had to be understood as a mechanism distinct from natural selection is that it is inherently problematic to propose that fitness explains secondary sex characteristics: if males differ from females by, say, having characteristic X, then X cannot be important for survival since the

[34] "From this fact we learn that the advantages which favored males derived from conquering other males in battle or courtship, and thus leaving a numerous progeny, are in the long run greater than those derived from rather more perfect adaptation to their conditions of life" (Darwin 1896 [1874]: 227). Hence there is no need to come up with natural selection–type explanations for why antlers are so great.

females seem to get along without it fine (also see Russet 1989: 79). But accepting this distinction sticks in the craw of the Panglossian vision; further, because it does not increase fitness, it can only be answered by detailed close analysis—no storytelling is possible.

The classic example has been the peacock's tail. Male peacocks have long tails with very freaky feathers. Peahens don't, and no one can find anything particularly useful about the big tails. Darwin's (1896 [1874]: 236) explanation is that there is something about these tails that just turns females on, and so males who have the flashiest tails were most likely to leave descendants. This is an altogether reasonable idea—the female has *some* principles for deciding who is a nice-looking male peacock, but like any set of rules, they can be gamed ("You like iridescent blue? I'll grow an iridescent blue *billboard* out of my butt!").[35]

Thus when you look at bird courtship rituals, you can't help but notice a lot of pretty tasteless strutting among the birds, which makes a Saturday night at Studio 54 in 1977 look in comparison like a University of Chicago study group.[36] But the normalizing mind isn't willing to accept the fact that males can do something stupid just to score, and so this is where the pathological theorizing kicks into gear, and pulls out a Tweedle.

And in fact, we see a perfect replication of the idea we saw before for humans, that a disutility can be turned into a utility. This was famously done by Amotz Zahavi (1975) in arguing that such plumage is a "handicap factor" for the male. That is, a male who can survive despite hauling around a mop of feathers shows how extremely fit he is. The very disutility is the utility; hence absolutely any outcome can be explained neatly.[37] Again, if you think "brilliant!" you have a fine career ahead of yourself as a pathological theorist. Because if this is accepted, unless there is independent evidence of when a handicap principle is actually employed, the system is unchallengeable. If females don't like males with parasites (as seems often to be the case), we can argue that this is because it is a "cue" for his (low) fitness. But if we find she actually prefers males who are tormented by multiple parasites, we now switch 180 degrees and say that the very survival of these males to the age of mating was a good sign that they had the "genetic quality" to resist parasites, and therefore pass on to their offspring a better chance for survival than the happy-go-lucky peafowl of unruffled plumage. When we have a theory that can

[35] In fact, more recent research has failed to confirm the original findings that (1) females selected males who had more eyespots; (2) that this correlated with their weight and (3) with their offspring's weight. See Takahashi et al. (2008). They just don't like males who have really ratty tails.

[36] Further, the word "ritual" is often misapplied; as for many birds, there is no particular ritualization to their actions—they just pogo up and down, shake anything they can, positively screaming "look at me look at me look at me!"

[37] As Immanuel Kant wrote (1987 [1790]: 259), one can find purposes even in the worst parts of nature—for example, we may say that lice are good because they force us to keep ourselves clean. These explanations, he noted, "provide an entertaining and sometimes also instructive outlook into the teleological order of things."

equally explain + and – findings, we are clearly inside the realm of Tweedle explanations, in which the only response is, if it were so, then it would be.

Further, as Darwin understood, fitness-based explanations should be at least mentally tested by looking for variation. Some birds pair bond while others are polygamous. Why does the handicap logic seem to work best for polygamous birds? How come pair bonders tend to look alike?[38] The trick here is not to come up with "an" explanation (pretty much any person with a few functioning neurons will be able to do this), but to come up with one for which there is independent evidence. This is not what our evolutionary psychologists have wanted to do.

In sum, we see that the problem isn't that there is anything intrinsically wrong with evolutionary arguments for behavior, even those that, for the purposes of simplification, assume a modularity to certain forms of behavior (e.g., we imagine for the sake of simplification that there is an "infanticide" module that can be selected for). But there is all the difference in the world between the statements "infanticide may be selected for because infanticide *does* increase the fitness of langurs *now* (visibly, measurably)" and "liking men with square chins was selected for because square chins *could have* been related to fitness *once* (imaginably, conceivably)."

The second (but not the first) allows for the complete development of a closed system of fanaticism in which anything can be explained, because things can become their opposites. Unconscious mechanisms can include rational action. Deficits can become pluses. This is the characteristic of all pathological science; as Freud himself understood, his own pathological system struck others as a suspiciously convenient, "heads I win, tails you lose" system, given that he felt free to count both evidence and the *absence* of evidence as proof of his claims.

Interestingly, this point was made quite clearly by the founder of sociobiology, E. O. Wilson, the great animal scientist (which is not to say he was immune to error). In fact, in his magnificent book *Sociobiology* he warned (1975: 27–31) specifically about these sorts of errors, where unfalsifiable claims that assumed what was to be proven were established through rhetoric, leading to insulated schools of thought that preach to the converted.

CONCLUSION

It seems that evolutionary psychology, of the Panglossian and pathological variety, is also slated to go down the tubes, and by the time this book is out, this may

[38] If you say because sexual selection is stronger for the polygamous (as it is), aren't you assuming what you set out to disprove—namely, that sexual selection is different from natural selection? There are, as Darwin himself (1896 [1874]) noted, pair bonders with divergent appearance (e.g., ducks), and we cannot rule out Roughgarden's (2010) suggestion that this might actually represent *natural* selection, as females might have a greater need to be inconspicuous during brooding.

seem like beating a dead horse. However, the chances are very good that something else will arise to replace it. Be on the lookout for a theoretical program that is extremely attractive to loudmouth types, that has an answer for everything, that makes arbitrary statements about subjectivity, that puts the imperative of selling books above all else, and that has a fundamentally selectionist logic at its heart with no firm measures of the quality variable. What will this be? My guess is that it would involve something about neural networks. I don't know why someone hasn't started this bandwagon rolling yet — but it may take a different guise.

We can be prepared for it. Selection is probably an indication, but selectionism is not in itself problematic, and certainly not wrong. More important is a theorized refusal to listen. Almost all forms of pathological theory in the human sciences have the researcher imputing subjectivity to actors without caring what the actors themselves say. Sure, you can come up with justifications for this, but the simple fact is, if you don't constrain yourself, you can basically say anything you want. Just like you wouldn't have a theory of geology that didn't care what rock samples were like, you can't have a theory of action that doesn't care what people say — one that tells them that they are "repressing" the truth, that they don't know the true psychological mechanisms driving their action, or that their preferences are only whatever makes your model fit.

The nice thing about the rational choice debate was that for a while, it looked as though people might actually try to resolve things by learning how people *did* think — and in some fields in psychology and decision theory, this did happen, and work continues. We may have dropped our interest because it *doesn't* allow for the formulation of arbitrary statements that can be marked "true." And perhaps, that's what we want. Certainly we didn't see a lot of interest among sociological evolutionary psychologists in what animal scientists had been learning about animal behavior. In fact, I think if they did, they could come up with some pretty interesting directions for theorizing. And that's where we'll go in the next chapter.

CHAPTER 5

What Does the Sociology of Animals Teach Us?

FEAR OF ANIMALS

Return to the Planet of the Apes

In the first chapter, I suggested that it might be more possible than we generally think to "invert" our knowledge by paying attention to how we tend to want to think, and then to question our assumptions. One way to do that might be to examine how we think about animal social behavior. The point isn't that in one arena (studying humans) we have prejudices and in the other (studying animals) we don't, it's that the shift to a new arena can help us generate insights that might be difficult for us to do at home. "What is it like to be a bat?" asked Thomas Nagel (1979). His answer was (eventually) that we will never know. But the reason to think about it, it seems to me, is that it can help us know what it is like to be a human.[1]

Now sociologists are rightly extremely suspicious of any attempt to learn general principles from the observation of nonhuman animals. This is, I think, for two reasons. The first is that it comes as no surprise to find that animals are extremely different from one another. Comparing humans to wolves gives us different lessons from the ones we produce if we compare humans to bees, and so on. Because of this variation, for a while some sociologists thought that we had to compare ourselves to our "closest" relatives based on current evolutionary theories, but this turned out to be largely incoherent. Although there are certainly *some* things that close relatives share, there are many, many, examples of closely related species that have antithetical social organization and behavior: hamadryas baboons have different social principles from savannah baboons, brown hyenas from spotted hyenas, and so on. On the other hand, we see similar principles of organization and action among very different species (hyenas and old-world monkeys share a great deal of social organization). The recognition of

[1] Here I would like to acknowledge the influence of discussions with Laurie Kauffman, who remains blameless for any errors I make herein.

the bonobo as a different species from the common chimpanzee perhaps permanently threw a wrench in the "planet of the apes" type analyses—both the bonobo and the chimpanzee are equally closely related to humans, and the two are rather different in habitus and social behavior. We would derive very different lessons for humans depending on whether we studied the bonobo or the chimpanzee.[2]

But even if an unambiguous "nearest neighbor" could be found, that has basically zero implications for human beings. Responding to those who argued that monogamy was not actually fundamental to humans since it was not seen in the other apes, Friedrich Engels (1942 [1891]: 29f) remarked, that's why *they're* still animals! It isn't at all a stupid thing to say. Speciation implies differentiation.

And it gets worse for the monkey modelers, because one of the big revolutions in animals studies over the late twentieth century was the realization of the great *variability* across times and places. Previously, each researcher assumed that all the members of a species were interchangeable, and while a few admitted that laboratory or zoo conditions could not be simply generalized to the wild, almost everyone assumed that one wild bunch was the same as any other.

But different groups are different. The eastern chimpanzees studied by Jane Goodall perpetrated fatal gang attacks on other chimpanzees, but the western ones studied by Boesch and others for twenty years never did anything like this (Perry 2008: 217; also Strum 1987: 73). Such variation doesn't always signal an end to the project of producing general knowledge, for it can be linked to other types of variation—most important, environmental. For example, studies of primates have pointed to the importance of density: where population density is high, there seems to be more conflict, and more change in ranking and leadership (Hrdy 1977: 274). Similarly, sex ratios can also greatly affect the degree of conflict in a group (see Zuckerman 1981 [1932]: 220). These population parameters may vary predictably with environmental factors, most obviously, concentration of resources (see, e.g., Moss 1988: 211 on elephants).

So groups differ, in part, by where they are. Further, even the same group can seem very different at different times. As Susan Perry (2008: 168) wrote, "One of the most important lessons I have learned in the past fifteen years about studying primate behavioral ecology is that if you want to have a simple story about what the animals are doing, you shouldn't study them for very long!"

---

[2] The idea that we are the "third species" of chimpanzee strikes me as almost completely irrelevant to our understanding of humans (and it seems to rely on what is certainly a common overestimation of the genetic overlap between human and chimpanzee that came from an earlier, incorrect assumption about the irrelevance of the repetition of certain stretches of genetic code). If we are simply one species of chimpanzee, we remain the only species of chimpanzee on whom it hath pleased the Almighty God to bestow an immortal soul.

Finally, a single individual can make a difference. Certainly, a group's overall relational "feel" can be changed by the style of a dominant animal, especially an alpha male (the highest ranking) in certain primate groups. But others can radically change how a group appears. In one case observed by Strum (1987: 129ff), the injury of a dominant baboon who had previously monopolized all hunting opportunities opened space for a younger—and possibly more creative—one who had always had an interest in meat. As our little hero came into his own, others came to join in, and the group developed a pincher type movement in which they converged on a victim. Further, the baboons began to *share* the kill, which is something they almost never do with food. They ended up displaying much more of what we consider a chimpanzee pattern.

An observer who had seen the troop earlier would have concluded that baboons are foragers and occasional opportunistic hunters but that the hunting was of minimal importance. One who watched during the later period might see baboons as being like chimpanzees. And, importantly, this behavior faded over time as new individuals came into the troop. This wasn't a step forward in evolution, it was just evidence of some monkeys being one way as opposed to another of the many ways they could be.

You might think I've beaten this into the ground, but in the Conclusion, we'll be able to draw on these lessons for improving our own theorizing. But for now, we also get a specific lesson for how to use animals in our thinking. When we recognize the degree of possible variability in behavior patterns, we realize that we are lost if we try to make "point estimates" as to what certain species are like, let alone use that to learn what *we* are like.

Anthropomorphizing and Anthropomondizing

But even when there are no deliberate attempts to draw parallels, our inability to sever our world from that of the animals can lead to distortions (and now we get to my second reason). This is because we see ourselves in the animals, reading into them the lessons we are supposedly drawing out. We often imagine that this is a problem of anthropomorphizing, but it is deeper and more subtle than that: we do not see animals as humans so much as we see them as instantiations of our own theories.

In the earlier days, some of this was just an assumption that "normal" animals were nice and functional and well behaved. When monkeys did things that didn't fit, like have group sex or same-sex contact, or eat each other's babies, it was dismissed as a pathology peculiar to the circumstances (Zuckerman 1981 [1932]: 390). Why ignore evidence? We have to understand that at the time, many in the behavioral sciences were attempting to wrest the study of human action away from the cultural sciences by claiming continuity with animal behavior.

That meant one had to be very choosy about one's neighbors. They tended to see animals as extremely human, in order to see *us* as relatively "animal."

The prime example here was sexology, the attempt to have a scientific attitude toward sex; this could be morally unobjectionable to nineteenth-century minds only if sex in nature was itself moral. So the argument involved emphasizing a chain-of-mental-being connecting all animals, as well as humanizing the animals. Hence August Forel (1929 [1906]: 107, 108, 145, 184, 194f; cf. Kinsey et al. 1948: 677), one of the first sexologists, argued, "The psychology of the higher apes is thus nearer our own than that of a dog. The psychology of the dog resembles ours more than that of the rabbit," and hence it was, he believed, not surprising that we find monogamous marriage among apes, and among some animals such as monkeys and parrots, a greater intensity of the "sentiments of sympathy and duty, as well as in love and conjugal fidelity," than possessed by most men. We put into the animals the lesson for humans that we want to draw out.

As a result, animals often do not help us resolve our debates about human nature—they rather exacerbate the differences. As the (English) philosopher Bertrand Russell (1995 [1927]: 23) wonderfully said, "One may say broadly that all the animals that have been carefully observed have behaved so as to confirm the philosophy in which the observer believed before his observations began. Nay, more, they have all displayed the national characteristics of the observers. Animals observed by the Americans rush about frantically, with an incredible display of bustle and pep, and at last achieve the desired result by chance. Animals observed by the Germans sit still and think and at last evolve the solution out of their inner consciousness."

There is a further distortion when we observe animals, which I will call "anthropomondizing." This is when we assume that the animals inhabit the same sort of world—that is, to use the language of Chapter 3, the same sort of phenomenal world—that we do. In particular, we are vision-oriented. In an open environment, we humans see things from farther away than we can hear or smell them. To us, when we see something that is far away, we believe that it is "there" in a way that wouldn't be the case if we were blind and deaf but smelled something that seemed 100 feet away. If we were relying on smell, we might think "I smell that something *was* once somewhere around here," but not that it still *is* "where" we smell it, because we think of light as instantaneous and air currents and dispersion as slow, and we're right.

But for many animals, their sight is relatively poor, and their hearing and smell are acute. Just like we don't think we were "wrong" if we see someone far away, but by the time we walk over, he's gone, so animals (maybe) don't feel wrong if they smell a trail but the source can't be located. They are probably "sensing" those things—your dog might well be "seeing" a squirrel through scent in a way somewhat more similar to how you see it through your eyes than we can understand. What is key is that you commit yourself to acting in a way that takes the existence of the squirrel into account. Both of you can be wrong — your eyes can fool you, the dog's nose can fool her. For animals in water, on the other hand, smell is slow and sight is really good only for nearby things. Light disappears quickly. But sound travels much better than in air. And so on. This affects who animals think are "near them," and hence can be vital for issues of social organization or for transmission of information.

Beyond this, we grow more speculative, but the work on honeybee spatial maps suggests that in their waggle dance, bees communicate not distance as we understand it, but *effort* (Wilson 1971: 265; we'll return to this example below). Given that bees are primarily oriented to air travel for long distances, it is quite reasonable that they understand space in terms of effort, at least to the extent that they "understand" at all, and this may be a common characteristic of many animals that lack long-distance sight. Cold-blooded animals may not have anything like our sense of time. They might well have two different time senses, an internal one (heat-time that, to us, changes with temperature), and an external one (light-time, that doesn't).[3]

We make errors in interpreting animal behavior, then, when we assume that they are primarily oriented to visual information, and more generally, that they live in the sort of experiential world that we do, not just when we imagine that their minds are like ours. If their worlds were like ours, their minds would indeed be a lot like ours; they'd *have* to be, for a mind is what you use to deal with a particular kind of world.

In sum, we need to make sure that our interpretations of animal behavior do justice to the world the animals are in. This will be especially important because, as we shall see, there is good reason to think that one thing we learn about action from animal studies is just that we need to incorporate the "worldliness" of behavior in our accounts. Of course, our interpretation of their worlds will still involve a lot of impressionistic guesswork and is certain to be wrong in some respects, but it is probably not quite as wrong as a simple assumption that they live in *our* world.

Tools, Not Models

Given these problems to studying animals as models for human social analysis, why suggest learning from animal studies? I will argue that the conceptual tools developed for the examination of animals, where we are forced to rely more on observation and less on our folk theories (also known as prejudices) about social

[3] Many reptiles can warm themselves up by simply moving; other creatures' time-senses might be more responsive to changes in external temperature.

life, may prove enlightening and perhaps useful for the study of social life in humans. That is, we do not take the *substance* of any particular species' social arrangements as a template for how we understand humans, but rather look for robust lessons — conclusions to which we are forced when we try to account for a wide range of behavior.

To do this, we would need to focus our attention on nondomesticated animals. The distinction between "wild" and "domesticated," like many important distinctions, is not an incredibly easy one to make in all circumstances — many nondomesticated animals have close, often necessary, interactions with humans and / or may have behavioral profiles that change dramatically when they are near human settlements. As Hrdy (1977: 61, 159) said regarding the langurs she studied (they're monkeys in India), they have been fed around temples and other human areas for many centuries, probably thousands of years. Do we consider them contaminated for analytic purposes by their human contact?

We need to imagine a continuum: on one end are some animals that can't really get along very well near humans, next to them are those that vary in degree of flexibility — some don't really mind if we are nearby so long as we don't kill them (e.g., rabbits); some can survive near us if they totally reorient (i.e., change from mostly predators to wholly scavengers); then there are those that seem to have already proved able to reorient so as to take advantage of our own built environment and food sources (e.g., rats and pigeons), such animals find many useful things near human society and hang around and have probably changed over the years accordingly; and at an extreme are those that have been long-term targets of artificial selection (e.g., cattle and dogs).

We cannot restrict our attention to only animals untouched by humans. But we can make some adjustments for *how* touched they are. We can exclude those at the far end of the continuum (pet and food animals, which tend toward neoteny) and we can make likely guesses as to the results of human contact, because there are regularities in how this contact shapes animal behavior. One of the things that humans do is concentrate good stuff. In sociology, we study this in terms of inequality, but to animals, it's a buffet. We make so much yummy fat, protein, and carbohydrates that we throw it away, and a clever animal can get more nutrition in a half hour in a dump than it could in ten hours of foraging. This, however, tends to lead to new behavior patterns. This was importantly realized by the great Jane Goodall (and her critics). To study chimpanzees in the wild, not in a zoo setting, she tried to make things a bit easier by luring them to hang out near her by provisioning them with bananas — and it is not a cartoon myth: chimpanzees really like bananas. But after a few years, as her understanding deepened, she saw that making bananas available led to new patterns of social interaction. Most important, there was more aggression, as there were more winner-take-all goods. But there was also a convergence of baboons and chimps in the same area, which led to a great increase in chimpanzee predation on baboon babies. (Perhaps they go well with bananas!) And finally, the general intensity of social life was just turned up a few notches. She noticed that whenever more bananas were given to apes who had been quietly resting, they would display a sudden burst of sexual activity (Goodall 1986: 52, 281, 450).

This is a general tendency: for animals with flexible foraging patterns, human settlements usually provoke a shift from what is called "scramble competition" to "contest competition." In the first, each animal goes off to gather food independently, as it is wasteful to attempt to take from someone else rather than getting your own—think of Rousseau's state of nature. The second is a zero-sum world where fighting is worthwhile to monopolize resources—Hobbes's vision. It's the concentration of good things that humans produce that has these indirect effects on social behavior. Population density goes up, group sizes often increase, the amount of social time increases, and so on. These aren't necessarily "unnatural" behaviors—they may be what would have been seen in a good rainy season in the absence of humans—but they are present for longer times and lead to different strategies being favored. Since we anticipate this effect of humans, we can bear in mind that we are often seeing one section of a distribution of possible behaviors, probably a more intense, and tense, one.

Some human contact, then, isn't deadly to our goals, but full-blown domestication is. There is a sense in which domesticated animals aren't animals at all—they're more like products (see Shepard 1996). Certainly normally wild animals raised in human households are very different from their wild conspecifics, and this is especially true of smart primates. And animals that are too intertwined with humans, even if they're not wholly domesticated, also have special characteristics. This is true even if we believe the animals domesticated *themselves* (and the domestication wasn't a brilliant plan of human beings).

Because no matter where one puts the agency, for animals to truly live with humans, they must lose certain instincts and move in a particular direction in the space of all possible ways-of-being. That in itself isn't unusual; species that become specialist parasites also move in a general direction as they become dependent on their hosts. It isn't simply that domesticated animals move in a particular "direction" in the space of all possible ways-of-being that is so worrisome, it's that this direction is related to our own understandings of the world. In general, sociologists might construct groups to investigate certain processes, but they're not allowed to construct groups of a certain type and then make conclusions about what groups in general "are like." With domesticated animals, we're basically making our theories about animals on animals we made. This will lead not only to bias but also to our ignoring some of the differences that we might be looking at animals to learn about. So we need to look at animals a bit farther from home than our house pets. Testing your theories on your dog is like testing them by interviewing yourself.

Now I do not pretend to be a Doctor Dolittle. However, the past thirty years have seen an explosion of work in animal sciences, including what was once called animal sociology—the examination of the social behavior and social intelligence of animals. Further, the quality of this work is extremely high. The long-overdue death of ideological behaviorism led to an increased verisimilitude of models of animals, as well as more in-the-wild studies. However, the growth of the field has reintroduced the rigor and, frankly, the skepticism that characterized some of the behaviorist work at its best, and which did not generally seem so important to the gorilla guerillas attempting to undermine behaviorism in the mid-twentieth century. Now, we're in a better position to get the best of both these traditions.

In many cases, animal sociology turns out to be amenable to the use of theoretical tools that are familiar to sociologists. But this isn't about applying sociology to animals, satisfying and reassuring though this is for those of us who might doubt that we've made any real scientific contributions. Instead, I discuss some recurrent lessons that I believe are coming to the attention of animal sociologists and that are generative of potential insights when it comes to human behavior.

WHERE IS COMPLEXITY AND INTELLIGENCE?

Flexible Worms

For years, animal scientists looked for intelligence in animals, hoping that we could determine that some did, and some did not, share that divine reason that God gave us when He made us in His image. Some scientists really hoped to find it, and may have seen something that was not there; others were sure that it wasn't there and so they ignored what didn't fit their preconceptions, or arranged for situations in which no animal could display much in the way of smarts. But the biggest problems came because "intelligence" is an ambiguous concept, often meaning "what I like about myself."

Who's to say who's smart? This has been a serious issue for animal researchers. For some time, they had judged many foraging species as being pretty stupid because the subjects couldn't always learn to choose the rewarded option in a test. Yet when people began investigating their behavior in the wild, they found that many seem to be downright brilliant, keeping track of where different plants are in the bloom-fruit cycle. Many researchers now think that for a forager never to return to a place just because there wasn't anything there when it came before would be pretty stupid. Things change. Refusing to "learn" not to approach a nonrewarded option was actually the better choice. Other animals are downright curious. And sometimes being curious means wanting to see if anything is in the empty box *now*. Finally, still other species, like the octopus, don't bother learning, say, how to open a jar—with eight arms, they just mess around with things and can trust that they'll open it each time pretty damn quick. Overlearning wouldn't be smart in any of these cases, but that's how *we* define intelligence; we assume that it's the sort of thing that would lead animals to get good grades in animal school. In other words, we tend to confuse tractability with intelligence.

But what would be a substitute for school-smarts, given that almost all animals are dropouts? *Flexibility* seems to be a clearer criterion. As we'll see, it turns out that animals in general are often more flexible than we would imagine. Still, it varies, and flexibility does go along with what we usually see as increased intelligence—which means that structure is for idiots. And that's the lesson for sociology.

Charles Darwin was probably a reasonably brilliant man, but his great breakthrough, as I mentioned in Chapter 4, was not to propose a theory of evolution nor even to emphasize the struggle for existence and its role in speciation (his grandfather Erasmus noted these) (King-Hele 1999). His contribution was his careful, repeated observation—unlike the florid poetry Erasmus used to describe his ideas. And this careful observation meant that Charles Darwin was able to find evidence that escaped others, including evidence of animal intelligence. Further, Darwin was (somewhat surprising to many of us, given the high correlation between mental rigidity and ritualistic citations to his name in our time) a profoundly creative and nondogmatic thinker—a truly open mind. I want to consider one of his later works—his examination of earthworms—that shows what a combination of open-mindedness and careful observation can accomplish (even though some of his conclusions seem to have been wrong).

Convinced that worms played an important role in the turning-over of earth, and hence the regeneration of plant life, in Europe, Darwin (1976 [1881]) set out to learn as much as he could about them. He writes, "Worms do not possess any sense of hearing. They took not the least notice of the shrill notes from a metal whistle, which was repeatedly sounded near them, nor did they of the deepest and loudest tones of a bassoon. They were indifferent to shouts, if care was taken that breath did not strike them. When placed on a table close to the keys of a piano, which was played as loudly as possible, they remained perfectly quiet." One has to love the idea of Darwin first bellowing at them, while watching them carefully, then moving the worms to the parlor, and having his wife (who was actually trained by Chopin) pound on the piano to see if the worms would move.

More to the point, Darwin knew from the literature that worms made burrows and that they dragged leaves into their burrows, for the purpose, it was assumed, of speeding up the process of decay. Never one to accept another's word, Darwin (1976 [1881]: 34, 45, 47) watched leaves decay under controlled conditions, with and without worm juice, rejected this explanation, and decided to study in greater detail how the worms brought the leaves in, putting out leaves to see how they were arranged the next morning. Of the 227 leaves, 181 were drawn into the burrows by the tips, which makes sense, as it is easier to get the narrow end into a hole first. So he then put out rhododendron leaves, which are narrower at the base than the apex, to see if the worms reorient or always grab the same part. Darwin found that two-thirds were drawn in through the base, which the worms usually avoid. "In this case, therefore, the worms judged with a considerable degree of correctness how best to draw the withered leaves of this foreign plant into their burrows; notwithstanding that they had to depart from their usual habit of avoiding the footstalk."

Now if you are a skeptical scientist, you would—and should—protest to Darwin that he was *assuming* intelligence, when it could be that trial and error with differential rates of success could lead to these results. Without seeing the *failures*, we don't know whether the worms have any idea of what they're doing; perhaps they just grab, and fail, and fail, and fail, and succeed.

So Darwin did more—he stayed up at night with a lantern, to watch exactly what the worms were doing. And he writes, at least when it comes to pine needles, many worms behave *differently* when they grab it by the foot. They seem to know that they have it the right way. Darwin (1976 [1881]: 49f) even did *in situ* experiments—tying pine needles together to see if the worms are just as likely to grab by the tip (which would now be successful, as the needles won't open up) as the base, and finds they still prefer the base.

What Darwin found was a kind of limited flexibility—he called it intelligence—among the earthworms to adjust their behavior to the environment. This sort of limited flexibility is characteristic of most animals—there is a range of situations that they can respond to; circumstances outside this can paralyze them, lead them to useless actions, or reveal their *lack* of intelligence in other ways. We tend to think of a vertical hierarchy of intelligence (us on top; worms way, way below). But rather than rank in terms of *height*, we should probably rank in terms of *breadth*: What is the range of activities for which an animal can respond flexibly to upset?

When we focus on breadth of flexibility as what we really mean by intelligence, we might then conclude that repetition, clarity, and structure are signs of a *lack* of intelligence, not a high degree of it. We have assumed that when animals are stupid, they wander around aimlessly, and that smart animals would (like Babar the elephant) make an orderly life for themselves. It may be the exact opposite. Not all insects have the sort of orderly life of the bees and ants (and indeed, many ants and wasps lack these social orders themselves). But the clear organization of such societies (to which we return below) certainly does not come because these animals are unusually flexible.

Structure and Anti-Structure

Let's consider mammals and first primates. A common form of primate organization is what is called the "fission-fusion" society; this is, a band that is decomposable into smaller units that go off to forage, either daily or when food is scarce, and reunite at times, often exchanging members (most frequently maturing young adults of one sex or the other). This grouping is seen most impressively in baboons such as the hamadryas which have multiple nested layers of organization (see Kummer 1968: 153; also 1995: 110; for Gelada, see Dunbar 1984: 17ff). But gorillas also seem to split into subgroupings, at least from large groupings with more than one silverback (Schaller 1963: 111) into one-silverback units; chimpanzees have such an organization but appear the most flexible of the apes, for anyone can come or go (if part of the club) and some go off on their own, sometimes for days at a time (Goodall 1986: 147).

Now let's turn to dolphins, which also have fission-fusion societies. In general, dolphins have proven tough for us to think about. Monkeys have hands and the sorts of eyes we have, and so they *look* as if they should be very much like us. They use implements the same way we do — it isn't hard for a monkey to grab a drumstick and play a drum, open a refrigerator, steer a vehicle. But dolphins don't have hands and they're hard to see because they swim underwater and are fast. Hence there have been extreme views of dolphins based on guesswork, fantasy, and misinterpretation of their morphology. One that many of us grew up with was that dolphins were as smart as people, only more peaceful. "They have a lot of love, for every living creature // the smile of a dolphin is a built-in feature!"

Actually, dolphins are one of the few mammals known to kill others for no particular purpose — they just bash porpoises to death (Connor et al. 2000: 102) which unfortunately does seem to suggest their intelligence — you need to be pretty smart to be that stupid. And they're not always so nice to each other. Every now and then, you'll see a story in the *Weekly World News* or the equivalent about some woman who's married a dolphin, because he's so much more sensitive than human men.[4] Well, actually some female humans — trainers, usually — have had sexual encounters with dolphins, and they tend to be extremely unpleasant

[4] I am not making this up. See "Gal Weds Dolphin — after the Lovesick Critter Seduced Her!" *Weekly World News*, July 9, 2002, p. 54. "He's the best lover I ever had, sensitive, uninhibited . . ." A similar story appeared in August 2, 1988 (yes, I used to subscribe, but now I get the *American Sociological Review* instead); Sharon Tendler, a British millionaire, did marry her dolphin, the male with the moniker Cindy, but she insisted that their relationship was nonsexual.

and certainly satisfy the definition of harassment as "persistent, unwanted and unencouraged sexual attention that reasonably interferes with one's ability to complete work assignments."

Dolphins are the bad frat boys of the animal kingdom; their normal mating procedures are very hard to distinguish from gang rape. This is because of the strength of male bonds; though female-female bonds form the core of dolphin societies (Wells 1991: 212), these seem to be weaker than male-male ties. Males often form groups of two or three close allies, generally used to capture females for consortship. Such groups tend to stay stable for years (Connor et al. 1992b: 987). Then there are alliances of these alliances, which are looser, and seem to be used to defend/steal consorts from other alliances (Connor et al. 2000: 111). In many cases (and this is relevant for our discussion of morality later), there seems to be strong evidence that different alliances help out one another in capturing females and have a sense of reciprocity (who owes whom help) (Connor et al. 1992a: 426f). All bottlenose dolphins seem to have this fission-fusion pattern, with group change happening often on a daily or hourly basis (Connor et al. 2000: 121, 91).

But in 1999, Connor et al. reported that a set of allies tended to form what they called a "super-alliance," namely, a pervasive sense of mutual defense between members of a large set of shifting smaller groupings. That is, this wasn't the same thing as the "second-order" alliance, as its units were the individuals, and not stable smaller alliances. This might seem totally uninteresting. So what if there's maybe *less* structure than you might imagine? That the larger one doesn't have well-ordered components?

I actually think that this suggests a leap forward in the organization of complexity—that the dolphins are able in some ways to take the *idea* of the structural form and apply it to their advantage without being *locked in* by it. That is, for most other groups, including elephants, the larger units in the "fusion" have as their units the smaller groupings and not the individuals; except for consortships (or young adults seeking to transfer), it doesn't seem that there are many well-documented cases of *optional* super- or subunits. It's as if the individuals themselves couldn't be trusted to order their relations in a sensible way.

But with the dolphins (or so it seems), it is more that they themselves understand the structural principles and can adapt them freely. It's a close analogue to what in sociology might be termed a shift from particularistic social structures to cultural templates, or "institutionalization."[5] This is exactly the point that Harrison White made (if any point that White made could be said to be made "exactly") in *Identity and Control* (1992) regarding "getting action"—the trick

[5] In the sense used in *Social Structures* (Martin 2009).

isn't to *develop* structure but to *cut through* structure. It is very difficult for social animals to function intelligently and flexibly.

If indeed, as I think we have seen, there is reason to think that more flexible, intelligent, action is often associated with *less* regularity of structure, then we might deduce a working hypothesis of a rough trade-off. The smartness can be (1) in the social *organization* of the animals, (2) in the *environment* of each individual seen as individual, or (3) inside each individual *as individual*. This is a pretty familiar idea in animal studies, and it seems plausible to me.[6] It also suggests that where there are well-structured environments, the subjectivity of actors can be much simpler than otherwise believed. And I think that animal sociology also helps explain how to think about this for human beings.

Complex Maneuvers, Simple Creatures

It would seem somewhat strange to say that we have learned something transferable to human society when we point to aspects regarding the simplicity of animal behavior. For one thing, we flatter ourselves as being more complex in mind and behavior than other animals, and with good reason. Second, we already have a well-developed tradition of cognitive science that emphasizes the simplicity of human cognition (Simon 1962, 1996). Why try to learn from animals what we already know? The answer is, because we've refused to learn this lesson — that is, we've rejected the idea that simple models should be invoked for human behavior because they seem implausible and they are often vague. What some recent animal studies have brought to our attention is (just as Simon himself understood) that iterated simplicity can lead to intelligent behavior.

We can begin by thinking in terms of the sorts of wonderful duplicity in communication that Goffman pointed out. In the social sciences, we tend to begin with a charming faith that better communication will solve all problems, as misunderstandings (and how, we wonder, could any conflict not be, at base, misunderstandings) will dissipate like clouds under the morning sun of reason. But communication is one of the ways in which organisms make each other's lives miserable — or short.

Like George Herbert Mead (1934), instead of beginning with the sender, someone who has some idea he wants to get across to the other, Goffman (1959) began analytically with the receiver. The receiver is watching the sender to get information about the sender. But there are two kinds of information: on the one hand, there are the *expressions* we deliberately *give out*—"I am not scared of you." But

[6] Only on editing this do I realize that these three possibilities correspond to the triad of involution, dependence, and stratification that I (2009) took from White (1992) and argued had wide structural applicability for the sources of organization. It's nice to be right.

there are also *impressions we give off*, whether we want to or not.[7] If I am sweating, the impression belies my expression. The receiver might have an advantage if he gets information that the sender doesn't realize she is broadcasting.

Of course, human beings, or other creatures with self-consciousness in Mead's terms, are the sorts of senders that can "take the role of the other" ("What would *I* look for in someone to assess her truthfulness, if I were she?"). This means that they can at least attempt to gain control of aspects of behavior that are being monitored because they are assumed to be out of control ("I'd look for wide eyes. Perhaps I can widen my eyes a bit."). There is no sign of sincerity that can't be faked. This leads to a game-theoretic understanding of communication: any regularity can be used for trickery, and so the "I know you know I know you know . . ." leads to an arms race. In some cases, smartness doesn't help too much (e.g., randomness is unbeatable in a rock-scissors-paper contest), but in others, the arms race leads to a victory for the most intelligent.

Such an arms race has developed between many predators and prey, perhaps especially cannibals. Here we look at a particular genus of jumping spiders that eat other spiders (*Portia*). As we all know, the fly that inadvertently lands in a web and sticks, struggles, sending a vibration across the web. This is akin, without intention, to "giving off" an impression. The spider knows that the vibration "means" to go eat the fly.

Portia rocks another's spider's web in such a way as to mimic the signals produced by a caught insect. It isn't trying (if we can speak loosely) to "imitate a fly" so much as to send the signals that mean "come hither" (Jackson and Cross 2011: 142). In Chapter 3 we saw that the meaning of a gesture, in Mead's terms, is what the other fellow is going to do about it, and some web vibrations mean "there is something to be approached quickly" while others mean "there is something to be approached cautiously." If the first attempt does not work, *Portia* uses trial and error to go through a series of vibration patterns until something gets the other's attention (Wilcox and Jackson 1998: 421). Then, it's lunch time.

Now let's shift to mating display behavior. When we think about animal behavior, we tend to go to one of two extremes—either we imagine that they are all out for some sort of dominance over every other animal (which actually turns out not to make much sense from an evolutionary standpoint), or we assume that they are doing something sensible for the good of the whole. Thus when it comes to mating ritual, we either (as we saw in more detail in Chapter 4) imagine that they are strutting their stuff like Charles Atlas at the beach, or they are helpfully giving out signals that will allow a willing mate to track them down in the

---

[7] Goffman (1959: 2) talked about *expressions* we give off and which cause an *impression* on others. Although this grammatically is correct, I think for mnemonic purposes it may help to introduce a dichotomy of expressions versus impressions.

confusing hustle and bustle of the wide, wide world. And when in fact we see this go awry, and, say, see a female devouring a conspecific male (that is, a male of her species), we generally assume that an error has been made — the signal wasn't strong or clear enough to announce this as a potential mate.

And in a way, yes, but in a way, no; a mistake for *someone*, surely, but maybe not everyone. Rather than mating ritual being a complex set of passwords and counterpasswords, it may be a disposition in one organism to make use of the preexisting dispositions in another. In our spiders, males may actually begin the "courtship" by sending exactly the sorts of signals that release predatory behavior in order to get the interest of females — a dangerous but effective tactic (Jackson and Cross 2011: 146). The male begins by trying to use signals that get the female's attention but not *too* well — because she may lunge and try to take a chomp out of him. It seems that at least in some cases (*Portia labiata*), the characteristic male posture of legs in front may not be an arbitrary ritual signal ("I am a male") but simply a way of guarding against female attack; however, this can in fact signal to the female that it is a male.

In some cases, insects have developed the capacity to "push the mating buttons" of other species in order to prey on them.[8] Fireflies' light pulse timing varies by species. Female fireflies of the species *Photuris versicolor* (one of a cannibalistic genus lacking their own production of the chemical that makes fireflies taste bad) can alter the frequency of their flashes, so that they are broadcasting on the same band that a different species of firefly uses. This is for the times when rather than mate, they'd prefer to attract, and then snack on, a male from this other species (e.g., *Photinus ignitus*) (Eisner 2003; Lewis and Cratsley 2008). In such a case, the sucker male has indeed made a mistake, though *she* hasn't. But what about our spiders — for sometimes a female eats a male of her *own* species? Why isn't this mistake weeded out by evolution? Because when the female eats the male, it is no more a mistake than when she eats anything else. She is hungry, and a sucker male is better than nothing. Indeed, nonreceptive (immature) females will "act receptive" by going through mating ritual movements, but then try to take bites at an approaching male (Jackson and Cross 2011: 143f).

What we are seeing is interesting from a Goffmanian perspective, but there is something else that might not always be appreciated. This incredible dance of deception, worthy of the counter-counterspies of the Cold War period, is being carried out by animals that are (by our standards) incredibly simple. Spiders actually are cognitively more flexible and impressive than most of us imagine given how tiny their brains are (though some manage to basically cram additional brains in their body outside of their heads). But still, just spiders. Human spies could

[8] Here I have learned from a class paper written by Bridgette Kragie.

easily have complete mental collapse under the strain of having to live three levels of deception deep ("I need to make them think that I want to make them think that I am trying to make them think that I believe them."). How can this be done by a simple creature? It seems that the key is that rather than try to live in multiple nestings simultaneously, successive iterations that respond to the results of the former allow for complex behavior on the part of simple creatures.

Iterated Action and Deception

There is little doubt that apes are capable of deliberate deception—that is, an attempt to evoke a subjectivity in another that does not correspond to the facts. But it is not clear that this capacity is shared by other animals, even those that carry out objectively deceiving sets of actions. For example, some ethologist (I forget whom) was struck that when a visitor occupied his dog's favorite easy chair, the dog would bark at the door, asking to be let out. When the visitor rose and crossed to the door, the clever dog would run over and jump into the now empty chair. It is not obviously impossible that this could have been planned, but it would also result if the dog's first choice was to sit in the chair, and the second to go out.

A more complex case was studied by Cheney and Seyfarth (2007), among others, one involving baboon infant handling. Baboons, especially young females, like many other primates, are inordinately interested in the babies of others. They want to touch them, pick them up, and carry them, and sometimes they do not treat these infants with particular care. Hence mothers of infants are wary of approaching female baboons—indeed, paranoid. Some of these would-be handlers approach the females from the back, groom them into a relaxed state, and only then reach for the infant. This could be a deliberate plan, or it could arise from the iterated nature of action (Barrett and Rendall 2010, who analyze Strum's case). Baboons, like many other primates, have a very hard time initiating social action vis-à-vis some other who is not looking at them. Hence the mothers turn their backs to avoid having the interaction even begin. Being socially agitated and seeing a back, the would-be handler may be likely to initiate grooming which would calm both her and the mother, and so on.

In other words, rather than think in terms of a "unit act" (as Parsons 1968 [1949] thought we should), we need to think of a larger unit, say, a "scene," in which each turn is conditional on the turns of others. Each action (turn) is a response to the current state of the environment, which includes, say, our two interacting animals, *A* and *B*. Thus, if we denote the state of the environment at time *t* as E_t, and the action of the first creature (*A*) at that time as A_t, and that of *B* as B_t, then our scene may be

$E_0 \rightarrow A_0$
$A_0 \rightarrow E_1$
$E_1 \rightarrow B_1$
$B_1 \rightarrow E_2$
$E_2 \rightarrow A_2$
$A_2 \rightarrow E_3$
$E_3 \rightarrow B_3$

With this sort of iterated action, animals can "deceive" one another without being able to actually "take the role of the other." Deception probably isn't the perfect litmus test of Meadian self-consciousness as it was first (reasonably) assumed.

Each animal, by acting, changes the environment to which the other responds. Overall, the succession of actions (A_0, B_1, A_2, B_3) may produce a complex interaction that only smart animals could have understood at time 0. Yet no animal has a representation of the interaction "(A_0, B_1, A_2, B_3)." Rather, what each has is a (possibly discrete) function $A_t = f(E_t)$—what to do in a situation of this general type. From such simple generative functions, an infinite number of complex interactions can be derived, depending on the conditions put in.

I am going to suggest—and defend in greater detail in the next chapter—that this principle holds for human action a lot more than we would probably want to admit. *Afterward*, we are able to *narrate* the interaction "(A_0, B_1, A_2, B_3)" and so come to think of it as a whole unit that we "did." And *sometimes* this may be true for us (while it might *never* be true for the spiders). But it is not always true. This will help explain some of our capacity to act in reasonable and interwoven ways, abilities that have often been ascribed to "roles" and "rules." Without denying the existence or importance of either of these, I think that animal studies give us some new insight on each, and I begin with roles.

ROLES

Queen Me

The concept of role is a central one in sociology; even those of us who do not make it a key part of our theoretical vocabulary tend to fall back on it when we are tired or distracted. The simplest definition of a role is one part in a recognizable interaction pattern, perhaps normatively defined as a set of rights and duties. This can often be seen as tied to a "status," a slot in social structure. The two correspond as verb and noun: the role of a mother is to mother, the role of a nurse is to nurse, and so on for father and doctor and the rest. Yet this definition seems to me somewhat inaccurate. Certainly, "doctor" makes sense as a role, and a doctor does have certain rights (prescribe drugs) and responsibilities (do no harm). But imagine a true regime of human rights, in which all persons treat each other as ends-in-themselves, all have a right to flourish and develop so long as they harm no one else (I did say we were imagining . . .). Is this position of "human," with its clearly defined rights and duties, a "role"? It seems to strain our definitions.

Further, now let's use what is another classic example of a "role," namely, "father." This strikes us as a more particularistic role than "doctor," for a doctor is a doctor even if she isn't *your* doctor. Of course, as Merton (1957) among others has said, the thing about roles is that they aren't single things, but sets. Thus, a doctor isn't just a doctor to her patients, she's a doctor to, say, the patient's teachers (and can say "please excuse John from school today, he was vomiting awfully much"). So a father may not be a father to anyone but his daughters and sons, yet he is *their* father to other people. The father still has rights and duties—the duty to take care of the child (and actually prevent said child from inflicting damage and destruction upon others) and the right to discipline the child, up to some limits.

But now how do we understand what is most distinctive about the things that we would understand as roles (that is, if we were to attempt to delineate the phenomenon)? To answer this, we often hazard guesses as to the origin, the reason, the wherefore of such roles, and conclude that roles "come about" for *functional* reasons. This in turn has affected our interpretation of animal societies. When we see what seems like specialization, we are likely to turn into Adam Smiths and imagine a functionality to the division of labor.

I am going to argue that this is *not* the essence of roles among animals, and that it may be that this is not how we should understand roles among people either. We can begin with the animals that are the obvious first choice for the examination of roles, namely, the social insects such as ants, which may be divided into several types with specific functions. Most common is the division into a queen or queens, other female reproductives, male reproductives, soldiers (or major workers), and regular workers.

This division of role is based on a division of phenotype—different roles have different bodies. They are born to fight, born to labor, born to mate, born to die. For this reason, the roles are often called "castes." *Within* a caste, there seems to be almost no specialization. For example, among regular worker ants, some may forage and others maintain the nest. But it seems that nest labor is a default choice—if you don't have anything else to do, "work" on the nest (Wilson 1971: 156). Somehow, reserve nest workers can be called out to patrol or to forage when necessary, but there is no reason to think that those working on the nest are any different except in age from their sisters who might have been called out earlier (Gordon 1999: 124–126). In fact, given the stunning inefficiency of ants' nest work, it is not clear if this is really a task at all, as opposed to "meddling" that achieves a reasonably tidy equilibrium, but does not do much good under normal conditions.

These actions within the minor workers, then, do not deserve to be called "roles"; they are merely tasks, like setting the table, taking out the garbage, feeding the dog, which in a household of anarchic but cooperative children might be allocated by a busy parent on the basis of who is at hand. That is different from what we think of roles in human society: just standing on the corner and teaching about Weber does not make one a professor; shooting a criminal does not make one a policeman or a judge.

To see what might be at the heart of "role" as a category, let's consider the queen. The queen doesn't do much queening. Our calling her a "queen" comes from our typically distorted way of seeing things — to put political relationships where they don't belong. The queen is a mother, a dependent super-mom who gets to produce many, many offspring.

Like the other roles, the queen is phenotypically made a queen, but the process whereby this takes place is a social one involving varying degrees of agonism. Among the social insects, the key thing is that the queen is the "normal" way that a female larva would develop, and the others come to be what they are by having some part of their development shut down. In fact, in the less-developed social insects, the queen, unlike the other females, is behaviorally complete, and at some point in her life cycle, she carries out every possible behavior that different castes are capable of (Wilson 1971: 151, 157). Like the old joke, the great thing about being a queen is that she can do it all, but thank God, she doesn't have to. In other species, the queen quickly specializes in being an egg-producer and *can't* do much else.

But all other females are *always* incomplete: sometimes sterile, sometimes able to produce only male offspring, sometimes only producing "trophic" eggs (snacks for the queen). They are often born or mature this way *because* there already is a queen. Her presence can suppress the development of other females into queens in a number of ways. Among some ants, the bigger larva are given *less* food than others if a queen is around — they're also licked and bitten more — which reduces their growth. Among honeybees, specific potential-queen-larvae cells are fed a special "queen substance" denied to other cells (Wilson 1971: 277, 303). If a queen is removed, within days, some workers' ovaries develop and they can lay eggs.

In some cases, the queen's odor is enough to suppress the full development of other females. In other cases, a more active approach seems called for: the first female ant born bites the wing buds off her nestmates as they appear, leading them to become workers. If hers are taken off experimentally, she too becomes a timid worker (Hölldobler and Wilson 1994: 90). Among honeybees, the first virgin queen emerging from her larval cell has sonic communication with her sisters who have not yet emerged, which seems to tell them "don't come out yet or I'll kill you." And she will indeed commit this sorocide if they emerge before she takes off on her nuptial flight.

Similar phenomena are common among termites; the queen — but also the "king" where there is a primary male breeder — releases a chemical to suppress the development of others into reproductives. But the suppression doesn't always take place chemically; sometimes it is a matter of rough and tumble. Thus among paper wasps, several queens start a nest but one dominates others by standing above them at frequent intervals; when the first crop of workers emerges, they drag out the loser would-be queens and expel them from the nest (Hölldobler and Wilson 1994: 86). In some other species, a number of females may all start out as egg layers, who attempt to lay their own eggs and eat those of the others. The one who ends up eating more of the others' eggs than they eat of hers takes charge, and so the "losers" end up being workers (299).

Thus the queen attains her special position in such cases by preventing her sisters from developing into full reproductives. Although the social insects are unique in the radical variation of the bodies of workers and the sterility of many, it turns out that the same dynamics are found among a number of mammals and birds, not merely insects: only a dominant female breeds. For example, among marmosets, subordinate females lack the hormone surge that leads to ovulation (Raleigh et al. 1991).[9] Similar dynamics exist in meerkats, canids, African hunting dogs, and tamarins; male orangutans have a similar suppression relation (Moss and Lee 2011: 193). The "slot" for breeder doesn't exist because of a cultural template; rather, it exists because of the suppression of others.

Control and Exclusivity

We've seen a way in which the presence of breeders suppresses the full development of others into breeders. It's a somewhat extreme example, but it might shed light usefully on a range of cases. When we define this large set of cases, however, we can be attentive to either the *form* or to the *content* of this phenomenon. The latter is to focus on the ways in which the hormonal system relevant for sexual development is sensitive to social processes. In particular, we can explore the responsiveness of hormone production to social status (Sapolsky 2004). Such responsiveness is found in many, perhaps all, monkeys and apes. For one well-studied example, it seems that high status among baboons leads to

---

[9] Most of this I first learned from a 2002 Rutgers paper by Jessica Horwitz.

patterns of hormone production that are related to reproduction. This is true for cortisol, but also for serotonin, at least for vervet monkeys. Low-ranking male vervets have lower levels, which in humans would predict higher levels of depression. The alpha has highest levels (at least in some captive groups studied) (Raleigh et al. 1984).[10] Because status is both a cause and an effect of such hormone levels, it is possible to manipulate the personality profile of animals (whether they are outgoing or fearful, ready to be near others or not) without manipulating the animals themselves, for example, by adding or subtracting more or less dominant others (McGuire et al. 1984). Thus the position of the animal in the social structure often affects hormonal development and hence sexual behavior.

So we certainly can focus on the *substantive* processes that we saw in the role creation through suppression. The second path of generalization, which we will follow here, would instead focus on the *formal* properties and on the *result* of the process — namely, the exclusionary nature of the position. I propose that this is what is key about a role. For example, the role of doctor doesn't come because the doctor helps you get better. I've been to plenty of doctors who didn't, and been healed by many non-doctors (e.g., parents and friends). The role of doctor comes because if you try to sell drugs without being one, someone may well shoot you or throw you in jail. A position, then, appears more like what we mean by a "role" when one who occupies is able to discourage others in a fundamental way from acting similarly. I am a "father" not so much because I have rights and responsibilities toward my son but because others are not allowed to have these rights. Further, when we focus on this exclusivity, we realize that the responsibilities, which generally are paramount when we think about the *functions* of the role, might not necessarily have as much connection to the role-fulness as do the rights.

Among primates, this sort of exclusion is often seen in the position of an "alpha male." Most social animals experience some degree of fighting and often figure out who is likely to beat whom. Humans tend to assimilate all such cases to the same Hobbesian world in which the one "on top" rules over the others. But "ruling" isn't simply about beating others up, it's about getting them to do something you want, something besides just running away. This is very rare in the animal world, for reasons Rousseau would have appreciated; when one animal gets another to do what it wants (except for running away and / or dropping something), it often relies on *leadership*, not dominance. Such leadership positions don't generally come as the result of fighting. For example, the "alpha male" of

[10] A failure to find the status / serotonin relation in cynomalgus monkeys (which are macaques) was reported by Shively et al. (1990), though in 1995, Shively et al. (1995) found a *reverse* relationship among females. Kaplan, Manuck, Fontenot, and Mann (2002) show dominant males and females here have higher levels of dopamine than subordinates.

the standard wolf pack is the father, and though wolves will fight (even to the death) for territory, their followers are mainly their own children (sometimes a hanger-on or two). There is often leadership without fighting, and where there is fighting, there may be no rule or "function" of the alpha position at all.

However, there are cases in which there is an alpha position that is achieved, not ascribed; it comes as a result of contest, not, say, by virtue of being a father, though this contest aspect is not mere brawling. And even more, in some cases, occupation of this role seems to be associated with the performance of duties. Sometimes the alpha protects against external enemies (though these may only be *his* enemies—other males).[11] For example, among rhesus monkeys, the alpha male—and not others—will respond to a stranger who presents a group threat (Bernstein 1964). And perhaps more important, often the alpha male preserves peace.

Among chimpanzees, the alpha male (frequently in partnership with the alpha female) keeps order largely by acting as a peace enforcer. He will enter a fight and intervene according to the simple but effective principle, "hit anyone who hits" (de Waal 1998: 117, 146). This generally means hitting the winning party who is less pleased with the premature end to the contest. (This is all the more notable because adult male chimpanzees tend to be winner supporters, in contrast to females, who perhaps have less reason to make opportunistic alliances [Smuts 1987b: 404].) But even outside such a melee, the alpha is more likely than other adult males to become a loser supporter or protector (see de Waal [1977: 260, 263] for the case of Java monkeys). This seems to help rally the masses behind the current alpha and puts any would-be challenger at a disadvantage (de Waal 1987: 427; 1998: 117, 146).

Yet these aspects of the alpha position seem to have less to do with farsighted strategic manipulation and more to do with a general orientation to control. We can say that one animal (*A*) "controls" another (*B*) when *A* can suppress *B*'s aggression to *C*, although the *A*–*B* tie is as close as, or closer than, the *A*–*C* tie (that is, this is not the same thing as a defensive alliance). There are some cases in which a mother monkey or an older brother will perform this function with a juvenile who is acting up with the member of another matrilineal family, purely for prudential reasons (although even this is rather rare). Picking on a juvenile of another matriline might seem like fun, but it could lead an older and meaner monkey to get in the mix, which would be bad for everyone. Therefore, thinks the mother, say, better to bite you now than for us both to get bitten later. Such actions within matrilines allow for *local* control roles, but we may also speak of a

[11] At the same time, the infanticidal tendencies of many new males can align the interests of the reigning alpha males and those of the females, since if they share children, his enemies are their enemies.

position of generalized *global* control. That is, *A* tries to make sure that *no B* is out making trouble. That's the way many medieval kings were understood — they were the lords who could tell other lords to stop fighting.

Goodall (1990: 137) gives an example of an older chimp who rescued a younger chimp attacked by a baboon he'd been teasing. However, when the young chimp began to tease the baboon again, the older one returned, and *this* time he attacked the younger chimp that he had previously aided. Moral transmitted: don't make trouble. (She notes that this older chimpanzee seemed cut out to be an alpha — as he soon was — not only because he was smart and courageous but also because "he could not tolerate disputes among his subordinates.") This sort of behavior — an aversion to trouble and a willingness to impersonally sanction troublemakers — is typical of alpha males in many primates.

This "control role" aspect, when it is present, gives, I believe, a qualitatively different nature to the position of the alpha. Yet it draws on the quantitative nature of the alpha (that he is the highest ranking male). This is because the thing about a global control role is that only one animal can do it. A second animal attempting to exert control through hitting a hitter is, in the eyes of the first control animal, simply another miscreant. As Hobbes would say, divided sovereignty is no sovereignty at all.

Thus the distinctive "control role" aspect of the alpha position arises with such clarity because by its very nature — its content, expressible as a set of action imperatives — it has a certain formal property of exclusivity. In some ways, this sort of position of sovereignty is the simplest role we can imagine, as its content is largely its form ("I have the sort of position that only one can occupy."). But other roles seem to have similar bases.

Marriage

A somewhat related form of exclusiveness is found among Hamadryas baboons in particular. Somewhere Friedrich Engels is smiling, for the relation between adult males and adult females is sometimes called "marriage" and other times "ownership." The ambiguity comes because both of these are in large part about exclusion. And this is a particularly asymmetric relation — a single male owns / marries one or more females; they don't have as much of an ownership claim over him, if only because none can protest the presence of *another* female. All females are married in that they are tied to a single primary male, but during swelling (their time of sexual receptivity around ovulation) they will copulate with others behind his back. If he catches one messing around, he bites her (not the other male). There is a way, then, in which the position of the female has less of a "role" about it (more than one can occupy the position, and indeed, they seem to have more "duties" and fewer "rights" than he).[12]

How do we understand this relationship? We can derive it as an extreme form of relations common among other baboons. Even savannah baboons (which don't share the "one male unit" based structure of the Hamadryas) have a sort of respect for property-in-another. A male who wants to try to get a female away from another male almost never approaches directly or interposes himself between the two; in fact, if they approach him, he'll probably move away. The males seem to be inhibited from taking a female if she and her consort partner maintain a normal relationship (Smuts 1985: 152, 174). Further, a male and a female will sometimes have a "friendship" in which the two seem to enjoy one another's company: the male friend may have more access to the female's infants, he may rush to her defense if she is threatened, and he may be more likely to go off on a consortship with her when she is in estrus. But females have no problem having more than one male friend.

For Hamadryas, the friendship has somehow consolidated to permanent marriages between one male and several females, probably related to increased sexual dimorphism. (Of course, if we were explaining the sexual dimorphism—that males are bigger than females—we might appeal to their social structure....) The respect that is seen in savannah baboons for existing relationships seems elevated to a positive fear of upsetting the sanctity of the marriage/ownership ties. Once a male basically shows interest in a female the others are inhibited—when forced into the company of a married pair, a male will find something "interesting" to look at elsewhere, and the husband will placate the (potential) rival by approaching and presenting (Kummer 1995: 170, 179f).

The key, then, to the emergence of this role is the *effective* ability to exclude others from it ("friends" don't have this—there's a relationship without a role, if we can think this way). If one male baboon is the mate of another, no one else *can* have this position. Further, this exclusive position is recognized by others (which isn't always the case for animals where breeding pairs are isolated from one another, and an interloper may have no inhibitions against mating with one of the pair). Could this be a good place for thinking about human roles? In Chapter 1,

[12] Hamadryas males won't desert their female partners, but it isn't clear whether this is something that the females appreciate (Kummer 1995: 16, 101, 105). Note that the fact (if it turns out to be one) that in their structural ur-form, roles tend to have more rights than responsibilities doesn't mean that as roles become unmoored from concrete structural definition and become more a matter of "culture" in the sense of Martin (2009), they retain this disproportionate focus on rights. That is, when roles become something we can "play," then they may carry a great deal of responsibility, if only because role-players are responsible for a continually successful performance if they are to retain their claim to the role. Thinking through these issues is complicated by the fact that we must focus on roles that are not defined by larger institutional structures (that is, a doctor is a doctor even if she does not work for a hospital, while a waiter ceases to be a waiter if he is not in a restaurant). Finally, we must bear in mind that rights and responsibilities are not necessarily benefits and costs, respectively.

we saw that there is a widespread but indefensible tendency in sociological theory to explain the existence of roles by their function — what they contribute (thereby assuming the existence of the role structure, that which is to be explained). It isn't that roles *can't* perform a function, but if the function they perform comes from people consciously deciding what they want to accomplish, functionalist explanations are just as pointless as the evolutionary psychological account in terms of unconscious psychological mechanisms that we explored in the previous chapter. So functionalism isn't necessarily wrong, but it has an unfortunate tendency to explain best what doesn't need to be explained. Hence this might not be a good way for defining our approach to roles. Thinking about roles as fundamentally about limited-occupancy might be a better way of starting out than in terms of what is being accomplished.

It isn't that occupants of roles don't do anything. But roles aren't about what one *does* — that is, what we mean by *tasks*. Roles aren't permanent tasks, simply because we know of many roles that just aren't—for example, the roles that can emerge in small group discussions—nor are they ones with rights and duties, because some roles don't have any rights or duties at all, yet they are recognized as roles. For example, the "class clown" doesn't have a right to goof off (he still goes to the principal's office), nor does he have any duty to do so. Yet there is something about many classrooms that they can support one and only one class clown. What seems to be distinctive about what we call a role is that not just anyone can enter it. It may be that more than one can, but there is something standing between a potential entrant and successful entrance: in the simplest cases, the current occupant. The rights, should there be any, then come from the fact of role institutionalization.

With roles, then, in analytic terms we can see a foundation for an idea of rights in the sense of privileges attached to a status or position. But could something similar help us understand "rights" in the sense of things that we actually think *are* right? If so, this might give us a different way of thinking about morality.

MORALITY (RULES)

Content and Form

There is nothing so popular now as feel-good books on the science of morality, and things like the origins of morality. I don't read these books, and I don't think you should either. Because almost invariably, what they mean by morality is "the sorts of behaviors you and I would approve of." Nowadays that's things like altruism and care, and so the "origins of morality" come from parental concern and so on. But it seems that it isn't hard to imagine a time when the origins of morality would be found in the fact that many animals go outside their nest to urinate, or that they bite anyone who bites them, because people would have a different understanding of what morality is all about.[13]

In other words, I think we need to dissociate the *content* from the *form* of morality. The problem with focusing on content is that either it's universal within a wide range of animals or it's not. If it's not, it doesn't help to look at animals and judge what we like about them, any more than we would judge their cuisine. If, however, we're talking about universals (or near universals for at least some animals, like infant care among mammals), we find that rather than speaking about morality, we seem to be speaking about self-interest and such. Although work on empathy is very revealing (it tells us something about the kinds of animals that are out there; e.g., Masserman et al. 1964), as Rousseau (1967 [1755]) emphasized, such *pité*, an instinctive aversion to witnessing other animals suffer needlessly, is not what we mean by morality.

Nor is morality just about whatever it is that makes us able to get along with others in our group — that would make it expedience, or prudence. Morality also seems to have to do with rightness — but what is this? Rightness, I propose (on the basis of animal evidence to be discussed shortly), seems to be a sense of the *legitimacy of expectations* in certain circumstances. When our expectations are upset by a force of nature, we do not feel wronged, although we may be unhappy. But there are certain expectations that we hold of others who (or so we think) are responsible actors. If they violate these expectations, the fault is not that *we* predicted wrongly, it is that *they* have violated our rights, and / or not fulfilled their duties. Or at least that's the way we think about it now, but even where "rights and duties" aren't the precise form used, there can be a sense of "shoulds and shouldn'ts."[14]

Further, as Durkheim (1961 [1902–3]) said in *Moral Education*, we usually think of morality in terms of violations. There is an assumption that people are moral unless proven otherwise, and this probably goes for any animals that have a budding moral sense as well. No one focuses on all the people you *didn't* kill. In contrast to ethical theories (like that of Augustine) that badness is the absence of good (theories of "privative evil"), it may well be that goodness is the absence of

[13] You might say, well there's nothing wrong with reading about the origins of "the sorts of behaviors that you and I would approve of." That's true, unless it drives out of our minds the capacity to understand what is distinctive about morality (if there is such a thing). Darwin (1896 [1874]) himself appealed to Kant for his definition of morality, and indeed tended to emphasize a feeling of *duty* when evaluating animal morality.

[14] Thus, according to this definition, morality is quite different from having a "beautiful soul," that sort of being that instinctively and gracefully acts selflessly (which Darwin himself confounded with morality in animals!), and different from intrinsic excellence (which some argue was inherent to Greek ideas of goodness). And so there *is* reason to think that this conception of "morality as legitimate expectation" isn't universal even among humans (here's another place where Turner [2010] has made my job more difficult!), but that doesn't mean that there aren't legitimate expectations everywhere. The jury is still out on this one.

badness. So morality may be about *failing* to live up to rights and duties, not about living up to them. Yet perhaps it isn't simply a cognitive understanding of a violation of an expectation. It also contains some feeling, not necessarily sympathy, but something that can be bruised. Our feeling that we have a *right* to our expectation may be just that — a *feeling*, and not a logical chain of reasoning.[15]

Not all animals have expectations of how others will act. But some apes certainly do, and I'm going to focus on chimpanzees here. Many times, their expectations are violated, and the expecting-but-disappointed animal has perhaps learned a valuable lesson. This usually does not indicate anything related to morality. But the violation of certain other expectations draws reactions that are explosive and often described by human observers as "tantrums." The classic American child's tantrum is accompanied by the wail, "It's not *fair*!" Parents often find it humorous that to young children, "fair" seems to mean "whatever I happen to want," but I believe that this is incorrect. It is true that by "fair" children certainly do *not* mean what American parents may think "fair" means, namely, "in accord with universal formal procedures." But that doesn't mean that it's nothing other than "what I want." Rather, to the children, *fair* seems to connote a conviction that their expectations had a sort of legitimacy. And I think things are similar with many apes.

Where, then, do we see such tantrums? A surprising number turn out to involve food sharing. Chimpanzees rarely share most kinds of food, but they often share meat. There have been some overstatements regarding the equanimity with which chimpanzees will part with a bloody hunk of carcass — they certainly don't sit down and divide up the kill among all group members — but they seem to have more rule-governed interaction here than in most of their interactions. Although they don't always respect the rule that possession equals property, they often do — males will beg for meat from (weaker) females at times, though sometimes they'll just try to grab it.

Here is an example of a tantrum witnessed by Goodall (1986: 308). The female Athena is in possession of a fawn carcass hotly desired by the strong male Figan, who is attempting to wrest it from her. She clings to it despite Figan's repeated attacks. Finally, he tries to calm her with reassuring touch — and then makes a lightning grab for the meat. As he scampers happily off with it, she has a tantrum. Interestingly, in another instance Figan had been begging for meat from a different female (Gigi) to no avail, and so he used the same duplicitous technique. Rather than a complete meltdown, however, Gigi's response was to blow off steam by whirling around and attacking another female.

---

[15] It is worth emphasizing that in contrast to eighteenth-century theories of a specific moral sense, here the moral sensibility does not tell us *what* the moral is in substantive terms. But a feeling of bruisedness of a special type is the indicator of the *formal* category of morality. It is close to what Kant called a "fact of reason."

Chimpanzees may also have tantrums when their begging for meat is ineffective (de Waal 1990: 47). And they've even been seen to throw tantrums when another monopolizes all the good foodstuffs without any sharing (de Waal 1996: 13). There seems to be something about the expectation of sharing the best foods, if you ask nicely, that seems more legitimate than other expectations, and an expectation that an owner has a right to be asked nicely—and to have her property respected if she says "no." That is, though it might initially be surprising, *both* sharing *and* ownership seem to be part of the same moral sense here.

There is one last case of a tantrum that I want to discuss, somewhat different from the others. This was the outcome of a prolonged Goffmanian arms race between two chimpanzees (Menzel 1988). In a study of communication, one female (Belle) was allowed to see where food had been hidden in a large enclosure while others were not allowed to see. She would lead the group there and they would all get some—except when the dominant male (Rock) was present. Because if he was there, once she uncovered it, he would attack her and take it all. The experiment, designed to examine whether chimpanzees can communicate, turned into an experiment on how chimpanzees can *avoid* communicating. Belle's response was to wait until Rock wasn't looking before getting the food. His counterresponse was to start pretending he wasn't looking. Her counter-counterresponse was to stop moving when he would race over after ceasing to pretend he wasn't looking, and his counter-counter-counterresponse was to try to follow her line of sight to anticipate where she was intending to go. She then began to lead him to *one* piece and then, while he grabbed this, to go off and find the main pile. This worked for a while but eventually Rock figured this out and would not be deceived. At this point, Belle was out of options, and she began to collapse in a tantrum.

We see here something else that is necessary for the tantrum—namely, helplessness. Tantrums are had by those who have no other control over the situation. The iterated actions may have reinforced Belle's sense of her cognitive superiority over Rock, but when she could not outsmart him, it may have seemed unfair, as she went from a world in which the brain was mightier than the brawn to the real world—and there was nothing she could do about it. Rock didn't have tantrums. He took her stuff.

Does this mean that Nietzsche (1966 [1886]) was right, and that what we mean by morality is rooted in a *ressentiment* of the inferior against their natural overlords? No, not even if our focus on these dynamics was simplified to the claim that this is "the root" of morality (my argument is not a genetic but an analytic one). The tantrum may indeed be seen only among those who can't do anything about it. Hence the tantrum is only a *sign* of the legitimacy of expectations when (1) the expectations are violated and (2) the expecting animal can't do anything. That doesn't mean, however, that the legitimacy of expectations is restricted to such situations. It's just that we don't have an obvious sign of it in other circumstances.

Punishment

What about punishment? We might imagine that when legitimate expectations are violated, and the expecting animal *can* do something about it, she or he will punish the offender. Is there evidence of this? Unfortunately, most of what is called "punishment" among animals can be understood as something very different: perhaps an animal's behavior to discourage certain actions by others, to exact vengeance, to demonstrate strength, a simple attempt to get its way with another, or to just blow off steam. If it is taken as a sign of a moral sensibility, punishment should have something a bit more impersonal about it. There are only a few examples of what might seem punishment for the violation of general norms. One possible example is the following: rhesus macaques who do not give food calls when they find food are more likely to be the target of aggression than those who give food calls (Clutton-Brock and Parker 1995: 211). Here the punishment doesn't seem to accomplish anything immediately instrumental (if the violation is noted, the food is now found), nor is it a simple frustration displacement (if there's food, be happy because the eating can begin!). But there are few of these cases, and the *way* in which the punishment occurs rarely shows any sense of outrage. (Of course, maybe we're just missing the outrage in our observations.)

In contrast, consider the following case (de Waal 1996: 91) of a reaction to what might be understood as a legitimate expectation. In a group of chimpanzees, an alpha male chasing another group member seemed to go beyond the "normal bounds" of bullying (e.g., chase for a while, then let the other go). The females began producing the "waoaw bark" sound that strikes observers as "indignant" and is usually given in response to intruders—that is, outsiders who should not be let it in. De Waal's interpretation is that this was in effect to let the alpha male know he had gone beyond a moral boundary. It's important to understand that this doesn't imply that they are reasoning analogically. ("How do I tell this guy he's gone too far and crossed a moral boundary? I'll make the same sound we make for those who are outside the group boundary.") Rather, it is (perhaps) that the same irritated / fearful feeling that they have when some chimp is not where it belongs (an outsider is here) is experienced when their idea of a legitimate punishment is violated.

Studies of punishment in animal groups are still in their early stages and, as is the case with morality, need to be placed in their proper context. There are important anecdotal reports of deliberately instructive punishment among domesticated dogs and even among wolves, reports that should be taken seriously; they may point to a pedagogical punishment that is disconnected from notions of legitimacy (that is, here the punishment is purely instrumental: "Well, *this* will help you remember not to do that!"). It may be that in some ways, our understanding of punishment is still too wrapped up with a model of rationality and reasoning. As we learn more about animals, we may find that we need to continually remind ourselves not to inject chains of logic where there may be none.

Guilt

The last issue I want to raise briefly, and which forms a nice bridge to the next section, is the issue of moral guilt. In sociology, we often make a distinction between *guilt* and *shame*. *Shame* is almost amoral and comes wholly from how we think others see us. *Guilt* is internal and involves a conscience. If people *think* they saw you wet your pants during class, you might be ashamed, even though it isn't true. On the other hand, if you were to switch your paper with that of your more industrious neighbor, so that you got the A and she was confused to get a D in the class, you might feel guilty, even though no one but you knows. Sociologists, especially followers of Mead, tend to imagine that guilt is internalized shame — that we, both as a species and as developing individuals, don't feel guilt until we internalize the perspectives of others, and I think that's a pretty reasonable idea, though by no means is the issue settled. So I'll be assuming that in animals, to look for guilt and to look for shame are connected — both are about seeing oneself through the eyes of others, and knowing that one is coming up wanting.

And once again, I am not arguing that here we identify the *source* of guilt, but rather, that we learn something about how we *might* be able to think about humans from seeing what we *need* to do to think about animals. Here we need to introduce the idea of a "theory of mind." The idea here is that a creature has a "theory of mind" (TOM) when it understands that *other* creatures have their *own* interiority, that they have beliefs, and — critically — that others' beliefs can be *incorrect*.

We can see that this TOM is related to the issues that Mead (1934) had raised regarding being able to see oneself through the eyes of the other. It seems that we can really do this only when we realize that the other *is* an other — one with his or her own self. Thus to Mead, we only gain self-consciousness when we truly understand the consciousness of others and borrow their own to see ourselves. Hence it was believed that the issue of TOM is crucial for understanding the selfhood of animals.

The first forays here tended to assume that a creature either did or did not have a TOM, so researchers wanted to investigate when children develop one, and what other animals might have one. The classic test for children was a false belief test. You sit a child down and take a doll or put a puppet on your hand,[16] introduce the puppet, have the kid talk to the puppet. The puppet watches you put some chocolate into a cupboard (actually a matchbox). The puppet says goodbye and "leaves." The chocolate is taken from the box and put somewhere else, such as in a bag. The puppet "returns" and the child is asked, Where does the puppet think the chocolate is? The kid says, "In the bag," which is where the *kid* knows it is (Wimmer and Perner 1983). The child, it was concluded, does not have a theory of mind, because she can't understand that the puppet has its own interiority and set of beliefs.

Of course, when you put it this way, we realize the kid is *right*, because the puppet *doesn't* have a mind—if it does, it's attached to that arm up the puppet's butt, which belongs to the experimenter. But actually, this isn't the problem with the original studies. It's that it isn't quite that kids don't have "a" TOM. It's that little kids are stupid. Lots of things that are easy for you are hard for them, and they also aren't always sure what we're talking about when we ask insane questions about puppet minds.

The kids who seem to fail the TOM test also fail similar tests that don't involve a TOM component. So in one great experiment, three-year-olds were given a task to find out what something in a tube is, sometimes able to see it, other times to reach in and feel it, or an accomplice can give them a hint ("Hey kid! It's the toothbrush in the tube!"). But when asked how they knew—whether they saw what was in the bag, they felt it, or they were told—three-year-olds are basically answering randomly. All they know is it's a toothbrush in there (O'Neill and Gopnik 1991). And that's when there really *is* a toothbrush there. When folks are lying or wrong, things are even worse. Negating *anything* is cognitively demanding for humans, and it can be a real struggle for kids, so they have a lot of problem with the idea of *false* belief—theirs or anyone's (Carey 2009: 207). As we perhaps saw in Chapter 3, a full human linguistic structure that allows for recursion (whereby we can think not just "X," but "he thinks 'X,'" where X itself could be "he thinks Y") makes this difficult task tractable for us, but little kids find it often stumps them. This difficulty is likely to be shared by a lot of animals. Even the crafty ones are, compared to us, very stupid.

We can't ask animals questions, and so a great deal of work on TOM among animals has turned on the issue of whether they can see themselves through others' eyes—whether they know when they can or can't be seen. We'll look at this in greater detail in a moment; for now, I want to focus on one single experiment with monkeys (de Waal 1996: 110), one that is key for the issue of guilt. A

[16] The original version used a doll. I like the puppet experiments because I like puppets. The original version used two different color cupboards, which later experimenters suspected might be too hard on some kids.

subordinate male is placed in a cage with a female with the alpha male not present. The two mate. They are released to rejoin the rest of the group. When the subordinate male sees the alpha later, he seems very cautious, more so than males that were also removed but didn't mate.

The explanation is that it has to do with the mating—that the subordinate knows this is the sort of thing the alpha might not like, and might in fact "punish." The alpha wasn't there, but the subordinate doesn't seem *quite* confident that he can be sure the alpha doesn't know.

And I think this is very reasonable—on the part of both the monkey and the analyst. Keeping track of who was where, who knows what, is all very difficult. And as said above, grasping another's *false* belief is extremely challenging for a nonlinguistic creature. When others are physically present, we can use them to help understand these issues—like rocks in a stream, the presence of others can be used to traverse complex problems that are nearly impossible in the abstract. In the case at hand, there's no reason to think that the monkey has *internalized* a super-ego in the form of the alpha and hence feels guilty; rather—like the little kid reaching into a cookie jar who pauses and calls out softly, "God? Are you watching?"—our male monkey's not entirely sure who knows what. Things are simplest in an open world, one where everybody is out and about and you can see them all; any additional complexities, like others coming and going, barriers to sight but not sound, and so on, present challenges for thinking and opportunities for action. We close by considering the nature of this world.

HAVING A WORLD

What Is a World?

Here it helps to take some terminology that was first developed in studies of human beings—specifically, phenomenological philosophy and psychology—and use them to understand animals (as was done by some of the phenomenological psychologists, such as Maurice Merleau-Ponty and W. Metzger).

We all naturally employ the term *environment* when thinking about animals and nature; it now has a positive connotation of nature and, increasingly, something that needs to be protected. But it was first introduced as a translation of the German *Umwelt*, used by Jakob von Uexküll to describe the phenomenological experience of the animal. To understand what he meant by this, think of an animal, say, a frog, sitting still and alert in the middle of a copse. Think of a (perhaps flattened) hemisphere that surrounds the frog—the frog at the center, and the sphere going up into the sky to some extent. From anywhere in this hemisphere may originate an impulse that will travel and impinge upon the frog's sensory system—a bird passes overhead, temporarily blocking the sun;

the ground underneath trembles slightly, due to a tractor 150 yards away; a dog barks from a different direction; or there is a scent of human wafting closer. The frog's position is central and it is aware, but it does not necessarily have a key to the integration of all of these experiences.

To have a *world* means to go beyond this. A world, at least, contains the following: First, it is a *neutral substrate* for representations (or "presentations"—objects, motions, and whatever else occurs *in* the realm of sensible experience).[17] We think of our neutral substrate as involving, more than anything, space and time. But this isn't necessarily the only possibility. Second, it is traversable in a particular way which, following Piaget (1970), may be understood in terms of *reversibility*. Although we can't go back in time, we understand that there are multiple pathways to the same place, and that we can go backward in space if we take the time. Further, we also understand that we can get *behind* things. A strictly *environmental* view does not have this "behind." Everything is a potemkin village: not to be sensed is not to exist. Third, we place *other organisms* in the same world as us. We don't need to believe that they have the same interiority that we do—and hence we don't yet need "selves" in order to have a world—but we do need to imagine that they can get to the same places that *we* can get to.

Do animals have worlds? It is hard to know, but it seems certain that *some* of them do. How can we tell? One way is to see whether they have "mental maps." It has been hard to comprehend how an animal can have a true mental map without having a world. Of course, just because we can't comprehend something doesn't mean it isn't possible. An animal is generally believed to have a mental map when it can do what is called "integration." Suppose you train an animal that if it goes ten meters north, then ten meters west, then ten meters south, it gets a treat. If it repeats this sequence the next time when it could very well just make a beeline for the treat, we assume it does not have a mental map. But if it just goes ten meters west, we assume it does.

[17] Most phenomenologists, in their zeal to stamp out the last vestiges of Cartesianism, deny the centrality of any such neutral substrate, arguing that there is no "empty substrate" but only positive existences, and then the configuration of relations between these (an argument easiest to make with regard to vision). There is a deep truth to this, but I think it is often misleading. On the one hand, it may well be that, contrary to Cartesian implications, this lived substrate is shaped by the particularities of the set of relations between sensibles—a space between two high walls *feels* and hence experientially *is* different from one running on top of a narrow ridge. But on the other hand, it is also the case that we have an *experienced* "position-ness" of many everyday objects such that we believe, trust, feel, and, I argue, *sense* that this space would remain were the object removed. (At least, this holds when we are confronted with a variety of medium and small objects. Being with a single incredibly large object can destroy our sense of space.) I further believe that this is *not* a simple and necessary function of the overall configuration of sensed objects, because I do not believe that all animals with vision necessarily produce this sense of a neutral substrate. Thus although we do not necessarily have (as Kant thought) Cartesian time and space as a prioris of sensibility, we may actually have a hardwired predisposition to induce a certain type of substrate from our sensations that not all animals share. In sum, phenomenological doctrines that are good for intra-species statements (which has been the focus of most phenomenologists) may be misleading in an inter-species comparison.

As the word "beeline" might suggest, bees can do this integration. Ever since von Frisch's (von Frisch and Lindauer 1956) amazing work, entomologists have known that honeybee foragers come back and report on the direction and distance of nectar sources by performing a "waggle dance." There's been controversy over some claims—in particular, that they do not follow a dance, suggesting that a flower is in an impossible place (e.g., the middle of a body of water) (see Gould and Gould 1999). Were these more radical claims correct, we might have to accept that bees have full-fledged mental maps. If they are not, it is possible to explain the integration with merely a dedicated module for this sort of operation. That is, integration does not necessarily imply a mental map, though a mental map implies (some degree of) integration.

Further, it's important to understand that a creature that does have a mental map rarely has a complete one. It's not like a human-made physical map, which is a convex surface, all internal parts of which are *terra cognita*. Indeed, even we humans' own mental maps often are not only incomplete but consist of parts that may be tied together with a thin thread. Thus, even if you have a good mental map of one area, and another of a second area, and understand that they are tied by a path, you might have no real sense of their reciprocal orientation. Thus we might be able to carry out integration tasks *within* either of the areas, but fail at tasks that *spanned* the areas.

A mental map seems to require a sort of flexibility in integration that a bee might or might not possess. Further, it requires that one be able to retain and speculatively "live in" the map—for example, not merely to integrate but to compile, and to do so in novel circumstances. This was proven for rats by the great Edward Tolman (Tolman et al. 1946a,b), though orthodox behaviorists just ignored him, refusing to believe his results. Several species of fish, and indeed, some octopuses seem to have these sorts of mental maps, since they can jump *out* of their own tidepool into another one that often forms in the same area (see, e.g., Guttridge et al. 2009: 6).

It seems obvious that having a world can allow for a certain kind of social action that would otherwise be very difficult. In particular, it is quite probable that it can be the basis for taking the role of the other; it is very hard to imagine this short of having a real world. However, I think that current studies suggest that having a world may make possible certain kinds of social action even *without* Meadian self-consciousness.

In fact, investigations of Meadian behavior by animals that almost certainly do have self-consciousness (chimpanzees) often led to surprising behaviors because a chimpanzee would seem to pass a "theory of mind" type test in one situation but then fail in another. Researchers were scratching their heads, wondering whether chimpanzees could see themselves from the outside. Many of the tasks that were assumed to require seeing oneself through others' eyes in fact were probably being done with a simpler heuristic—namely, *seeing others' eyes.* (As the truck bumpersticker says, "If you can't see my mirrors, I can't see you.")

Now even when chimpanzees *can't* see the eyes of those who are watching them, they can clearly model the line of sight of another sentient primate and conduct themselves accordingly—that is, they can sneak. But they do this only when they have a good reason.[18]

And what constitutes a good reason depends on who you are. Rosati, Santos, and Hare (2010: 129) find that subordinate chimps are more likely to choose the food that a dominant one *can't* also see, while dominants are more likely to take the food that the subordinate *can* see (food that is thus at risk of being taken). Now it could be that one hypothetically transports himself into the other's mind and says, "If I were he, what can I see?" and in fact this may be done in certain complicated tasks. But the thing about living in a world is that we can read off many of the answers we need to these tasks without modeling another's subjectivity. In fact, chimpanzees may have that same sort of Platonic theory of sight that seems the natural first guess of most humans—that eyes shoot out beams. That means that you can see what the other fellow sees not by taking his role but by seeing his sight. Phenomenologically, chimpanzees and many monkeys are good at seeing what another animal is *tending toward*—What is the other's focus of attention? Where is it likely to go? This may lead to an ellipse of space, a personal bubble, that they can enter or stay out of as they choose.

And I believe that similar processes are far more important for humans than we have believed. Modeling—that is, formulating a clear representation of the physical and mental states of others so as to make inferences—is, I am increasingly persuaded, almost never done outside of linguistically mediated interactions. It's just too hard. We have these various tests of false knowledge, but (except for the suppression of information from others) they are extremely artificial. As we saw in Chapter 3, it's rather difficult to construct a case in which we would form the idea that someone else's knowledge is incorrect outside of an actual interaction in which this other person says "X is Y" and we know—and say—it isn't. It's not that it's impossible to imagine something like this, but it's hard to explain why it would be worth the cognitive effort if there's a simpler way of getting what you want.

Thus, having a world allows for animals to carry out tasks that would defeat even a much smarter animal that could not hang its thinking on the pegs of actual objects—looking at the eyes of others, seeing the simultaneous interrelations of three things at once as a triad as opposed to having to piece them

[18] Chimpanzees turn out to fail at many theory-of-mind tasks that are about *cooperation*, when they can carry these out under circumstances of *competition*. The problem seems to be not that the task is too hard—they're still stuck on the idea, "this stranger wants to *help* me?!?" Chimpanzees are mostly not very nice people.

together from three (or six) dyadic relations, and so on. This turns out to shed light on issues of social intelligence that have been confusing us for some time, namely, the nature of imitation and of culture.

The Problem of Learning

"Monkey see, monkey do." There is a great deal of truth to this—but we have often taken the wrong lesson. We assume that stupid animals can "ape" others—merely imitate—as opposed to figuring things out on their own. To have a true *culture* in the sense of subjective traditions of dealing with the world that are passed down (nongenetically), well *that*, we suppose, is far beyond any of the animals. And yet, once we understand the way in which having a "world" is used in cognitive and social actions, we find that the reverse is true. Culture, as we'll see in the next section, is pretty easy to acquire (which doesn't mean that some baboon will be the next Shakespeare). Actual imitation, as it is currently defined by animal scientists, turns out to be extremely difficult and complex. It is we, not apes, who are experts at "aping."

To begin, we need to be clear on what we mean by learning more generally. Classical behaviorism assumed that all animals could learn, but only through piecemeal conditioning. Further, this learning did not become "knowledge" in the sense of information that is "globally available" to mental processes. That is, not only do we humans know *how* to grab a snake when we see a snake, but we can reflect on this when we are *not* confronted with a snake, and, for example, perhaps model it using a rope. But an animal can "know how" to do something without "knowing that" it knows (it can have "procedural" memory without the corresponding "declarative" memory).

Classical behaviorism was wrong in many ways; perhaps most important was in its refusal to entertain the possibility of what Köhler (1925 [1917]) called insight: when an animal sees a problem as a whole and how the parts contribute to the solution. Then its action can be guided by the future—its *goal*, and not its past. For example, a chimpanzee staring in frustration at a hanging banana would suddenly run off and return with a crate on which he could climb—no interminable bouts of random variation and positive reinforcement needed. Because insight seemed the sort of successful thinking that we do when we are *smart* (Ah-ha! I understand it now!), it was assumed that granting insight to animals implied a wholesale upgrading of our estimation of their think-power. Both behaviorists (doubters) and Gestalt theorists (believers) made this assumption. Certainly insight implies something more than the unconscious reinforcement posited by behaviorists, but insight might not be as remarkable as it sounds. I'm going to argue that the thing about having a world is that you don't need to be an Einstein to "see" a solution all at once; if it's actually in the world and all the pieces are near you, it's a lot easier to see a solution than to learn it.[19]

Social Learning

So, to return to learning, animal scientists defined "social learning" as one animal learning about the world by observing or interacting with others. We might immediately imagine that this involves "teaching," but examples of true teaching are very rare in most of the animal kingdom, and some of these (e.g., mother cats teaching kittens how to hunt) may not involve the mother's *awareness* of the kittens' ignorance (Cheney and Seyfarth 1990: 223).[20] But even when mothers do not teach, offspring learn.

For a classic example, roof-rat offspring learn to open pinecones by watching their mothers do it. Yet they do not imitate. The mother opens pinecones by stripping scales; young try to get seeds from her; as they grow older, they grab partially opened cones and continue the process themselves. Those whose mothers knew how to do it, learned; those whose mothers didn't, didn't learn. But this is not imitation because it seems that the actions of the mother only focus the attention of the young on the pinecones and (largely by accident) give them partially done examples that they can figure out how to finish (Galef 2007: 209).

Why don't they just copy what the mother is doing? After all, they want to eat the seeds, too. Imitation seems to be hard because it requires a mapping of one's own body onto another's, and in many cases, a mapping of subjectivity to subjectivity as well.[21] That is, it involves knowing

1. I want to eat pinecone seeds.
2. She wants to eat pinecone seeds.

[19] And who knows—Einstein probably "saw" the solution to special relativity in the Lorentz equations that he could put on a single sheet of paper . . . .

[20] A few well-known examples of ape teaching are fascinating because they are so rare in non-language-trained apes. Yet language-trained apes have taught each other signs.

[21] The importance of mirror neurons in no way supports the idea that true imitation is common for primates (Rizzolatti and Craighero 2004: 170). Quick review: monkey brain area F5 has two types of neurons. First there are canonical neurons, which respond to presentation of an object. They also fire when an actor performs the action on an object and when the object is observed. Barrett and Henzi (2005: 1870) argue that "What this means is that the affordances of an object (its possibilities for action) are built directly into our perceptual representation of it." That's as much as to say, by the way, that the Gestalt and ecological psychologists were right after all.

Second, there are mirror neurons that respond when a monkey sees object-directed action, whether the hand grasping something is a monkey's hand or a human's hand. It seems that actions that are recognized as such are mapped onto the observer's motor system; those that don't are recognized on a purely visual basis without motor involvement (Rizzolatti and Craighero 2004: 179). They indicate "action understanding," it seems. But that doesn't imply the possibility of imitation.

3. She is doing something with her paws and teeth.
4. I have paws and teeth like hers.
5. Hence, I will use my paws and teeth like she uses her paws and teeth and accomplish for myself the goal she has set out to accomplish for herself.

This is actually mentally complex, so it is not surprising that while "monkey see monkey do" holds well for monkeys, it holds even more for human infants. That is, human infants are likely to copy *exactly* the motions that another makes, while other primates are more likely to use *convenient* motions to accomplish the same *goal* that the observed animal is meeting.[22]

So what are the animals learning? Here we must introduce a key piece of terminology used in ecological psychology (e.g., Gibson 1986 [1979]) and also social psychological field theory — namely, affordances. Affordances are the characteristics of objects that give them potentials for our actions. A rock affords throwing, a strawberry eating, an oak tree climbing. Ecological psychologists argue that animals need to be understood to have the capacity to directly perceive these affordances, and I believe that this is correct (see footnote 21). But animals often need to *learn* about the affordances in order to perceive them (Tomasello 1996). Watching a conspecific achieve a certain type of success does not, I believe, allow the observer to *imitate* the *action*, but it tells the observer that this *can be done*. This pinecone affords stripping. That is, the animals literally perceive the objects differently. And this is the sort of change that can happen with insight: when a chimpanzee suddenly sees a large box as "something that can be stood on" and reaches the banana.

A justly well-known piece of work along these lines comes from Dugatkin's (1996) studies of female mate choice among guppies. Guppy females are more likely to choose a male that they have seen a *different* female choose. Presumably, this is because of the cheap information: if someone else chooses something, maybe she knows more than you do, so why not copy? Or that's our logical re-creation. Presumably, the *way* this happens is that the male guppy *looks* more attractive in the same way that the pinecone now *looks* openable.

---

[22] I am aware of some fascinating work that suggests the prevalence of true imitation based on intersubjective reasoning, such as the five steps outlined earlier. The gist of the experiments (Range et al. 2007) is to have subject animals observe other animals (the "models"), reaching a valued goal. All models use a somewhat strange method (e.g., a dog uses a paw to pull a lever), but in half the cases, there is an obvious reason for this (e.g., the dog has something in its jaws)— call these the "burdened" cases. In the "unburdened" cases, there doesn't seem to be reason for the model to use the unusual method. The observers paired with burdened models did *not* mimic the action exactly, seeming to reason that "one can use one's jaws to pull; it's just that this model has something in his." The animals observing the unburdened model, lacking a plausible account for the strange action, used their own paws. I do not doubt the results, but I find it difficult to accept that the dogs are going through the imitative thought process laid out above; it doesn't fit with other things we know about dogs. This is a lot of chains of reasoning even for a smart pup.

Thus, animals may be unlikely to "imitate" in the way we might have first imagined, but they don't need to, at least, not if they live in a world. Stuff in the world carries information about itself — some things *look* light, or graspable — and, with experience, we can learn how to "see" what we can do with this stuff. Even more, we can change the world. Humans make it very easy to know what to do with things, because we write on them — stuff like "push down and turn" or "squeeze from the bottom up." But even without writing, acting on the world can solve epistemic problems: we can take one object over to another to *see* whether it will fit (Kirsh and Maglio 1994). Animals can do similar things. And for this very reason, it turns out that culture is extremely common in animals, because all it requires is that animals shape and respond to their own worlds.

Culture

Scientists first assumed that animals imitated; the real question was whether they could by any stretch of the mind be said to have *culture*. By culture, folks generally meant traditions of behavior that varied across groups and were passed down intergenerationally, but not genetically. This cut against the "animal-as-programmed-machine" view that many skeptics held. Their assumption was that every animal comes basically fully programmed out of the box with a set of innate behavior patterns, and given certain stimuli, it would spit out its programmed behavior. If put in the wrong environment, it would simply carry out actions that were suboptimal at best, or perhaps completely senseless.[23]

I've said that culture is easy, because it involves changing the world. Change the world for other animals and you change their behavior. You can change the world physically by reorganizing matter: building a mound, tramping down a path, ripping out a tree. Or you can change the world of experience by changing the perceived affordances of objects. Since most intelligence is in the environment, this leads to highly "intelligent" action — even on the part of somewhat dim actors.

Kaplan and Rogers (2000: 33) related the story of an orangutan at a rehabilitation program intended to "graduate" harmed apes back into the wild. But this one was so very attached to her human caregivers that she would not leave the area when released. And so they would drop her off farther and farther from the center, and she would still manage to make her way back. Then they took her

[23] Classic behaviorism, with its emphasis on learning, did not make this assumption, and it is important to bear in mind that the ethological studies that did were an important *advance* over behaviorism, which treated all animals as if they were rats or pigeons — super-flexible learners.

beyond what they expected was her range of travel. Later that day, a bus pulled up at the stop near the center, and the orangutan got out. She had walked to the bus stop, boarded the bus without hesitation, and gotten off at the right stop. She was happy to see her friends again.

We might think, "What an amazing thing. Isn't she smart!?" And that's true if we mean "she's nearly as smart as we are!" But the real thing is that we aren't individually smart, it's that we have a constructed environment that makes it easy to be smart. For example, we have buses that arrive at the same place every day at the same time. They even say where they are going, for those creatures that can read. In many ways, this is a lot easier to grasp mentally than the likely path of a jaguar who is sneaking up on you.

In other words, a great deal of the organization of animal life, even the social aspects of this organization, come from the shaping of the environment. If there's a cliff on one side and a lake on the other, all the animals walk a certain way. Once they walk one way once, they're often more likely to walk there again. Small animals like ants may leave comforting odor trails; larger ones have tramped down vegetation to make it an easier trip. As the animals act, they transform their environment in such a way as to channel future action.

Thus collectivities form habits that are not merely embodied in their minds and muscles, but in the world outside. It seems that most of the ants' and termites' organization is that sort of collective physical habit. We might be tempted to say that the smarter the organism, the more the habit is inside as opposed to outside, but it's not clear that this is so.

But animals also change their world (that is, their experienced world) by changing the affordances of the objects around them. A bear cub watching its mother pull open a picnic basket learns that picnic baskets afford eating (Mazur and Seher 2008). And for this reason, we see divergences in behavior across groups of the same species. Some of the classic stories here are still contested, but certainly for apes and many monkeys, as well as corvids like crows and ravens, we see such cultural behavior. It isn't a secret anymore that apes make and use tools, but tool use differs across chimpanzee groups because they live in different environments and discover different things. (See the essays collected in Wrangham et al. 1994, especially those of McGrew on tools, and Huffman and Wrangham on medicinal use of plants.) Indeed, animals that display culture also often have "fads" or "fashions" that sweep through a group and are then abandoned (Köhler 1925 [1917]: 85; Goodall 1986: 92, 144ff.). When crows discover that a lion in a zoo can be tormented, they may find playing this game to be irresistible, while other crows may not know that a lion "affords" teasing. But sooner or later, the game gets boring.

CONCLUSION

Spiders are different from dolphins; crows are different from rhesus monkeys. And it may not be that we are closer to chimpanzees than to monkeys, and closer to monkeys than to other mammals, let alone to birds, in terms of our basic cognitive workings. We can't learn about our "true nature" from studying animals. Instead, what we learn from animal studies is that we may have theoretical prejudices that come from the fact that (to simplify greatly) the linguistically oriented part of our mind, the one that writes books and conducts research (among other things), tends to assume that it is in charge of everything. Its job, however, is not to lead the body in all respects. It is to interact with others, to solve certain types of novel problems, and whenever it has free time, to continue its wonderful history that it is writing—in true Joe Bob Briggs (1988) style, it is "the history of the world, or, my main accomplishments."

But sometimes it seems that the body is off behaving a bit differently from the way the narrator describes things. Of course, this basic idea is not new, and we see in Merleau-Ponty a very compelling rendering of the general approach. However, what the animal studies suggest is that it is not merely the iterative re-shaping of our environment that allows for intelligence, but also that key aspects of our structure come from when we can and cannot displace others. In the last chapter, I make a simple suggestion of how we can build on these premises for human action.

CHAPTER 6

"The Gentleman Is to Let the Lady Enter the Door First"

Or How the Environment Tells Us What to Do

MOTIVES AND TENDENCIES

Go Figure

When we're tired, or in a hurry, or focused on something else, almost all of us in sociology fall back on what I'll call "good old-fashioned action theory" (GOFAT). Almost no sociological theorist would defend it, and yet we use it almost all the time. We try to attach fancier or newer terms to this basic structure (and recognize the "practical" nature of this or that), but such qualifications don't seem to have gone very deep into our way of thinking about action. (Of course, there are some people who put forward very different ideas, but these haven't convinced the rest. I think that we *should* be able to convince them, and that's the goal of the current chapter.)

GOFAT links actions to motivations, first and foremost. These motivations, in turn, usually come from some sort of mixing process that, even if not a true calculus, can take inputs from "values" and from "interests," and use some form of rational or quasi-rational deliberation if necessary to make all this work together. The fact that people are being moved by the same values, or by systematically related interests, produces regularity in actions and allows us to explain them. In fact, for a long time, interests alone were understood as sufficient to guarantee the possibility of social science. One thing about rational interests, as Hirschmann (1977) said, is that unlike other passions, they are predictable. Although there are conflicts of interest between persons, we can at least learn to make a social order that contains them or works with them, as opposed to the conflict implying chaos.

However, this sort of order wasn't quite orderly enough for the sociologists, and so they emphasized the importance of *values*. Parsons (1968 [1949]) in particular argued that just having actions be motivated by interests would lead to a war of all against all which, even if predictable, lacked the kind of order that springs to mind when we use the term "orderly." Nowadays, we compromise, admitting that *both* interests *and* values lead to action (Parsons joined these in a great-chain-of-normative-being). Actors think about things and decide to do one of a number of possibilities, taking into account the means and materials at their disposal, and the likely results, as well as all the moral prescriptions and proscriptions around. Further, we assume that an act is a naturally meaningful unit. People commence an act as a means to their end, and when they emerge out of it, with success or failure to their credit, the act is done.

This might seem so obvious that we forget other ways of beginning—other ways in which the orderliness of action can be approached. One of these is related to older ideas of action, prescriptive accounts turning on virtue, and this is to understand people as having "characters"—abiding profiles of tendencies that come from the inner nature of each one. And indeed, I will argue that "character," despite its antiquated ring, will turn out to be a nontrivial form of regularity for social action. Another possibility has often been considered only in terms of *weakness* of character, and this is the importance of "situational factors"—certain situations tend to call out certain types of actions from persons, no matter what their values or interests. Recognizing the importance of situational factors is often understood to imply positing the weakness of character, for those with strong characters are the same in all circumstances (think of Scott's men politely freezing to death in turn at the South Pole).

Now I think there are good *empirical* reasons to jettison GOFAT. That is, I think the evidence doesn't support it, and instead points in other directions. However, that isn't always enough to lead us to reject a theory, and in some cases, it *shouldn't*. This is especially true if we can't come up with any coherent alternative. We're always going to think in *some* way, and if we stick with a false theory, at least we'll know *which* way. But in this case, there *are* alternatives. Here, drawing on the results of the previous chapter, I want to propose that there is a coherent, largely situation-based (though character-sensitive), approach to explaining action.

What Are Motivations?

One of the greatest pieces in sociological theory was C. Wright Mills's (1940) article on motivations. Inspired by American pragmatism and its (I think still) revolutionary reappraisal of the nature of action, Mills turned his attention to motives. According to GOFAT, motivations precede actions: "First you gotta tell yourself you're gonna do it, and then—you gotta do it!" In Hobbes's (1909 [1651]) version, a stirring in the imagination rattles around in the nervous system, sending some sort of impulse—*"Now I want you to pick up that pipe"*—to the hand. The motive is the cognitive version of the act; in some ways, it is the ideal expression of the act itself. In the beginning were the words—*"Pick up the pipe"*—and then, lo, there was the action.[1]

Mills basically asked us to put our folk theories on hold, and be empiricists, at least for a while. Where do we actually *see* "motives" appear? Introspection actually has a tough time uncovering it. I just typed eight words and fifty characters in the previous sentence. Did I have a motive to type the "p" in *introspection*? Or was that not an act? Did I have a motive to type *introspection*? Was *that* an act? Or was the act the typing of the sentence *Introspection actually has a tough time uncovering it.*? But when I started, I didn't even know I would end with the word *it*. Was it writing this book that was the act that was preceded by the motivation? But I'd already formulated portions before I had the idea of writing a book, and the decision to put them together in a book came as I was impulsively lying to an editor, assuring him that I planned to write a book of essays on theory while working on a larger project, so that people would know I was still alive. "Sounds like a good idea," I thought to myself, as I heard the blatant fabrication.

This actually seems to be rather typical of actions. They usually don't have a "pre-" action stage whereby the motive *could* be formulated.[2] The means are often their own ends. And so on. So if we don't find a clear "motive to write this book" or "motive to go to college" or "motive to go shopping" when we seriously introspect recent concrete activities, where *do* we see motives? Mills's answer was that we see them *after* the event. Sometimes these come in the form of "accounting"—when we attempt to excuse ourselves if our actions are challenged. "Why didn't you water the lawn?" "Well, it looked like it might rain, so I thought I'd save the water and wait to see . . ." But even outside of the challenge-account couplet, motives emerge after the act, when the actor is involved in social

[1] Most neurologists would say that there's strong evidence against this, since instruments will pick up changes in the neural system that precede our conscious awareness of wanting to do an act. But it isn't quite a closed case, because it's so hard to compare the timings of different parts of the nervous system. As you can imagine, it might also take some time to go from wanting to do something to knowing you want to do something to remembering to press a button to actually have your finger press a button indicating "I want to make a movement." So I'm happy to consider this an open issue, and one that might go nowhere if it turns out we are attempting to split up things that are indivisible.

[2] Colin Campbell's (1996: 58f) response to this critique is to say that the critics are looking in the wrong places (such as, right before typing "it"), so of course they aren't finding the formulation of a coherent subjective motive. Rather, we should use the presence of such a motive to determine where an act begins and ends. So, for example, if today I go to the post office, as I currently intend, that would be a good example of an act, and it has a motivation that in fact existed in a stage of deliberation ("I should go to the post office to mail that letter.") before the act. This is entirely acceptable, but it means that, from the moment the alarm clock rang today to the time I fall asleep, this is likely to be the *only* "act" I have accomplished—as I didn't think like this before I made coffee, went to work, picked up reading where I had left off, and so on.

dialogue.[3] It turns out that often these professed motives aren't empirically very sound; even when they're trying to be honest, people seem to do better at explaining why they *would do* that action *now* than they are at recalling the precise constellation that existed *then*. But even if our offered motives are as accurate as accurate can be, they're still a selection, said Mills, of different *vocabularies* of motive. A person can "become" a doctor "because" she didn't want to be poor, because she wanted to help people, because she found math (her true love) too hard, and so on. In certain circumstances, Mills argued, one of these vocabularies may be favored over another, and for no (scientifically) good reason.

So I have said (correctly) that I didn't have "an" idea for this book before the writing. Even further, in some ways, I didn't write it so much as it used me to write itself. This section was added because it became obvious that it needed to be here, when I read over the third draft. If you had read it, you'd probably have added this section, too. Of course, maybe not—there are branches in the paths that lead through the space of all possible outcomes, which is why we can assume that the thousand monkeys don't all type the same thing. But the book as it was, my local environment, called for someone to add this in. I just happened to be here as the first responder. This idea—that action is really a dialectic, a continuous interaction with the world, yada yada—certainly isn't new (an elegant formulation tied to more specific claims should be forthcoming in a book by Ira Cohen). And that's why I hadn't put it in the earlier drafts—because everyone knows it already.

Or do they? We often assent to this vision of action, yet also claim that action can be explained as rule following, not understanding that this completely contradicts the dialectical understanding of action. As we'll see, this dialectical vision instead is compatible with a different understanding of the nature of social action, one more in tune with pragmatism. That is, most of the sociologists I talk to do acknowledge that GOFAT might exaggerate the degree to which motivations are always conscious. But they reject Mills's idea of considering motives as coming *after* action. "So just call the mental things that come before the action 'motivations,' even if they aren't well-formed, propositional beliefs." *Before*? This still assumes that action naturally breaks up into droplets, unit acts, each with its own subjective preface. If this isn't so—and I think every last bit of evidence tells us, and has told us, for 2000 years, that it isn't so—then this is to stick with a fundamentally misleading understanding of action, just to avoid rethinking our vocabulary. The chunking whereby one part of the stream of

[3] Some ethnomethodologists distinguish between *excuses*—when we lessen our degree of attributed control over some outcome, recognizing that it was a dispreferred outcome—and *justifications*, when we believe that we can demonstrate that our actions were defensible and thus do not need to lessen our agency (Scott and Lyman 1968).

behavior turns into "an" act only comes in the accounting after the fact. The "act" as such doesn't exist for it to have a motive. That doesn't mean there aren't cognitive components of action, but we can't rely on a minor modification of GOFAT to understand them.

Deliberation and Liberty

It is not that the pragmatist tradition, on which Mills drew, denied that people ever thought before acting. Rather (and here Dewey [e.g., 1930 (1922)] is our chief exemplar), their understanding was that action is an alternation between nonproblematic, habitual action, and problems. Problems are thrown up by the world. They call for readjustment, recalibration, and sometimes even deliberation.

Thus if we want, we can certainly find examples of deliberation before action through introspection. Indeed, many of us spend countless hours (often around 1 AM) deliberating over what to do. But when translating these data to our theoretical understanding, we can easily make two mistakes. The first is to hold on to this "deliberation-first" mode as the fundamental one for our theory of action, when it seems to be the exception. This is an easy mistake to make, for if we try to think about our action, by definition, we are reflecting. It's easy then to say that a key part of *anything* is the presence of this sort of reflective consciousness. But that's formally akin to concluding that the light is *always* on inside the refrigerator, because every time you open it to check, it's on![4]

The second mistake is that we easily confuse the fact that deliberation often arms us with justifications for our action, which is certainly true, with the thesis that deliberation is responsible for the choice—this is an empirical question, and the evidence is not great in its favor. Indeed, it may well be that deliberation is not a part of a process of *making* a decision but more what it feels like when one is *unable* to make a decision. At least, when I am awake at night, you could call it "deliberation" or "obsession" or "indecision" with equal justification. It doesn't have much to do with those (few) actions that I successfully implement.

[4] Archer (2003) has suggested structured differences in the type of reflection that people use, which gives us a much richer sense of the nature of internal dialogue, though the question of its proportionate weight in explaining action remains open. Indeed, it may well be that her empirical work is not immune to the refrigerator problem—by asking respondents about their reflection, and then categorizing them by their responses to *her*, Archer may not simply be assuming what some of us doubt, the centrality of deliberation, but indeed *creating* the particularities (one cannot help noticing that the category of "meta-reflexives" are PLUs—"people like us"—who, themselves academics, know how to express a thoughtful accounting that will push another academic's buttons). Thus, what appears to be an avenue to the innermost subjectivity of others may be a joint production of the interview situation.

Although deliberation, then, often does take place, it does not do so "before" the act has begun. Instead, any truly weighty decision is actually a conglomerate, most of which consists of nondecisions and nonactions: before you can "decide" to be a doctor, you need to have taken enough biology courses to go to medical school; if you took a lot of religion and history classes, you've already embarked on a path that makes the decision to forget about medical school a *fait accompli*; and so on. By the time of the "deliberation" and the discursive reasoning, almost all the "decision" has already taken place, because we have already shaped our environment so that we only need to look around to figure out where we have already guided ourselves, by means of previous actions that have foreclosed enough options that a calculus is not as silly as it would be for a more open-ended choice. If deliberation is prolonged, it may simply be that we have failed at a successful trajectory.

In sum, the fact that we often deliberate — run through different possibilities, attempting to weigh the positives and negatives — doesn't mean that we have found evidence for GOFAT. We only count it as evidence if we assume what is in question — that these sorts of psychic events are the causes of later action. And here is where orthological (and not substantive) considerations come in.

Tendentious Tendencies

What are motivations? Clifford Geertz (1973: 96) gives a classic formulation: "A motivation is a persisting tendency, a chronic inclination to perform certain sorts of acts and experience certain sorts of feeling in certain sorts of situations." That, at least, seems a pretty safe definition. But it can encourage some dangerous leaps of faith.

When one is trying to explain a phenomenon but doesn't quite understand it, the most appealing sort of explanation is often a pseudo-explanation, whereby we try to take the phenomenon we're trying to explain, and stuff it back into the object of explanation. We can then pull it out like a rabbit from a hat. Perhaps the most generic one is the idea of "tendency." We try to explain *X*'s appearing some way or doing something by saying that it has a tendency to do so. You might think this is so obviously silly that no one with a brain would propose something this vacuous — at least, not since the early modern period. After all, thanks to Molière, we're all familiar with the foolish scholastic explanations that only restated what was to be explained — thus opium's effects are due to its "soporific tendencies."

Yet it turns out that it is often hard to avoid the tendency to invent tendencies — indeed, the realist theorist examined in Chapter 3, Roy Bhaskar (1975), deliberately tried to rescue the idea of tendency for scientific explanation.[5] I confess that I found myself relying on the idea of "structural tendencies" as I tried to formulate an understanding of how social structure emerges (Martin 2009: chapter 1). Once I realized that (in early drafts) I had actually inserted a tautology and dressed it up like an explanation, I was distraught, and it took quite some time before I was able to specify it nontautologically if vaguely as actual sentiments experienced by actors.

It turns out that it isn't quite the tautological nature of the idea of tendency that is the problem. That may bring the problem to our attention, but it is only a polar position of a continuum of problematic usages. In all cases on this continuum, there is something, some phenomenon *X*, that we are attempting to explain. So we take *X* and somehow push it, in some materialized form, into the entity responsible for the phenomenon. For example, the phlogiston theory of combustion was that there is something potentially fiery in objects (phlogiston), and objects burn because the phlogiston in them comes out and is actualized. These theorists were too hasty, and needed to remember that the only place they empirically saw evidence of fire was in the burning, not the pre-burning. It was overly convenient to assume it into the objects. And that's our theory of motivation. It's the action, stuffed into the head of the actor, idealized, but not fundamentally changed. It should raise a dozen danger flags.

Now consider another form of the tendency argument, one on which I've relied a great deal, namely, the idea of "quality." A quality, Peirce (1955 [1875–1910]: 85ff) said, is a *potential* for experience—that doesn't mean it isn't *real*, for it can be a real potential.[6] Thus we may say that the quality of redness is the potential of something to induce a qualia of "looking red" in a human observer who sees it under certain conditions. To say that its redness is *explained* by its quality of redness is completely circular and a waste of breath.

But that doesn't mean that the idea of quality is useless. Formulaically, we can say that if a quality is an attribute of some set of elements S (not necessarily a single element), say, $Q(S)$, that is defined by its propensity to produce some event on S, say, $E(S)$, that is a transformation in other attributes of S, we don't get any purchase by saying $Q(S) \rightarrow E(S)$. However, that doesn't mean that we don't get purchase if we say $Q(S) \rightarrow E(T)$, where $T \cap \sim S \neq \varnothing$ (that is, T includes something that S doesn't). Further, we may be able in many cases to say something about $Q(S)$ other than $\rightarrow E(S)$. It turns out (as we remember from Chapter 3) that we can say a lot of interesting and nontrivial things about the quality of redness in

[5] Bhaskar (1975: 175, 229–231) has a great deal to say about this issue, as he often does for things about which there isn't much to say.

[6] In general, there is a close formal relation between tendency and potential, though we seem to use them somewhat differently, and, though perhaps I can't defend it here, it seems less problematic to claim that a "potential" exists even when it isn't actualized than it is to claim that an entity has a tendency not being put into practice.

addition to its leading things to look red to us. It can signify infection, heat, receding, or what have you.[7]

Further, there is a way in which "quality" turns out to be a *relation* (e.g., a wine tastes fantastic to you and stanky to me), and we might argue that rather than some action being due to the quality of an object (I bought it because it was good wine) or of some characteristic of the actor (I am an oenophile), it is a function of their interaction, giving the two analytic independence from the act. We'll return to this interaction below.

But for now, our lesson is simply that we should always be suspicious when an explanation is of the tendentious form. In many cases, it is a pure tautology that makes us appear to be saying something when we are actually saying nothing at all. However, sometimes inserting a nearly tautological tendency is not at all problematic, if it allows us to link other theoretical elements.[8] Further, there are times when the tendency argument *isn't* tautological — it is wrong. This is when the tendency we insert is not of the contentless variety — something like "whatever-it-is-that-leads-things-like-this-to-do-things-like-that"— but rather, has a specific nature. In the case of motivation, our tendency is a homunculus version of the act, an iconic representation of what the motivation is supposed to cause. And that's our voo-doo doll theory of action.

So it isn't that there aren't things in the actors' heads, or bodies, or both, that explain the action. There certainly must be. But it's overly convenient to imagine that these are action-ideas, representations of the action, or anything like that. It's just like the early modernist scientists who scoffed at the scholastic explanation of opium. The true explanation, they were sure, was that the opium particles were round and smooth, and thus soothed the nerves as they rolled up and down them (Shapin 1996: 57). This isn't a tautology, but it's overly convenient, hoping that "soothingness" can be seen, as such, in the entity. Looking for "motives" for our action in our minds is like doing an fMRI (functional magnetic resonance imaging) on subjects as they talk and expecting to see the words they speak lighting up, spelled out in Times New Roman letters on their brain.

If this model of "motives" is as wrong as I think it is, this realization has some serious implications for one of the issues that is most associated with what are often understood as "cultural" emphases in sociology — namely, the idea that we

---

[7] Take the idea of "habitus," especially as used by Pierre Bourdieu. I'm sure that somewhere this has been criticized for being tautological. Indeed, I myself have argued that there is something wrong when we try to explain, say, someone's choice of an authoritarian political candidate by the actor's "authoritarianism." Isn't this an argument by recourse to habitus? It certainly is, but Bourdieu's wasn't. That is, Bourdieu didn't announce, I can explain everything anyone does — I'll just tell you what his or her habitus is. Rather, if habitus itself can be partially explained, then it is neither tautological nor irrelevant as part of an explanation as a whole.

[8] Note that I am not in any way saying that quality or habitus *is* tautological — both are subject to empirical exploration and have specifiable measurable aspects. However, pursuing their empirical and physically measurable aspects is unnecessary for the argument at this point.

follow rules (or norms, or schema, or whatever). We saw in Chapter 2 that it doesn't make much sense to say that culture constrains us—but does it make sense to say that rules do?

WHO FOLLOWS RULES AND WHEN?

Rules Are for Fools

Since so many of us don't like rules and feel ourselves beset and oppressed by them, it seems undeniable that they are there. Further, since many of us also suffer grievously, time and time again, for violating them, it seems that they matter. Finally, it also seems that these rules must be stored in our heads, and when we don't break them, it's because these rules, in our head, are guiding our actions. Left to your own devices, you are free to drive your automobile any way and anywhere you want. In circles in the middle of the park, up on the neighbor's porch, 100 miles per hour on the left side of the street. But if you drive 55 on the right side, it is because you know that this is what you are supposed to do.

This can't, and so shouldn't, be denied. Yet there seems to be something wrong in our current understanding of rules. For one small thing—probably, you *don't* drive 55, even where that's the law. You might still feel like you are following some sort of rule when you do what basically everyone else is doing. You believe, and you know it isn't so, that it's okay if everybody's doing it. You have a set of things rattling about in your mind—an understanding of the law, a sense of what is typical, and many other different justifications that you can use to explain to your child why you're breaking the law, and which you should probably keep to yourself if you're pulled over by a cop.

More generally, there are indeed patterns of action that we *call* rules, things like you're not allowed to initiate touch with strangers who are your status equals, or that you say "Good morning!" in a perky voice to co-workers but not to good friends, or that when someone asks you "Howzit goin'?" you say "Fine." And so, when we ask (if we do), "Why do people say 'Fine' when asked 'Howzit goin'?" we come up with the answer, "Because they are following the rule."

This does seem to adequately explain the cases of rule following, but it still isn't an acceptable answer if we're looking for a theory of action. We can indeed explain every instant in which we did not put our elbows on the table by appealing to our internalization and memory of "Don't put your elbows on the table," but if this is taken as support for the norms view, then it is only fair that every instant in which we *do* put our elbows on the table is taken as evidence *against* this theory. The problem is that we *do* put our elbows on the table and we *do* hit, and so on. To get a complete "explanation," we must allow one to bring in *other* norms and explain why *in this case* it was permissible to hit or put our elbows on the table.[9] We find that rather than there being "some" norms, there are many, so many, in fact, that it seems that basically *any* action could be described as being in consonance with the larger set of norms. We realize, then, that these "norms" are "ethnomethods"—vocabularies that actors use to *justify* their actions, not *causes* of their actions.

Impressive empirical studies—most important, D. L. Wieder's (1974) work—suggest that, at least in everyday informal action, the rules are something that actors invoke *after* the action to explain, excuse, or condemn it. The "rule" exists only in interactions, when one person attempts to manipulate another's action (whether for good or bad reasons) or to account for his or her own. Thus, argued Wieder, rules aren't things that lie behind and *shape* action, they are things that actors *use* in action—with typical flexibility and perplexing illogicality. There may be a pattern, and the pattern may be theorized by actors, and the actors may formulate this as a rule, but we must not therefore assume that the rule causes the pattern.

The similarity to our previous finding—that the motives appear *post actum*, not *pre actum*—should be worrisome. We saw in Chapter 3 that we need to beware of any argument that sounds substantively impressive but works just as well no matter what we drop in. There our pattern was "X couldn't exist in a people without language," because we had inadvertently substituted '*X*'—that is, the linguistic ideas associated with the term '*X*'—for X itself. So, too, there is a danger in arguments of this form: "Y doesn't lie behind action, because *Y* exists only in social action." The reason is that if empirically we can see things only when they are "in social action," then this is always true and doesn't add much.

Or perhaps it does. There are times when a statement that is true for everything you substitute in is still nonvacuously true. A humorous example is, "You cannot read this sentence without thinking of an *X*." Substitute elephant, submarine, or violin, and it's actually true. And there are claims that we may not be able to dismiss even if they are false, which is frustrating, but they are neither empty nor tautological. Imagine I claimed that blood in your arteries was red, because it was oxygenated, and blood in your veins was blue because it wasn't. Let's also say that even the fair skinned among us get outside enough that we can't see right through pale skin (we are imagining, remember!). You ask where a big vein is, and I trace one on your arm. Emboldened by the quest for knowledge, you stick a pin in your vein and draw out red blood. "Your theory is wrong!" you triumphantly conclude. "But any blood we see has mixed with oxygen and is therefore red," I respond. "Hey, no fair. Your theory is then unfalsifiable! There is

[9] We could also appeal to our animalistic or satanic nature, but this has become unpopular in sociology, because admitting that we all might have enough devil in us to override society requires understanding humans as having a presocial "essence," which we've all agreed to ignore as a possibility. I actually think that's a wise choice, though maybe that's just one of the devil's tricks . . . .

no variation," you complain. I understand your frustration. Without going beyond pinpricks, we can't know the truth. The answer, though, isn't to reject my argument, it's to go beyond pinpricks. The limitation isn't in our thoughts but in our methods.

So, too, there may be something very important in the realization that all the things we're putting in people's heads are ideas that have actually come from their interactions with others. That doesn't mean that *nothing's* in their heads, but if there is something there, it isn't necessarily things like "rules." We must be cautious, but we don't need to automatically withdraw from exploring this idea simply because it might be — not *is*, but *might* be — one of these formulae that work for any X we put in.

Indeed, we shouldn't refuse to entertain that problematic thought experiment, our imaginary world of speechless human beings. These individuals interact but don't talk. In this imaginary world, would there be anything like a "motive" in the sense we understand it? Well, we know there wouldn't be one if we defined motive as the thing-that-is-raised-in-social-interaction. We need to first imagine what we might mean by "motive" in such a way that it isn't impossible in our speechless species by definition. But I actually have a hard time figuring out what sort of motive they might have. It seems that our very idea of motives, our belief that there are such things, may come from the social practice of answering questions and explaining things. We can imagine a motive being something like "drink to quench my thirst." But I find it hard not to conclude that in this speechless world, to the extent that we thought about why we did things, we would not be thinking about ourselves but about our *environments*. Our drinking of water would likely appeal to the qualities of water, not the thirst of the actor.[10] It is, just as Mead would have it, the switch to reflexivity in a certain type of interaction that puts a self in our thoughts, and a motivation is an account that makes use of this self.

Well, this exercise isn't determinative. First, as said above, our inability to imagine something is never a proof; further, even if it were true that speechless beings wouldn't have motives at all yet would still act, this doesn't mean that *we* act without these motives. Maybe speech changes us big time. But perhaps now we can start to imagine a kind of rule following that is dissociated from ex post facto challenge and defense. We can use this to approach the issue of who follows rules and when.

[10] Armchair theorizing often claims that at the root of any action must be a *lack* that motivates us. Phenomenologically, this is extremely implausible and represents an introjection of self-monitoring where there is no reason to expect it. The presence of thirst isn't necessarily experienced as an absence of drink, and water looks refreshing (because it is), often even when we didn't *know* we were thirsty until we saw the water saying "drink me." Sure, the starving person or the stranded crawler in the desert might indeed have a different relation of his inner sensation to his action — but using the stranded crawler as our default model for action might be like using the person blinded by sunlight for our default theory of vision.

Good Morning!

Now let's handle a simple imaginary problem: At 9:04 AM on Friday, Reginald enters his new workplace and says "Good morning!" in a perky voice to Archibald, Elizabeth, and Ronnie, who all work in the same office room. Why did he do this? Was it because of the rule, "You say 'Good morning!' in a perky voice to co-workers but not to good friends"?

Perhaps we can distinguish between:

1. A *pattern*: For example, on Monday, Tuesday, Wednesday, and Thursday, all four people in Reginald's office said "Good morning!" in a perky voice to whoever was already in the office when each arrived.
2. Reginald *seeing* this pattern: "You know, on Monday, Tuesday, Wednesday, and Thursday, everyone in the office said 'Good morning!' in a perky voice to whoever was already in the office when each arrived." I'm going to follow my previous (2011: 303) usage and call this his subjective understanding of (1) *patterning*, and use *pattern* for the underlying regularity.
3. Reginald *extrapolating* from this: "Here it seems that, in general, people say 'Good morning!' in a perky voice to whoever is already in the office."
4. The *descriptive rule*: "People [always] say 'Good morning!' in a perky voice to whoever is already in the office."
5. The *prescriptive rule*: "People should say 'Good morning!' in a perky voice to whoever is already in the office."

If Reginald held (5), this could be used to explain his action. Of course, there could be a somewhat different version that does not involve (5). Instead, there are two other planks:

6. Those who violate descriptive rules are conspicuous.
7. I do not want to be conspicuous.

It seems to me that the "rules" account is happy with either the (1–5; prescriptive) or (1–4, 6–7; descriptive) versions of these. Although in a philosophical sense they are worlds apart (one normative, the other instrumental), both are indeed saying that the rule guides action. But what if we come up with a modified form of (6), call it (6′), that goes as follows: "Those who violate patterns are conspicuous," and propose an account that accepts 1–3, 6′ and 7, but not 4 or 5? This seems to be just as satisfactory. Yet it lacks the idea of the rule (though it does assume that the focal actor will only avoid violating *patternings*, because he won't know about *all* the possible patterns). Of course, it might be that this is splitting hairs — there is no real difference between (2) and (3) and (4). And yet, it seems that there is. There must be thousands and thousands of empirical behavioral regularities ("patterns") in Reginald's office. Not all are recognized as such (and therefore become "patternings"). And so they certainly aren't all rules, which means that breaking such patterns might not be noticed at all, and certainly wouldn't make one conspicuous. For example, if one is left-handed and picks up one's coffee cup with one's left hand, it might not be noticed, and if it was, it might be immediately forgotten.

Some of these patterns can be important for understanding social action. For instance, it appears that in large unstructured spaces with many people going in opposite directions (e.g., the lobby of a train station in rush hour), people dramatically increase their average speed of travel by tending to walk behind someone going in the same direction (Couzin and Krause 2003: 19). They may know they do this, and they certainly wouldn't deny it were it brought to their attention, but that doesn't mean that they do it because they hold the norm. They might actually be swept into the slipstream of other people simply by following a heuristic such as "try to go forward and keep a 2.5′ radius of space around you." Yet they don't have it in the form of a rule that could itself explain their action as due to rule following. And that's because someone who *doesn't* follow isn't perceived as violating the rule, he's just perceived as standing in your way.

Still, so far I've really only demonstrated that patterns (2) aren't the same as descriptive rules (4). But are "patternings" (3) really distinguishable from rules? Can we identify patternings that aren't rules? Or can we figure out what makes a patterning a rule? To do this, let's consider cases in which four things hold: first, an actor *A* can reach generalizations of form (3) above; second, *A* believes that such generalization is generally available — that is, every other *B* in the situation should have a similar generalization. It seems that this second criterion is necessary for a patterning to be a descriptive rule: if we didn't think that others were aware of the patterning, we wouldn't say they were following a rule. In any case, the third thing we'll assume is that there is some *B* who violates the patterning; and the fourth, that this inconveniences *A*. In such a case, *B* may well be perceived as violating *something*, and this may need to be ascribed to *B*'s lack of *knowledge* of the patterning, to *B*'s lack of *ability* to execute the patterning, or to *B*'s lack of *goodwill*. Especially when we go with the last of these, we are likely to see the patterning as more rule-like.

What we are finding—and this is by no means a new argument, it was taught to me by my advisor, Ann Swidler, and I'm stealing her ideas right and left here—is that it isn't the regularity itself that leads to (6), it's that some sorts of regularities have *meaning*. Not saying "Good morning!" is different from how you pick up your cup. Why? Because it is one of the things that can be scrutinized by those who are trying to draw out information on others, with or without their knowledge. Not following a general pattern when it inconveniences *me* means that you are not respecting me, which means that you are a jerk, and a great way to explain your jerkiness is to appeal to the widely understood rule. That is, following the results of the last chapter, something moral emerges as we see the expectations associated with the patterning as legitimate expectations to hold.[11]

On Valentine's Day — which is a pretty stupid holiday honoring a religious figure that even most Catholics don't give a hoot about — we give presents to our true love. Maybe most people do this. Maybe it's a rule. But that's not why we do it, or not exactly. And certainly it's not because we want to pay tribute to Saint Valentine (since no one is even sure who he was). Forgetting Valentine's Day can be a big deal because it's the sort of thing someone who didn't care about his or her true love might do. That's why we all give presents. And it's because "we" all do it, that it has meaning that *you* didn't (and no, it's *not* okay!). If we all didn't, your noncompliance would carry no information.

Now here's the thing: if we all *really* gave chocolates on Valentine's Day, it wouldn't be a rule. Why? Because there would never be occasion to say "You (jerk) *broke the rule. You* forgot *Valentine's Day.*" In my elementary school, there were rules against giving wedgies, cheating, and leaving the campus to get candy, because we — some of us, sometimes — gave wedgies, cheated, and left the campus. There were no rules against lighting children on fire, eating glass, or teaching the class yourself, because no one ever did this.

Sometimes it turns out to be true — that things don't exist unless they're talked about. It's not always true, and in the 1970s some sociology seemed very silly because folks liked the shock value they got by implying that if you didn't mention it, a Sherman tank would bounce right off of you. Power doesn't come from talking. You can call a policeman "my little pony" and not "officer" but that doesn't mean he won't sock you with a billy club. But rules, at least in the way in which we use the idea in sociology, might well only appear *as rules* from the talking about them.

Talking 'bout Rules

This doesn't mean that everything we might want to call a rule has this communicative nature as its core. So thinking back to elementary school, I remember

---

[11] I recognize that one could also argue that there is something pre-existingly moral about the nature of the individual, and it is this that leads to the belief in the legitimacy of expectations here. But this doesn't seem to get at what is distinctive about these situations, at least among people and places where we don't treat people as behaving immorally for accidental wrongs made in ignorance (though they still might be held responsible).

observing and breaking some rules. Some fit the semiotic version: I didn't play with the girls, because that would have semiotic import, so long as other boys weren't playing with the girls; or I didn't pledge allegiance *because* it was a rule, and so disobeying could be meaningful. But other observances and nonobservances lacked this meaning-focus: I didn't tattle, because I didn't want to be punched (pure self-interest); or I didn't copy my neighbor's paper even if it would have been in my self-interest to do so. (Though, interestingly, note that I can't say "I wouldn't have cheated, even if it weren't a rule not to," because if there isn't a rule against it, it's not cheating!)

And yet, there is a way in which to the extent that the *rule-ness* of the rules acted in a distinctive manner for my action, the semiotic component comes to the fore. That is, there were lots of things I didn't do because I didn't want to be punched (not that I wasn't, anyway). Whether they were rules or not didn't really enter my subjectivity. In fact, it might be that (as Hobbes would have said) there is really only one rule of the playground: do not do to another that which is likely to lead you to end up getting punched. Although you could *describe* the action using the idea of rules, there's no reason to think that the subjectivity of the actors was oriented to these rules. The regularity generally comes from somewhere else. Rules appear as rules when there is contestation over them, and when it can be meaningful (or can be made meaningful) to be seen as in or out of compliance with them.

If so, then we can't stick with an explanation of the regularity of action that turns on our walking around with catalogues of rules and following them. What else do we have?

I CAN ONLY OPEN THE DOOR

A Field-Theoretic Account

In other works (especially Martin 2011), I have argued that the importance of field theory is that it provides us a more plausible account of how persons act in regular ways; more plausible, that is, than GOFAT and its kin. I personally think that the field-theoretic account does not fall afoul of the strictures laid out in the preceding chapters, yet I acknowledge that it has been substantively weak. Here I want to see if—in part, drawing on the results of the last chapter—we can push forward an attempt to offer a serious alternative to the norms-driven account.

The running example here, for reasons I will explicate below, will be the norm "The Gentleman Is to Let the Lady Enter the Door First." According to GOFAT, when I am a Gentleman and in the environment is a door and a Lady, I recall the norm, find that it fits the condition ("when a Gentleman and a Lady come to a door . . ."), understand the conclusion (". . . the Gentleman should let the Lady enter the door first."), and hence I let the Lady enter the door first.

In contrast, I have claimed that actors are not guided by such norms and that they do not even carry them around in their heads (though I will clarify this misleading claim below). There have been two justifications for this claim. First, there is the argument of implausibility: it seems hard to imagine that we really carry around norms for every form of regularity in social action. The second justification was parsimony: if we do not need to have an internal rule for all forms of regularity, and we therefore have some other way of producing regularity from the environment, it may be more parsimonious, or at least more intellectually pleasing, if we imagine that all forms of regularity arise thusly—they do not correspond to general norms but rather to regularities in the environment that we experience (here see especially Reed 1996).

These are not actually very strong justifications, especially given what should be an apparent weakness in the critique of GOFAT, namely, that on the one hand, we *do* have verbal formulae for many norms (e.g., don't put your elbows on the table, don't hit, and so on), and on the other hand, it is quite obscure what it means to claim (as I did) that the environment contains the information on how we are to act. It is therefore reasonable for explanations to revert to the norm-driven version until stronger justifications are provided for the field-theoretic approach.

I will try here to provide such stronger justifications—and thereby demonstrate that the principles introduced by Bourdieu (1984 [1979]) in *Distinction*, often taken to be a good if limited account for "culture" (whatever that is) but obviously inadequate as a general theory of human action, are in fact of the broadest relevance. But first, I must turn to what I think is a possible misstatement that those of us who put forward an ecological approach to action in place of a normative one may be prone to make. We often make it seem as if it were impossible that the rules could be "in the heads" of the actors because there isn't sufficient room. But this can't be so. If people can use the rules to account for the action *after the fact*, presumably the rules were there *before* the fact as well. So why could they not inspire the action, as well as account for it?

One can't deny that we can memorize many verbal formulae and later recite them. That doesn't mean that they guide our action.[12] Think of some comic-relief character from a novel (probably an old-timer) who makes self-righteous I-told-you-so comments in the form of proverbs but will alternate between opposing

[12] We saw something like this with the example of baboon baby handling in Chapter 5. Strum's argument was that the mother (*A*) who wants to prevent the other female (*B*) from handling her infant turns her back to *B*. *B*, seeing a back, and being a bit agitated, grooms *A*'s back. This relaxes *A*. Seeing *A* relaxed, *B* now successfully grabs the baby. I doubt that baboons have propositional norms, but a naïve student might propose that the baboons have internalized the rule "you must first groom before you may handle." This might seem to explain the behavior but be quite incorrect; the chances are good that in a different environment (one in which, say, turning around was not a practical strategy of the mother), this "norm" would not be followed.

pairs such as "look before you leap" and "he who hesitates is lost," depending on the situation. Just as this character is unable to know which maxim should guide action in the current situation *before* the fact, so, too, we with our norms. And that is because it is not the "rule" in the abstract that would be costly to hold in our heads, but the detailed information on the *applicability* of the rule.

To return, then: the immediate problem with the rules approach is that we often violate the rules, and although a rules-theorist can always explain why in this case but not that we observed the rule, one feels less like an impressed observer of scientific progress and more like a teacher having to listen to one excuse after another from a student. We don't have a science, we have special pleading. It isn't that these claims are wrong, it's that because they are mobilized selectively to account for discrepancies, we are pretty sure that nearly anything can be explained—not in the good way, but because there's an instability or unidentifiability in our system. We have enough rules, meta-rules, counter-rules, precedents, and so on, that in any particular situation, we could account for an action or its opposite with equal confidence.

More important, thinking about the situations in which we *do* put our elbows on the table and so on may help us understand in what way the environment tells us what to do. We do not put our elbows on a *fancy* table—but a fancy table is not merely recognized as such by its physical construction and what sits on it, but by who sits around it and how they act at the table. Drawing from the principles reached in the previous chapter, we can accept that the way in which others influence our actions comes not (or not *always*) through a direct transmission of subjectivity (or one mediated by symbolic communication), nor by modeling others (I watch how they act to figure out how *I* should act)—though these *do* occur—but rather, by changing the perceived qualities of the environment.

Let's now consider the action for which the norm "The Gentleman Is to Let the Lady Enter the Door First" may be expected to be relevant. I find this a good example for the following reasons.[13] First, it is one that not only can be and has been expressed in propositional form, but it is one that many readers may well have been explicitly taught at some time. Second, it is one with differential implications: unlike "thou shalt not kill," the action imperative of the "same" norm is different depending on whether we are a Gentleman, a Lady, or neither. Third, it is one whose moral status has been contested and we can imagine subpopulations among which the norm has different meanings.

---

[13] Schutz and Luckmann (1973: 176) also considered a very similar norm; I find their treatment unsatisfactory, though only because of their starting point.

Ladies and Gentlemen . . .

Let's first begin in a simple world in which everyone is either a Gentleman or a Lady, and everyone accepts the validity of this norm. What does it mean to tell someone, "The Gentleman Is to Let the Lady Enter the Door First"? Most obviously, it is not that "The Gentleman Is to Let the Lady Enter the Door First" in any literal sense. For example, a Gentleman and a Lady walking into the large garage-door style opening that constitutes the door of a Costco warehouse would not slow down to make sure that the Lady preceded him across the threshold. That would be strange and rude. On the other hand, should a Gentleman and a Lady be walking down a corridor that begins to narrow to a width of 36 inches, though there is no door, the Gentleman may slow down so that the Lady goes first.

There are two likely ways of saving the norm account. The first is the many-norms response that I raised above and found wanting (that is, we say that in the Costco warehouse a *different* norm was governing action). The second is to say that the literally expressed norm is not the *actual* norm. This *actual* norm, say, pertains to deference, or to symbolic protection. But because "deference" is a complex issue and hard to explain in simple rule form, children are taught a number of less ambiguous norms that lead the socialized child to re-create the underlying principle of deference and be able to make practical adaptations when it comes to particular circumstances. Thus the norm in question is really a subnorm of the supernorm "The Gentleman must show deference to Ladies."

But this new version of the norm-theory produces its own difficulties. If the Lady clearly indicates that she is planning to hold the door for the Gentleman, the Gentleman may indeed go through and account for this as a successful application of the "deference" supernorm, and therefore explain the violation of the norm "The Gentleman Is to Let the Lady Enter the Door First." The vague nature of the supernorm means that it is possible to explain why an interaction that seems successful was in fact an application of a norm, and an interaction that seems unsuccessful was a violation. The appeal to vague supernorms is thus not very different from the solution invoking many particular norms. There can always be a post hoc explanation of any action. In other words, such supernorms don't actually save the norm-driven account at all because they don't provide the rules that could be used to guide action. Rather than being something that explains behavior, *this* now becomes what we need to explain: What counts as deference, to whom, in what situations? Once again, we are forced to accept the ethnomethodologists' point that such accounts are not causes of action, but are used by actors to justify or criticize actions.

Consider the following scenario: a Gentleman and a Lady in a hall come to a normal size exit door with a large metal bar that must be pushed to open the door; after the door, the hall continues (see Figure 6.1). There may be a number of norms that could be invoked in the quiet of retrospective debriefing: "The Gentleman Is to Let the Lady Enter the Door First," "The Gentleman Is to Do Strenuous Tasks for the Lady and Prevent Her from Dirtying Her Hands," "A Gentleman Should Not Turn His Back to a Lady," and "The Gentleman Should Not Force the Lady to Pass Closely to the Front of His Body." The problem is that if he does not open the door for the Lady, she will have to press the metal bar hard—perhaps it will require un-Ladylike exertion to open. But if he goes first (violating *one* rule) he has another problem. Yes, he has spared her the un-Ladylike exertion, but once he has opened and walked through the door, what does he do? It will only open 90°, meaning that he can neither get it completely out of her way nor stand behind it. If he holds it for her, he forces her to walk dangerously near his front, but turning his back on her while holding the door is also a problem. Finally, opening it and allowing it to slam closed toward the Lady might also be extremely rude.

Such practical issues sometimes do in fact arise, and sometimes lead to explicit and agonized deliberation of the form that I have outlined here. But the surprising thing is that similar situations are navigated all the time without such thought; they do not stick out, and no repair or explanation is necessary, and so no "norm" is invoked. The very smoothness of the action can make it hard to analyze; making things more complex can facilitate an understanding of the processes involved in regular (nonproblematic) action.

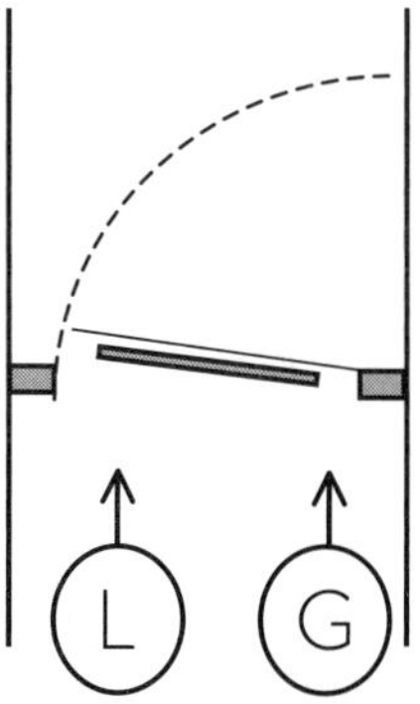

FIGURE 6.1: What to do?

Let's now introduce further heterogeneity in our population: there are two types of Ladies (or beings that a Gentleman is likely to believe to be a Lady—he may be wrong), one type possesses what we shall call "old-fashioned femininity" (OFF) and the other does not (~OFF). In other words, we introduce two types of "character." (Here one may see Gerth and Mills [1954: 13] for a discussion of the character of the OFF lady.) OFF Ladies agree as to the validity of the norm (which does not mean that this necessarily guides their behavior, it is just what they use to interpret behavior), whereas ~OFF Ladies do not, and in fact believe that a Gentleman should *not* spare Ladies from exertion nor engage in symbolic protection. Indeed, they believe that such acts communicate a *lack* of deference. Our one type of Gentleman, however, cannot tell the difference between OFF and ~OFF Ladies. What a potential recipe for disaster! There is clearly an insoluble dilemma: any action may not only fail to reach the normative goal, but also may send the wrong message and insult the Lady.

With that sort of mock objectivism so well fitted to mask anticipated *schadenfreude*, we situate ourselves near the door, ready to enjoy (I mean, observe) the pragmatic failures that are sure to result. Yet pair after pair of Gentleman–Lady duos proceed through without seeming to even notice the door. What has happened?

The situation as I described it above was reproduced in Figure 6.1. The door with the bar is ahead of the Lady (L) and the Gentleman (G). The arrows indicate the direction and speed that the Gentleman and the Lady are traveling. Now consider the sketches in Figures 6.2 and 6.3, respectively. Two things are different: the position of the Lady is altered somewhat, and we have added the "envelope" of personal space that surrounds her. Let's also postulate that all our subjects have a relatively clear agreement as to how much space a Lady must be afforded before one has changed the situation in some way that requires justification. Further, they have a phenomenological *sense* of this, as opposed to a *theory* of it. Finally, personal space toward the front increases with our velocity, and we notice that in Figure 6.2, the Lady is a tiny bit faster than the Gentleman, and her personal envelope is a bit larger to the front than it is in Figure 6.3, where she has slowed down a bit. We can see, merely for reasons of fluid dynamics, that the Gentleman in Figure 6.2 seems very unlikely to be squeezed to the front position, while the one in Figure 6.3 is very likely to open the door.

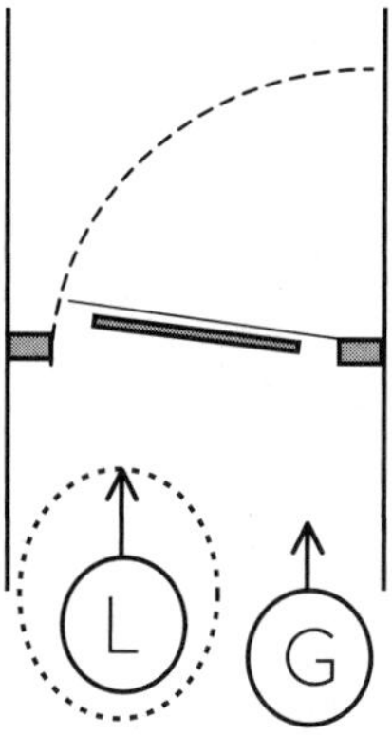

FIGURE 6.2: An ~OFF lady

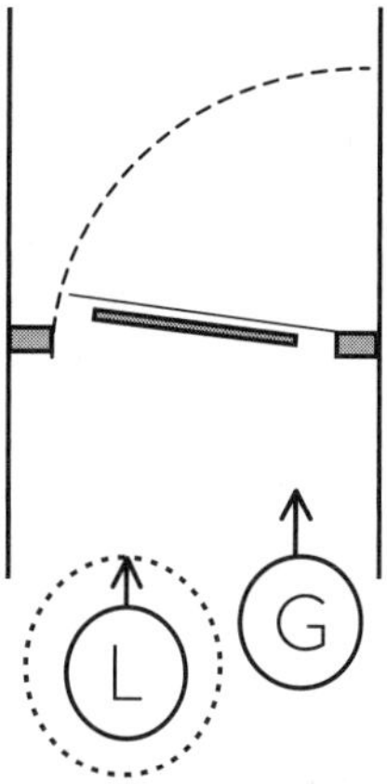

FIGURE 6.3: An OFF lady

The norm-driven response might be that the man has taken his lead from the woman, and that the woman has decided whether to treat the norm "The Gentleman Is to Let the Lady Enter the Door First" as a valid one for her or to respect it in the breach. And of course, there will never be a situation that cannot, with suitable creativity, be described ex post facto as in conformity with norms, since there are so very many of them. The question for us now is whether the field account has a different and a plausible explanation. It does.

Affordances and Action

As we saw in the previous chapter, objects have affordances for us, affordances that are available on inspection; in Gibsonian terms, these are qualities of the objects that are available in the ambient optic array (that is, it's there in all that light bouncing around that you are free to direct your eyes to). Further, these qualities that the objects perceivably have tell us what to do about them. Field theories, as I have emphasized, note that these qualities, though retaining intersubjective validity, vary in predictable ways for different persons. The force field of a heavy iron bar is different for an ~OFF Lady than for an OFF Lady—the first it perhaps attracts, the second it repels (see Figures 6.4 and 6.5, respectively). It is this that explains the different positions of the Lady in Figure 6.2 and in Figure 6.3.

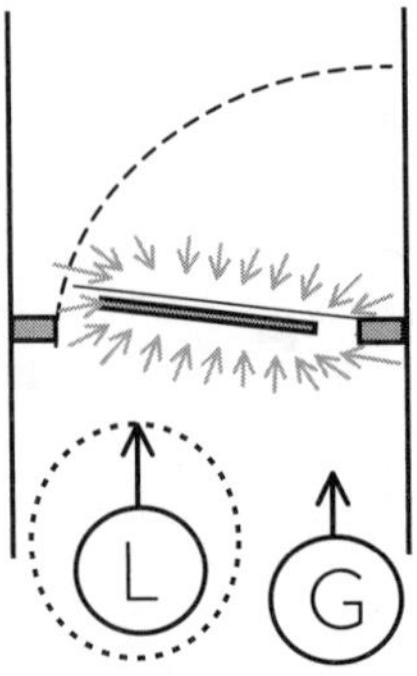

FIGURE 6.4: An ~OFF attracted

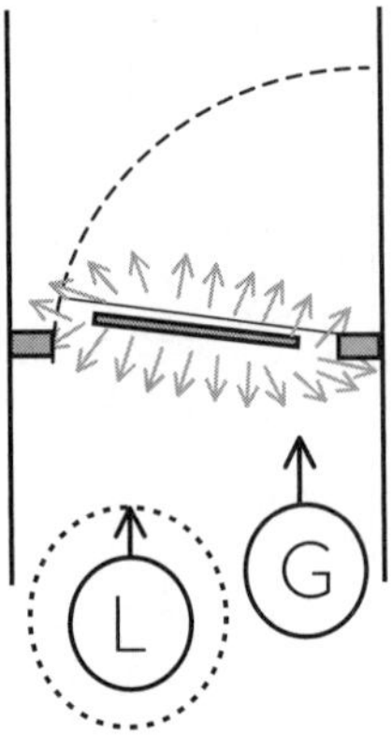

FIGURE 6.5: An OFF repelled

It is important not to impatiently dismiss what may seem to be an over-elaborated and over-schematized adumbration of a very uninteresting and obvious set of actions. "Of course," we might snap, "the OFF Lady doesn't want to touch the door, or wants to communicate that she doesn't want to, and so by slowing down, she signals to the Gentleman to go first." But that was never in doubt. The question was *how* she did this, and I am claiming that she does this *not* by invoking any of the norms but by responding to the qualities of physical objects in her physical environment. Even though we explain her response by the qualities, and the qualities are all qualities *of* physical objects, she responds differently than does an ~OFF because the qualities of the situation are conditional on character. Since the qualities of objects tell us about our potentials for doing things with them, their attributes such as "coarseness" or "heaviness" do not have merely to do with them, but with our own constitutions.[14] The same pole that seems to say "throw me" to one person, announces just as definitely "I am too big for you to wield" to another.[15]

Thus we explain action by the qualities of the objects in the environment; as these qualities are reciprocal to the actions of particular types of actors, they produce a regular, structured, but also differentiated world. This does not mean, however, that there are never times when things do not run smoothly when there

[14] And that's because it's about what *we* are going to do with the objects; people judge objects to be "heavier" when their distribution of mass is such that they are difficult to wield (Turvey et al. 1999).

[15] I used to be incredulous that Kurt Lewin (1951) thought his formula $B = f(P,E)$—that behavior is a function of the personality *and* the environment—was even worth writing down, let alone that scores of his students saw it as a profound statement. Now I get it. It's the core of field theory—about the interaction of valenced objects in the environment and sensitized (hysteresized) actors.

are dilemmas that arise that are consciously grappled with.[16] For example, if our OFF Lady speeds up as she goes through the door, the Gentleman may not hold it, but fling it open, as her force field pushes him on; but if she is on the more sensitive side, and our Gentleman large, she may treat him as having a very large envelope, and thus slow down or remain slow, leading him to slow down, which will mean he is still in the door, possibly — given his large envelope — forcing her too close to the wall.

In such cases of failure, reasoning from norms may well be all that our hapless actors can rely on (and recall that *knowing* the norms doesn't automatically help our actor know how to *apply* them, because of the overlapping relevance of different norms with contradictory action implications). But this does not mean that these processes are those that will explain the nonproblematic situations. If Dewey was correct that we are jolted out of habit into intelligence (or what contemporary psychologists might speak of as a change from basal parallel assimilative processes to prefrontal serial reasoning processes), then simple reflection is not enough to determine which processes are used in nonproblematic circumstances. It is, as said above, akin to opening the door to see whether the refrigerator light is on, even when the door is closed. To reflect on action is to turn on that part of the mind that reflects, and we know from much neurological research (Gazzaniga 1970; Wegner 2002) that this portion boastfully if sincerely claims control of things it has not really done.[17]

Further, what the field-theoretical approach can explain is not just how there is regularity, but how we perceive our actions as regular and norm-conforming despite the variety of situations in which we find ourselves. Different halls, different arrangements of doors, different types of door pulls and handles, different placements of them call for improvisations that are cognitively demanding for a norm follower but *may* be traversed easily by attending to what the environment affords. It is only when there is turbulence — no easy way of traversing

[16] Further, although it goes beyond the purely theoretical goals of the current work, contemporary neurology does seem to support the idea that objects directly tell us what to do with them, and when we do not actually obey, this is due to a secondary suppressive reaction that can, among healthy individuals, be inhibited under load, and can be completely missing in persons with certain forms of neurological damage (e.g., they will reach out and pick up anything that goes by [McBride et al., forthcoming]; Lhermitte [1986] calls this "Environmental Dependency Syndrome"). Although this will be a tough sell, I think our best model of the actor is Reed's (1996) of roughly hierarchically organized coupled oscillators with higher orders suppressing lower ones, and an extremely perceptive but not omniscient consciousness that selects aspects of the states of these, should they become available, for narrative purposes.

[17] It might seem that reflection could *never* produce or confirm the account given here. But this is not so. A good first step, one I presume Dewey used in his initial researches, is simply to have one's conscious mind first remember, then keep track of, the sorts of situations when it is present, or when it "comes to life."

lines of force—that we become aware of the "problem" that seemed to call for deduction.[18]

To sum up, it seems that the field approach's claim that what we are to do is stored not in mental norms but in the environment, is a plausible and consistent account. It *does* have a partiality; it is good at explaining how the environment tells us what to do, and not so good at telling us when (as discussed in note 16) we decline to obey. One of the puzzles is how to differentiate those aspects of character that *facilitate* our response to the environment (generally understood as arising from repeated experience *with* the environment—that is, habit) from those that *dampen* our responsiveness ("character" as understood in the old sense). *Logically*, we introduce all sorts of problems if we allow for an explanatory factor that is "resistance-of-the-agent-to-doing-what-my-theory-suggests." *Psychologically*, however, there is no doubt that such resistance to environmental affordances is a measurable factor that exists as both "state" (it changes for us as individuals over time) and "trait" (it differentiates one individual from another). *Sociologically*, we had better *know* something about such character before we shoot off our mouths about it, and it seems like the field approach is in as good a position as anything else to get us started here.

The reader may likely object that this example is trivial, and indeed it does seem trivial, but it is not clear why it seems so, and whether its seeming triviality is at all relevant for analytic purposes. First, we must acknowledge that the example does involve normative considerations, and these are considerations that have been taken quite seriously in the past century. Does the presumed triviality arise because we are speaking about actions that are merely persons moving their bodies through space? Perhaps. But how easy do we think it will be to claim that there are actions that are *not* about organisms moving their bodies in physical space? (I'll give this critique a stronger form below.)

The best objection would be that this account is not actually more parsimonious than that of the norm-driven account. Recall our finding that for GOFAT to account for actual behavior, we needed to bring into play more and more

---

[18] For a nice example, the Booth Graduate School of Business at the University of Chicago put in large double glass doors that have hidden pivots, and steel rods as handles. On the *inside*, the handle is (as is conventional) horizontal, but on the *outside*, the handle runs vertically down the entire jamb side of the door. Since the horizontal handle is visible through the transparent door, the vertical handle is often mistaken as the pivot, and so many people first try to open the doors by pushing on the side opposite the vertical bar, even though this is the fixed point. A Gentleman who positions himself here to open a door for an OFF Lady finds himself in a difficult position. She will be near the door, and he must reach across her body, effectively blocking her path and perhaps violating her envelope, in order to get a portion of the handle with which he can exert sufficient torque to open the door. But if the Lady does not react to this as a violation of her envelope, the whole interaction will be nonproblematic. I suspect that the behavior at this door is more predictive of career success than anything that happens once they are inside.

norms other than "The Gentleman Is to Let the Lady Enter the Door First," some having to do with deference, some with exertion, and so on. But the field approach also begins to bring in more things, not the simple spatial constriction of the doorway, but the envelope of each person, the affordance of the door, and, were we to pursue other concrete cases, other qualities of the environment (perhaps placement of fire extinguishers on walls, whether the door leads to stairs and, if so, whether they go up or down, the color of the door, and so on).

It seems to me that the difference is that the things appealed to in the field account, unlike those appealed to by the norm account, are *already there*. Further, the properties of the things are there and the relation of these properties to action imperatives is usually clear. For example, let's say that an ~OFF Lady and a Gentleman approach a door in the same size hall, and yet, unlike the scenario graphed in Figure 6.4, in this case, the Gentleman holds the door for the Lady. If an analyst accounts for the discrepancy by pointing to the presence of a fire extinguisher that projected 10 inches from the wall, 3 feet from the door (see Figure 6.6), the explanation does not bring into the situation something that was not already obviously there. That cannot be said for something like the norm "the Gentleman should symbolically protect the Lady." There is no independent evidence that this norm *was* there before the analyst (whether or not this person is the same as the actor) has brought it into existence.

The claim that physical features of our spatial environment contain the information on how we are to act, including what it means to do the right thing,

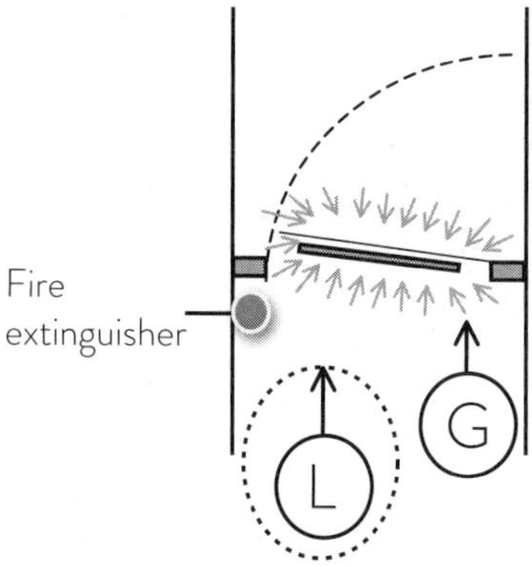

FIGURE 6.6: A new factor

might seem a stretch—but that is only because our conventional sociological theory has allowed us to smuggle in a form of scholastic idealism that none of us would defend. Bear in mind that you will have a great deal of hard work to do to establish that there is anything at all other than objects in space (including grimacing and talking objects like ourselves, and artifacts that we have made and put in places to shape our behavior). The problem with the field-theoretic account, then, is not that we think it is implausible. In a way, we all necessarily accept it. The question is whether it is *tractable*, and it seems to me quite likely that it is for a wide class of interesting problems (though see Latour et al. 2012: 7 for a serious critique). Movement of bodies in space is one, and a fine place to start, finally, trying to produce a serious science of social action.

Extensions

I noted above that this example might seem to be of a particular nature because it involves people moving their bodies in physical space. I gave a cute response to that, pointing out that unless you are a spiritualist, you accept that *all* social action is bodies moving in space. Still, one could respond that although all action may involve bodies moving in space, often the *meaning* of the action isn't as clearly tied to where the bodies are, but rather to what they accomplish. It's one thing to say that the environment holds information about what we are to do when it comes to navigating the environment in direct ways, but what about when we see our action in terms of meaningful accomplishments, and not position? Maybe then we'd find that, in fact, everything *is* about the observance or nonobservance of social rules?

I think we find that the principles uncovered here remain important. In many cases, the environment tells us what to do, but we have to remember that we (that is, we humans) construct the environment for that very reason. That might seem to make things more complex, but it allows us to simplify our theory of action for the same reason that it simplifies tasks for the actor. I don't know which fork you use for what, and I can't tell a salad fork from a dessert fork, but I do know that one is supposed to start with the implements farthest from the plate and work inward. The environment is set up so that I can follow the arbitrary norms without actually knowing them. And the person who sets the table need not know about the use–norm either, actually.

One may object that this example is just as trivial as the other. A true understanding of behavior needs to deal not simply with etiquette, or not with it at all, but with the more fundamental things like morality—not foofie forks but things like murder.

But as we recall from Chapter 5, we generally don't murder. And most of these "more serious" moral rules turn out to be (as Durkheim emphasized) about what *not* to do. Of course, the environment doesn't have information on all the things we *don't* do. All that stuff is imaginary. If you *do* kill someone, however, it might well be that you follow some rules, and then the theoretical claims above should be relevant. But *not* doing things isn't automatically following rules — every day, I don't kill people, but I think it would be silly to say that I am following the don't-kill-people rule, because I don't *want* to kill any people. (Then again, I haven't read the reviews of this book yet. Just kidding reviewers! No worries!)

Put in other words, if morality is "negatively privative" in that goodness is the absence of evil, that would fit with what we've seen here regarding rules. The fact that conduct is moral doesn't mean morality is constraining conduct, and the fact that we act within rules doesn't mean we're following rules. Rather, when people believe — or can make a credible show to others that they believe — that another has acted in a way in which she or he can be taken to account, rules may well be invoked. The application of these cognitive constructs for meaningful disruptions of patterns doesn't need to explain the pattern following itself (see especially Vollmer 2013). That, rather than being privatively defined, is positively defined — what we *do* do — and it seems parsimonious, plausible, and consistent with other findings that this is largely guided by the physical aspects of our environment and what it affords.

CONCLUSION

The good-old-fashioned-action-theory feels right to most of us. But that doesn't mean it's correct. Its two main planks — the importance of conscious or paraconscious motivation before action, and the importance of rules in leading to the orderliness of sociological action — both have serious difficulties. Many of these difficulties are empirical, which is outside of the scope of the current work. But some of the support for GOFAT seems to come from making the sorts of errors that orthological investigations can uncover — in particular, the idea that rules constrain or guide action.

All this is old, indeed, very old, hat. But despite such critiques, as a discipline, we haven't moved very far from GOFAT, and not only because GOFAT seems intuitively correct. We also haven't had a compelling alternative spelled out for sociology. Although the basis of a plausible theory was offered by John Dewey, and later by Pierre Bourdieu, both were marginalized not only because they were vulnerable to a crushing critique ("You are saying we act *only* on the basis of habit?"), but because they had difficulty with the combination of, on the one hand, the culturally constituted and individually variable nature of the character of the actor, and on the other, the physical fundament for the qualities of the objects that called out for action. They had difficulty, but they got it right. However, it was easy for readers to lose the thread of the argument, and think that things weren't solved that were solved. All theories have problems; good ones solve their problems. It seems to me that the approach discussed here comes from a tradition that is solving its problems. That's a good place to work from.

CONCLUSION

ON LUCK

I like watching automobile racing, including Indy formula racing, although I know that most people in my world don't share this appreciation. They think it is very boring to watch the nearly identical cars go around and around and around. But I find something aesthetically pleasing about watching a first-class machine at work. I have a somewhat similar feeling about most of what we consider sociological theory. Even if theorists are just going around and around in circles, as I think they do and must, we often see first-class minds in operation. Circles may not, as the scholastics thought, represent perfection, but you could do worse.

My colleague Andrew Abbott once said that the history of theoretical innovation in sociology seemed, if not such a circle, then a wander over the surface of a globe, in which progress was just returning to a place where no one had been in a very long time. This is in some sense undeniable and might be taken as cause for despair or for cynicism, but now I think it shouldn't be. The circles we go in are where we want to be. They arise from the combination of our preexisting conceptual momentum and the pull of our dedication to understanding the world (call it the real world, if you want). That's what we're circling *around*. In this book, I've emphasized "thinking straight." But in a warped space, that doesn't rule out curves! If we were going in a straight line, we'd be shooting out into the space of silliness.

Pursuing the metaphor, we might say that the quality of our thoughts here is inverse to the radius of our orbit. There can be a better or a worse, even if it's hard for us to compare the better-worser-ness of very different theories. (Think in terms of polar coordinates — different theories may have very different angles, but that doesn't mean we can't compare their radii. Sometimes we need to change our angle to allow us to get around a blockage that prevents us from changing our radius.) It might be that we can never get all the way there, and certainly, as our radius decreases, it seems we might speed up to a dizzying extent. So far, it does seem that no one's been able to get closer than a certain point without a crash landing into mysticism.[1]

So perhaps there's a chance of theoretical progress. Even if not, it does seem that in social science, we're often going to need to say things that require a certain amount of conceptual scaffolding. That is, we'll need some theory, even if our theory can't get any better. As a result, there isn't anything inherently wrong with system building, even castle-in-the-sky-building. Consider this the construction of the scaffold in a zero-gravity environment — it makes things easier, but might lead us to want to check our resulting structure very carefully before using it to bear weight. Still, in most cases, sociological theory is, as we might say, "mostly harmless." Even when it is very wrong, nothing terrible happens, because usually no one bothers to consult it before acting, including practicing social scientists. Even those who think they are strongly attached to one theoretical tradition or another, and that their work is focused on a contribution to this tradition, tend to write books whose first chapter you could pull out, switch it with the first chapter in another book at random, and probably no one would notice. I am actually inclined to think that this is a good thing, although for a sociological theorist it's professionally somewhat discouraging.

But sometimes, the way we think about things (and we must think about them in *some* way) makes it hard for us to understand what is going on about us. In such cases, system building doesn't help, and in fact makes things worse. We can distract ourselves from our real problems by repeating to ourselves our theories — that is, our mishmash of unfounded substantive assertions and our favorite words — as if this little prayer could keep scientific failure at bay. To pursue the structural analogy, we make it harder for the fundamental problem to be identified, as we nail up all sorts of temporary supports and wrap everything with duct tape. For such situations, orthological researches (as we might laughingly call them) are potentially important. Unfortunately, our biggest problem is usually simply coming to recognize that we are in a situation calling for such orthological investigation. Most of us seem to feel that our own ideas are just "obviously true, you idiot," or "already said by someone very famous, fool" or "the kind of thing only a bad person would deny, creep."

Often the only thing that can trigger our search for a serious consideration of our own formal theoretical structure is a kind of vigilance that is the last thing our discipline encourages, and this is a vigilance based on a suspicion of things that look too good. Most of us now understand that if a Nigerian prince needs *your* help to smuggle $12 million out of Russia and is willing to split it with you,

[1] The problem with this version of the metaphor is that, really, I think our progress is best understood as an *away from* error, and not a progress toward truth, which would imply that the quality of our ideas is proportional (and not inversely proportional) to the radius. But combining the two metaphors becomes ungainly.

this is too good be true. But we don't look a gift horse in the mouth in our own work, neither methodologically nor theoretically. Regarding the former, if we do what seems like a very conservative longitudinal analysis and yet we get three asterisks by our favorite coefficients, we go right to the press. We don't think, "Hmmm, have I rested too much on a linearity constraint for a temporal change, such that I'm reparameterizing time as if it were a causal effect?" He who hesitates is lost. Or so we think (which is why we're *all* lost—as Thurber said, "He who hesitates is sometimes saved.").

Similarly, we don't think, "Huh! My theory explains everything I was interested in, in just the way I thought it would, using my favorite terms, *and* it shows that I'm morally superior to most other social scientists! Too good to be true." But it is. Only one person was that lucky, and he's buried in the Highgate Cemetery—and even he was often a pain in the ass to his friends.

So, strangely enough, when things are good is precisely when we should be worried, and when we should see whether we are making an argument that sounds important, but isn't what it appears to be. In such cases, we may have slipped in the sorts of problems that are outlined here.

Such orthological considerations are the first word, not the last. We should all become so good at the rules of straight thinking that we know when and how to break them. Because, for example, at a certain point, the law of self-identity breaks down. Things *aren't* themselves. An acorn isn't an acorn, it is an oak tree, . . . and it isn't. There are mysteries pertaining to duration, to the limited transitivity of identity, and even (but don't tell your professors you know this!) problems of reification. But that's not the place to start. We start as simply as we can, and try to walk as straight as we can. Don't worry—the crazy landscape we walk on will introduce plenty of twists and turns. As we go along, there are a few principles that can be used to guide us in the right direction, think-wise. I close by providing what I believe to be some of the robust rules for sociology, mostly drawing on work by generations of others, and emphasizing their relevance for theory construction.

BONUS: THE NEWEST RULES OF SOCIOLOGY

The idea of the basic rules of sociology was started by Vernon K. Dibble, whose first rule, justly lost to history, was "the sociologist knows." His second rule is now known as the first rule of sociology, and the one I give as second is also from the Columbia school at around this time.

1. Some Do, Some Don't

This is so deeply important that every sociologist should have it tattooed on her or his forehead. We generalize, and that is fine. We talk about averages, and that is fine. But in part because of our disciplinary vision of social life as the average plus "error," we tend to be seriously hampered in thinking about variation. Admitting it often seems like confessing ignorance. Hence, when we are hostile to others, and they use a comparison, we may play a card that seems a version of this rule, misunderstood as some sort of triumphant negation: "You compared German X to French X—thereby assuming homogenization within the groups." Really? Since when does a comparison of means imply absence of variance? Unless you think Germany and France are random draws from the same bag of marbles, there's nothing wrong with a comparison.

Isn't it silly that we, who have a science *based* on the assumption that we should study groups, aggregates, societies, or whatever, because these things are fundamental, and that individuals have no epistemic priority, and so on and so forth, turn around and slash at each other for pooling individuals? I think this is because we really haven't come to grips with the truth that even when our comparisons are okay, and our normal methods are doing just fine, some do and some don't. It isn't bad sociology, it's not error of *any* type—it's life.

And the real problem with our ignoring this principle doesn't arise in comparisons like this illustration, it happens when we *aren't* comparing—when we are giving our "story" as people increasingly say these days, that is, our interpretation and conclusions. Then there isn't any comparison at all to alert us to the problem—there's just a fantasy of an abstract "what people do." At the time of writing this, I actually just finished an unintentionally humorous piece in a top journal on racial prejudice in hiring decisions that concluded "employers discriminate against . . ." and so on. (The evidence indicated that *some* employers discriminated, . . .) My point isn't that saying that employers discriminate is morally just as wicked as saying that nonwhite employees steal. It's that where it really counts—in our conclusions, what we take away—we are often unable to bear in mind not only that some do and some don't, but that this can matter.[2]

And most important, if you find yourself making a theory that starts out "people do X . . . ," watch out. Something's probably wrong. Even if you are sure that a society where people don't do X couldn't last five minutes, or that our ancestors *must* have been selected for X, it's just not that way. We've seen the errors

[2] Because this is outside the theoretical issues in this book, I won't go on about it, but the obsession with the "average treatment effect" in causal and policy studies is just as bad. The average is just a meaningless compositional artifact. Any serious investigation should be focusing on causal heterogeneity, and we now finally have statistical tools for this.

people made in animal studies by assuming homogeneity, and it's not going to get better with people.

2. It's Different in the South

This was understood as the third rule in 1960s Columbia, and it is indeed a good one, at least for any country that has a South (and that's lots of 'em). That's the cool thing about having a rotating sphere to live on: south versus north is different from east versus west. Going farther west can change things, but it doesn't have to. This seemingly wholly substantive lesson speaks to a more general point for sociological theory that we only admit when we can make it sound fancy-schmancy ("I draw attention to the emplacedness of human action . . .") but ignore otherwise. It isn't just that where we are matters, it matters in a material way. Because early sociologies (or the sorts of things that would turn into sociology) often were (by today's view) embarrassingly direct, blunt, and simplistic in how they linked culture to climate, it's been considered insane to say that the physical qualities of where people are matter in any way you could figure out. That's overly pessimistic. There are plausible things to say, and they matter. You can't go to the library where there isn't one. Rain and cold keep people inside. If the only road where you live goes east, you go east to get stuff. It matters where the people are and the stuff is. And as we saw in Chapter 5, culture is about how we transform the environment that shapes our action. And this gets to a third principle.

3. Composition Is Nine-Tenths of the Law

We often read about how America, say, is changing, again, as if there were a single person (or maybe two, Mr. and Mrs. America) who once did things one way, but now do them differently. But America—and not just America—is a big bunch of different types of people, and the relative proportion of these people has been changing. Guess what? Sociology actually works. We can find out a lot about social action, and even our usual suspects for explanations—the "master statuses" like age, sex, race, occupation, education, and income—do a lot here.

Most of what we think of as cultural change is really change in the composition of populations. Industrial revolution means fewer farmers. Deindustrialization means fewer union members. Aging of the population means (you guessed it) more old folks. Before we theorize about *aggregate* changes, we need to think through what would be a null model of no change in the *conditional* action of persons (conditional on the sorts of people they are).

Sociological theorists do need to be comfortable working with abstractions. But too often they seem to be comfortable *only* with abstractions—they run from any encounter of the concrete with terror. But theorizing about an abstraction like "the changing American character" isn't sociological theory. It isn't social theory. It isn't anything but the roar of the wind.

4. Ask a Sociologist a Question, You'll Get a Sociological Answer

This is true even if there is no reason to think a priori that the question should have one. Not all things that seem to be questions have answers, not all questions that could in principle be answered can be answered in practice, and not all of those questions that can be answered have sociological answers. For example, if you are wondering what caused ethnic cleansing in the 1990s, if you ask a sociologist you will probably get an answer that involves sociological phenomena. It is quite possible that the answer to this question is a political one that political scientists will get to but not sociologists, and so on. If you're a sociologist, you probably have an occupational blindness here. If you assume that the answer is always under your realm of professional competence, you're more likely to need orthological fixes in the future.

5. Everybody Always Thinks Something

Sociologists are good at understanding that just because scientists say something, doesn't mean it's true. "We now know . . ." should set your b.s. detector on full power, especially if someone is trying to sell you (or your insurance plan) something. The fact that there is uniform agreement *right now* shouldn't sway you. There was a day when everyone knew that bloodletting was pretty much all you could do for a case of smallpox. And so it goes.

And yet, sociologists allow the fact of universal agreement (that is, among everyone we know, *now*) to dismiss sociological *theories*. Something that is no longer believed to be a good idea "by everybody" is assumed to be validly ignorable. But if indeed pretty much anything in sociology has been thought up at least *once*, everything's already been dismissed, as will whatever we all think now. That can't be a good way of proceeding—to dismiss something because we all know that it is worthy of being dismissed. And related to this is the one principle perhaps most important for theorizing, explained next.

6. The New Law of Large Numbers

You have heard it said that the law of large numbers pertains to issues of inference under random sampling. All that is well and good, but there is a different law of large numbers, which, if understood, would completely reorient our current theoretical practice. It is simply this: the world is a big place. Many things come in "lots of 'em." For such things, chances are that whatever *kind* you think of, you can find one, if you look.

That means to have a general theory and to *illustrate* it with a case is a waste of everyone's time. You wouldn't propose that "in general," people are named "John" because you can find one, two, three, or however many of them, would you? Yet people make all sorts of claims based on the one thing that they have found — often because they were looking for just something like this.

Take for granted that you can find one of anything: unions that run bottom up, corporations that produce religious conversion, four-leaf clovers, even mermaids. Unless there was a strong theory that denies that such a thing should *ever* be found, it's just not important. Don't cross the street to look at them, let alone write a dissertation on them.[3]

7. Think about How You Know What You Think You Know

Every now and then, there are reasonable questions raised about the level of political debate in the United States. We wonder why, given that there are serious problems our country might want to deal with, we spend so much time yelling about whether, say, some senator likes to watch the giraffes in the zoo humping each other. It's easy to say that Americans are prurient, or idiots, or whatever, but more sociological analyses will remind us that we can only argue about what we know about. If the newspapers print scandal stories, that's what we'll know about. If they print negative stories — and, as Schudson (2011) shows, they disproportionately do — we'll tend to think that most politicians are creeps and liars. But we can adjust our ideas if we take into account the *processes* that bring this news to our attention.

So, too, when it comes to theorizing, a lot of the story is over before you even start thinking, because it all depends on what you have in your head to think with. You often need to take a step back and try to see if you can figure out what got into your head, and what didn't, and where it comes from. You can't do much of this, but you can do some, and most of us don't do any at all. Absolutely, we think "from a place," but the key thing here usually isn't about who we are ("I'm a guy") or what we value ("I hate fascism")— and those things are easy to take into account. More difficult is to understand how certain ideas and information reach us; even when we are active, going out and about to gather perceptions, we don't always understand how the paths we take affect what ends up in our heads. We have to—as well as we can—get a sense of the stuff that *didn't* reach us. We even need to go out of our way to get some of it.

---

[3] That goes for mermaids; remember, they're *really* bad luck.

8. You Can Be Too Smart

All men are mortal. Socrates is a man. Therefore, Socrates is mortal. QED. The logic is perfect. Of course, really, we're not 100.000 percent sure that all men are mortal. Perhaps someone born among us right now will never die. And who knows—maybe Socrates is a very unusual type of squirrel, or of angel, or he is an alien. Still, if we are even just 99 percent sure of the two first statements, we can still conclude that Socrates is a mortal with 98 percent (= 99% × 99%) certainty.

But suppose that instead of a classic syllogism, we had sixty-eight different links in a chain of reasoning. Now, even with 99 percent certainty in each link, our conclusion is basically a toss-up. What's the point? That you can be too smart.

This actually was a refrain my grandfather said, or that I thought he said, but with his thick Russian-Yiddish accent, I often had a hard time understanding him. My father thought it was "you can't be too smart," but as he pointed out, the two things really mean the same thing: there is a zone in which increasing smartness can make things worse, not better.

Why? To answer, let me give you a sad, bitterly funny scene that has unfolded time and time again in different ways. I'll give the classic form I grew up with. In a room, an ideologue who has no real idea what he is talking about is mouthing slogans. Someone else who knows much more and, for whatever reason, has a significantly greater share of smarts than the ideologue, is nodding appreciatively, and allowing himself to be corrected. Our anti-hero is quite willing to discard things he has learned, things that are perhaps true or reasonable or both, to gain the approval of the narrow-minded, perhaps insane, ideologue. What's up with this?

Our anti-hero was too smart for his own good. He could reproduce a long chain of reasoning, each link with some plausibility, that connected his fundamental goal such as the liberation of all humanity on one end, to his kissing butt to some numbskull on the other. Unfortunately, this is a very general phenomenon. Many con men will look for those who are "smart" in the sense of having a verbal and complex intelligence, and avoid those who just seem to have common sense. Because the "smart" person can turn into a co-conspirator, he'll be better than any con man at coming up with plausible explanations for why the deal is suddenly changing, and is better at reducing dissonance than someone who may not be able to talk uninterrupted for an hour but knows when he smells a rat.

Okay, so what's the point for sociological theory? It's a vital one—being too smart is working through a chain of reasoning that, if you properly took into account the uncertainty of each link, you'd realize was bringing you to a conclusion that seems air-tight, but is better seen as improbable. We need to understand the difference between *chains* and *ropes* of reasoning. Chains are "serial," one after the other. A chain is only as strong as its weakest link. Ropes are "parallel," in that each thread is side by side with the others. If one breaks, the whole doesn't. In one kind of logic, adding more things makes your argument stronger, but in another, it actually makes it weaker. We need to know when we are piling up ideas in parallel, as opposed to in serial arrangement. The funny thing is that, as I think Thomas Reid (1969 [1785]: 730) suggested, it's common-sense stuff, the sort of thing you don't need a prodigious memory to comprehend, that tends to work in parallel. It's the complex chains that only a smart person can keep in mind that are serial. If there's a ratio in which you divide smarts by common sense, you want to keep that low. Many of us theorists don't have a lot of common sense. If we did, we would keep our reasoning in plausible bounds, where we might have a chance of sticking with things that we can understand.

9. Everything Is Somewhere

And this gets to one of the running themes of this work: we need to be attentive to where things are. We found a number of times that initially very impressive claims about the way things *really* happen, the sorts of things we're likely to march around trumpeting when we are in a very scientific mood, things like "causality" and "facts," turned out to be far more intrinsically *mental* than they first appeared. That is, they weren't in the things *outside* our minds, they were *in* our minds. There's nothing intrinsically wrong with using your mind—it's pretty hard to be smart otherwise—but it is important to know what we *should* be committed to as sitting happily in the world *outside* our minds (the transphenomenal), and what we should accept as a human way-of-working.

This is where the principle of everything-is-somewhere comes in handy. A zebra is not a giraffe, and no zebras ride the Staten Island Ferry. Now a zebra, say, Zelda the zebra, can be somewhere outside of your mind, and it is fine to say that the zebra, outside of your mind, isn't a giraffe (even outside your mind, that is, she isn't a giraffe—it isn't your mind that turns Zelda into a zebra). But the not-giraffeness of Zelda, if you want to treat it as an element, has to be somewhere. Where could it be? It *can't* be in the trans-phenomenal world, which only includes things that *are*, so chances are, it's in your mind. Where is the Staten Island Ferry? Probably somewhere in the Upper New York Harbor between Staten Island and lower Manhattan. Where is the absence of zebras on the ferry? It isn't there. It's only in your mind, and in mine.

Why should one be so punctilious about this matter? Because pathological theorizing always involves claiming that absences are in the trans-phenomenal world. We've seen in Chapter 2 how such claims throw our attempt to think through causality into a mess, but it gets worse. What would you think are the likely signs of being obsessed with, say, cheese? You might talk about cheese a lot, eat it a lot, or just put up pictures of it. But if absences can be real, you might propose that someone who is truly obsessed with cheese might *never* mention it—and refuse to eat it. Of course, this sounds reasonable, in a way, because it *could* be true. But there isn't any good reason to think it *is* true, or *always* true. And (again), it gets worse. If an absence of cheese-talk is a real thing in the world (cheese-avoidance) that (somewhat paradoxically) indicates a cheese-obsession, guess what else is real? The absence of cheese-avoidance, the double-whammy technique of the *truly* cheese-obsessed. Sometimes the truly cheese-obsessed will mention cheese, thereby *negating* their cheese-avoidance, which they employ to *negate* their cheese-obsession.

Do you think this is very silly? If so, don't tell your psychoanalyst, because this was exactly how Sigmund Freud was able to go from his botched experiences with a few patients that he mis-treated (and mistreated) to an elaborate set of doctrines that still compel the unreasonable adherence of many today. (And if you think I'm exaggerating, see his analysis of Dora, which precisely argued that the disorderly absence of an orderly absence indicated the truth of his own twisted projections.)

But it's not just that. Keep going. Why don't the working classes accept whatever version of dumbed-down Marxism you are trying to peddle to them? Well, again, make the *absence* of their doing what *you* think they should a real thing in the world, and start populating the real world with *equally* imaginary entities to explain this. We saw in Chapter 2 that this actually starts to feel *more* successful and *more* scientific than when we don't include all the imaginary thingamabobbies. But when you take absences out of mind, where they exist, and put them in the world, you open a hatch through which all sorts of your own demons will flood in, and contaminate your trans-phenomenal with the phenomenal to the point that there's no longer any reason to do science. You might as well just write fiction and call it nonfiction.

FROM HERE ON

These are the best of times and the worst of times. Methodologically, our field has grown far more sophisticated, and we have even learned some core principles that allow us to productively understand the processes whereby we produce data as social situations of specific kinds that have their own dynamics. That's pretty advanced for a social science. But we're not always doing a very good job with the tools we have, in part because they're difficult to use properly, but also because they need to be guided by a theoretical vision that has certain architectonic properties. Otherwise, we find things, but actually do not know what we find. This book, I hope, helps us produce such theoretical structures.

REFERENCES

Adorno, Theodor W. 1973 [1966]. *Negative Dialectics*, translated by E. B. Ashton. New York: Seabury Press.

Akerlof, George. 1970. "The Market for 'Lemons': Quality Uncertainty and the Market Mechanism." *Quarterly Journal of Economics* 84: 488–500.

Alexander, Jeffrey C. 2003. *The Meanings of Social Life*. New York: Oxford University Press.

Aquinas, Thomas. 1952. [*Disputed Questions on*] *Truth*, translated by Robert W. Mulligan, S. J. Volume I. Chicago: Henry Regnery.

Archer, Margaret S. 2003. *Structure, Agency and the Internal Conversation*. Cambridge: Cambridge University Press.

Ashwander, Dan Scott. 1999. *Am I Insane*. Boston: Kooks Press.

Austin, J. L. 1975 [1962]. *How to Do Things with Words*, second edition. Cambridge, Mass.: Harvard University Press.

Barnes, Barry. 2000. *Understanding Agency: Social Theory and Responsible Action*. London: Sage.

Barrett, Louise and Peter Henzi. 2005. "The Social Nature of Primate Cognition." *Proceedings of the Royal Society, Series B*. 272: 1865–1875.

Barrett, Louise and Drew Rendall. 2010. "Out of Our Minds: The Neuroethology of Primate Strategic Behavior." Pp. 570–586 in *Primate Neuroethology*, edited by Michael L. Platt and Asif A. Ghazanfar. Oxford: Oxford University Press.

Batten, Mary. 1992. *Sexual Strategies*. New York: Putnam.

Becker, Gary S. 1981. *A Treatise on the Family*. Cambridge, Mass.: Harvard University Press.

Bell, Daniel. 1973. *The Coming of Post-Industrial Society*. New York: Basic Books.

Bernstein, Irwin S. 1964. "Role of the Dominant Male Rhesus Monkey in Response to External Challenges to the Group." *Journal of Comparative and Physiological Psychology* 57: 404–406.

Bhaskar, Roy. 1975. *A Realist Theory of Science*. Leeds: Leeds Books.

Bhaskar, Roy. 1979. *The Possibility of Naturalism*. Atlantic Highlands, N.J.: Humanities Press.

Bornstein, Marc H. 1987. "Perceptual Categories in Vision and Audition." Pp. 287–300 in *Categorical Perception*, edited by Steven Harnad. Cambridge: Cambridge University Press.

Bourdieu, Pierre. 1984 [1979]. *Distinction: A Social Critique of the Judgment of Taste*, translated by Richard Nice. Cambridge, Mass.: Harvard University Press.

Briggs, Joe Bob. 1988. *A Guide to Western Civilization, or: My Story*. New York: Delacorte Press.

Brock, Thomas D. 1988. *Robert Koch: A Life in Medicine and Bacteriology*. Madison, Wis.: Science Tech.

Buss, David M. 1994. *The Evolution of Desire*. New York: Basic Books.

Campbell, Colin. 1996. *The Myth of Social Action*. Cambridge: Cambridge University Press.

Carey, Susan. 2009. *The Origin of Concepts*. Oxford: Oxford University Press.

Carroll, Lewis. 1946 [1896]. *Through the Looking Glass, and What Alice Found There*. New York: Random House.

Cartwright, Nancy. 2004. "Causation: One Word, Many Things." *Philosophy of Science* 71: 805–819.

Cheney, Dorothy L. and Robert M. Seyfarth. 1990. *How Monkeys See the World*. Chicago: University of Chicago Press.

Cheney, Dorothy L. and Robert M. Seyfarth. 2007. *Baboon Metaphysics*. Chicago: University of Chicago Press.

Clutton-Brock, T. H. and G. A. Parker. 1995. "Punishment in Animal Societies." *Nature* 373: 209–216.

Cohen, I. Bernard. 1985. *Revolution in Science*. Cambridge, Mass.: Harvard University Press.

Coleman, James S. 1990. *Foundations of Social Theory*. Cambridge, Mass.: Harvard University Press.

Collins, Randall. 1975. *Conflict Sociology: Toward an Explanatory Science*. New York: Academic Press.

Collins, Randall. 1986. *Weberian Sociological Theory*. Cambridge: Cambridge University Press.

Collins, Randall. 2004. *Interaction Ritual Chains*. Princeton, N.J.: Princeton University Press.

Connor, Richard, Michael R. Heithaus, and Lynne M. Barré. 1999. "Superalliance of Bottlenose Dolphins." *Nature* 397: 571–572.

Connor, Richard C., Rachel A. Smolker, and Andrew F. Richards. 1992a. "Dolphin Alliances and Coalitions." Pp. 415–443 in *Coalitions in Humans and Other Animals*, edited by Alexander Harcourt and Frans B. M. DeWaal. Oxford: Oxford University Press.

Connor, Richard C., Rachel A, Smolker, and Andrew F. Richards. 1992b. "Two Levels of Alliance Formation among Bottlenose Dolphins." *Proceedings of the National Academy of Sciences USA* 89: 987–990.

Connor, Richard C., Randall S. Wells, Janet Mann, and Andrew J. Read. 2000. "The Bottlenose Dolphin: Social Relationships in a Fission-Fusion Society." Pp. 91–126 in *Cetacean Societies*, edited by Janet Mann, Richard Connor, Peter L. Tyack, and Hal Whitehead. Chicago: University of Chicago Press.

Couzin, Iain D. and Jens Krause. 2003. "Self-organization and Collective Behavior in Vertebrates." *Advances in the Study of Behavior* 32: 1–75.

Darwin, Charles. 1896 [1874]. *The Descent of Man, and Selection in Relation to Sex*, Second edition. New York: Appleton.

Darwin, Charles. 1976 [1881]. *The Formation of Vegetable Mould through the Action of Worms with Observation on Their Habits*. Ontario, Calif.: Bookworm.

Darwin, Charles. 1958. *The Autobiography of Charles Darwin, 1809–1882*, edited by Nora Barlow. London: Collins.

Davis, Lance E. 1986. "Comment on Wallis and North." Pp. 149–161 in *Long-Term Factors in American Economic Growth*, edited by Stanley L. Engerman and Robert E. Gallman. Chicago: University of Chicago Press.

Dewey, John. 1930 [1922]. *Human Nature and Conduct: An Introduction to Social Psychology*. New York: Modern Library.

Dewey, John. 1929. *Experience and Nature*. New York: W. W. Norton.

DiMaggio, Paul. 1997. "Culture and Cognition." *Annual Review of Sociology* 23: 263–287.

DiTomaso, Nancy. 1982. "'Sociological Reductionism" from Parsons to Althusser: Linking Action and Structure in Social Theory." *American Sociological Review* 47: 14–28.

Dugatkin, Lee Alan. 1996. "Interface between Culturally Based Preferences and Genetic Preferences: Female Mate Choice in *Poecilia reticulata*." *Proceedings of the National Academy of Sciences* 93: 2770–2773.

Dunbar, R. I. M. 1984. *Reproductive Decisions*. Princeton, N.J.: Princeton University Press.

Durkheim, Emile. 1933 [1893]. *The Division of Labor in Society*, translated by George Simpson. Glencoe, Ill.: Free Press.

Durkheim, Emile. 1961 [1902–3]. *Moral Education*, translated by Everett K. Wilson and Herman Schnurer. New York: Free Press.

Durkheim, Emile. 1979 [1908]. "La Morale positive: examen de quelques difficultés." *Bulletin de la Société Française de Philosophie* 8: 189–200, reprinted as "A Discussion on Positive Morality" in *Durkheim: Essays on Morals and Education*, edited by W. S. F. Pickering and translated by H. L. Sutcliffe. London: Routledge and Kegan Paul.

Durkheim, Emile. 1995 [1912]. *The Elementary Forms of Religious Life*, translated by Karen E. Fields. New York: Free Press.

Einstein, Albert, Boris Podolsky, and Nathan Rosen. 1935. "Can Quantum-Mechanical Description of Physical Reality Be Considered Complete?" *Physics Review* 47: 777–780.

Eisner, Thomas. 2003. *For the Love of Insects*. Cambridge, Mass.: Harvard University Press.

Elder-Vass, Dave. 2010. *The Causal Power of Social Structures*. Cambridge: Cambridge University Press.

Elder-Vass, Dave. 2012. *The Reality of Social Construction*. Cambridge: Cambridge University Press.

Ellwood, Charles A. 1899. "Prolegomena to Social Psychology. II. The Fundamental Fact in Social Psychology." *American Journal of Sociology* 4: 807–822.

Engels, Frederick. 1942 [1891]. *The Origin of the Family Private Property and the State*, from the fourth edition. New York: International.

Eriksson, Nicholas, Shirley Wu, Chuong B. Do, Amy K. Kiefer, Joyce Y. Tung, Joanna L. Mountain, David A. Hinds, and Uta Francke. 2012. "A Genetic Variant Near Olfactory Receptor Genes Influences Cilantro Preference." *Flavour* 1: 1–22.

Feuerbach, Ludwig. 1957 [1843]. *The Essence of Christianity*, translated by George Elliot. New York: Harper.

Fine, Gary Alan. 2002. *Shared Fantasy: Role Playing Games as Social Worlds*. Chicago: University of Chicago Press.

Fischer, David Hackett. 2004. *Washington's Crossing*. Oxford: Oxford University Press.

Fleck, Ludwik. 1979 [1935]. *Genesis and Development of a Scientific Fact*, translated by Fred Bradley and Thaddeus J. Trenn. Chicago: University of Chicago Press.

Forel, August. 1929 [1906]. *The Sexual Question*, translated by C. F. Marshall. Brooklyn: Physicians and Surgeons Book Company.

Frederick, Shane, George Loewenstein, and Ted O'Donoghue. 2002. "Time Discounting and Time Preference: A Critical Review." *Journal of Economic Literature* 40: 351–401. Freud, Sigmund. 1961 [1924]. "The Economic Problem of Masochism." *Standard Edition of the Works of Sigmund Freud*, translated and edited by J. Strachey. London: Hogarth Press. Volume 19: 155–170.

von Frisch, K. and M. Lindauer. 1956. "The 'Language' and Orientation of the Honey Bee." *Annual Review of Entomology* 1: 45–58.

Gadamer, Hans-Georg. 1975 [1965]. *Truth and Method*, translated by Garrett Barden and John Cumming from the second edition. New York: Seabury Press.

Galef, Bernard G. Jr. 2007. "Social Learning by Rodents," pp. 206–215 in *Rodent Societies: An Ecological and Evolutionary Perspective*, edited by Jerry O. Wolff and Paul W. Sherman. Chicago: University of Chicago Press, 2007.

Gazzaniga, Michael S. 1970. *The Bisected Brain*. New York: Appleton-Century-Crofts.

Geertz, Clifford. 1973. *The Interpretation of Cultures*. New York: Basic Books.

Gerth, Hans, and C. Wright Mills. 1954. *Character and Social Structure*. London: Routledge and Kegan Paul.

Gibson, James J. 1986 [1979]. *The Ecological Approach to Visual Perception*. Hillsdale, N.J.: Lawrence Erlbaum.

Giddens, Anthony. 1976. *New Rules of Sociological Method: A Positive Critique of Interpretative Sociologies*. London: Hutchinson.

Giddens, Anthony. 1979. *Central Problems in Social Theory*. Berkeley: University of California Press.

Giddens, Anthony. 1984. *The Constitution of Society. Outline of the Theory of Structuration*. Cambridge: Polity.

Gode, Dhananjay K. and Shyam Sunder. 1993. "Allocative Efficiency of Markets with Zero-Intelligence Traders: Market as a Partial Substitute for Individual Rationality." *Journal of Political Economy* 101: 119–137.

von Goethe, Johann Wolfgang. 1970 [1810]. *Theory of Colours*, translated by Charles Lock Eastlake. Cambridge, Mass.: MIT Press.

Goffman, Erving. 1959. *The Presentation of Self in Everyday Life*. New York: Anchor Books.

Goffman, Erving. 1974. *Frame Analysis*. London: Harper and Row.

Goldthorpe, John H. 2007. *On Sociology*, second edition, Volume I. Stanford: Stanford University Press.

Goodall, Jane. 1986. *The Chimpanzees of Gombe*. Cambridge, Mass.: Harvard University Press.

Goodall, Jane. 1990. *Through a Window: My Thirty Years with the Chimpanzees of Gombe*. Boston: Houghton Mifflin.

Gordon, Deborah. 1999. *Ants at Work*. New York: W. W. Norton.

Gould, James L. and Carol Grant Gould. 1999. *The Animal Mind*. New York: Scientific American Library.

Gould, Roger. 2000. *The Rational Choice Controversy in Historical Sociology*. Chicago: University of Chicago Press.

Gould, Stephen Jay and Richard C. Lewontin. 1979. "The Spandrels of San Marco and the Panglossian Paradigm: A Critique of the Adaptationist Programme." *Proceedings of the Royal Society of London* B 205: 581–598.

Gouldner, Alvin W. 1970. *The Coming Crisis of Western Sociology*. New York: Basic Books.

Granovetter, Mark. 1985. "Economic Action and Social Structure: The Problem of Embeddedness." *American Journal of Sociology* 91: 481–510.

Groff, Ruth. Forthcoming. *Ontology Revisited: Metaphysics in Social and Political Philosophy*. New York: Routledge.

Guttridge, Tristan L., Arthur A. Myrberg, Ila F. Porcher, David W. Sims, and Jens Krause. 2009. "The Role of Learning in Shark Behaviour." *Fish and Fisheries* 10: 1–20.

Habermas, Jürgen and Niklas Luhmann. 1971. *Theorie der Gesellschaft, oder, Sozialtechnologie — Was leistet die Systemforschung?* Frankfurt: Suhrkamp Verlag.

Hacking, Ian. 1983. *Representing and Intervening*. Cambridge: Cambridge University Press.

Hall, Stuart and Tony Jefferson, editors. 1993 [1976]. *Resistance through Rituals: Youth Subcultures in Post-War Britain*. London: Routledge.

Hesse, Mary B. 1980. *Revolutions and Reconstructions in the Philosophy of Science*. Bloomington: Indiana University Press.

Hirschman, Albert O. 1977. *The Passions and the Interests*. Princeton, N.J.: Princeton University Press.

Hobbes, Thomas. 1909 [1651]. *Leviathan*. Oxford: Clarendon Press.

Hölldobler, Bert and Edward O. Wilson. 1994. *Journey to the Ants*. Cambridge, Mass.: Harvard University Press.

Horne, Christine. 2004. "Values and Evolutionary Psychology." *Sociological Theory* 22: 477–503.

Hrdy, Sarah Blaffer. 1977. *The Langurs of Abu*. Cambridge, Mass.: Harvard University Press.

Humphreys, Paul. 1989. *The Chances of Explanation*. Princeton, N.J.: Princeton University Press.

Hutchins, Edwin. 1995. *Cognition in the Wild*. Cambridge, Mass.: MIT Press.

Iannacone, Laurence R. 1995. "Voodoo Economics? Reviewing the Rational Choice Approach to Religion." *Journal for the Scientific Study of Religion* 34: 76–89.

von Ihering, Rudolf. 1913 [1877]. *Law as a Means to an End*, translated by Isaac Husik. Boston: Boston Book.

Ingrao, Charles. 1985. "The Hessian Military State and the American Revolution." *Studies in History and Politics* 4: 115–124.

Jackson, Robert R. and Fiona R. Cross. 2011. "Spider Cognition." *Advances in Insect Physiology* 41: 115–174.

Jacobs, Jane. 1992 [1961]. *The Death and Life of Great American Cities*. New York: Vintage Books.

James, William. 1950 [1890]. *The Principles of Psychology*. New York: Dover.

Kanazawa, Satoshi. 2001. "De Gustibus Est Disputandum." *Social Forces* 79: 1131–1163.

Kanazawa, Satoshi. 2004. "General Intelligence as a Domain-Specific Adaptation." *Psychological Review* 111: 512–523.

Kant, Immanuel. 1950 [1787]. *Critique of Pure Reason*, translated by Norman Kemp Smith. London: Macmillan.

Kant, Immanuel. 1987 [1790]. *Critique of Judgment*, translated by Werner S. Pluhar. Indianapolis: Hackett.

Kaplan, Gisela and Lesley J. Rogers. 2000. *The Orangutans*. Cambridge, Mass.: Perseus.

Kaplan, Jay R., Stephen B. Manuck, M. Babette Fontenot, and J. John Mann. 2002. "Central Nervous System Monoamine Correlates of Social Dominance in Cynomolgus Monkeys (*Macaca fascicularis*)." *Neuropsychopharmacology* 26: 431–443.

Keynes, John Maynard. 1935. *The General Theory of Employment, Interest and Money*. New York: Harcourt, Brace.

King-Hele, Desmond. 1999. *Erasmus Darwin: A Life of Unequalled Achievement*. London: Giles de la Mare.

Kinsey, Alfred C., Wardell B. Pomeroy, and Clyde E. Martin. 1948. *Sexual Behavior in the Human Male*. Philadelphia: W. B. Saunders.

Kirsh, David and Paul Maglio. 1994. "On Distinguishing Epistemic from Pragmatic Action." *Cognitive Science* 18: 513–549.

Kiser, Edgar and Hechter, Michael. 1998. "The Debate on Historical Sociology: Rational Choice Theory and Its Critics." *American Journal of Sociology* 104: 785–816.

Köhler, Wolfgang. 1925 [1917]. *The Mentality of Apes*, translated by Ella Winter. London: Routledge and Kegan Paul.

Köhler, Wolfgang. 1938. *The Place of Values in a World of Fact*. New York: Liveright.

Korenbrot Carol C., Claire Brindis, and Fran Priddy. 1990. "Trends in Rates of Live Births and Abortions Following State Restrictions on Public Funding of Abortion." *Public Health Reports* 105: 555–562.

Kuhn, Thomas S. 1962. *The Structure of Scientific Revolutions*. Chicago: University of Chicago Press.

Kummer, Hans. 1968. *Social Organization of Hamadryas Baboons*. Chicago: University of Chicago Press.

Kummer, Hans. 1995. *In Quest of the Sacred Baboon*, translated by M. Ann Bierderman-Thorson. Princeton, N.J.: Princeton University Press.

Kurzman, Charles. 1988. "The Rhetoric of Science: Strategies for Logical Leaping." *Berkeley Journal of Sociology* 33: 131–158.

Lakatos, Imre. 1970. "Falsification and the Methodology of Scientific Research Programmes." Pp. 91–195 in *Criticism and the Growth of Knowledge*, edited by Imre Lakatos and Alan Musgrave. Cambridge: Cambridge University Press.

Latour, Bruno. 1987. *Science in Action*. Cambridge, Mass: Harvard University Press.

Latour, Bruno. 2004. "Why Has Critique Run Out of Steam? From Matters of Fact to Matters of Concern." *Critical Inquiry* 30: 225–248.

Latour, Bruno, Pablo Jensen, Tommaso Venturini, Sébastian Grauwin, and Dominique Boullier. 2012. "The Whole Is Always Smaller Than Its Parts: A Digital Test of Gabriel Tarde's Monads." *British Journal of Sociology* 63: 590–615.

Laudan, Larry. 1977. *Progress and Its Problems: Towards a Theory of Scientific Growth*. Berkeley: University of California Press.

Levine, Phillip B., Douglas Staiger, Thomas J. Kane, and David J. Zimmerman. 1999. "Roe v Wade and American Fertility." *American Journal of Public Health* 89: 199–203.

Lewin, Kurt. 1951. *Field Theory in Social Science*, edited by Dorwin Cartwright. New York: Harper.

Lewis, David. 1986. "Postscripts to 'Causation.'" Pp. 172–213 in *Philosophical Papers*, Volume II. Oxford: Oxford University Press.

Lewis, David. 2004. "Causation as Influence." Pp. 75–106 in *Causation and Counterfactuals*, edited by John Collins, Ned Hall, and L. A. Paul. Cambridge, Mass.: MIT Press.

Lewis, Sarah M., and Christopher K. Cratsley. 2008. "Flash Signal Evolution, Mate Choice, and Predation in Fireflies." *Annual Review of Entomology* 53: 293–321.

Lhermitte, F. 1986. "Human Autonomy and the Frontal Lobes. Part II: Patient Behavior in Complex and Social Situations: The 'Environmental Dependence Syndrome.'" *Annals of Neurology* 19: 335–343.

Lieberson, Stanley. 1985. *Making It Count*. Berkeley: University of California Press.

Lieberson, Stanley and Joel Horwich. 2008. "Implication Analysis: A Pragmatic Proposal for Linking Theory and Data in the Social Sciences. 2008. *Sociological Methodology* 38: 1–50.

Little, Daniel. 1991. *Varieties of Social Explanation*. Boulder, Colo.: Westview Press.

Lizardo, Omar. 2012. "Analytical Sociology's Superfluous Revolution." *Sociologica* 1: 1–12.

Locke, John. 1924 [1700]. *An Essay concerning Human Understanding*, edited from the Fourth edition by A. S. Pringle-Pattison. Oxford: Clarendon Press.

Lucy, John A. 1997. "The Linguistics of 'Color.'" Pp. 320–346 in C. L. Hardin and L. Maffi, eds., *Color Categories in Thought and Language*. Cambridge: Cambridge University Press.

Makkreel, Rudolf A. 1990. *Imagination and Interpretation in Kant*. Chicago: University of Chicago Press.

Mandeville, Bernard. 1924 [1732]. *The Fable of the Bees*. Oxford: Clarendon Press.

Manski, Charles F. 1995. *Identification Problems in the Social Sciences*. Cambridge, Mass.: Harvard University Press.

Martin, John Levi. 2001a. "On the Limits of Sociological Theory." *Philosophy of the Social Sciences* 31(2): 187–223.

Martin, John Levi. 2001b. "*The Authoritarian Personality*, 50 Years Later: What Lessons Are There for Political Psychology?" *Political Psychology* 22: 1–26.

Martin, John Levi and Matt George. 2006. "Theories of Sexual Stratification: Toward an Analytics of the Sexual Field and a Theory of Sexual Capital." *Sociological Theory* 24: 107–132.

Martin, John Levi. 2009. *Social Structures*. Princeton, N.J.: Princeton University Press.

Martin, John Levi. 2011. *The Explanation of Social Action*. New York: Oxford University Press.

Marx, Karl. 1906 [1867]. *Capital,* Volume I, edited by Frederick Engels, translated from the third German edition by Samuel Moore and Edward Aveling. Chicago: Charles H. Kerr.

Marx, Karl. 1968. *Theories of Surplus Value,* Part II, edited by Frederick Engels, translated by S. Ryazankaya. Moscow: Progress.

Masserman, Jules H., Stanley Wechkin, and William Terris. 1964. "'Altruistic' Behavior in Rhesus Monkeys." *American Journal of Psychiatry* 121: 584–585.

Mazur, Rachel and Victoria Seher. 2008. "Socially Learned Foraging Behavior in Wild Black Bears, *Ursus americanus*." *Animal Behavior* 75: 1503–1508.

McBride, Jennifer, Petroc Sumner, Stephen R. Jackson, Nin Bajaj, and Masud Husain. 2013. "Exaggerated Object Affordance and Absent Automatic Inhibition in Alien Hand Syndrome." *Cortex*, in press.

McGuire, Michael T., Michael J. Raleigh, and Gary L. Brammer. 1984. "Adaptation, Selection, and Benefit-cost Balances: Implications of Behavioral-Physiological Studies of Social Dominance in Male Vervet Monkeys." *Ethology and Sociobiology* 5: 269–277.

Mead, George H. 1934. *Mind, Self, and Society: From the Standpoint of a Social Behaviorist*, edited by Charles W. Morris. Chicago: University of Chicago Press.

Menzel, Emil W. 1988. "A Group of Young Chimpanzees in a 1-Acre Field." Pp. 155–159 in *Machiavellian Intelligence*, edited by Richard W. Byrne and Andrew Whiten. Oxford: Clarendon Press.

Merton, Robert K. 1957. "The Role-Set: Problems in Sociological Theory." *British Journal of Sociology* 8: 294–303.

Merton, Robert K. 1968. *Social Theory and Social Structure*, second edition. New York: Free Press.

Messner, Michael A. 2000. "Barbie Girls versus Sea Monsters: Children Constructing Gender." *Gender and Society* 14: 765–784.

Metzinger, Thomas. 2003. *Being No One*. Cambridge, Mass.: MIT Press.

Michell, Joel. 2012. "'The Constantly Recurring Argument': Inferring Quantity from Order." *Theory and Psychology* 22: 255–271.

Mills, C. Wright. 1940. "Situated Actions and Vocabularies of Motive." *American Sociological Review* 5: 904–931.

Moss, Cynthia J. 1988. *Elephant Memories*. New York: William Morrow.

Moss, Cynthia J. and Phyllis C. Lee. 2011. "Female Reproductive Strategies." Pp. 187–223 in *The Amboseli Elephants*, edited by Cynthia J. Moss, Harvey Croze, and Phyllis C. Lee. Chicago: University of Chicago Press.

Nagel, Thomas. 1979. *Mortal Questions*. Cambridge: Cambridge University Press.

Nelson, Richard R. and Sidney G. Winter. 1982. *An Evolutionary Theory of Economic Change*. Cambridge, Mass.: Harvard University Press.

Neurath, Otto. 1944. *Foundations of the Social Sciences*, Volume II, No. 1 of *International Encyclopedia of Unified Science*. Chicago: University of Chicago Press.

Nietzsche, Friedrich. 1966 [1886]. *Beyond Good and Evil*, translated by Walter Kaufmann. New York: Vintage.

O'Neill, Daniella and Alison Gopnik. 1991. "Young Children's Ability to Identify the Sources of Their Beliefs." *Developmental Psychology* 27: 390–399.

Owens, B. Robert. 2010. "Producing Parsons' Reputation: Early Critiques of Talcott Parsons' Social Theory and the Making of a Caricature." *Journal of the History of the Behavioral Sciences* 46: 165–188.

Panofsky, Aaron. 2006. *Fielding Controversy: The Genesis and Structure of Behavior Genetics*. PhD dissertation. New York: New York University.

Parsons, Talcott. 1968 [1949]. *The Structure of Social Action*, two volumes. Glencoe, Ill.: Free Press.

Parsons, Talcott. 1951. *The Social System*. Glencoe, Ill: Free Press.

Parsons, Talcott and Edward A. Shils. 1954 [1951]. *Toward a General Theory of Action*. Cambridge, Mass.: Harvard University Press.

Passie, Torsten, John H. Halpern, Dirk O. Stichtenoth, Hinderk M. Emrich and Annelie Hintzen. 2008. "The Pharmacology of Lysergic Acid Diethylamide: A Review." *CNS Neuroscience and Therapeutics* 14: 295–314.

Peirce, Charles. S. 1984–2010 [1867–1890]. *Writings of Charles S. Peirce*, Volume 2, edited by Nathan Houser et al. Bloomington: Indiana University Press.

Peirce, C. S. 1955 [1875–1910]. "The Principles of Phenomenology." Pp. 74–97 in *Philosophical Writings*, edited by Justus Buchler. New York: Dover.

Pepper, Stephen. 1961. *Concept and Quality*. LaSalle, Ill.: Open Court Press.

Perry, Susan. 2008. *Manipulative Monkeys*. Cambridge, Mass.: Harvard University Press.

Piaget, Jean. 1970. *Structuralism*, translated by C. Maschler. New York: Basic Books.

Polanyi, Karl. 1957 [1944]. *The Great Transformation*. Beacon Hill: Beacon Hill Press.

Porter, Eleanor H. 1913. *Pollyanna*. Boston: L. C. Page.

Posner, Richard A. 1992. *Sex and Reason*. Cambridge, Mass.: Harvard University Press.

Proctor, Ian. 2000. "'I do': A Theoretical Critique of Becker's Rational Choice Approach to Marriage Decisions." Pp. 147–166 in *Rational Choice Theory: Resisting Colonisation*, edited by Margaret S. Archer and Jonathan Q. Tritter. New York: Routledge.

Raleigh, Michael J., Michael T. McGuire, Gary L. Brammer, and Arthur Yuwiler. 1984. "Social and Environmental Influences on Blood Serotonin Concentrations in Monkeys." *Archives of General Psychiatry* 41: 405–410.

Raleigh, Michael J., Michael T. McGuire, Gary L. Brammer, Deborah B. Pollack, and Arthur Yuwiler. 1991. "Serotonergic Mechanisms Promote Dominance Acquisition in Adult Male Vervet Monkeys." *Brain Research* 559: 181–190.

Range, Friederike, Zsófia Viranyi, and Ludwig Huber. 2007. "Selective Imitation in Domestic Dogs." *Current Biology* 17: 868–872.

Reed, Edward S. 1996. *Encountering the World: Toward an Ecological Psychology*. New York: Oxford University Press.

Reed, Isaac Ariail. 2011. *Interpretation and Social Knowledge*. Chicago: University of Chicago Press.

Reid, Thomas. 1969 [1785]. *Essays on the Intellectual Powers of Man*. Cambridge, Mass.: MIT Press.

Rickert, Heinrich. 1902. *Die Grenzen der naturwissenschaftlichen Begriffsbildung*. Tübingen: Verlag von J. C. B. Mohr.

Rickert, Heinrich. 1986 [1929]. *The Limits of Concept Formation in Natural Science*, fifth edition, translated by Guy Oakes. Cambridge: Cambridge University Press.

Rizzolatti, Giacomo and Laila Craighero. 2004. "The Mirror-Neuron System." *Annual Review of Neuroscience* 27: 169–192.

Rosati, Alexandra G., Laurie R. Santos, and Brian Hare. 2010. "Primate Social Cognition: Thirty Years after Premack and Woodruff." Pp. 117–143 in *Primate Neuroethology*, edited by Michael L. Platt and Asif A. Ghazanfar. Oxford: Oxford University Press.

Rosch, Eleanor. 1978. "Principles of Categorization." Pp. 27–48 in *Cognition and Categorization*, edited by Eleanor Rosch and Barbara B. Lloyd. Hillsdale, N.J.: Lawrence Earlbaum.

Roughgarden, Joan. 2010. *The Genial Gene*. Berkeley: University of California Press.

Rousseau, Jean-Jacques. 1967 [1755]. *Discourse on the Origin of Inequality*, edited by Lester G. Crocker. New York: Washington Square Press.

Russell, Bertrand. 1995 [1927]. *An Outline of Philosophy*. London: Routledge.

Russet, Cynthia Eagle. 1989. *Sexual Science*. Cambridge, Mass.: Harvard University Press.

Sapolsky, Robert M. 2004. "Social Status and Health in Humans and Other Animals." *Annual Review of Anthropology* 33: 393–418.

Satz, Debra and John Ferejohn. 1994. "Rational Choice and Social Theory." *Journal of Philosophy* 91: 71–87.

Sayer, Andrew. 2010. *Method in Social Science: A Realist Approach*, second edition. London: Routledge.

Schaller, George B. 1963. *The Mountain Gorilla*. Chicago: University of Chicago Press.

Schelling, Thomas C. 1978. *Micromotives and Macrobehavior*. New York : W. W. Norton.

Schudson, Michael. 2011. *The Sociology of News*, second edition. New York: W. W. Norton.

Schutz, Alfred and Thomas Luckmann. 1973. *The Structures of the Life-World*, Volume 1, translated by Richard M. Zaner and H. Tristram Engelhardt Jr. Evanston, Ill.: Northwestern University Press.

Schwartz, Barry and MiKyoung Kim. 2002. "Honor, Dignity, and Collective Memory: Judging the Past in Korea and the United States." Pp. 209–226 in *Culture in Mind: Toward a Sociology of Culture and Cognition*, edited by K. A. Cerulo. New York: Routledge.

Scott, Marvin B. and Stanford M. Lyman. 1968. "Accounts." *American Sociological Review* 33: 46–62.

Shapin, Steven. 1996. *The Scientific Revolution*. Chicago: University of Chicago Press.

Shepard, Paul. 1996. *The Others: How Animals Made Us Human*. Washington, D.C.: Island Press.

Shively, Carol A., Gary L. Brammer, Jay R. Kaplan, Michael J. Raleigh, and Stephen B. Manuck. 1990. "The Complex Relationship between Behavioral Attributes, Social Status, and Whole Blood Serotonin in Male Macaca fascicularis." *American Journal of Primatology* 23: 99–112.

Shively, Carol A., M. Babette Fontenot, and Jay R. Kaplan. 1995. "Social Status, Behavior, and Central Serotonergic Responsivity in Female Cynomolgus Monkeys." *American Journal of Primatology* 37: 333–339.

Simon, Herbert A., 1962. "The Architecture of Complexity." *Proceedings of the American Philosophical Society* 106: 467–482.

Simon, Herbert, 1996. *The Sciences of the Artificial.* Cambridge, Mass.: MIT Press.

Smith, Adam. 1997 [1759]. *The Theory of Moral Sentiments.* Washington, D.C.: Regnery.

Smith, Adam. 1976 [1776]. *An Inquiry into the Nature and Causes of the Wealth of Nations.* Chicago: University of Chicago Press.

Smith, Christian. 2011. *What Is a Person? Rethinking Humanity, Social Life, and the Moral Good from the Person Up.* Chicago: University of Chicago Press.

Smuts, Barbara B. 1985. *Sex and Friendship in Baboons.* New York: Aldine.

Smuts, Barbara B. 1987b. "Gender, Aggression, and Influence." Pp. 400–412 in *Primate Societies*, edited by Barbara B. Smuts, Dorothy L. Cheney, Robert M. Seyfarth, Richard W. Wrangham, and Thomas T. Struhsaker. Chicago: University of Chicago Press.

Spencer, Herbert. 1896 [1873]. *The Study of Sociology.* New York: Appleton.

Spickard, James V. 1998. "Rethinking Religious Social Action: What Is 'Rational' about Rational-Choice Theory?" *Sociology of Religion* 59: 99–115.

Spitzer, Manfred. 1999. *The Mind with the Net.* Cambridge, Mass.: MIT Press.

Stammler, Rudolf. 1896. *Wirtschaft und Recht nach der Materialistischen Geschichts Auffassung.* Leipzig. Verlag Von Veit & Comp.

Steinmetz, George. 1998. "Critical Realism and Historical Sociology." *Comparative Studies in Society and History* 40: 170–186.

Stinchcombe, Arthur L. 1982. "Should Sociologists Forget Their Mothers and Fathers?" *American Sociologist* 17: 2–11.

Strum, Shirley C. 1987. *Almost Human: A Journey into the World of Baboons.* New York: W. W. Norton.

Strum, Shirley C., Deborah Forster, and Edwin Hutchins. 1997. "Why Machiavellian Intelligence May Not Be Machiavellian." Pp. 50–85 in *Machiavellian Intelligence II: Extensions and Evaluations*, edited by Andrew Whiten and Richard W. Byrne. Cambridge: Cambridge University Press.

Svenningsson P., A. C. Nairn, and P. Greengard. 2005. "DARPP-32 Mediates the Actions of Multiple Drugs of Abuse." *AAPS* (American Association of Pharmaceutical Scientists) *Journal* 7: E353–E360.

Swidler, Ann. 2001. *Talk of Love.* Chicago: University of Chicago Press.

Swift, Jonathan. 1960 [1726]. *Gulliver's Travels.* Boston: Houghton Mifflin.

Takahashi, M., H. Arita, M. Hiraiwa-Hasegawa, and T. Hasegawa. 2008. "Peahens Do Not Prefer Peacocks with More Elaborate Trains." *Animal Behaviour* 75: 1209–1219.

Tetens, Johann Nicolas. 1777. *Philosophische Versuche über die menschliche Natur und ihre Entwicklung*, Volume 1. Leipzig: Weidmanns.

Tilly, Charles. 2004. *Contention and Democracy in Europe, 1650–2000*. Cambridge: Cambridge University Press.

Tolman, Edward C., B. F. Ritchie, and D. Kalish. 1946a. "Studies in Spatial Learning. I. Orientation and the Short-Cut." *Journal of Experimental Psychology* 36: 13–24.

Tolman, Edward C., B. F. Ritchie, and D. Kalish. 1946b. "Studies in Spatial Learning. II. Place Learning versus Response Learning." *Journal of Experimental Psychology* 36: 221–229.

Tomasello, Michael. 1996. "Do Apes Ape?" Pp. 319–346 in *Social Learning in Animals: The Roots of Culture*, edited by C. M Heyes and B. G. Galef Jr. San Diego: Academic Press.

Townsend, John Marshall and Timothy Wasserman. 1997. "The Perception of Sexual Attractiveness: Sex Differences in Variability." *Archives of Sexual Behavior* 26: 243–268.

Turco, Catherine J. 2010. "Cultural Foundations of Tokenism: Evidence from the Leveraged Buyout Industry." *American Sociological Review* 75: 894–913.

Turner, Stephen P. 2010. *Explaining the Normative*. Oxford: Polity Press.

Turvey, Michael T., Kevin Shockley, and Claudia Carello. 1999. "Affordance, Proper Function and the Physical Basis of Perceived Heaviness." *Cognition* 73: B17–B26.

Vaughan, Diane. 1996. *The Challenger Launch Decision*. Chicago: University of Chicago Press.

Vollmer, Hendrik. 2013. *The Sociology of Disruption, Disaster and Social Change: Punctuated Cooperation*. Cambridge: Cambridge University Press.

Vosniadou, Stella and William F. Brewer. 1992. "Mental Models of the Earth: A Study of Conceptual Change in Childhood." *Cognitive Psychology* 24: 535–585.

de Waal, Frans. 1977. "The Organization of Agonistic Relations within two Captive Groups of Java-Monkeys (Macaca fascicularis)." *Zeitschrift für Tierpsychologie* 44: 225–282.

de Waal, Frans. 1986. "Deception in the Natural Communication of Chimpanzees." Pp. 221–244 in *Deception: Perspectives on Human and Nonhuman Deceit*, edited by Robert W. Mitchell and Nicholas S. Thompson. Albany: SUNY Press.

de Waal, Frans. 1987. "Dynamics of Social Relationships." Pp. 421–429 in *Primate Societies*, edited by Barbara B. Smuts, Dorothy L. Cheney, Robert M. Seyfarth, Richard W. Wrangham, and Thomas T. Struhsaker. Chicago: University of Chicago Press.

de Waal, Frans. 1990. *Peacemaking among Primates*. Cambridge, Mass.: Harvard University Press.

de Waal, Frans. 1996. *Good Natured*. Cambridge, Mass.: Harvard University Press.

de Waal, Frans. 1998. *Chimpanzee Politics*, revised edition. Baltimore: Johns Hopkins University Press.

Watterson, Bill. 1990. *The Authoritative Calvin and Hobbes*. Kansas City: Andrews and McMeel.

Weber, Max. 1946 [1918]. "Politics as a Vocation," in *From Max Weber: Essays in Sociology*, translated and edited by H. H. Gerth and C. Wright Mills. New York: Oxford University Press.

Weber, Max. 1978. *Economy and Society*, edited by Guenther Roth and Claus Wittich. Berkeley, two volumes, California: The University of California Press.

Wegner, Daniel M. 2002. *The Illusion of Conscious Will*. Cambridge, Mass.: MIT Press.

Wells, Randall S. 1991. "The Role of Long-Term Study in Understanding the Social Structure of a Bottlenose Dolphin Community." Pp. 199–226 in *Dolphin Societies*, edited by Karen Pryor and Kenneth S. Norris. Berkeley: University of California Press.

Whitaker, Daniel J., Tadesse Haileyesus, Monica Swahn, and Linda S. Saltzman. 2007. "Differences in Frequency of Violence and Reported Injury between Relationships with Reciprocal and Nonreciprocal Intimate Partner Violence." *American Journal of Public Health* 97: 941–947.

White, Harrison C. 1992. *Identity and Control*. Princeton: Princeton University Press.

Whitehead, Harriet. 1987. *Renunciation and Reformulation: A Study of Conversion in an American Sect*. Ithaca, N.Y.: Cornell University Press.

Whyte, William Foote. 1981 [1943]. *Street Corner Society*, third edition. Chicago: University of Chicago Press.

Wickler, Wolfgang. 1973. *The Sexual Code*, translated by Francisca Garvie. Garden City, N.Y.: Anchor Books.

Wieder, D. L. 1974. *Language and Social Reality*. The Hague: Mouton.

Wilcox R. Stimson and Robert R. Jackson. 1998. "Cognitive Abilities of Araneophagic Jumping Spiders." Pp. 411–434 in *Animal Cognition in Nature*, edited by Russell P. Balda, Irene M. Pepperberg, and Alan C. Kamil. San Diego: Academic Press.

Williamson, Oliver E. 1985. *The Economic Institutions of Capitalism*. New York: Free Press.

Wilson, E. O. 1971. *The Insect Societies*. Cambridge, Mass.: Harvard University Press.

Wilson, E. O. 1975. *Sociobiology*. Cambridge, Mass.: Harvard University Press.

Wimmer, Heinz and Josef Perner. 1983. "Beliefs about Beliefs: Representation and Constraining Function of Wrong Beliefs in Young Children's Understanding of Deception." *Cognition* 13: 103–128.

Windelband, Wilhelm. 1915 [1882]. "Was ist Philosophie?" Pp. 1–54 in *Präludien: Aufätze und Reden zur Philosophie und ihrer Geschichte*, Volume 1. Tübingen: Mohr / Siebeck.

Wolfram, Stephen. 2002. *A New Kind of Science*. Champaign, Ill.: Wolfram Media.

Wrangham, Richard W., W. C. McGrew, Frans B. M. de Waal, and Paul G. Heltne. 1994. *Chimpanzee Cultures*. Cambridge, Mass.: Harvard University Press.

Wrong, Dennis H. 1994. *The Problem of Order*. New York: Free Press.

Zahavi, Amotz. 1975. "Mate Selection — A Selection for a Handicap." *Journal of Theoretical Biology* 53: 205–214.

Zuckerman, S. 1981 [1932]. *The Social Life of Monkeys and Apes*. London: Routledge and Kegan Paul.

INDEX

A
Abbott, Andrew, 245
Adorno, Theodor, 109
affordances, 212–14, 237–42
Akerlof, George, 151
alpha position, of animals, 194–97
altruism, 139–42
analysis levels, theory construction and, 38–40
animal behavior, 175–215
  animal sociology field, 182
  communication between animals, 121–25, 187–89
  deceptive behavior, 190–91
  environment and, 206–14
  "fission-fusion" societies of, 185–87
  human behavior compared to, 177–79
  intelligence and, 182–85
  morality and, 199–206
  rationality and, 137, 160–61, 170–72
  relevance of, to sociology, 179–82
  roles and, 191–99
  study of, 175–77
  theory construction and, 43–44
Aristotle, 15, 27
attribution theory, 43
Austin, J. L., 121

B
baboon behavior, 190, 197–99
balance theory, 41
Becker, Gary S., 149
bee behavior, 179, 193–94, 208
Bhaskar, Roy, 94–95, 99, 112, 125
Bourdieu, Pierre, 17–18
Buss, David, 162, 169

C
causality, 45–75
  comparison and, 62–65
  comparison and etiology, 65–71
  constraint, defined, 52–56
  counterfactualist approach to, 63, 67, 74
  culture as constraint and, 45–52
  defining, 56–61
  mechanisms of, 71–74
  processes of, 74–75
  theory construction and, 37–38
Challenger Launch Decision, The (Vaughan), 35
change, as exogenous, 31–32
change score models, 35–37
Cheney, Dorothy L., 190
chimpanzee behavior, 176, 196, 197, 201–2, 208–9
classical behaviorism, animal behavior and, 210
Collins, Randall, 147–48
communication, animal behavior and, 121–25, 187–89
concept formation, realism and, 98–105
Connor, Richard C., 186
consistent phenomenology, 78
constraint
  culture as, 45–52
  defined, 52–56
  see also causality
"contest competition," 181
control, animal behavior and, 194–97
core premises, theory construction and, 18–19, 20–21, 23–26
"correspondence" theories of truth, 110–13
critical realism, 77, 94–98, 100–102
critique, theory construction and, 9–10, 15–18
culture
  animal behavior and, 213–14
  as constraint, 45–52
  "culture constrains and enables," defined, 46
  norms and, 231–43

D
Darwin, Charles, 163, 170–72, 183–84
Darwin, Erasmus, 183

deception, animal behavior and, 190–91
decision making. *See* rational choice theory
degenerative research programs, 107–8
delineation, causality and, 59–60
de Wall, Frans, 203–4
Dewey, John, 12, 110, 114, 125, 239
dialectical materialism, 114–15
Dibble, Vernon K., 247
dolphin behavior, 185–86
Dugatkin, Lee Alan, 212
Durkheim, Emile, 3, 29, 87, 200

E
earthworm behavior, 183–84
Elder-Vass, Dave, 99–100
Engels, Friedrich, 176
environment, 217–44
 animal behavior and, 206–14
 motives and tendencies, 217–25
 norms and, 231–43
 rules of, 225–31
essentialism, 65, 93
evolutionary psychology
 consciousness and, 168–70
 generally, 158–63
 selectionist arguments and, 163–68
 sexual *versus* natural selection, 170–72
Evolution of Desire (Buss), 162
exchange theory, 143–49
existence, causality and, 64–65, 68–71, 74–75
experience, realism and, 125–26
Experience and Nature (Dewey), 125
Explanation of Social Action, The (Martin), 56

F
Fable of the Bees (Mandeville), 150
facts, constraint and, 54–56
Feuerbach, Ludwig, 114–15
Fine, Gary Alan, 43
"fission-fusion" societies, 185–87
Fleck, Ludwik, 55
Forel, August, 178
Frederick II, 153–54
functionalism, Parsons on, 20–21, 32

G
Geertz, Clifford, 222–25
generalization, theory construction and, 5–8
George, Matt, 146
gestures, animal communication and, 121–25, 187–90
Gibson, David, 106
Goffman, Erving, 187
Goldthorpe, John H., 142–43
Goodall, Jane, 176, 197, 201–2
"good old-fashioned action theory" (GOFAT), defined, 217
guilt, animal behavior and, 204–6
guppy behavior, 212

H
Habermas, J., 12
habit theories, 17–18
Hamadryas baboon behavior, 197–99
Hobbes, Thomas, 53–54, 218–19
Horwich, Joel, 6
Hrdy, Sarah Blaffer, 160–61, 180

I
idealism, 78
Identity and Control (White), 186–87
individualism, 38–40
"inside-outside" questions, of theory construction, 32–37
instability, theory construction and, 13–15
intelligence, of animals, 182–85
"interests," rationality and, 8–9
"is-ought" problem, 30, 31–32

J
James, William, 110

K
Kanazawa, Satoshi, 169
Kant, Immanuel, 79–80
Kaplan, Gisela, 213–14
Keynes, John Maynard, 167
knowledge, realism and, 81–85, 86, 95, 129

L
Lakatos, Imre, 107–8
language, culture and, 49–51
learning, animal behavior and, 210–13
Levine, Phillip B., 156
Lieberson, Stanley, 6
Locke, John, 87
Luhmann, Niklas, 12

M
Mandeville, Bernard, 150
Mannheim, Karl, 33
"marriage" roles, animal behavior and, 197–99
Martin, John Levi, 24, 56, 146
Marx, Karl, 19, 163
mating behavior, of animals, 188–90
Mead, George H., 121, 187–88
mechanisms
causality and, 71–74
realism and, 85
Merleau-Ponty, Maurice, 206
Metzinger, Thomas, 22
Mills, C. Wright, 218–21
modeling
animal behavior and, 209
rational choice theory and, 134–35
Moral Education (Durkheim), 200
morality
animal behavior and, 199–206
environment and, 242–43
motivation
for actions, 217–18
defined, 218–21
deliberation and, 221–22
tendencies and, 222–25

N
naïve realism, 78, 80
nominalism
causality and, 56–57
realism and, 77, 86
norms, environment and, 231–43

O
orangutan behavior, 213–14
organizational culture, decision making in, 34–35
orthologics, theory construction and, 10–13, 40
"outside in" error, of theory construction, 37–38

P
paradox
rational choice theory and, 138–49
theory construction and, 11–12
Parsons, Talcott
as conservative, 19, 20–21
on motivation, 217–18
rationality and, 136
study of theorists and "theory-ology," 2–3
theory premises of, 23–24, 29–30
"peephole epistemologies," 108–10
Peirce, Charles
environment and, 223
realism and, 110, 112–13, 114, 120, 126, 127–28
perlocutionary speech, 121–24
Perry, Susan, 176
phenomenology, realism and, 77–78, 81–85
Piaget, Jean, 207
Popper, Karl, 79
positivism, 92
Posner, Richard A., 137
power
causality and, 57
theory construction and, 7
practice, theory of, 17–18
pragmatism
"correspondence" theories of truth, 110–13
nonpropositional truth, 121–24
predicates and truth, 124–25
truth, defining, 126–28
truth and propositions, 113–21
see also realism
prejudice, of theories, 21–23
prototypes, causality and, 59, 61
punishment, animal behavior and, 203–4

Q
quality, tendency and, 223

R
rational choice theory, 131–73
altruism and, 139–42
consequences, 149–58
defining rationality, 136–38
disagreement about, 131–34
evolutionary psychology and, 158–72
exchange theory and, 143–49
modeling and, 134–35
satisficing and, 142–43
substantive and formal rationality, 25–28
theory construction and, 6, 8–9, 14, 19, 40
utilitarianism and, 138–39

realism, 77–129
  concept formation and, 98–105
  critical realism, 77, 94–98, 100–102
  experience and reality, 125–26
  issues of, 77–81
  knowledge and, 81–85, 86, 95, 129
  nonpropositional truth, 121–24
  phenomenology and, 77–78, 81–85
  pragmatism and, 110–16
  predicates and truth, 124–25
  social constructionism *versus,* 86–94
  supporting claims and, 105–10
  truth, defining, 126–28
  truth and propositions, 116–21
"revealed preferences," 139
Rickert, Heinrich, 87
Rogers, Lesley J., 213–14
roles
  animal behavior and, 191–99
  functionalism and, 32
romantic/sexual pairing, 146–49
roof-rat behavior, 211–12
rules
  defined, 225–27
  norms and, 231–43
  patterns of, 228–30
  semiotic component of, 230–31
Russell, Bertrand, 11–12, 178

S

Samuelson, Paul, 139
satisficing, 142–43
Schelling, Thomas C., 151
"scramble competition," 181
selection, rational choice theory and, 144–45, 146–49, 163–68, 170–72
sexology, 178
Seyfarth, Robert M., 190
Simon, Herbert, 83, 142
Smith, Adam, 150–51
social constructionism, realism *versus,* 86–94
social learning, animal behavior and, 211–13
Social System, The (Parsons), 20, 29
Sociobiology (Wilson), 172
speech, types of, 121–24
status, animal behavior and, 191–99
Strum, Shirley C., 177
subjective judgment, theory construction and, 28–30
substantive claims, 25–28
Swidler, Ann, 47, 229
Swift, Jonathan, 19
systems theory
  as conservative, 19, 20–21
  theory premise and, 23–24, 29–30

T

tautology, theory construction and, 13–15
tendency, 222–25. *See also* motivation
terminology, theory construction and, 8–9, 42
theory construction, 1–44
  conception of theory, 3–5
  defining, 1
  identifying core premises for, 18–19, 20–21, 23–26
  "inside-outside" questions of, 32–37
  "is-ought" problem of, 30, 31–32
  levels of analysis for, 38–40
  "outside in" error and, 37–38
  prejudice of theories, 21–23
  "rules" of sociology for, 247–54
  subjective judgment and, 28–30
  substantive and formal rationality, 25–28
  tautology and, 13–15
  theoretical progression and, 245–47
  theory as critique, 9–10, 15–18
  theory as generalization, 5–8
  theory as vocabulary, 8–9, 42
  "theory-ology" of, 2–3
  theory-work as orthologics, 10–13, 40
  "unthinking," 15, 40–44
  see also animal behavior; causality; environment; rational choice theory; realism
"theory of mind," 204–6
Theory of Moral Sentiments (Smith), 150–51
"theory-ology," defined, 2–3
Tilly, Charles, 72–73
"tipping" phenomenon, 151
"tool kit," culture as, 51–52
transcendental idealism, 79–80
"trans-phenomenal" world, 78, 81–85
Turner, Stephen, 15

U

"unidentifiability," 140
utilitarianism, rational choice theory and, 138–39

V
values, 217–18
Vaughan, Diane, 35
vocabulary, theory construction and, 8–9, 42
von Frisch, K., 208
von Uexküll, Jakob, 206

W
"waggle dance" (bees), 179, 208
Wealth of Nations, The (Smith), 151
Weber, Max, 2, 26, 57–58, 157–58
White, Harrison, 186–87
Whitehead, Harriet, 42
Whyte, William, 36
Wieder, D. L., 226
Wilson, E. O., 172
"worker bee studies," 6
Wrong, Dennis, 24

Z
Zahavi, Amotz, 171